Challenges and Transitions in Education in Times of Crisis

Leah Purpuri
Lacey Township School District, USA

Sancha Gray
Kean University, USA

A volume in the Advances in Educational Marketing, Administration, and Leadership (AEMAL) Book Series

Published in the United States of America by
IGI Global
Information Science Reference (an imprint of IGI Global)
701 E. Chocolate Avenue
Hershey PA, USA 17033
Tel: 717-533-8845
Fax: 717-533-8661
E-mail: cust@igi-global.com
Web site: http://www.igi-global.com

Copyright © 2024 by IGI Global. All rights reserved. No part of this publication may be reproduced, stored or distributed in any form or by any means, electronic or mechanical, including photocopying, without written permission from the publisher.
Product or company names used in this set are for identification purposes only. Inclusion of the names of the products or companies does not indicate a claim of ownership by IGI Global of the trademark or registered trademark.

Library of Congress Cataloging-in-Publication Data

Names: Purpuri, Leah Nicole, 1987- editor. | Gray, Sancha K., 1969- editor.
Title: Challenges and transitions in education in times of crisis / Edited by Leah Purpuri, Sancha Gray.
Description: Hershey, PA : Information Science Reference, [2024] | Includes bibliographical references and index. | Summary: "The objective of this book is to examine the challenges that were experienced through the COVID-19 crisis in education, and to view them from a lens of opportunity"-- Provided by publisher.
Identifiers: LCCN 2023053014 (print) | LCCN 2023053015 (ebook) | ISBN 9798369315071 (hardcover) | ISBN 9798369315088 (ebook)
Subjects: LCSH: Internet in education. | Social distancing (Public health) and education. | Education--Effect of technological innovations on. | COVID-19 Pandemic, 2020- | Community and school.
Classification: LCC LB1044.87 .C4196 2024 (print) | LCC LB1044.87 (ebook) | DDC 371.33/44678--dc23/eng/20231211
LC record available at https://lccn.loc.gov/2023053014
LC ebook record available at https://lccn.loc.gov/2023053015

British Cataloguing in Publication Data
A Cataloguing in Publication record for this book is available from the British Library.

All work contributed to this book is new, previously-unpublished material.
The views expressed in this book are those of the authors, but not necessarily of the publisher.

For electronic access to this publication, please contact: eresources@igi-global.com.

Advances in Educational Marketing, Administration, and Leadership (AEMAL) Book Series

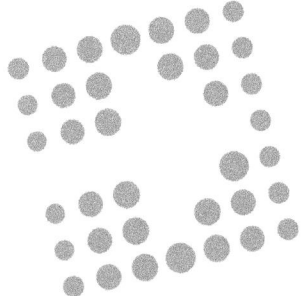

MISSION

Siran Mukerji
IGNOU, India
Purnendu Tripathi
IGNOU, India

ISSN:2326-9022
EISSN:2326-9030

With more educational institutions entering into public, higher, and professional education, the educational environment has grown increasingly competitive. With this increase in competitiveness has come the need for a greater focus on leadership within the institutions, on administrative handling of educational matters, and on the marketing of the services offered.

The **Advances in Educational Marketing, Administration, & Leadership (AEMAL) Book Series** strives to provide publications that address all these areas and present trending, current research to assist professionals, administrators, and others involved in the education sector in making their decisions.

Coverage

- Direct marketing of educational programs
- Educational Leadership
- Educational Management
- Educational Marketing Campaigns
- Marketing Theories within Education

IGI Global is currently accepting manuscripts for publication within this series. To submit a proposal for a volume in this series, please contact our Acquisition Editors at Acquisitions@igi-global.com or visit: http://www.igi-global.com/publish/.

The (ISSN) is published by IGI Global, 701 E. Chocolate Avenue, Hershey, PA 17033-1240, USA, www.igi-global. com. This series is composed of titles available for purchase individually; each title is edited to be contextually exclusive from any other title within the series. For pricing and ordering information please visit http://www.igi-global.com/book-series/advances-educational-marketing-administration-leadership/73677. Postmaster: Send all address changes to above address. Copyright © IGI Global. All rights, including translation in other languages reserved by the publisher. No part of this series may be reproduced or used in any form or by any means – graphics, electronic, or mechanical, including photocopying, recording, taping, or information and retrieval systems – without written permission from the publisher, except for non commercial, educational use, including classroom teaching purposes. The views expressed in this series are those of the authors, but not necessarily of IGI Global.

Titles in this Series

For a list of additional titles in this series, please visit: www.igi-global.com/book-series

Teaching and Assessment in the Era of Education 5.0
Ghizlane Chemsi (University of Hassan II, Morocco) Imane Elimadi (University Hassan II, Morocco) Mounir Sadiq (University Hassan II, Morocco) and Mohamed Radid (University Hassan II, Morocco)
Information Science Reference • copyright 2024 • 443pp • H/C (ISBN: 9798369330456)
• US $275.00 (our price)

Inclusive Educational Practices and Technologies for Promoting Sustainability
Santosh Kumar Behera (Kazi Nazrul University, India) Atyaf Hasan Ibrahim (University of Diyala, Iraq) and Faten Romdhani (Regional Board of Education, Bizerta, Tunisia)
Information Science Reference • copyright 2024 • 310pp • H/C (ISBN: 9798369369555)
• US $165.00 (our price)

Inclusivity and Indigeneity in Education for Sustainable Development
Santosh Kumar Behera (Kazi Nazrul University, India) Atyaf Hasan Ibrahim (University of Diyala, Iraq) and Faten Romdhani (Regional Board of Education, Bizerta, Tunisia)
Information Science Reference • copyright 2024 • 297pp • H/C (ISBN: 9798369328026)
• US $165.00 (our price)

Global Insights on Women Empowerment and Leadership
Malika Haoucha (University Hassan II of Casablanca, Morocco)
Information Science Reference • copyright 2024 • 315pp • H/C (ISBN: 9798369328064)
• US $245.00 (our price)

Exploring Educational Equity at the Intersection of Policy and Practice
José Sánchez-Santamaría (Universidad de Castilla-La Mancha, Spain) and Brenda Boroel Cervantes (Autonomous University of Baja California, Mexico)
Information Science Reference • copyright 2024 • 336pp • H/C (ISBN: 9798369316146)
• US $245.00 (our price)

701 East Chocolate Avenue, Hershey, PA 17033, USA
Tel: 717-533-8845 x100 • Fax: 717-533-8661
E-Mail: cust@igi-global.com • www.igi-global.com

Table of Contents

Preface xiv

Chapter 1
Virtual Learning and School Refusal: Understanding Complex Dynamics in
the COVID-19 Era 1
    Ryan J. Eckert, Monmouth University, USA

Chapter 2
The Family Perspective and Experience: How the COVID-19 Pandemic
Interrupted and Impacted Education 32
    Gabriella Hall, Monmouth University, USA
    Ryan J. Eckert, Monmouth University, USA

Chapter 3
Wait, We Have to Do What? How Teachers Entering the COVID-19
Shutdown Paved New Pathways for Education 54
    Jamie Sassano, Lacey Township School District, USA

Chapter 4
COVID-19 and Mathematics Students at a Suburban New Jersey Middle
School 77
    Kaitlyn M. Sorochka, Monmouth University, USA

Chapter 5
Laboratory at Home: Science Instruction During COVID-19 96
    Kyle Seiverd, Ocean County Vocational Technical Schools, USA
    Jennifer Huey, Toms River Regional School District, USA

Chapter 6
Secondary School Learners' Experiences During COVID-19 in Africa and
Beyond: A Systematic Review 115
    Daniel L. Mpolomoka, UNICAF University, Zambia
    Petronella Mwaka, Zambian Open University, Zambia
    Joseph Mandyata, University of Zambia, Zambia

Chapter 7
Leading Through Uncertainty: Stakeholder Dynamics in PK-12 Education
During the COVID-19 Pandemic 135
    Silvana Zircher, Monmouth University, USA
    Ryan J. Eckert, Monmouth University, USA

Chapter 8
Challenges in Online Education During the COVID-19 Pandemic: A Case
Study in Higher Education Institutes of Rural Areas of Birbhum District of
West Bengal, India 156
    Tirthankar Mandal, Krishna Chandra College, India

Chapter 9
Online Education and Its Commercial Viability With Reference to the
COVID-19 Pandemic 185
    Kapil Kumar Aggarwal, Chandigarh University, India
    Satakshi Agrawal, Ajay Kumar Garg Institute of Management, India

Chapter 10
Fostering and Maintaining Student Communities: Persistence of Business
Students Through COVID-19 197
    Jenna Cook, Gabelli School of Business, Fordham University, USA
    Marisa Villani, Gabelli School of Business, Fordham University, USA

Chapter 11
Relationship Between Student Involvement, Leadership, and Belonging
Before and During the Pandemic: Points of Comparison and Differentiation... 228
    Dayna S. Weintraub, Rutgers University, New Brunswick, USA
    Ralph A. Gigliotti, Rutgers University, New Brunswick, USA
    Tori Glascock, Rutgers University, New Brunswick, USA
    Gregory Dyer, Rutgers University, New Brunswick, USA
    Salvador B. Mena, Rutgers University, New Brunswick, USA

Compilation of References 258

About the Contributors 305

Index 311

Detailed Table of Contents

Preface xiv

Chapter 1
Virtual Learning and School Refusal: Understanding Complex Dynamics in
the COVID-19 Era 1
   Ryan J. Eckert, Monmouth University, USA

This book chapter presents a study on the complex dynamics of school refusal in the context of the COVID-19 pandemic's move to virtual learning, asking whether this transition could be beneficial for students previously struggling with school refusal, a form of chronic absenteeism with emotional roots. Contrary to expectations, these students showed equal or lesser academic outcomes and sustained unwillingness to engage in remote learning, challenging the pre-pandemic notion that online learning could effectively address school refusal. With a complex interplay of causal factors, a mere change in setting from physical to virtual is insufficient to address the core issues of this difficult problem. The chapter thus advocates for adoption of multi-faceted intervention models encompassing mental health supports, integrating social emotional learning, and taking a proactive approach toward building positive school culture.

Chapter 2
The Family Perspective and Experience: How the COVID-19 Pandemic
Interrupted and Impacted Education... 32
> *Gabriella Hall, Monmouth University, USA*
> *Ryan J. Eckert, Monmouth University, USA*

This chapter provides a comprehensive analysis of the impact of family dynamics on children's educational experiences during the COVID-19 pandemic. The pandemic's effect on education, necessitating a shift to remote, virtual, and hybrid learning models, underscored the importance of family support in maintaining continuity in children's education. The chapter delves into factors that shape family dynamics, such as socioeconomic status, family composition, and the educational background of parents or caregivers. These elements not only affect the level and quality of parent-child interaction but also contribute to educational challenges, disparities, and learning gaps, which were further magnified during the pandemic. The narrative further explores the diverse experiences and challenges faced by families of students with special needs. By examining the interplay of these dynamics, the chapter aims to offer insights into the complex relationship between family support and educational success, providing a nuanced understanding of the diverse family experiences during a global crisis.

Chapter 3
Wait, We Have to Do What? How Teachers Entering the COVID-19
Shutdown Paved New Pathways for Education... 54
> *Jamie Sassano, Lacey Township School District, USA*

This chapter delves into the multifaceted challenges faced by educators and during the the COVID-19 crisis, examining the emergent issues, experiences, and solutions in navigating remote teaching and learning. From technological constraints to the emotional toll of isolation, educators grappled with unprecedented challenges in adapting to online instruction while striving to maintain meaningful connections with students. Despite these challenges, the pandemic also spurred the emergence of new instructional techniques born out of necessity. Educators worldwide innovated in real-time, leveraging digital platforms and creative approaches to engage students and foster learning. Success stories highlight the resilience and adaptability of educators, as well as the transformative potential of technology-enhanced teaching practices. Looking ahead, the chapter explores the outlook for future teachers and educational systems, emphasizing the importance of integrating lessons learned from the pandemic into long-term contingency planning.

Chapter 4
COVID-19 and Mathematics Students at a Suburban New Jersey Middle School 77
Kaitlyn M. Sorochka, Monmouth University, USA

School closures in response to the COVID-19 pandemic caused students to experience new and different learning environments in public schools. This chapter focuses on the experiences of mathematics students in a large suburban middle school in New Jersey from 2019 through 2023. These perspectives elucidate the state of middle school mathematics achievement in the present day. Each pandemic school year is reviewed individually throughout the chapter for the school of study, highlighting several key factors, such as the student learning environment, instructional modalities, pandemic variables impacting student education, technology utilized, student success, and the overall student school-based experience. Student achievement data highlights the impacts of student learning experiences from the pandemic years on their knowledge attainment. The chapter concludes with a summary of the key details and the needs moving forward for middle-grade mathematics general and special education following the end of the pandemic.

Chapter 5
Laboratory at Home: Science Instruction During COVID-19 96
Kyle Seiverd, Ocean County Vocational Technical Schools, USA
Jennifer Huey, Toms River Regional School District, USA

Every course has elements that make it special. These special qualities can be due to the personality of the teacher, atmosphere of the school, set up of the class, or more. Science classes are one of the only courses to provide students with laboratory activities. These activities are often hands-on and done under teacher supervision. However, when COVID-19 forced learning to go virtual, providing laboratory activities to students became one of the biggest challenges. This chapter will provide an overview on the purpose of laboratory activities, how labs were changed to accommodate virtual learning, and the challenges educators faced when making these changes.

Chapter 6
Secondary School Learners' Experiences During COVID-19 in Africa and
Beyond: A Systematic Review.. 115
    Daniel L. Mpolomoka, UNICAF University, Zambia
    Petronella Mwaka, Zambian Open University, Zambia
    Joseph Mandyata, University of Zambia, Zambia

This chapter is informed by findings of a study that explored the lived experiences of learners who survived COVID-19 in secondary schools of Kasama District. The study emanated from the backdrop that while these experiences by COVID-19 survivors in their communities and society at large are well documented, little is known about such experiences involving learners as COVID-19 survivors in school environments which are much more vulnerable and delicate communities. A Systematic Literature Review (SR) was conducted on the subject. Specific search engines were employed with a distinct inclusivity and exclusivity criterion applied. Findings indicate that schools recorded COVID-19 cases among the learners more especially during the time when schools were in session. Literature abounds that confirms that schools had learners who experienced and survived the ills of the COVID-19 who required support system from their teachers, peers, and the school within the school community for the experience that they went through with COVID-19.

Chapter 7
Leading Through Uncertainty: Stakeholder Dynamics in PK-12 Education
During the COVID-19 Pandemic.. 135
    Silvana Zircher, Monmouth University, USA
    Ryan J. Eckert, Monmouth University, USA

This chapter delves into the transformative effects of the COVID-19 pandemic on PK-12 education, emphasizing the adaptive leadership and stakeholder dynamics that emerged. It begins by highlighting early challenges faced by educational leaders in ensuring continuity and equity in learning amidst the shift to remote education. The narrative then transitions to the evolution of educational practices, underscoring the integration of technology and the reimagining of pedagogical approaches. Central to this discussion is the focus on the digital divide and the efforts to bridge disparities in access and digital literacy. It further explores the collaborative dialogues between educational leaders and community stakeholders, crucial in formulating effective, inclusive responses. Concluding with reflections on the lessons learned and future implications, it not only recounts historical events but also provides insights and strategies for managing future crises in education, underlining the importance of resilient, adaptive leadership and community engagement.

Chapter 8
Challenges in Online Education During the COVID-19 Pandemic: A Case Study in Higher Education Institutes of Rural Areas of Birbhum District of West Bengal, India 156
    Tirthankar Mandal, Krishna Chandra College, India

COVID-19 has had a serious impact on all aspects of society, all citizens, and all institutes around the country. In India, educational institutions have compulsorily changed their traditional teaching methods to an online platform. The transition to online mode has been an abrupt one due to the unprecedented lockdown imposed to manage COVID-19, and all the educational institutes did not have time to design and adopt the course contents for an online delivery system. Several obstacles like infrastructure, internet service, e-resources, communication gap, rural-urban gap, financial constraints, social and family burden, etc. have made the education and learning system far behind the previous system. The present study has tried to find out the difficulties students face to continue smooth learning such that a skilled and technologically efficient generation will arise soon.

Chapter 9
Online Education and Its Commercial Viability With Reference to the COVID-19 Pandemic 185
    Kapil Kumar Aggarwal, Chandigarh University, India
    Satakshi Agrawal, Ajay Kumar Garg Institute of Management, India

Over the past few years, online education has been an exciting research topic. Many educationists are working on the future and the scope of online education. Due to the COVID-19 outbreak, it has become a significant source of imparting knowledge among the youth, keeping in mind the health and safety of the children. While talking about EdTech, internet connectivity and the lecturer play a crucial role in defining the effectiveness of online education. The chapter mainly focuses on online education as a new emerging business in the country. The chapter also discusses its growing role and increasing contribution to GDP during the COVID-19 pandemic. Earlier, there was less awareness and trend of online learning; however, it is interesting to know that the pandemic has highlighted the importance of online learning, and it has emerged as a rare business that has shown an upward trend in crises. Online learning has emerged as an affordable, convenient and time-efficient method of gaining knowledge.

Chapter 10
Fostering and Maintaining Student Communities: Persistence of Business
Students Through COVID-19 197
    Jenna Cook, Gabelli School of Business, Fordham University, USA
    Marisa Villani, Gabelli School of Business, Fordham University, USA

The purpose of this mixed-methods study was to understand how the Gabelli School of Business at Fordham University's academic and co-curricular interventions that led to a remote, virtual, and hybrid experience during the period of the COVID-19 Pandemic (March 2020 to May 2022) impacted student academic persistence and experience. Built on the Interpretative Phenomenological Awareness qualitative methodology, this chapter examined how the perceived student experience and student persistence were impacted by the pandemic in four specific areas: academic experience, community and social experience, academic persistence, and academic support resources. Students who were enrolled from May 2020 to March 2023 were invited to participate. The researchers found that enrollment and retention rates were maintained and identified three main takeaways from the qualitative responses: Community and engagement are critical, intentionality in building academic experiences matter, and student support systems need to connect in more meaningful ways to the institution.

Chapter 11
Relationship Between Student Involvement, Leadership, and Belonging
Before and During the Pandemic: Points of Comparison and Differentiation... 228
    Dayna S. Weintraub, Rutgers University, New Brunswick, USA
    Ralph A. Gigliotti, Rutgers University, New Brunswick, USA
    Tori Glascock, Rutgers University, New Brunswick, USA
    Gregory Dyer, Rutgers University, New Brunswick, USA
    Salvador B. Mena, Rutgers University, New Brunswick, USA

The COVID-19 pandemic dramatically changed the college experience; however, it also provided an opportunity to engage with and support students differently. The COVID-19 pandemic dramatically changed the college experience; however, it also provided an opportunity to engage with and support students differently. Participation and leadership in college organizations at many institutions has traditionally been an in-person experience; however, during the first two years of the pandemic, this practice shifted to a fully or partially remote setting for many colleges and universities. This chapter compares two years of data from the Multi-Institutional Study of Leadership (MSL) in 2018 and 2021 and explores the pandemic's effect on the relationship between student involvement and leadership experiences and feelings of belonging. Results show slight declines in involvement and leadership experiences and decreased feelings of belonging during the pandemic. The chapter concludes with crucial questions for leaders in education to consider regarding the cultivation of student involvement and leadership in the aftermath of the pandemic.

Compilation of References 258

About the Contributors 305

Index 311

Preface

COVID-19 served as a rapid accelerator for change, compelling educators to transition from theoretical discussions to actionable strategies almost overnight. Professional development sessions had long emphasized the importance of a growth mindset, but the pandemic made it an urgent necessity. Echoing Winston Churchill's words, "Never let a good crisis go to waste," the pandemic period became a decisive period for innovation and transformation in education.

Systemic inequities in education were quickly exposed and exacerbated by the pandemic, revealing missed opportunities and compelling the entire educational ecosystem to re-engage and rethink. This crisis-driven reflection necessitated a reevaluation of student learning outcomes and the creation of multiple pathways to support their growth and achievement.

The pandemic brought significant uncertainty and despair, yet it also sparked unprecedented opportunities for exploration, experimentation, and innovation. Educators were compelled to transition from learning to application, and from application to synthesis, in ways never before imagined. This book deliberately shifts the focus away from narratives of learning loss, instead highlighting the resilience and adaptability demonstrated through lived experiences, practical adjustments, and crisis-driven research.

This book highlights the remarkable contributions of educators from PK-12 to higher education. Throughout this work, readers will encounter a broad range of authors' viewpoints on the impact of COVID-19, through both experiential and literary lenses. The earlier chapters examine experiences at the onset of the pandemic, discussing its impact first on K-12 education and later on higher education. Inspired by these challenges, it distills essential lessons, offering insights to navigate future crises. Through collaboration, empathy, and forward-thinking, we can continue to evolve and improve the educational landscape, ensuring that every crisis becomes an opportunity for growth and betterment.

The editors and contributing authors, with hundreds of years of combined professional experience, have crafted this academic resource carefully. We hope that these cumulative perspectives demonstrate the valuable insights that can emerge from a time of crisis, as Churchill would have wanted.

As editors, we envision *Challenges and Transitions in Education in Times of Crisis* as a beacon of hope and resilience, guiding educators and stakeholders towards a brighter, more understanding future. We invite readers to embark on this journey with us, navigating challenges, embracing opportunities, and envisioning a more resilient educational landscape, regardless of what lies ahead.

CHAPTER 1

Virtual Learning and School Refusal: Understanding Complex Dynamics in the COVID-19 Era

Ryan Eckert

This book chapter presents a study on the complex dynamics of school refusal in the context of the COVID-19 pandemic's move to virtual learning, asking whether this transition could be beneficial for students previously struggling with school refusal, a form of chronic absenteeism with emotional roots. Contrary to expectations, these students showed equal or lesser academic outcomes and sustained unwillingness to engage in remote learning, challenging the pre-pandemic notion that online learning could effectively address school refusal. With a complex interplay of causal factors, a mere change in setting from physical to virtual is insufficient to address the core issues of this difficult problem. The chapter thus advocates for adoption of multifaceted intervention models encompassing mental health supports, integrating social emotional learning, and taking a proactive approach toward building positive school culture.

Preface

CHAPTER 2

The Family Perspective and Experience: How the COVID-19 Pandemic Interrupted and Impacted Education

Gabriella Hall, Ryan Eckert

This chapter provides a comprehensive analysis of the impact of family dynamics on children's educational experiences during the COVID-19 pandemic. The pandemic's effect on education, necessitating a shift to remote, virtual, and hybrid learning models, underscored the importance of family support in maintaining continuity in children's education. The chapter delves into factors that shape family dynamics, such as socioeconomic status, family composition, and the educational background of parents or caregivers. These elements not only affect the level and quality of parent-child interaction but also contribute to educational challenges, disparities, and learning gaps, which were further magnified during the pandemic. The narrative further explores the diverse experiences and challenges faced by families of students with special needs. By examining the interplay of these dynamics, the chapter aims to offer insights into the complex relationship between family support and educational success, providing a nuanced understanding of the diverse family experiences during a global crisis.

CHAPTER 3

Wait, We Have to Do What? How Teachers Entering the COVID-19 Shutdown Paved New Pathways for Education

Jamie Sassano

This chapter delves into the multifaceted challenges faced by educators and during the the COVID-19 crisis, examining the emergent issues, experiences, and solutions in navigating remote teaching and learning. From technological constraints to the emotional toll of isolation, educators grappled with unprecedented challenges in adapting to online instruction while striving to maintain meaningful connections with students. Despite these challenges, the pandemic also spurred the emergence of new instructional techniques born out of necessity. Educators worldwide innovated in real-time, leveraging digital platforms and creative approaches to engage students and foster learning. Success stories highlight the resilience and adaptability of educators, as well as the transformative potential of technology-enhanced teaching practices. Looking ahead, the chapter explores the outlook for future teachers and educational systems, emphasizing the importance of integrating lessons learned from the pandemic into long-term contingency planning.

CHAPTER 4

COVID-19 and Mathematics Students at a Suburban New Jersey Middle School

Kaitlyn Sorochka

School closures in response to the COVID-19 pandemic caused students to experience new and different learning environments in public schools. This chapter focuses on the experiences of mathematics students in a large suburban middle school in New Jersey from 2019 through 2023. These perspectives elucidate the state of middle school mathematics achievement in the present day. Each pandemic school year is reviewed individually throughout the chapter for the school of study, highlighting several key factors, such as the student learning environment, instructional modalities, pandemic variables impacting student education, technology utilized, student success, and the overall student school-based experience. Student achievement data highlights the impacts of student learning experiences from the pandemic years on their knowledge attainment. The chapter concludes with a summary of the key details and the needs moving forward for middle-grade mathematics general and special education following the end of the pandemic.

CHAPTER 5

Laboratory at Home: Science Instruction During COVID-19

Kyle Seiverd, Jennifer Huey

Every course has elements that make it special. This uniqueness can be due to the personality of the teacher, atmosphere of the school, set up of the class, or all three. Science classes are one of the only courses to provide students with laboratory activities. These activities are often hands-on and done under teacher supervision. However, when COVID-19 forced learning to go virtual, providing laboratory activities to students became one of the biggest challenges to remedy. This chapter will take the reader through the purpose of laboratory activities, how labs were changed to accommodate virtual learning, and the challenges educators faced when making these changes.

CHAPTER 6

Secondary School Learners' Experiences during COVID-19 in Africa and Beyond: A Systematic Review

Daniel Mpolomoka, Petronella Mwaka, Joseph Mandyata

This chapter is informed by findings of a study that explored the lived experiences of learners who survived COVID-19 in secondary schools of Kasama District. The study emanated from the backdrop that while these experiences by COVID-19 survivors in their communities and society at large are well documented, little is known about such experiences involving learners as COVID-19 survivors in school environments which are much more vulnerable and delicate communities. A Systematic Literature Review (SR) was conducted on the subject. Specific search engines were employed with a distinct inclusivity and exclusivity criterion applied. Findings indicate that schools recorded COVID-19 cases among the learners more especially during the time when schools were in session. Literature abounds that confirms that schools had learners who experienced and survived the ills of the COVID-19 who required support system from their teachers, peers and the school within the school community for the experience that they went through with COVID-19.

CHAPTER 7

Leading Through Uncertainty: Stakeholder Dynamics in PK-12 Education During the COVID-19 Pandemic

Silvana Zircher, Ryan Eckert

This chapter, as presented by the authors, delves into the transformative effects of the COVID-19 pandemic on PK-12 education, emphasizing the adaptive leadership and stakeholder dynamics that emerged. It begins by highlighting early challenges faced by educational leaders in ensuring continuity and equity in learning amidst the shift to remote education. The narrative then transitions to the evolution of educational practices, underscoring the integration of technology and the reimagining of pedagogical approaches. Central to this discussion is the focus on the digital divide and the efforts to bridge disparities in access and digital literacy. It further explores the collaborative dialogues between educational leaders and community stakeholders, crucial in formulating effective, inclusive responses. Concluding with reflections on the lessons learned and future implications, it not only recounts historical events but also provides insights and strategies for managing future crises in education, underlining the importance of resilient, adaptive leadership and community engagement.

CHAPTER 8

Challenges in Online Education During COVID-19 Pandemic: A Case Study in Higher Education Institutes of Rural Areas of Birbhum District of West Bengal, India

Tirthankar Mandal

COVID-19 has had a serious impact on all aspects of society, all citizens, and all institutes around the country. In India, educational institutions have compulsorily changed their traditional teaching methods to an online platform. The transition to online mode has been an abrupt one due to the unprecedented lockdown imposed to manage COVID-19, and all the educational institutes did not have time to design and adopt the course contents for an online delivery system. Several obstacles like infrastructure, internet service, e-resources, communication gap, rural-urban gap, financial constraints, social and family burden, etc have made the education and learning system far behind the previous system. The present study has tried to find out the difficulties students face to continue smooth learning such that a skilled and technologically efficient generation will arise soon.

CHAPTER 9

Online Education and Its Commercial Viability with Reference To COVID-19

Kapil Kumar Aggarwal, Satakshi Agrawal

Over the past few years, online education has been an exciting research topic. Many educationists are working on the future and the scope of online education. Due to the COVID-19 outbreak, it has become a significant source of imparting

Preface

knowledge among the youth, keeping in mind the health and safety of the children. While talking about EdTech, internet connectivity and the lecturer play a crucial role in defining the effectiveness of online education. The paper mainly focuses on online education as a new emerging business in the country. The paper also discusses its growing role and increasing contribution to GDP during the COVID-19 pandemic. Earlier, there was less awareness and trend of online learning; however, it is interesting to know that the pandemic has highlighted the importance of online learning, and it has emerged as a rare business that has shown an upward trend in crises. Online learning has emerged as an affordable, convenient and time-efficient method of gaining knowledge.

CHAPTER 10

Fostering and Maintaining Student Communities: Persistence of Business Students Through COVID-19

Jenna Cook, Marisa Villani

The purpose of this mixed-methods study was to understand how the Gabelli School of Business at Fordham University's academic and co-curricular interventions that led to a remote, virtual, and hybrid experience during the period of the COVID-19 Pandemic (March 2020 to May 2022) impacted student academic persistence and experience. Built on the Interpretative Phenomenological Awareness qualitative methodology, this chapter examined how the perceived student experience and student persistence were impacted by the pandemic in four specific areas: academic experience, community and social experience, academic persistence, and academic support resources. Students who were enrolled from May 2020 to March 2023 were invited to participate. The researchers found that enrollment and retention rates were maintained and identified three main takeaways from the qualitative responses: Community and engagement are critical; intentionality in building academic experiences matter; and student support systems need to connect in more meaningful ways to the institution.

CHAPTER 11

Relationship Between Student Involvement, Leadership, and Belonging Before and During the Pandemic: Points of Comparison and Differentiation

Dayna Weintraub, Ralph Gigliotti, Tori Glascock, Gregory Dyer, Salvador Mena

The COVID-19 pandemic dramatically changed the college experience; however, it also provided an opportunity to engage with and support students differently. Involvement and leadership in college organizations for many institutions has traditionally been an in-person experience, yet, for two years, this practice shifted into a fully or partially remote setting. This chapter compares two years of data from the Multi-Institutional Study of Leadership (MSL) in 2018 and 2021, describes student involvement and leadership experiences and levels of sense of belonging, and explores the pandemic's effect on the relationship between student involvement and leadership experiences and feelings of belonging. Results show slight declines in involvement and leadership experiences and decreased feelings of belonging during the pandemic. The chapter concludes with crucial questions for education leaders to consider regarding approaches to cultivating student involvement and leadership in the aftermath of the pandemic.

As editors of *Challenges and Transitions in Education in Times of Crisis*, we stand at the conclusion of a journey that has been both enlightening and humbling. The chapters within this book provide a panoramic view of the educational landscape during the COVID-19 pandemic, capturing the resilience, adaptability, and innovation that emerged in response to unprecedented challenges.

From the swift pivot to remote learning in PK-12 education to the transformative shifts in higher education, each chapter offers valuable insights into the multifaceted impacts of the pandemic and beyond on educators, students, families, and communities. We have explored the challenges encountered, the strategies devised, and the lessons learned, all through a lens of opportunity and growth.

Throughout this book, we have witnessed the emergence of educational leaders who rose to the occasion, the resilience of students navigating new learning modalities, and the innovative approaches adopted by educators to ensure continuity of learning. We have delved into the complexities, the importance of inclusive and resilient classroom environments, and the critical role of digital transformation in shaping the future of education.

Preface

Reflecting on the collective wisdom shared within these pages, we are reminded of the power of collaboration, empathy, and forward-thinking in navigating crises. The COVID-19 pandemic has tested the resilience of education systems worldwide, but it has also sparked innovation and transformation on an unprecedented scale.

We envision this book as more than just a collection of chapters; it is a testament to the indomitable spirit of educators and stakeholders in the face of adversity. It serves as a beacon of hope and inspiration for those navigating the complexities of education in times of crisis.

Our heartfelt gratitude is extended to the contributors who have generously shared their expertise, experiences, and insights. We also thank our readers for embarking on this journey with us, as we navigate the challenges, embrace the opportunities, and envision a more equitable and inclusive educational landscape.

As we look to the future, let us carry forward the lessons learned and the resilience gained from this transformative period. Together, let us continue to strive for excellence, innovation, and equity in education, ensuring that every student has the opportunity to thrive and succeed.

DEDICATION

To our husbands.
To our children.
And last, but not least:
To our outstanding contributing authors.

Leah Purpuri
Lacey Township School District, USA

Sancha Gray
Kean University, USA

Chapter 1
Virtual Learning and School Refusal:
Understanding Complex Dynamics in the COVID-19 Era

Ryan J. Eckert
https://orcid.org/0009-0001-5818-096X
Monmouth University, USA

ABSTRACT

This book chapter presents a study on the complex dynamics of school refusal in the context of the COVID-19 pandemic's move to virtual learning, asking whether this transition could be beneficial for students previously struggling with school refusal, a form of chronic absenteeism with emotional roots. Contrary to expectations, these students showed equal or lesser academic outcomes and sustained unwillingness to engage in remote learning, challenging the pre-pandemic notion that online learning could effectively address school refusal. With a complex interplay of causal factors, a mere change in setting from physical to virtual is insufficient to address the core issues of this difficult problem. The chapter thus advocates for adoption of multi-faceted intervention models encompassing mental health supports, integrating social emotional learning, and taking a proactive approach toward building positive school culture.

School refusal, a complex phenomenon marked by a student's persistent avoidance of school due to emotional distress, presents a significant challenge in educational settings. In order to address this issue, it is essential to understand its nuances and underlying causes, which often remain obscured by broader patterns of chronic absenteeism (Malkus et al., 2020; Townsley, 2020; Wimmer, 2013). This chapter aims to explore the intricacies of school refusal, particularly in the context of the transformative shift to virtual learning triggered by the COVID-19 pandemic.

DOI: 10.4018/979-8-3693-1507-1.ch001

Copyright © 2024, IGI Global. Copying or distributing in print or electronic forms without written permission of IGI Global is prohibited.

UNDERSTANDING SCHOOL REFUSAL

School refusal is characterized not just by absenteeism but by an emotional aversion to attending school, which can stem from anxiety, fear of negative social interactions, or other stress-related conditions. Unlike truancy, school refusal involves the awareness and sometimes the involvement of the parents, adding a layer of complexity to its management. The condition is often a response to specific negative stimuli within the school environment and can manifest as physical symptoms that conveniently subside once the threat of school attendance is removed. Despite extensive research, gaps remain in fully understanding the triggers and most effective interventions for this condition.

The Impact of COVID-19 and Virtual Learning

The onset of the COVID-19 crisis and the subsequent abrupt transition to virtual learning provided an unprecedented opportunity to study school refusal in a new light. With schools closing their physical doors and switching to online platforms, the traditional triggers associated with school refusal were ostensibly removed or altered. This shift not only accelerated advancements in virtual learning technologies but also offered a unique experiment to see if such a format could better accommodate students who resist traditional school settings. However, the reality was more nuanced, as the move online also introduced new challenges and stressors, complicating the dynamics of school refusal.

This change in the educational landscape opens up fresh avenues for research. By examining the impact of virtual learning on students who exhibited school refusal prior to the pandemic, we can gain insights into how different the dynamics of school refusal are in a virtual setting. This chapter presents three case studies of students who struggled with school refusal before the pandemic, providing a detailed look at their experiences with virtual learning during the school closures.

The primary goal of this chapter is to offer a deeper understanding of school refusal within the context of both traditional and virtual learning environments. By analyzing how the shift to online education has affected students with a history of school refusal, we aim to identify potential improvements in educational practices and interventions. Additionally, this exploration will help educators and policymakers better support at-risk students and potentially leverage virtual learning as a more tailored approach for those who find traditional school settings challenging.

In summary, this chapter seeks to enhance our understanding of school refusal, assess the impact of the COVID-19-induced shift to virtual learning, and explore how these insights can inform future educational strategies and policies. This analysis will contribute to a more nuanced view of how educational environments can adapt to meet the diverse needs of all students, particularly those struggling with school refusal.

The Dynamics of School Refusal in the Context of Virtual Learning

This chapter presents three case studies based on interviews with students who exhibited school refusal behaviors prior to the onset of COVID-19. These students were invited to share their experiences and perceptions during the school closures prompted by the pandemic, providing insights into how the transition to virtual learning influenced their patterns of school refusal. Historically, intervention strategies for school refusal have primarily focused on returning students to in-person instruction, based on the belief that school refusal stems from negative stimuli within the physical school environment rather than a general disinterest in education (Kearney, 2007). This traditional view suggested that removing a student entirely from the in-person setting might eliminate the aversive stimuli contributing to their refusal, hence the closures due to COVID-19 presented an opportunity for students with school refusal to potentially thrive in a virtual environment. However, the findings from this study reveal a more complex reality.

Contrary to earlier assumptions, the students involved in the study were equally reluctant to engage in schooling, even remotely. The academic outcomes they achieved through virtual learning were comparable or inferior to those from their previous in-person experiences. The shift to a virtual format, while mitigating some existing factors that contributed to school refusal, also intensified other factors and unveiled new potential causes. These results highlight a novel and specific dynamic of school refusal that manifests in virtual settings. Simply changing the learning environment from physical to digital was insufficient to alter the students' fundamental aversion to school.

This data is critical as it provides valuable insights for school districts and families in making informed decisions on allocating time, energy, and resources to most effectively support this at-risk group. For educational leaders, it underscores the need to develop a deeper understanding of the unique dynamics of school refusal in an era increasingly dominated by digital learning. Ultimately, the COVID-19 pandemic has demonstrated that virtual learning may not be a viable solution for all students, particularly those experiencing school refusal.

LITERATURE REVIEW

This literature review delves into the multifaceted nature of chronic absenteeism, exploring its causes, consequences, and the related phenomenon of school refusal. It aims to provide a comprehensive overview of the various factors contributing to absenteeism, including socioeconomic, emotional, and physical elements, and how these factors interplay with the educational outcomes and well-being of students. The review further distinguishes between chronic absenteeism and school refusal, highlighting how different motivations and underlying issues lead to absence from school. By examining a range of interventional strategies and the evolving role of virtual learning, especially in the wake of the COVID-19 pandemic, this review seeks to shed light on potential solutions and the changing dynamics in addressing these educational challenges. Through this exploration, the literature review aims to contribute to a better understanding of how to effectively support at-risk students and improve attendance and engagement in educational settings.

CHRONIC ABSENTEEISM

To understand the nature, causes, and consequences of school refusal, it is crucial to first examine chronic absenteeism from a broader perspective. Chronic absenteeism refers to student absence exceeding a predetermined number of days for various reasons. The most commonly used gauge of chronic absenteeism defines a chronically absent student as one who misses more than 18 days (or 10%) of the school year. A multitude of factors contribute to chronic absenteeism, including socioeconomic, cultural, emotional, and physical factors, often intermingling. Some cases are directly linked to physical illnesses, where students suffering from chronic ailments like asthma, dental pain due to untreated tooth decay, vision impairment, and diabetes show significantly higher absenteeism rates than the national average (Richardson et al., 2018). Poverty also plays a critical role, as it presents numerous logistical challenges that can impede a guardian's ability to ensure consistent school attendance. In single-parent households prevalent in low-income districts, for instance, the absence of a parent during critical morning or evening times often forces students to take on adult responsibilities such as working late hours or caring for younger siblings, further complicating their ability to attend school regularly (Jensen, 2009).

Effects of Chronic Absenteeism

Chronic absenteeism is associated with a range of negative outcomes. Students who are chronically absent are less likely to graduate from high school, as chronic absenteeism is the factor most closely correlated with dropout rates (Jensen, 2009). According to a Robert Wood Johnson Foundation report (2016), students who are chronically absent between grades 8 and 12 are seven times more likely to drop out. The same report suggests that high school dropouts are less likely to obtain gainful employment, more likely to engage in unhealthy behaviors, and on average live approximately nine years less than those who complete high school. A study by Gottfried (2015) indicates a significant relationship between chronically absent students and a corresponding decline in performance among their classmates. Teacher attention can be seen as a finite resource: when students are chronically absent, they require a disproportionate amount of teacher attention due to falling behind academically. Other students are thereby deprived of their fair share of teacher time, energy, and attention and suffer academically as a result (Gottfried, 2015). According to the same study,

In essence, chronically absent students produce both an individual effect by decreasing their own learning and increasing social disengagement from having missed excessive amounts of school, and also a congestion effect on the public good by frequently slowing instruction and reducing the educational outcomes for others in the class when actually present in the classroom. (p. 6)

While many studies show the negative effects of chronic absenteeism, there are also studies that inversely demonstrate the positive effects of reducing chronic absenteeism. Schools provide a language-rich environment and opportunities to develop skills like social competence, cooperation, and teamwork (Kearney & Graczyk, 2014). Belfanz and Byrnes (2018) demonstrated that even among students with poor attendance, significant increases in credit accumulation and academic indicators occurred as attendance was improved. Higher standardized test scores, higher future employment rates, and decreased likelihood of future incarceration are also among the many benefits associated with regular school attendance (Kearney & Graczyk, 2014).

SCHOOL REFUSAL

School refusal, *school anxiety*, and *school phobia* are all terms used to describe a collection of related issues that challenge students, parents, and schools. Reasons for these issues may include separation anxiety, conflict with peers or teachers, fear for personal safety, social phobia, depression, anxiety, learning difficulties, or any number of other stressors originating from within the school. Affected students often lack the ability to identify and articulate the source of their stress, and simply act on it by avoiding school altogether (Brand & O'Conner, 2004).

Generally, there are a number of criteria present in the majority of cases. The onset of school refusal symptoms can develop gradually, often starting to manifest after a holiday or illness (Freemont, 2003). At-risk students typically show severe reluctance toward attending school or staying until the end of the school day and present severe emotional distress including fearfulness, angry outbursts or temper tantrums, or complaints of illness when faced with going to school (Brand & O'Conner, 2004). Often, these physical symptoms—such as abdominal pain, headaches, stomachaches, dizziness, or nausea—present themselves in the morning before school, only to quickly vanish if the child is allowed to stay home (Elliott, 1999). Most school-refusing students can be classified with broader psychological disorders associated with their behaviors, including separation anxiety, social phobia or another specific phobia, anxiety, or major depressive disorder (Brand & O'Conner, 2004). Research shows that approximately 90% of students who refuse school have some form of psychiatric diagnosis (Ek & Eriksson, 2013).

School Refusal vs. Truancy

It is important to distinguish school refusal as a unique form of chronic absenteeism, separate from others such as chronic physical illness or truancy. In contrast to school refusal, truancy generally describes illegitimate absence without parental permission; time spent away from school is often spent without parental supervision. According to Rogers (2014), "truancy is distinct from absenteeism in that the student is deliberately spending time away from school *and* from home" (p. 185).

A key differentiator between truancy and school refusal is the type of stimuli behind the student's disengagement from school: often, truant students are motivated by more appealing stimuli outside of school, whereas school-refusing students are motivated to stay away due to negative stimuli from within the school setting (Kearney, 2007). Truant students generally "skip school" without parental permission or knowledge, while school-refusing students tend to remain at home with the knowledge of parents during school hours (Elliott, 1999).

The underlying causes leading to school refusal versus truancy were further reinforced in a study by O'Shea (2010) that considered 70 variables related to chronic absenteeism. It was found that there are different factors correlated with the prediction of each; according to the study, "school phobics and truants have non-attendance in common, however there are significant discrepancies in their social, emotional, family, and school histories" (p. iii).

Causes of School Refusal

In addition to the larger generalized factors shown to influence chronic absenteeism, there are several factors particularly associated with school refusal. Fundamentally, there are typically one or more stressors, real or perceived, present within the school or home environment. Contemporary research most closely associates school refusal with some combination of specific and generalized phobias, anxiety, and depression (Brand & O'Conner, 2004). Consequently, school refusal should be considered a "heterogeneous and multicausal syndrome" according to Freemont (2003). According to Brand and O'Conner (2004), school refusal can be understood by identifying a number of common factors among school-refusing students, including

a high level of anxiety, a power struggle between students and one or both parents about the students' perception of helplessness, an inability to resist a powerful parent or parents, fear of not measuring up, thoughts that love is conditional on meeting parental standards, a tendency to avoid difficult situations, and fear of criticism or failure (p. 56).

Impacts of School Refusal

School phobia, like any other anxiety disorder, can create significant short- and long-term consequences if left untreated (Freemont, 2003). Potential consequences include poor academic performance, parental conflict, difficulty forming peer relationships, academic failure, school dropout, and development of post-adolescent psychiatric disorders such as panic, anxiety or depression that can last long into adulthood. A significant number of adults suffering from neurotic disorders, such as agoraphobia, were school refusers earlier in life, and school refusers tend to apply for psychiatric help more often as adults than individuals from the general population (Elliott, 1999). Parents who were formerly school-avoidant themselves may be inclined to pass on negative associations with school and education to their own children, creating a perpetuating cycle (Morrison-Gutman & McLoyd, 2000).

School refusal can also become self-reinforcing, as the longer the child remains home, the harder it becomes to return. School-refusing students fail to progress academically and socially along with their peers, which makes attention surrounding their return to school itself an increasingly daunting secondary stressor (Freemont, 2003; Havik et al., 2015).

INTERVENTIONAL STRATEGIES FOR SCHOOL REFUSAL

School administrators, lawmakers, counselors, teachers, parents, and therapists have developed a range of strategies that are used to treat school refusal, with varying degrees of success. In any case, prompt and timely intervention is key. According to O'Shea (2010), "there is a definitive acute phase that precedes the chronic phase, and as is the case in any number of disorders, early treatment is the most effective course of action" (p. 87).

Clinical assessment of school-refusing students is the first step in establishing a treatment plan. If an organic cause of physical complaints is ruled out by medical examination, the child typically is assessed by a child psychologist or psychiatrist, when, according to Elliott (1999), "consideration should be given to the child's affective, cognitive and behavioral functioning, both generally and in relation to the specific circumstances of the refusal" (p. 1003). Typically, a variety of procedures are employed: child self-reporting and self-monitoring, child and parent interviews, teacher- and parent-reported data, and behavioral observation at home and in school.

Following clinical evaluation, treatment plans are developed based on the child's individual needs. A 2003 study by Layne et al. found cognitive behavioral therapy to be the most efficacious treatment for depression, school phobia, and separation anxiety, with its effectiveness further enhanced when combined with additional added emphasis on social skills training, social exposure, and anxiety management. A study by Garvey and Hegrenes (1966) reported successful use of progressive desensitization techniques over the course of three weeks. The therapist and the affected student made incremental progress as they walked together toward the school entrance, entered the building, made steps closer toward the classroom, met with the teacher, and sat in the classroom with two classmates. Eventually, over the course of three weeks, the child was able to fully return to attending school. A follow-up after two years showed that the child had not relapsed and continued to attend school regularly after the intervention (Garvey & Hegrenes, 1966).

Virtual Learning and School Refusal

Immersion or desensitization-based therapeutic techniques are another option; there is strong evidence to support the effectiveness of a forced or rapid return rather than a graduated approach, particularly in cases where there have been no prior symptoms of school refusal behavior (Elliott, 1999). One nationwide study (Kearney & Beasley, 1994) showed that forced return was used in only 11.6% of school refusal cases, despite a nearly 100% success rate. The relatively low popularity of forced return may be due to the emotional stress it places on both child and parent, making it somewhat objectionable in the eyes of clinical practitioners and school leaders alike.

A more novel approach to desensitization therapy was considered in a 2009 University of Barcelona study (Gutiérrez-Maldonado et al.) in which Virtual Reality Exposure Therapy was used to successfully treat school phobia in a group of at-risk students. Mirroring the classic immersion model, like that of Garvey and Hegrenes (1966), students progressed incrementally from less to more stressful stimuli, but used a computer program that simulated entering the school, sitting in class, solving a problem on the board, and addressing the class by introducing themselves. In the simulation's most advanced level, the student is tasked with enduring "expressions of discontentment and pejorative comments" from virtual classmates (Gutiérrez-Maldonado et al., p. 230). The intervention was successful in lowering student self-reported fears and anxieties toward attending school.

Proactive Systemic Interventions

There are a number of measures that school leaders can take to help broadly increase student attendance on an organizational level, representing intervention that is proactive rather than reactive. For example, improved communication between school and families can make a tangible impact. A 2016 study by Rogers and Feller involved sending home letters to three groups of parents, each with incrementally more detail; improvements in attendance increased correspondingly. Letters that simply reminded parents of the importance of attending school increased attendance by 8%, while letters that also included a count of the student's total absences increased attendance by 10%. The third group of letters, which included a count of the student's total absences along with "relative absences" compared to other students, increased attendance by 11% (Rogers & Feller, 2016). Gottfried (2015) demonstrated that students who participated in school-based Pre-K programs went on to have demonstrably lower rates of absenteeism, as it acclimatized parents to the routine of sending their children to school daily and figuring out the accompanying logistics such as transportation and childcare.

From a building management perspective, school administrators can reduce school refusal by improving school culture. Bullying, truancy, classroom disruption, hostile teacher-pupil relationships, and other negative school-cultural factors are all correlated to higher incidents of school refusal (Elliott, 1999). Since depression and anxiety can be hard to identify in children and adolescents, thorough, school-wide initiatives in support of mental health and wellness are an important component of building school culture (Ek & Eriksson, 2013). A comprehensive support system including properly trained teachers, administrators, counselors, and school nurses is critical for timely and effective intervention in school refusal cases (Tyrrell, 2005). Teacher training should include strategies for interacting with school-refusing students in the classroom, where teachers should "resist the temptation to engage the child in lengthy inquisitions that may result in the child becoming defensive and more anxious" (Elliott, 1999, p. 1008).

VIRTUAL LEARNING

All of the interventions discussed to this point share the idea of returning to physical school as the ultimate goal. Virtual learning—or online-based, remote instruction that takes place outside the school campus—is another option that has been available for students, families, and school districts for the last several decades. Typically, this route has been seen as a temporary fix or measure of last resort (Tyrell, 2005). The COVID-19 crisis, however, has served as an outside catalyst for exponential growth and change in the related fields of remote instruction and virtual learning (Fisher et al., 2021).

Pre-COVID-19

There are a number of groups to whom virtual learning presents advantages making it particularly suited to those learners. It offers time flexibility and greater access for those who are geographically remote, physically disabled, have emotional and/or cognitive disorders, or are otherwise unable to easily participate in in-person classes (Abedi & Badragheh, 2011). For students who meet these criteria, virtual learning may be ideal. On the other hand, learning remotely requires a measure of self-discipline and time management compared to in-person learning, and entails a lack of face-to-face interpersonal interaction (Abedi & Badragheh, 2011). Students and their families who struggle with school refusal may find it difficult to balance virtual learning's benefits with its disadvantages. Virtual learning may resolve the acute conflict between students and parents over attending in-person school but may also delay resolution of underlying chronic psychological issues that contribute to school refusal in the first place (Kearney, 2007). Additionally, the lack of interpersonal interaction with both teachers and peers is often considered a significant element of the educational experience that is lost when students are not present in school (Neuman & Guterman, 2016). In contrast, some virtual schooling advocates suggest that much of the peer interaction in public schools is negative socialization, such as bullying, harassment, and profanity; children who opt out are still free to experience positive socialization, such as participation in local recreational sports, church activities, 4-H clubs, and so on (Wayne, 2019). Of course, this would require students who choose to learn virtually to also participate actively in the non-virtual world, which is not always feasible, such as during the COVID pandemic.

Critics of virtual schools point to educational standards that may not correspond with state or national standards; lack of collegial support among virtual teachers, leading to high rates of attrition; inadequate student support and counseling services; and lack of legal and/or fiscal oversight, such as in the 2013 case of the Pennsylvania Cyber Charter School founder and CEO convicted of embezzling millions in federally provided funds (Herold, 2013; Toppin & Toppin, 2016). Additionally, studies about the objective quality and effectiveness of cyber charter schools are emergent and limited (Beck et al., 2014; Collins et al., 2015; Waters et al., 2014). In contrast, arguments in favor of cyber charter schools parallel those for brick-and-mortar charter schools; competition from profit-driven charter schools, proponents contend, raises the bar for improved educational and economic efficiency necessary for public schools to keep up in an open marketplace. The effect of such free-market competition is to drive innovation and ultimately improve education for all students (Gulosino & Miron, 2017; Mann et al., 2016).

VIRTUAL LEARNING AND THE COVID-19 CRISIS

The landscape of American education experienced a sudden, vast, and transformative moment when the COVID-19 crisis caused schools to close for safety reasons on a massive scale. Ultimately, few states issued specific guidelines, and it was left to individual districts to devise and implement their own plans for a virtual learning model; predictably, results varied widely (Schwartz, 2020) Nevertheless, some guiding principles began to take shape: the emergent majority opinion suggested school be mindful of accommodation of both students and teachers, be flexible with student deadlines, emphasize relationships, and focus on essential learning (Schwartz, 2020).

The transition to virtual learning during COVID must be considered in the larger context of the global pandemic in which it took place. All actors involved, including school leaders, teachers, families, and students, were placed under great emotional duress, in addition to the omnipresent threat to their physical health and well-being. These circumstances helped lead to a renewed emphasis on the social-emotional component of P12 education (Belsha, 2020). Numerous experts suggested that teachers engage students in genuine human connection, checking in on their mental and emotional well-being, albeit in a virtual setting (Cipriano & Brackett, 2020; Fisher et al., 2020; Haavik, 2020). Unfortunately, many students who were most at risk were rendered unable to receive help from caring adults at school. Reported incidences of child abuse and neglect actually declined during the COVID quarantine; sadly, many observers believed this likely did not reflect a reduction in actual abuse, but rather an increase in cases going unreported (Belsha, 2020; Cramer, 2020).

MAKING THE CONNECTION: VIRTUAL LEARNING AND SCHOOL REFUSAL

On its face, virtual learning would seem like an ideal solution for students who are reluctant to attend in-person school, but only if that virtual experience is able to deliver high-quality instruction with objectively measurable academic outcomes. Additionally, in order for virtual learning to be a fully viable substitute for in-person learning, it should acknowledge and address the social-emotional component of schooling which, today, has largely been nonexistent for students not attending in-person school (McAuliffe, 2002; Neuman & Guterman, 2016). This hinges on the question of whether or not the future of virtual learning can provide successful delivery of both enriching academic and social-emotional content. Ongoing development in virtual learning suggests that significant advances in both areas are possible (Fisher et al., 2021). This may ultimately lead to virtual learning proving to be a more effective and efficient interventional approach for school-refusing students, especially in light of the exponentially accelerated evolution in the field prompted by the COVID pandemic.

Fundamentally, it has been established that chronic absenteeism is a strong predictor of high school dropout rates (Bridgeland et al., 2006; Jensen, 2009), and one survey of high school dropouts indicated that greater than 80% blame their decision on lack of direct engagement and/or difficulty fitting into a rigid, traditional school schedule (Bridgeland et al., 2006). Virtual learning has been shown to increase student engagement, especially among those who struggle with traditional schooling

Virtual Learning and School Refusal

hours (Abedi & Badragheh, 2011; Kearney, 2007), so it would stand to reason that, *ipso facto*, use of virtual learning can lead to reduced rates of chronic absenteeism. Yet no studies to date have specifically measured the effect of districts expanding virtual options to increase retention rates.

Questions remain about the use of virtual learning for school-refusing students. The COVID-19 pandemic's sudden and unexpected upheaval caused within the world of virtual learning has led directly to rapidly accelerated innovation and development in the field (Malkus et al., 2020). Virtual learning as a potential solution for school-refusing students is an area that has, to date, been under-researched and yielded inconsistent results. The next logical step, then is to help fill this gap in the scholarship about virtual learning for school-refusing students by examining the impacts of the large-scale shift away from in-person school and toward virtual learning brought about by the COVID pivot.

INTERVIEWS

The purpose of this study is to examine the impacts of the shift to virtual learning caused by the COVID-19 crisis on students who formerly displayed school refusal behavior. The researcher first identified students who were chronically absent during the 2018–2019 and/or early 2019–2020 school year(s), and from among that population categorized a subgroup of students who were chronically absent specifically due to school refusal. Attendance history was considered as a criterion for inclusion, as well as teacher, counselor, and administrator recommendation, which were considered to determine whether the cause of absence met the criteria of school refusal as defined for the purposes of this study: an avoidance of negative stimuli from within the school that is fundamentally emotionally based (Kearney, 2007; Wimmer, 2013). The study focuses on three case studies of students identified as demonstrating school refusal behavior.

Subjects were interviewed for the study, focusing on their attitudes toward school before, during, and after the forced shift to virtual learning. There were five key areas in which inquiry was directed, and each interview prompt was related to one or more of these themes. Specifically, the five thematic areas guiding the study were based on inquiry into how the shift to virtual learning instruction affected school-refusing students' a) academic outcomes; b) own perceptions of learning; c) willingness to complete schoolwork; d) perceptions toward school overall; and e) attitudes toward their academic futures.

Methods

Questions were designed to be broad to start, moving toward more specific questions as the interview progressed. Students were given a series of interview questions regarding their experiences with virtual learning and how it affected them with an emphasis on the five identified themes as detailed above. Responses to initial, broader questions were used to guide and shape the progression of the interview. For example, when a student stated early in the interview that they were home alone while their parents went to work, the remainder of the interview was contextually framed in light of that student's independent/unsupervised participation in virtual learning instruction, and so on.

Student interviews were transcribed, coded, and analyzed using an inductive method rooted in a constructivist approach to grounded theory (Creswell, 2012). Being that this is an emerging field of research in a novel area, there is no "off the shelf" theory available to test. Consequently, analysis of the data sought to construct an explanation that is grounded in the data itself (Creswell, 2012). Analysis of the interviews followed both a cross-sectional and analytical case study approach (Patton, 2015). The investigation considers commonalities expressed by participants, but also considers the unique experiences of each individual. Three case studies are presented in a linear-analytic structure, followed by broad inductive conclusions about the students' overall experiences with online learning.

Participants

Both male and female student participants were recruited, ranging in age from 13–17 years. In order to focus specifically on school refusal behavior, the study did not consider chronically absent students who were absent due to truancy, medical illness, family vacations, or any other reasons. Ethnicity, special needs, and socioeconomic status were not factored into the selection process, although students did need home internet access and a connected device to participate in the interview via online teleconference (i.e., Google Meet). Once the participants were selected, information, including student report card grades, was obtained in order to contextualize each individual student's experiences more distinctly.

The researcher also engaged in conversation with parents or guardians of the student subjects before, during, and after the student interviews. Parents of each student were informed ahead of time that the content of their individual discissions pertaining to the student would be eligible for inclusion in the study. While these discussions were not the initial emphasis of the study, they yielded a number of astute revelations and valuable insights and contributed to the creation of the overall explanatory construct.

CASE STUDY #1: O.W.

OW is a 16-year-old White male currently in 10th grade. According to his parents, his school refusal behavior began to manifest itself in 5th or 6th grade, when getting him out of bed and on his way to school quickly became a daily conflict. His parents—themselves also attempting to get ready and go to work each morning—found it very difficult to maintain this battle day after day, and his requests to stay home have been granted with increasing frequency as time has gone on. OW has been diagnosed with depression and anxiety and has seen a therapist on and off over the last few years; his parents do not believe a pharmacological intervention would be in his best interests. He does not have an IEP or 504 plan in place at school.

OW has also been diagnosed with a relatively uncommon chronic illness that is linked to psychosomatic symptoms and can be associated with a number of problematic behaviors, including avoidance behavior. There is a lack of universal consensus about this illness and its diagnosis in the medical community, but his family is confident that the diagnosis is correct. Consequently, the illness and its symptoms have become an omnipresent factor in their lives. OW's mother explained that those symptoms can be mitigated, according to his doctor, through careful diet and avoiding certain foods. However, OW has been generally resistant to following those dietary guidelines and they are not always strictly enforced in the home.

OW's parents have recently divorced, with a provision of 50/50 split custody. The parents' relationship is cordial but not highly cooperative; they often undermine or contradict one another's decisions related to OW and the rules he is expected to follow. His only sibling—a brother who is three years older—is a high-performing student academically and has had no attendance issues. His brother certainly has the potential to serve as a positive role model, but OW does not show a strong inclination to emulate his brother's behavior.

Academic Outcomes

In the 2019–2020 school year, prior to the virtual shift prompted by COVID, OW was in ninth grade. His rate of absenteeism decreased compared to the previous year, and his grades reflected some improvement. When instruction moved to a virtual setting in March of 2020, OW's performance dropped. His attendance in his online classes was extremely poor, and he earned failing grades in every class.

Perceptions of Learning

OW feels like he "hasn't learned anything" since the move to online instruction. He believes he "won't pass...[because] I'm too stupid and can't learn anyway." He blames this on a number of factors, including a lack of support from teachers, and a feeling that "the school doesn't care, or want to help."

Willingness to Engage

OW has been largely unwilling to engage in virtual learning. He is not interested in logging on to his classes, even with his camera off. He cites difficulty with online assignments and inability to stay focused: "The online stuff is so painful… there's too much work. They want you to pay attention for 80 minutes, but [I'm] lost after five." He further indicates an emotional disconnect, stating "Teachers don't know [me] at all," adding to his discouragement.

Perceptions of Schooling

School serves no purpose for OW, who has "zero interest" in schooling in general: "They only have college prep and don't have anything for people who don't want to go to college." He feels that there is no incentive or reward for attending school or getting an education, as he maintains the curriculum taught has no connection to any of his passions or interests. The specifics of what those passions or interests might be, however, are fairly ambiguous.

Attitudes Toward the Future

Before COVID, OW was not really sure what he wanted to do after high school. Recently, he has developed a slightly clearer picture of his ideal plan for the future: he knows he would like to drop out of high school and pursue some type of career as quickly as possible. While there is no strong sense of aspiration for a particular vocation, he does have a passing interest in pursuing a career as a chef. Any ambition he does have to pursue that career, however, is not combined with any specific plans to achieve that goal. He is of the belief that he has been "shortchanged" by his school district's lack of vocational/technical training in the culinary arts field, and he consequently feels he has little chance of realistically obtaining a career in that field on his own. At least one of his parents shares this belief, as they believe a transfer to a different nearby school district which does offer more electives could do wonders to motivate him in school.

Overall

Despite a marginal improvement in attendance and school engagement in the months prior to the COVID shift, OW shut down completely once school moved to virtual instruction. His predominant attitude is that if he stays home and refuses to participate in virtual school now, he can still figure things out at some point in the future. He has a broad desire to do something with his life at some point, but he is not sure what. Moreover, he does demonstrate a full understanding of the connection between his current actions and the actions that he needs to take in order to achieve his goals in the future. Regardless, he is convinced that the high school education he is currently expected to complete is not relevant to whatever path his life will ultimately take.

CASE STUDY #2: I.G.

IG is a 15-year-old Black male currently in 9th grade. He is the youngest of five adopted children living with his adoptive mother, who is White. His adoptive father died when he was 7 years old, leaving him to be raised by a single parent. His siblings, who are also adopted Black children, are not biologically related to one another, but they are a fairly tight-knit and mutually supportive family unit. He has been diagnosed with depression, anxiety, and severe attention deficit hyperactivity disorder (ADHD), along with an auditory processing disorder. He is classified as a special education student as a result of associated cognitive impairments and has an IEP that his teachers must follow.

School refusal began to manifest in Grade 6 after IG had a traumatic experience stemming from an interaction between himself and his guidance counselor. He met with his counselor to discuss what he describes as a disturbing dream he had, which included suicidal ideation; according to his mother, he had been experiencing night terrors semi-regularly for some time prior. The content of this conversation was interpreted by his guidance counselor as sufficient to send him for an immediate evaluation by psychiatric emergency screening services, which ultimately resulted in him being sent to an inpatient behavioral healthcare treatment facility. The result was a sense of extreme confusion, anxiety, and fear: "They asked why [I] was there and I said it was because of this dream. They were totally annoyed at me. I didn't understand it at all... You're in there with no cellphone, nobody knows I'm there. You're in there all alone."

This experience left both IG and his mother feeling that his comments were considered out of context and that the school blew things out of proportion. Fundamentally, IG and his family felt like the trust they had placed in school officials had been violated. Further, this incident resulted in bullying from other students when IG returned as word of his circumstances spread among his peers. He was assailed with extremely uncomfortable questions upon his return from an already traumatic experience: "They said stuff like, wow, you're still alive? Did you really try to kill yourself and go to a mental hospital?" Consequently, IG still harbors significant resentment and distrust toward the school system as a whole.

Most recently, IG has reconnected with his birth family, including his biological mother, a brother who is 11 months younger, and several other older siblings and cousins. This has been a source of happiness, but also one of upheaval and conflict. He would like to make a deeper connection with his birth family, but expressed frustration with his perception that this desire has not been strongly reciprocated: "Our family's always busy, their family's always busy... I don't know, whatever." This perceived lack of reciprocal desire to connect may be rooted in a significant disparity in cultural norms existing between IG's adoptive family and biological family, a source of substantial friction among all involved. At an age where the process of social development already weighs heavily on most young people, these events have led to a feeling of significant uncertainty about his own identity and place in the world.

Academic Outcomes

Since the move to virtual learning, IG has been almost entirely unwilling to participate in his virtual classes. As a result, he is failing virtually every subject. He does have accommodations and modifications in place per his IEP, but teachers have been unable to establish enough communication to even begin to implement those accommodations. His academic progress in a virtual setting to date has been effectively nil.

Perceptions of Learning

IG doesn't feel that he has learned anything since the move to virtual learning. He believes that his teachers harbor a certain amount of bias against him, primarily due to his status as a special education student. "No one is on [my] side," he states, ever since the shift away from in-person schooling took place. "I think they think [an] ADHD student is just a pain... like, I'm not getting paid extra to deal with this."

Willingness to Engage

As stated previously, IG was almost unwilling to participate in virtual learning. Many days he did not log on to his class meetings; when he did, he was often non-participatory, with his camera turned off. He would complete assigned tasks periodically, sometimes by googling the answer key to the given assignment. The overall impression he gave is that the transition to virtual learning has been a virtually insurmountable obstacle. This belief is shared by his family; his mother believes that his preexisting ADHD and anxiety make it extremely difficult for him to adapt to changes in his daily routine, and the COVID-19 crisis has been a huge source of stress. According to IG, he and his mother eventually reached a compromise: "[She] said, just sign on, I don't care if you go back to sleep. Just sign on."

Perceptions of Schooling

IG's overall perceptions of schooling are framed by a fundamental sense of broken trust and resentment toward the school system. The shift to virtual learning caused by the COVID crisis did little if anything to ameliorate that preconception. IG's perception of school is that of a place of uncertainty and insecurity. His feeling of anxiety fueled by that insecurity has manifested itself variously as avoidance, withdrawal, hostility, and aggression. For IG's family, the simple act of getting him up, out of bed, and logged on to his virtual classes represents a victory in itself. Taking the next steps, such as engaging with his teachers and classmates, appears to be far from imminent.

Attitudes toward the Future

The future is uncertain for IG. He reports no specific goals or aims after graduating from high school. According to IG's mother, when she initiates discussions with "*When* you go to college…" he is receptive. However, when the conversation shifts toward specific plans—whether for college, vocational training, or the workforce—he is generally ambivalent. His mother believes that this ambivalence may be rooted in his diagnosed clinical depression, which frequently presents as an overall affect of malaise. "I just don't really care," is his usual default response when asked about the future; when pressed, he sometimes voices interest in the field of social work and/ or helping at-risk teenagers someday. Even though he has not attended much virtual schooling since the COVID shift began, he still enjoys hanging out with friends, both in person and via online multiplayer games. His mother believes that allowing him to maintain social contact, rather than taking it away as punishment for school nonattendance, is of greater net benefit to his emotional wellbeing.

Overall

IG's chronic avoidance behavior can be understood as a manifestation of unfocused resentment and mistrust toward school as a whole, inclusive of peers, teachers, and administrators. Upheaval and turmoil associated with the COVID pandemic has made this fragile relationship even more tenuous. In recent months, his avoidance has begun to shift toward outright aggression, his mother explained. "There was a time when one of his teachers called him a 'crybaby' which he took very personally," she said. "Now, he has the attitude that nobody's ever going to do that to me again." IG himself put it more succinctly: "I'm not gonna be anybody's bitch."

A number of sentiments expressed by IG throughout the interview indicate that his attitudes toward schooling may be informed by additional racial, ethnic, and/or cultural factors. These factors involve a degree of complexity and nuance that could not be treated adequately within the limited confines of this study.

CASE STUDY #3: J.B.

JB is a 14-year-old White female currently in 9th grade. Her school refusal behavior started around 3 years ago, roughly around the time her parents initialized divorce proceedings. As an only child, she lives with her mother exclusively now that her parents' divorce is finalized. Prior to the pandemic, her mother struggled to get her out of bed and off to school, and she ended up staying home about twice a week. Some days, however, she was willing to go to school without much of a protest at all. JB has been diagnosed with ADHD, depression, and anxiety, but she does not have an IEP or 504 plan for special accommodations.

Academic Outcomes

The shift to virtual learning prompted by COVID in March 2020 yielded academic outcomes that were fairly similar to the grades JB had earned previously during in-person schooling. She failed two classes, Language Arts and Spanish, and earned Bs and Cs in others. The discrepancy in performance between classes seems to align with her personal preferences. "[Language Arts] is boring and stupid, and my Spanish teacher doesn't know anything," she explained.

Perceptions of Learning

JB was notably self-aware when it came to her ability to learn successfully in a virtual setting. "I wouldn't really learn anything, because I'd get distracted every second, or else fall asleep," she said. "Teachers don't know how to assign the right amount of work. Too much is discouraging and too little, I would finish right away and take a nap, then sometimes sleep through my next classes." When asked if she understood the material she said, "No, not really. In the moment I got it, but afterwards I [would] have no idea." Several teachers made attempts to contact her directly via email or by setting up 1:1 video chat, but JB explained, "I don't really check my email, so I didn't see it until way later."

Willingness to Engage

Self-reported engagement in virtual classes ranged from minimal to moderate, based on interest in the subject matter. However, even in the classes where moderate engagement took place, JB admits a tendency to lose focus: "I hate virtual. Teachers don't really pay attention to us. When I zone out, the teacher isn't there to call my name and make me listen." Regardless of engagement level, JB is unwilling to show herself on camera. "I used to turn my camera off, but an administrator came into our [Google] Meet, and my teacher got in trouble. Now we have to have it on. We have to show some part of our head, so I just point it at my forehead."

Perceptions of Schooling

Unlike the other students surveyed, JB's overall perceptions of schooling actually improved somewhat after the COVID shift, albeit in an unexpected way. Rather than seeing virtual learning as a welcome alternative to the in-person instruction she had been so adamant about avoiding, the virtual shift caused JB to arrive at a greater appreciation for in-person school: "Being virtual is too hard. I tried to follow along as best as I can but there's too much work. I want to go back in-person. I realized in-person is better. Some days I still don't feel like getting ready and stuff, but my mom makes me." She also reflected on the lack of personal connection with her teachers that made in-person school preferable to virtual learning. "Teachers, I would say, need to figure out how to help people learn more easily on virtual," she said. "Most of my teachers don't even know who I am. Before, at least I could see my teachers in the hall and stuff, and they know me."

Attitudes Toward the Future

After an uninspiring experience with virtual learning, JB looks forward to a return to in-person schooling post-COVID. Her intention is to try to improve her attendance, at least to the extent that it will enable her to graduate from high school. She believes some sort of post-secondary education is in her future, but she doesn't have any further details figured out just yet. "College? Yeah. I don't know what for, though, really," she speculated when asked. "Some days I just want to stay in bed all day though."

Overall

JB demonstrated a degree of self-awareness when considering the reasons for her poor academic performance and overall dissatisfaction with virtual learning. She found it too difficult to stay focused and engage with her virtual classes consistently while at home. Even though attending in-person school was no longer an issue, regular clashes in the household continued: "I used to fight with my mom about getting up and going to school, but when we went virtual, we still fought the same amount, just about other things I guess… because, I don't know, she's my mom?"

SUMMARY OF FINDINGS

The study was guided by an examination of five foundational questions: how the shift to virtual learning affected school-refusing students' academic outcomes, own perceptions of learning, willingness to complete schoolwork, perceptions toward school overall, and attitudes toward their academic futures. Academic outcomes were poor, with all students failing multiple classes, and two of three students failing all classes. The students' own perceptions of learning were negative, as exemplified by quotes such as "I really didn't learn anything" and "I don't know, it was dumb." The students' willingness to complete schoolwork was extremely limited, with one student participating with regularity in some classes and not in others, another student participating very rarely, and a third student effectively demonstrating zero participation. Perceptions of school overall were unanimously negative, with varying degrees of resignation: one student conveyed dissatisfaction with school but admitted a begrudging willingness to return, while the remaining two expressed a strong antipathy toward school and schooling as a whole. Finally, attitudes toward their academic futures varied: One student expressed a desire to enter the workforce, and another planned to attend college, but both were at a loss when asked what specific steps they intended to take to realize those goals. The third student surveyed voiced no feelings about the future one way or the other, an attitude which his mother suggested may be at least partially attributed to his diagnosed clinical depression.

In short, there were no areas among the five investigated that indicated substantive change took place as a result of the change from in-person to virtual instruction. Just as the virtual shift was not a simple fix for the problem, there is also no simple explanation for the lack of impact that the virtual shift had on the sample group. Every student's experience is different as school refusal is a symptom of a complex web of contributing factors. However, there were also several overarching emergent concepts that made themselves apparent over the course of the interview study, from which a broad concept of the dynamics of school refusal in a virtual environment may be drawn.

DYNAMICS OF SCHOOL REFUSAL IN A VIRTUAL ENVIRONMENT

Household Dynamics

On the whole, the school-refusing students studied came from households with a number of similar characteristics, including complex and sometimes acrimonious intrafamilial dynamics. In all cases, these parents felt they had to walk a delicate line between being overly permissive on one hand or pushing the child away by being overly authoritarian on the other. As a result, household expectations for behavioral norms were often unclear and applied inconsistently.

Emergent Concepts

Several concepts emerged regarding the student subjects and their fundamental relationships with school. Each student demonstrated a series of avoidance techniques that can be characterized as reinforced learned behaviors. This uncanny ability to effectively avoid anxiety-provoking stimuli may be seen as the net product of many years of implicit positive and negative reinforcement, transmitted to each student through interactions with the many individuals who may have contributed to the child's social development, including parents, family members, teachers, school personnel, and peers. Finally, all students interviewed expressed a general, nonspecific dislike toward school and schooling.

These factors that were identified and drawn from the data collectively represent emotionally based sources of disaffection. Since school refusal is, at its core, an emotionally based phenomenon (Wimmer, 2013), consideration of these concepts is of vital importance toward constructing an understanding of how and why the shift to virtual learning had a minimal impact on these students' engagement with school.

Shared Responsibility

Another commonality of school-refusing students observed in the study was a pattern of learned and reinforced avoidance behavior. According to Kearney (2007), school refusal may present acutely as a direct response to a particular stimulus or may be chronic as avoidance becomes habitualized. In all cases observed, the behavior was chronic, and by the time these students had reached middle- to high school-age it was fairly well-established and ingrained. In truth, all parties involved share a certain degree of complicity in reinforcing this behavior through their actions, whether they realize it consciously or not. When speaking with the parents of these students, all acknowledged that a measure of complicity and responsibility for the behavior pattern could be ascribed to themselves.

Misplaced Antipathies for School in General

This pattern of behaviors exemplifies a tendency to associate negative feelings and emotions to all things broadly related to school that is present among school-refusing students. According to Woolfolk (2014), children and adolescents often lack the ability to pinpoint the source of negative feelings, and further lack the vocabulary to express those feelings in a specific way. Consequently, a handful of individual negative experiences within the school setting can manifest as an aversion to all things connected with schooling.

For example, one of the subjects of this study initially refused to join a video chat with the researcher—according to the parent, "Why should I volunteer to waste my time with people who said I was unteachable?" was the student's response when asked why they would not participate. Upon further discussion, it was revealed that the student, now a high school freshman, was referring to a statement they recalled overhearing a teacher make in elementary school. This exchange was one among several self-described negative experiences in their school career to date, but one that clearly made a lasting impression.

The phenomenon of misdirected anger toward school in general, rather than limiting resentment toward a specific negative stimulus that caused emotional discomfort, is to be expected among adolescents. Moreover, it further reinforces the fundamental conclusion of this study, which suggests a change of setting from in-person to online remote instruction is not a cure-all for school refusal behavior. Ultimately, the findings of the study served to indicate that school refusal is a complicated and difficult condition, which requires a holistic approach with a variety of remedies in place to overcome.

IMPLICATIONS FOR SCHOOL LEADERS

School refusal, as characterized by Freemont (2003), is a "heterogeneous and multicausal syndrome" requiring an equally multi-faceted and nuanced interventional approach. The findings of this study suggest several additional action steps to address school refusal in hybrid or fully remote settings.

Mental Health Services

Increasing access to mental health services for students, whether on-campus or off, is crucial. There is a wealth of research and literature exploring how schools can approach this issue. For example, this could include forming partnerships with external clinicians, therapists, and mental health organizations to provide regular counseling services for students. These partnerships can offer both in-person and virtual therapy sessions, making mental health support accessible to students regardless of location. Another approach is to employ or expand in-house counseling staff, ensuring students have access to trained professionals who understand their unique challenges. These counselors should be equipped to handle a range of issues, from academic stress to emotional wellbeing.

Professional development programs for teachers, administrators, and staff can further enhance this support. Training in mental health awareness, cultural sensitivity, and trauma-informed approaches helps educators recognize early signs of mental health struggles in students, allowing for timely interventions. Additionally, schools can implement mental health programs aimed at normalizing discussions around mental health, reducing stigma, and encouraging students to seek help when needed. This could include regular workshops, assemblies, and classroom discussions on mental health topics. Finally, fostering peer support networks where students can share their experiences and offer mutual support is vital. This not only helps destigmatize mental health struggles but also builds a sense of community and solidarity among students.

School Culture

Building a positive school culture is paramount and should encompass key components such as training for staff, community partnerships, and student support programs. A proactive approach is needed to prevent student withdrawal in virtual classrooms or disengagement in physical settings. This can be achieved by promoting active student engagement and destigmatizing and normalizing students' mental health struggles, vulnerability, and self-reflective behavior. Rather, schools should focus on encouraging positive peer engagement, empathy, and mindfulness (Jensen, 2009). Teachers and school leaders must adapt to changing student needs and evolving learning environments. Professional development should focus on best practices for hybrid and virtual learning, ensuring staff, teachers, and administrators are equipped to support students effectively.

CONCLUSIONS

School refusal is an emotionally based learned avoidance behavior and a significant problem for educational leaders. However, it is complex, multifaceted, and deeply ingrained. Students often lack the ability to identify and verbalize the specific factors prompting a flight response from school, resulting in broad negative associations and general disengagement with school overall. A change of instructional venue from an in-person to a virtual learning platform was insufficient to change this established negative association among the students in this study.

The solution for improving attendance is the renewal and maintenance of student engagement. The way forward to achieve this goal, whether in-person or virtually, is to promote a culture of empathy, involve all students in SEL from a young age, and establish school as a safe place with caring, trustworthy adults.

Virtual learning should not simply consist of traditional 20th-century instructional practices transposed into an alternate platform. Instead, it should be designed thoughtfully and purposefully to maximize its effectiveness within the framework of the unique advantages and disadvantages presented by schooling in an online setting. The potential for future utilization of virtual learning represents a world of possibilities and flexible options academically, but it must also encompass methods of socioemotional engagement that utilize this distinct medium in a novel and innovative way.

REFERENCES

Abedi, M., & Badragheh, A. (2011). Online classes vs. traditional classes: Comparison between two methods. *The Journal of American Science*, 7(4), 307–314.

Balfanz, R., & Byrnes, V. (2012). *The importance of being in school: A report on absenteeism in the nation's public schools*. Johns Hopkins University Center for Social Organization of Schools.

Balfanz, R., & Byrnes, V. (2018). Using data and the human touch: Evaluating the NYC inter-agency campaign to reduce chronic absenteeism. *Journal of Education for Students Placed at Risk*, 23(1–2), 107–121. 10.1080/10824669.2018.1435283

Bauer, L., Liu, P., Schanzenbach, D. W., & Shambaugh, J. (2018). *Reducing chronic absenteeism under the every student succeeds act*. The Brookings Institution.

Beck, D. E., Maranto, R., & Lo, W.-J. (2014). Determinants of student and parent satisfaction at a cyber charter school. *The Journal of Educational Research*, 107(3), 209–216. 10.1080/00220671.2013.807494

Belsha, K. (2020, November 23). *Across the U.S., fewer students are being identified as homeless. Educators say that's actually a bad sign*. Chalkbeat.

Brand, C., & O'Conner, L. (2004). School refusal: It takes a team. *Children & Schools*, 26(1), 54–64. 10.1093/cs/26.1.54

Bridgeland, J. M., DiIulio, J. J., & Morrison, K. B. (2006). *The silent epidemic: Perspectives of high school dropouts*. Bill & Melinda Gates Foundation.

Centers for Disease Control and Prevention. (2020). *Interim guidance for administrators of US K–12 schools and childcare programs: Plan, prepare, and respond to coronavirus disease (COVID-19)*. Centers for Disease Control and Prevention.

Chang, H., & Romero, M. (2008). *Present, engaged and accounted for: The critical importance of addressing chronic absence in the early grades*. National Center for Children in Poverty.

Chiland, C., & Young, J. G. (1990). *Why children reject school*. Yale University Press.

Chingos, M. (2013). Questioning the quality of virtual schools. *Education Next*, 13(2), 1–8.

Cipriano, C., & Brackett, M. (2020). *Teacher interrupted: Leaning into the social-emotional learning crisis amid the COVID-19 crisis*. EdSurge News.

Collins, K. M., Green, P. C.III, Nelson, S. L., & Madahar, S. (2015). Cyber charter schools and students with disabilities: Rebooting the IDEA to address equity, access, and compliance. *Equity & Excellence in Education*, 48(1), 71–86. 10.1080/10665684.2015.991219

Cramer, M. (2020, October 5). Parents face murder charge in death of girl with severe lice. *The New York Times*.

Creswell, J. W. (2012). *Educational research: Planning, conducting, and evaluating quantitative and qualitative research*. Pearson.

Dodge, K. A. (1993). Social-cognitive mechanisms in the development of conduct disorder and depression. *Annual Review of Psychology*, 44(1), 559–584. 10.1146/annurev.ps.44.020193.0030158434896

Ek, H., & Eriksson, R. (2013). Psychological factors behind truancy, school phobia, and school refusal: A literature study. *Child & Family Behavior Therapy*, 35(3), 228–248. 10.1080/07317107.2013.818899

Elliott, J. (1999). Practitioner review: School refusal: Issues of conceptualization, assessment, and treatment. *Journal of Child Psychology and Psychiatry, and Allied Disciplines*, 40(7), 1001–1012. 10.1111/1469-7610.0051910576531

Fisher, D., Frey, N., & Hattie, J. (2021). *The distance learning playbook: Teaching for engagement & impact in any setting*. Corwin.

Freemont, W. (2003). School refusal in children and adolescents. *American Family Physician*, 68(8), 1555–1561.14596443

Garvey, W. P., & Hegrenes, J. R. (1966). Desensitization techniques in the treatment of school phobia. *The American Journal of Orthopsychiatry*, 36(1), 147–152. 10.1111/j.1939-0025.1966.tb02301.x5904485

Gottfried, M. A. (2015). Can center-based childcare reduce the odds of early chronic absenteeism? *Early Childhood Research Quarterly*, 32, 160–173. 10.1016/j.ecresq.2015.04.002

Gulosino, C., & Miron, G. (2017). Growth and performance of fully online and blended K–12 public schools. *Education Policy Analysis Archives*, 25(124), 124. 10.14507/epaa.25.2859

Gutiérrez-Maldonado, J., Magallón-Neri, E., Rus-Calafell, M., & Peñaloza-Salazar, C. (2009). Virtual reality exposure for school phobia. *Anuario de Psicología*, 40(2), 223–236.

Haavik, M. (2020, October 12). % of Minnesota's educators are considering quitting. *KARE News Minneapolis*.

Hanushek, E., & Woessmann, L. (2020). *The economic impacts of learning losses*. OCED.

Havik, T., Bru, E., & Ertesvåg, S. K. (2015). School factors associated with school refusal- and truancy-related reasons for school non-attendance. *Social Psychology of Education*, 18(2), 221–240. 10.1007/s11218-015-9293-y

Herold, B. (2013, August 6). Federal indictment fuels concerns about Pa. cyber charters. *EdWeek*.

Jensen, E. (2009). *Teaching with poverty in mind: What being poor does to kids' brains and what schools can do about it*. ASCD.

Kearney, C. A. (2007). *Getting your child to say "yes" to school: A guide for parents of youth with school refusal behavior*. Oxford University Press. 10.1093/oso/9780195306309.001.0001

Kearney, C. A., & Beasley, J. F. (1994). The clinical treatment of school refusal behavior: A survey of referral and practice characteristics. *Psychology in the Schools*, 31(2), 128–132. 10.1002/1520-6807(199404)31:2<128::AID-PITS2310310207>3.0.CO;2-5

Kearney, C. A., & Graczyk, P. (2014). A response to intervention model to promote school attendance and decrease school absenteeism. *Child and Youth Care Forum*, 43(1), 1–25. 10.1007/s10566-013-9222-1

Layne, A. E., Bernstein, G. A., Egan, E. A., & Kushner, M. G. (2003). Predictors of treatment response in anxious-depressed adolescent with school refusal. *Journal of the American Academy of Child and Adolescent Psychiatry*, 42(3), 319–326. 10.1097/00004583-200303000-0001212595785

Malkus, N., Christensen, C., & West, L. (2020). *School district response to the COVID-19 pandemic: Round 1, districts' initial responses*. American Enterprise Institute.

Mann, B., Kotok, S., Frankenberg, E., Fuller, E., & Schafft, K. (2016). Choice, cyber charter schools, and the educational marketplace for rural districts. *Rural Educator*, 37(3), 17–29.

McAuliffe, G. (2002). *Working with troubled youth in schools: A guide for all school staff*. Bergin & Garvey. 10.5040/9798216038818

Morrison-Gutman, G., & McLoyd, V. (2000). Parents management of their children's education within the home, at school, and in the community: An examination of African-American families living in poverty. *The Urban Review*, 32(1), 1–24. 10.1023/A:1005112300726

National Center for Education Statistics. (2018). *Percentage of public school districts with students enrolled in technology-based distance education courses and number of enrollments in such courses by instructional level and district characteristics.* NCES.

National Center for Education Statistics. (2019). *What percentage of elementary and secondary schools offer distance education?* NCES.

Neuman, A., & Guterman, O. (2016). Academic achievements and homeschooling—It all depends on the goals. *Studies in Educational Evaluation*, 51, 1–6. 10.1016/j.stueduc.2016.08.005

New Jersey Department of Education. (2019). *NJ school performance report.* Author.

O'Shea, S. M. (2010). *A study of school phobic students on selected psychodynamic variables.* Available from ProQuest Central; ProQuest Dissertations & Theses Global. (756399330).

Patton, M. Q. (2015). *Qualitative research and evaluation methods* (4th ed.). Sage.

Richardson, K. L., Weiss, N. S., & Halbach, S. (2018). Chronic school absenteeism of children with chronic kidney disease. *The Journal of Pediatrics*, 199, 267–271. 10.1016/j.jpeds.2018.03.03129706492

Robert Wood Johnson Foundation. (2016). *The relationship between school attendance and health.* Robert Wood Johnson Foundation.

Rogers, T., & Feller, A. (2016). Reducing student absences at scale. Working paper, Harvard University, Cambridge MA.

Schwartz, S. (2020, May 13). States all over the map on remote learning rigor, detail. *EdWeek*.

Stempel, H., Cox-Martin, M., Bronsert, M., Dickinson, L. M., & Allison, M. A. (2017). Chronic school absenteeism and the role of adverse childhood experiences. *Academic Pediatrics*, 17(8), 837–843. 10.1016/j.acap.2017.09.01328927940

Toppin, I. N., & Toppin, S. M. (2016). Virtual schools: The changing landscape of K–12 education in the U.S. *Education and Information Technologies*, 21(6), 1571–1581. 10.1007/s10639-015-9402-8

Townsley, M. (2020). Grading principles in pandemic-era learning: Recommendations and implications for secondary school leaders. *Journal of School Administration Research and Development*, 5(1), 8–14. 10.32674/jsard.v5iS1.2760

Tyrell, M. (2005). School phobia. *Journal of Nursing (Luton, England)*, 21(3), 147–151.15898849

Waters, L. H., Barbour, M. K., & Menchaca, M. P. (2014). The nature of online charter schools: Evolution and emerging concerns. *Journal of Educational Technology & Society*, 17(4), 379–389.

Wayne, I. (2019, February 4). Benefits of homeschooling. *The New American Magazine*.

Wimmer, M. B. (2013). Implementing evidence-based practices for school refusal and truancy. *National Association of School Psychologists Communique*, 42(4), 18–20.

Woolfolk, A. (2014). *Educational Psychology: Active learner edition* (12th ed.). Pearson.

Yin, R. K. (2018). *Case study research and applications: Design and methods* (6th ed.). Sage.

Chapter 2
The Family Perspective and Experience:
How the COVID-19 Pandemic Interrupted and Impacted Education

Gabriella Hall
Monmouth University, USA

Ryan J. Eckert
https://orcid.org/0009-0001-5818-096X
Monmouth University, USA

ABSTRACT

This chapter provides a comprehensive analysis of the impact of family dynamics on children's educational experiences during the COVID-19 pandemic. The pandemic's effect on education, necessitating a shift to remote, virtual, and hybrid learning models, underscored the importance of family support in maintaining continuity in children's education. The chapter delves into factors that shape family dynamics, such as socioeconomic status, family composition, and the educational background of parents or caregivers. These elements not only affect the level and quality of parent-child interaction but also contribute to educational challenges, disparities, and learning gaps, which were further magnified during the pandemic. The narrative further explores the diverse experiences and challenges faced by families of students with special needs. By examining the interplay of these dynamics, the chapter aims to offer insights into the complex relationship between family support and educational success, providing a nuanced understanding of the diverse family experiences during a global crisis.

DOI: 10.4018/979-8-3693-1507-1.ch002

The Family Perspective and Experience

INTRODUCTION

A student's educational experience, beginning in the earliest stage of preschool all the way through high school and higher education, is significantly influenced by family support. More specifically, a child's home life and associated support can impact academic outcomes, student engagement, persistence, perseverance, and psychological well-being (Roksa & Kinsley, 2019). The quantity and quality of parents' and caregivers' interaction with their children can also significantly impact a child's learning and academic progression (Kuhfeld et al., 2020). The level of support that a family can provide, along with the quality and quantity of parent-child interaction, depends on various factors. These include, but are not limited to, geographical location, socioeconomic status, family composition, dynamics, and the educational background of parents or caregivers. Each family possesses distinct influential factors that may create educational challenges and disparities, contributing to learning gaps among students. The challenges, disparities, and learning gaps associated with family dynamics were further exacerbated by the COVID-19 pandemic. This became increasingly evident as society endeavored to navigate the novel territory of delivering instruction through remote, virtual, and hybrid learning models.

The COVID-19 pandemic undoubtedly impacted education and the ways in which students received instruction and engaged in learning. When schools abruptly closed, families found themselves compelled to facilitate remote, virtual, and hybrid models of learning. This shift necessitated adequate time, space, and access to technology, resources that many families struggled to accommodate or secure. Furthermore, family composition and the employment status of caregivers, particularly whether they were required to report to their own jobs, significantly influenced the situation. Childcare emerged as a major issue and source of stress for families. These unique factors underscored the varied ways in which families' capability to facilitate and sustain learning was profoundly impacted by the pandemic.

The COVID-19 pandemic, while a shared global experience, had varied impacts on the day-to-day lives of individual families, leading to unique circumstances and diverse perspectives. This chapter aims to highlight these diverse experiences and viewpoints of families. It will also share specific accounts of how educators collaborated with families, offering unprecedented levels of support to mitigate and alleviate the burdens brought about by the pandemic.

This chapter will explore the diverse experiences and perspectives of families, focusing on several critical factors. Firstly, family dynamics will be examined, considering aspects such as family composition, the challenge of maintaining a work-life balance, and the educational background of parents. Secondly, the impact of family income will be discussed, including access to essential resources, childcare arrangements, and issues related to food security. Lastly, attention will be given to families with exceptional needs. This includes an exploration of special education services, the specific challenges faced by families of children with autism spectrum disorder, and the importance of early childhood education. Through this comprehensive analysis, the chapter aims to provide a nuanced understanding of the varied experiences of families during the COVID-19 pandemic.

FAMILY DYNAMICS

The dynamics of families before and during the pandemic greatly impacted ways in which individual families experienced and responded to school closures. The rapid shift in education and sudden closure of schools presented a number of obstacles, barriers, and struggles for children and their families who were expected to facilitate learning within their homes. Certain family dynamics contributed to heightened risks of learning loss, limited access to resources, and increased stress and anxiety levels among both children and parents. The family dynamics with the most significant impact on education during school closures were 1) family composition; 2) work-life balance; and 3) parent education. These factors collectively influenced families' abilities to establish effective school routines at home, ensure access to necessary resources, and provide adequate support and guidance. Additionally, these dynamics affected the capacity of families to effectively communicate and collaborate with teachers, as well as to manage stress and anxiety. Each of these aspects played a crucial role in the educational experiences of families during the period of school closures.

Family Composition

Family composition refers to the makeup and structure of a family based on the members and living arrangements within the home. The composition of individual families can be unique, nuanced, and ever-changing. Families vary significantly in their structures and living arrangements. Some families consist of two parents, while others are led by a single parent. There are instances where families operate across two separate homes, with children traveling between them, and others where the family lives and functions primarily in one home. Family sizes also differ, with some being small and others larger. Despite these differences, each family operates in its own unique way, reflecting the diverse nature of family dynamics in society. These factors shape the educational environment and experiences of children in various ways, highlighting the importance of family structure and dynamics in the context of educational outcomes and experiences. In short, the compositional factors

The Family Perspective and Experience

of families significantly influence how children experience education under normal circumstances, even without the added challenges of a global pandemic.

The parenting dynamic present within the home can prove particularly impactful on children's academic performance and success. Divorce and the changes it creates can often have unintended ripple effects on all members of a family, especially pertaining to education. In families with divorced or separated parents, this can include shifts in living arrangements, the introduction of new family members like stepsiblings or stepparents, and differences in parenting styles between households. Additionally, there may be a decrease in parental involvement, particularly from the non-resident parent. This situation often leads to access to fewer resources, which can further affect the educational environment and opportunities available to children. These factors collectively play a significant role in shaping the educational journey of children from families with divorced or separated parents (Härkönen et al., 2017). Children from single-parent homes in comparison to two-parent homes drop out of high school at higher rates, are more likely to attain a General Equivalency Diploma (GED), perform lower on standardized testing, receive overall lower grade point averages, and read at a lower level (Hampden-Thompson, 2013; Härkönen et al., 2017).

The influence and impact of family composition on education became increasingly pronounced when schools were forced to shut down during the COVID-19 pandemic, and this period saw many new challenges for families with divorced and separated parents. Communication and co-parenting were brought to the forefront while parents navigated disputes over custody and at-home learning. Divorced parents reported co-parenting as a major source of conflict and indicated that disagreements over school decisions and interactions were at the root of many of their co-parenting conflicts (Goldberg et al., 2021). Remote learning was identified as a major catalyst of this sort of conflict, with newly created friction emerging over how to balance and share responsibility for facilitating remote learning (Goldberg et al., 2021). Parents were quick to point out the challenge posed by managing educational responsibilities alongside full-time work. For example, one parent reported that they closely monitor virtual learning when they have the children every other week, being sure to provide updates to the other parent for continuity. Frustratingly, they felt the other parent's involvement in return was minimal, often leaving the children to their own devices and not providing any information back (Goldberg et al., 2021). These kinds of stories exemplify the ways in which divorced and separated parents struggled with co-parenting during the pandemic, and how co-parenting impacted children and their experiences with remote learning.

The shift to at-home learning meant that parents were suddenly responsible for managing and supervising their children's education in a more hands-on way. Many parents were required to set aside time during their day to help children with their schoolwork, but this created an issue of time management, especially for parents with multiple children. More than one child in the household created an issue of balancing heavier workloads, facilitating additional learning, and supporting diverse learning abilities. Some parents described the challenge of assisting two children simultaneously with different subjects; another parent noted the difficulty of managing three children at varying skill levels, each with different motivations and abilities to focus on tasks (Garbe et al., 2020). Moreover, parents reported an added burden when managing remote learning for both school-aged and preschool-level children. The unique situation of preschool children, with their need for more support, inability to navigate online platforms, and shorter attention spans for sedentary learning, created additional challenges. These struggles were further amplified for parents who also had to cater to the needs of other children in the household (Garbe et al., 2020).

Work-Life Balance

Families' ability to manage remote learning during school closures was highly influenced by their parent(s)' work-life balance. At a minimum, remote learning required some level of parental supervision during times when children would have otherwise been occupied and supervised by their educators, and more often necessitated greater parental involvement to ensure children were grasping new concepts (Lee et al., 2021). The level of parental supervision needed to facilitate productive remote learning was dependent on a number of factors, such as family size, children's age(s) and ability, and specific learning needs. Students who receive special services through an Individualized Education Plan (IEP) often require additional supervision and supports in the classroom, and the period of remote learning was no different. The obligation to assist and support children's remote learning and adequately meet their individual needs was especially difficult for parents who were also managing their own work responsibilities. In one 2022 study conducted by Roy et al., families of 606 children were surveyed to better understand the COVID-19 experience in terms of the family dynamic. A number of challenges posed by remote learning were identified, including the balance between remote learning and work responsibilities (Roy et al., 2022). The burden of maintaining a productive and healthy work-life balance, managing stress levels, and adequately supporting children's schooling became even more pronounced for single parents who lacked a partner to share responsibilities with (Lee et al., 2021). Working parents, particularly essential workers who had to report to work outside the home, encountered significant challenges in securing childcare due to social distancing guidelines and concerns about virus transmission. The combination of a lack of childcare and work responsibilities made it challenging for parents to manage their children's remote learning experiences. This situation often led to heightened levels of anxiety, stress, and exhaustion.

Parent Education

Parental education can also impact a child's educational experiences, including ways in which they acquire new knowledge. The vocabulary parents use with and around their children, for example, can significantly impact linguistic development (Harris & Goodall, 2008). Early language development can serve as an important gateway for future learning, in addition to impacting the ability to understand new information, communicate with others, and interact socially. When children attend school, they are exposed not only to the vocabulary used by their parents but also to the language and vocabulary of their teachers and peers. Such exposure aids in building a more extensive vocabulary inventory. However, during school closures, with education primarily delivered through remote and virtual platforms, children's exposure to diverse language significantly diminished. Consequently, the language and vocabulary spoken by parents at home became more influential. Parents with higher education levels had the advantage of relating to their children's schoolwork and using their own educational experiences to aid their children in understanding and completing assignments. Additionally, parents' own schooling experiences influence their views and perceptions of education, which can directly impact how their children value school and how parents approach supporting remote learning at home.

Family Dynamic Discussion

Family dynamics are an important contributing factor in educational outcomes; this was true before and during the COVID-19 pandemic and remains relevant today. It is important that educators and stakeholders, including parents, consider how individual family dynamics influence the ways in which children access education, the attitudes and habitats they cultivate around the value of education, and the levels of support they receive from members of their households. When schools were forced to close in March of 2020, families had to quickly adapt their homes and lifestyles to accommodate remote learning. Parents, many of whom already supported their children's education in many ways, were suddenly responsible for facilitating and managing day-to-day schooling as well. Besides the fact that many parents lack formal training in teaching, parents were also faced with a number of other obstacles that made accommodating remote learning difficult. Each family's experience was unique and influenced by their own distinctive dynamics, such as family composition, work-life balance, and parent education. The composition of individual families significantly influenced how parents managed co-parenting and shared responsibilities. The number of children in a family affected the amount of remote learning that parents needed to juggle. Parents' work situations determined the level of support they could provide. Moreover, parents' own educational levels and experiences shaped their attitudes towards remote learning and their capability to facilitate learning at home. These factors not only impacted the effectiveness of remote learning and contributed to potential learning loss during school closures, but they also continue to be crucial considerations for educators, stakeholders, and parents in the preparation, implementation, and support of learning both currently and in the future. If educators thoughtfully acknowledge the importance of family dynamics in children's learning experiences, they are more likely to provide the necessary support that certain families may require. They are also better equipped to make effective adaptations in their instruction and delivery of information, thereby making learning more accessible and engaging for diverse learners.

FAMILY INCOME LEVELS

Gaps in learning and academic achievements are an ever-growing issue in education. The root cause of achievement gaps is often debated but many have argued that this phenomenon is often correlated to an imbalance of opportunity. Opportunity is largely related to access, and not all children have equal or equitable access to important resources that assist in advancing their educational experiences. These resources can include quality schools, highly trained teachers, tutoring, internet access, possession of electronic devices, reliable and supportive childcare, food insecurity, and the means necessary to sustain physical and mental health. Aside from resources that enhance education, some children lack access to everyday necessities like food, water, and shelter. When children's basic needs are not met, their ability to effectively engage in meaningful learning is greatly hindered. This inequitable access and opportunity became alarmingly evident when schools abruptly closed during COVID-19. Children who had previously received essential meals through their schools faced dire food shortages at home, and an inability to access the necessary technology resources for remote learning not only impaired children from lower socioeconomic backgrounds, but also significantly limited their ability to participate in education, broadening an already existing achievement gap.

Pre-Existing Achievement Gaps

Prior to schools closing during the COVID-19 pandemic, achievement gaps among minority and economically disadvantaged students already existed. Research collected and analyzed before the pandemic indicates disparities in reading levels,

The Family Perspective and Experience

math levels, school attendance, and matriculation rates among children of color and lower socio-economic status in comparison to white and Asian children and children from higher socio-economic backgrounds (Gee et al., 2023). Some contributing factors include parent education levels (Hung et. al., 2020), adverse home environments, familial stress levels (Dahl & Lochner, 2005), and quality of schools and teachers (Porter, 2007). Although some contributing factors of the achievement gap have been identified, the research varies and it appears the inequity is much more nuanced and multifaceted (Gee et al., 2023). The inability to clearly identify the root cause of the achievement gap, coupled with a failure to draft, initiate, and sustain effective solutions, results in the continuation of inequities in education. During crises, these existing inequities and disparities are often exacerbated, highlighting the urgent need for more effective educational strategies and interventions.

Access to Internet and Digital Devices

When school shut down and learning shifted outside of the brick and mortar school building, families, especially families of lower socio-economic status, scrambled to secure adequate ways to support remote learning from home. In order to support remote learning families needed access to the internet and access to digital devices. The digitalization of education during school closures created barriers for children and families who were either unable to access the internet and or had limited access to multiple devices. Even though many schools and other entities offered children temporary use of devices, practically attaining those devices and accessing quality reliable internet service was challenging for many. For families that live in apartment buildings or multi-family homes, internet stability was often challenging given the number of devices working on a single source of service. Additionally, some parents and caregivers were unfamiliar with using digital technology which made it difficult for them to support their children through the remote learning process. This was especially true among younger children, who often required much more guidance and assistance to access and navigate remote learning formats. The digital divide between families with ample access to reliable internet and multiple devices and those without shed light how income inequity impacts opportunity, consequently creating barriers to equitable attainment of effective and meaningful education.

The Impact of COVID-19 on Achievement Gaps

The impacts of the pandemic and school closures were far reaching and potentially long lasting. The effects the pandemic had on academic growth and educational participation for minority families and families of lower socio-economic status appear to be more detrimental in comparison to white families and families of higher socio-economic status (Gee et al., 2023). Research findings suggest that, in general, non-school related factors are a leading contributor to academic disparities (Hung et al., 2020). These findings are based on data that reports larger academic loss and regression among minority and lower SES children during school recessions, such as holiday breaks and summer vacation (Hung et al., 2020). The same trend in academic loss was observed during school closures caused by COVID-19. The exact reason behind this disparity is not clearly identified but research data indicates that while schools were shut down and or operating on partial hybrid models, minority children and children of lower socio-economic status suffered greater academic loss in areas of math and reading, especially those at the elementary level, and had increased levels of absenteeism (Gee et al., 2023). Underlying causes of increased chronic absenteeism could be related to disproportionate exposures to illness, as well inconsistent access to stable housing and/or reliable transportation. These barriers contribute to the widening of the achievement gap in the United States and demonstrate the significant impact of socio-economic factors on educational equity.

Childcare

School shutdowns and quarantine mandates presented a significant childcare dilemma for many families, who found themselves needing to balance work responsibilities with caring for their children, now at home full-time. As Zhang, Sauval, and Jenkins (2023) noted, the abrupt closure of many facilities led to a rapid increase in the demand for childcare, while the supply was severely limited. This situation posed particular challenges for families with young children and for those with caregivers who were still required to work outside the home. Securing childcare became increasingly difficult as facilities shut down, and babysitters or other caregivers were concerned about the risk of spreading the virus. Families that relied on grandparents and other elder relatives for childcare also faced the dilemma of balancing their need for assistance with family members' health and safety. In addition to needing someone to attend to children's needs and supervise their safety and well-being, many children needed adult guidance to engage in education at-home. The lack of childcare meant not only were families unable to coordinate adult supervision, but they were also unable to assist their children through the remote learning process, creating yet another barrier between educational access and opportunity among families with limited resources.

A lack of access to childcare throughout the pandemic and school shutdowns may have also exacerbated achievement gaps and disparities. Many families faced inequitable access to high quality, affordable childcare and early childhood education (ECE), even prior to the pandemic. These disparities in equitable access to childcare and ECE disproportionately impact children of color, lower socio-economic status,

The Family Perspective and Experience

and those living in more rural communities (Zhang et al., 2023). Although little to no data exists that indicates an exact measurement of academic regression or differential impact, it is evident that certain groups of children were more likely to experience a loss of access to childcare and or ECE during the pandemic. In turn, this can be associated with academic regression, missed opportunities for development and growth, and higher stress levels among caregivers suddenly expected to facilitate childcare and education within the home.

Food Security

Food insecurity was another obstacle many families faced during this period, as a lack of access to school, childcare, and familial support, along with potential loss of wages, all contributed to levels of food insecurity that surged during the pandemic (Moreland et al., 2020). The disruption of food security due to school shutdowns had a reciprocal effect, as food insecurity hindered families' ability to engage meaningfully in remote learning opportunities provided during school closures or hybrid formats. Gundersen and Ziliak (2015) have demonstrated that food insecurity can significantly negatively affect the physical and mental health of families and children. This, in turn, directly impacts children's cognitive, academic, and socioemotional development, as highlighted by Alaimo et al. (2001). The pandemic undoubtedly had physical and mental health impacts on a vast majority of families, but disproportionately impacted low-income families, among whom it had much more immediate negative effects (Benner & Mistry, 2020). A number of federal and state government programs worked to mitigate food security issues and increase low-income families' access to food services (Coronavirus Aid, Relief, & Economic Security Act, 2020; Families First Coronavirus Response Act, 2020), and although such services were much appreciated and indeed offered a necessary support, parent reporting indicated that the psychological toll it had on their families was not necessarily alleviated by such measures. In some cases, parents reported that accepting charitable food resources actually increased feelings of anxiety and depression (Fang et al., 2021). The intertwined nature of food security and educational engagement is just one among many multifaceted challenges faced by families during periods of educational disruption.

Family Income Discussion

Family income levels had a profound influence on education during the pandemic, with limited resources such as reliable internet access, digital devices, childcare, and food security playing crucial roles. School closures in many cases exacerbated existing inequities in addition to introducing new challenges. For low-income families, these additional burdens restricted their ability to access, engage in, or facilitate at-home learning. Reports indicated higher stress levels and unstable psychological well-being among lower-income families during COVID-19, with childcare and food instability being major stress triggers (Patrick et al., 2020). The correlation between family income and pandemic experiences, as well as its impact on effective learning at home, is evident from both family reports and research.

Understanding how families experienced the pandemic based on income levels can inform the types of support necessary for equitable education access for all children. Equitable access to the internet and digital devices is crucial, even during regular in-person school operation, as it can mitigate disparities. The internet's role in research and networking can significantly influence a child's academic trajectory, and familiarity with the internet and digital devices is vital for future job skills and career opportunities. Thus, ensuring all students have equitable opportunities to access internet-based programs and software is essential.

Childcare and access to high-quality ECE are also important factors for academic growth. Childcare is an ongoing issue, particularly for working families and those with lower incomes. The misalignment of school and work schedules and the cost of before and after care programs can exacerbate socio-economic disparities. The expense of ECE programs often creates inequality in the quality of accessible programming, affecting early childhood opportunities.

Furthermore, meeting children's basic needs is critical, as these needs lay the foundation for all learning. When these needs are unmet, children's capacity to learn and their long-term academic success are jeopardized. The pandemic underscored the vital role schools play in providing lower-income families with reliable food sources and highlighted the stigma associated with relying on such resources. This stigma might also affect children receiving services at school, emphasizing the need for discretion in resource distribution and potentially advocating for more universal food programs to avoid singling out any child.

FAMILIES WITH EXCEPTIONAL NEEDS

When schools shut down during the pandemic, not only was in-person instruction halted, but children with Individual Educational Plans (IEPs) were no longer able to access in-person services which provide necessary modifications and accommodations. A lack of access to such services created barriers for students with IEPs and added stress to home environments as parents struggled to meet the unique needs of their children and facilitate at-home learning, even without adequate training or knowledge about supporting learners with unique needs. During an already stressful time, parents reported significant levels of anxiety due to increased behavior

The Family Perspective and Experience

issues, regression in skills, and/or inability to accommodate at-home learning for their children with exceptional needs. A lack of access to special education services meant that children who needed such interventions and support were at greater risk for academic regression and social emotional distress.

Special Education Services

Although social distancing was reported as an effective measure to mitigate the spread of the COVID-19 virus, social distancing measures, such as school closures, had potentially negative impacts on childhood development, especially for those with special needs (Houtrow et al., 2020). The impacts of the pandemic were immediately felt by families with special needs children who had to quickly scramble to secure necessary support, services, and supplies; remote learning formats proved challenging for families for a variety of reasons, but this was an exceptionally difficult time for families with special needs children (Houtrow et al., 2020). This can be attributed to increased difficulty to remain focused, the need for more one-to-one assistance, inadequate access to necessary accommodations and modifications, and a loss of intervention and special services such physical therapy, occupational therapy, and speech. Many parents were expected to facilitate learning at-home with minimal access to resources and support.

The abrupt shift in instruction format not only directly impacted the learning experience for children with special needs, but also had significant effects on their families' stress levels. Even without the added stress of a global pandemic, parents and caregivers of children with special needs already face unique challenges associated with their children's disabilities. Parents and caregivers report worrying about managing and affording the cost of therapies and interventions, receiving a lack of social support, and coping with ways in which chronic needs can have an impact on their child's quality of life (Siracusano et al., 2021). The pandemic both exacerbated many of these worries and created new challenges and obstacles. Researchers who aimed to assess parent stress levels during the pandemic, with direct comparisons drawn between parents of neurotypical children and parents of children with disabilities, indicated overall higher stress levels among parents of children with disabilities, regardless of specific diagnoses or identified disabilities (Siracusano et al., 2021). The highest levels of stress were reported among parents of children with autism spectrum disorder (ASD), suggesting that the pandemic and school closures may have had the most significant impacts on children with ASD.

Children With Autism Spectrum Disorder

Many children with ASD prefer to follow repetitive schedules and express a preference for sameness and consistency. These characteristics of ASD were especially challenging during the pandemic as predictable routines were thoroughly disrupted. Whereas school programs typically provide highly structured environments and tailored schedules for children with ASD, remote learning environments within the home were relatively unstructured and less predictable. Parents of children with ASD reported increased levels of stress and worry during the pandemic and did so at relatively higher levels than parents of neurotypical children (Genova et al., 2021).

Their concerns were not only based on conjectured fear of potential issues developing, but rather a result of actual reported increases in problem behaviors. Parents reported that their children displayed increased stimming behaviors, toileting issues, aggression, and meltdowns. Along the same lines, many felt their children were left out of virtual socialization, were falling behind in school, and appeared to be less prepared to return to in-person school (Genova at al., 2021). In contrast, parents of children with ASD did report some positive changes in their children's anxiety levels, but oftentimes these positive shifts were in connection with reduced demands to socialize, the net effect of which may have actually added to parents' worries about a regression in social skills and development. Overall, children with ASD and their families endured a number of particular challenges, and their educational experience was impacted due to specific characteristic behaviors, unique needs, and a lack of necessary support.

Special Education Discussion

Families of children with special needs typically present educational leaders with a greater need for support and resources. Children with disabilities who have IEPs rely on the services they receive in school, and the consistency of those services are an important element in their progress and development. The unique experiences among families of children with disabilities during the pandemic sheds light on the importance of special education services, as well as the continued need for schools to prioritize special education funding and secure high quality teachers, service providers, supervisors, and administrators. Educators in the special education field should also receive ongoing training and professional development to ensure they are up to date on best practices for effective strategies, techniques, interventions, and supports. The pandemic revealed the vulnerability of children with special needs and how these needs inherently impact their families' day-to-day life the overall well-being.

The Family Perspective and Experience

EARLY CHILDHOOD EDUCATION

Education at the early childhood (EC) level was drastically altered when schools shut down and instruction was offered remotely. Prior to school closures, remote and virtual learning formats in ECE were foreign in concept and completely undeveloped. Younger students had little to no experience navigating virtual platforms, and early childhood teachers had rarely, if ever, incorporated virtual learning in their traditional instruction. The abrupt shift to remote learning at the EC level prompted a rapid reconceptualization of instructional design that was vastly different from typical instruction. Consequently, the switch to remote and virtual learning created unique problems for young learners and their families (Timmons, 2020; Yamamura & Tsustsui, 2021).

The shift to remote learning in ECE was difficult for a number of reasons, and the challenges of offering this new format of learning posed risks for young developing learners and their families. ECE plays an important role in children's growth and development and helps lay the foundation for learning. The learning that takes place in the primary level (generally Pre-K through Grade 2) helps children acquire important language, literacy, and mathematical skills (Piasta, 2016). Young children develop and grow these skills in a number of ways, but primarily EC educators foster such growth and development through tailored, differentiated instruction that relies heavily on inquiry- and play-based learning experiences (Timmons et al., 2021). Meaningful play experiences offer children opportunities to develop and practice numeracy skills, sorting, creating patterns, and estimating (Hunting, 2010), as well as exercise the use of creative language and develop an understanding of their own interests and curiosities. This type of enriched learning, however, requires hands-on learning experiences and educators who actively foster meaningful interactions with children, both of which were difficult to realize through remote learning formats.

The ability to deliver developmentally appropriate instruction during school shutdowns and through remote learning avenues was quite challenging, requiring much assistance from families. One main obstacle that emerged was related to the means by which instruction is presented in ECE. Best practices advise EC educators to utilize play-based and inquiry-based approaches to teaching and learning. Young children need to be actively involved and participating in hands-on learning experiences that involve movement, sensory engagement, and the ability to explore and investigate. Those types of developmentally appropriate learning experiences proved difficult to facilitate through virtual avenues such as teleconference or pre-recorded videos. When something approximating traditional instruction was offered by means of remote learning, it frequently required a parent or caregivers participate in the role of facilitator.

The unique requirement for parents and caregivers to take on the primary role as educator for their young children often created stress and frustration as logistical challenges emerged. Parents and caregivers reported feeling ill-equipped and uniformed about child development and how to appropriately facilitate learning. They scrambled to find adequate time to dedicate to their children's learning, and they worried their children were missing out on critical time to build essential social skills (Timmons et al., 2021). Reports from educators and parents indicate that family involvement was essential in aiding EC students to access remote learning, but the requirement for adult facilitation meant that parents and caregivers had to fully understand learning expectations and effective ways to support such learning (Timmons et al., 2021). This level of participation was quite challenging for many parents to accommodate, especially working parents and those who had to simultaneously look after other children. Given the important role ECE plays in the early development of social skills, many parents reported a high level of worry about diminished opportunities for their children to experience socialization and peer interaction (Timmons et al., 2021).

Timmons et al. (2021) reported some of the specific sentiments expressed by parents of EC students, regarding how the COVID pandemic affected them in a number of areas:

Time and participation requirements: "If I was working full time, I really don't know that I would be able to do it like this. I would have to take a leave of absence, or I don't think that I would have been able to get done as much as I am now" (p. 891).

Training in early childhood education: "I haven't taught kindergarten before, but I know enough to know the questions to ask and how to navigate through tasks, whereas I'm assuming for parents that have no background in teaching that it would be really challenging to try and navigate" (p. 891).

The need for social interactions: "I think it would be really good for my child to still interact with their teachers and their peers... I think that's a piece that's really missing for them, for him specifically" (p. 893).

Lack of instructional differentiation: 'She's bored out of her mind watching it. And so, watching that lesson for 30 min and then trying to do the worksheet, we've actually pulled out of the math days" (p. 893-4).

Early Childhood Discussion

Offering ECE remotely proved to be a challenge, with all parties involved often finding it difficult to facilitate meaningfully and effectively. Given the nuanced nature of ECE and the unique needs of young children, it is apparent that high-quality, developmentally appropriate programming is crucial. The experiences

The Family Perspective and Experience

and perspectives that families shared revealed the critical role EC educators play in the growth and development of young children and reinforced the need for young children to be engaged in hands-on, sensory-rich learning experiences alongside their peers. When instruction is too teacher-directed or offered in a one-size-fits-all manner, young children often lose focus and fail to make meaningful connections to learning. The experiences that families and young children had while engaging in remote learning offer useful insight into why ECE is important and how ECE should be facilitated. As ECE continues to evolve and expand, it is vital for educators and families to partner and expand equitable access to quality early learning. This is a key element toward ensuring that all children have ample opportunity to develop critical foundational learning skills for later success. Additionally, EC educators and administrators must ensure the use of developmentally appropriate teaching practices that empower young children to be active learners who are engaged in exploring, investigating, and building meaningful connections.

REFLECTION

The COVID-19 pandemic, which prompted abrupt school shutdowns and an often hasty shift to remote learning, undoubtedly impacted education and the learning experiences of all children. Families were suddenly responsible for facilitating remote learning which proved difficult for many, especially depending on certain unique factors which in some cases made it very difficult to initiate and sustain remote learning throughout the pandemic. Feedback from individual families revealed that family dynamics, family income levels, and specialized learning needs were among some of the unique factors that created obstacles for some children to meaningfully engage in learning remotely. The complex dynamics of families, including household composition, caregivers' educational backgrounds, and successfully navigating work-life balance all played a role in how families managed remote learning. Families with lower incomes faced disadvantages in obtaining resources such as internet access, digital devices, childcare, and even basic needs like food and water. Families with exceptional needs who had children in special education or early childhood encountered a lack of access to necessary services and supports and had trouble facilitating meaningful and or sustainable learning at home.

In light of the insights gained from the COVID-19 pandemic regarding family dynamics and their impact on remote learning, educational leaders can take proactive steps to better prepare for future crises. One fundamental lesson is the importance of flexibility and adaptability in educational approaches. When faced with the next crisis, educational systems should have robust plans in place for seamless transitions between in-person and remote learning. This includes ensuring all students have access to the necessary technology and internet connectivity, a challenge that was highlighted during the pandemic, especially for families with lower incomes.

Furthermore, the pandemic underscored the need for schools to develop stronger partnerships with families. Educational leaders must prioritize creating channels for ongoing communication with parents and caregivers, ensuring they are equipped to support their children's learning at home, regardless of the circumstances. This involves offering training and resources tailored to the needs of diverse families, including those with children requiring special education services.

Another implication for educational leaders is the importance of integrating mental health support into the curriculum and providing additional resources to students and families. The stress of navigating education during a crisis can significantly impact mental health, and schools should be prepared to offer support and referrals to professional services.

Investing in teacher training is also crucial. Educators need to be prepared to adapt their teaching methods to a variety of formats and to support students who may be facing additional challenges outside of school. This includes training in using digital tools effectively, as well as strategies for engaging students and supporting diverse learning needs remotely.

Finally, educational leaders should advocate for policies that address the root causes of educational disparities, such as socioeconomic inequality and access to technology. By working towards a more equitable educational system, schools will be better prepared to support all students during a crisis.

In preparing for future crises, educational leaders have the opportunity to apply the lessons learned from the pandemic to create more resilient and inclusive educational systems. By focusing on flexibility, strong family-school partnerships, mental health support, teacher training, and systemic equity, schools can ensure that they are better equipped to support students and families, no matter what challenges lie ahead.

The educational barriers, divides, and obstacles that were revealed throughout the pandemic offer insight into how educational reform can work towards mitigating such disparities. Most fundamentally, educators must consider the individual needs of families and build strong connections and partnerships with parents and caregivers to establish strong support systems for children. Each family is unique, and their overall dynamics most certainly can impact a child's behaviors, attitude, ability, and/or interest in learning. Our best educators get to know their students and their individual backgrounds, leaving teachers better equipped to offer educational opportunities that suit their students' diverse needs.

Systemic change is also necessary to mitigate socio-economic barriers that many children face. All children need equitable access to quality educational programming and the tools to help support these programs, such as a reliable internet connection and suitable devices to access online resources. Schools and communities must

The Family Perspective and Experience

ensure that children's basic needs are met so they can feel safe, comfortable, and ready to learn. Special education and ECE programs must be prioritized as a means of creating equitable opportunities for all. Although the pandemic prompted many unsolicited yet substantial changes in education, it also created opportunities for growth and development. There is much to be learned from the distinct experiences of families and children, and such knowledge provides educators with invaluable perspectives. These insights will be instrumental in enhancing and refining educational experiences to benefit all children, both now and in the future.

REFERENCES

Alaimo, K., Olson, C. M., & Frongillo, E. A. Jr. (2001). Food insufficiency and American school-aged children's cognitive, academic, and psychosocial development. *Pediatrics*, 108(1), 44–53. 10.1542/peds.108.1.4411433053

Benner, A. D., & Mistry, R. S. (2020). Child development during the COVID-19 pandemic through a life course theory lens. *Child Development Perspectives*, 14(4), 236–243. 10.1111/cdep.1238733230400

Cheng, S., Yang, Y., & Deng, M. (2021). Psychological stress and perceived school success among parents of children with developmental disabilities during the COVID-19 pandemic. *Journal of Autism and Developmental Disorders*, 52(1), 1–8.34322825

Coronavirus Aid, Relief, and Economic Security Act. (2020). Pub. L. No. Public Law 116-136, 9001 15 USC.

Dahl, G. B., & Lochner, L. (2005). The impact of family income on child achievement. *The American Economic Review*, 102(5), 1927–1956. 10.1257/aer.102.5.1927

Families First Coronavirus Response Act. (2020). Pub. L. No. Public Law 116-127, 2601 29 USC.

Fang, D., Thomsen, M. R., & Nayga, R. M. Jr. (2021). The association between food insecurity and mental health during the COVID-19 pandemic. *BMC Public Health*, 21(1), 1–8. 10.1186/s12889-021-10631-033781232

Feinberg, M. E. A., Mogle, J., Lee, J. K., Tornello, S. L., Hostetler, M. L., Cifelli, J. A., & Hotez, E. (2022). Impact of the COVID-19 pandemic on parent, child, and family functioning. *Family Process*, 61(1), 361–374. 10.1111/famp.1264933830510

Garbe, A., Ogurlu, U., Logan, N., & Cook, P. (2020). COVID-19 and remote learning: Experiences of parents with children during the pandemic. *American Journal of Qualitative Research*, 4(3), 45–65.

Gee, K. A., Asmundson, V., & Vang, T. (2023). Educational impacts of the COVID-19 pandemic in the United States: Inequities by race, ethnicity, and socioeconomic status. *Current Opinion in Psychology*, 52, 101643. 10.1016/j.copsyc.2023.10164337442079

Gee, K. A., Hough, H., & Chavez, B. (2023). Chronic absenteeism postpandemic: let's not make this our "new normal." *Ed Policy*. https://edpolicyinca.org/newsroom/chronic-absenteeism-post-pandemic

Genova, H. M., Arora, A., & Botticello, A. L. (2021, November). Effects of school closures resulting from COVID-19 in autistic and neurotypical children. *Frontiers in Education*, 6, 761485. 10.3389/feduc.2021.761485

Goldberg, A. E., Allen, K. R., & Smith, J. Z. (2021). Divorced and separated parents during the COVID-19 pandemic. *Family Process*, 60(3), 866–887. 10.1111/famp.1269334227099

Goudeau, S., Sanrey, C., Stanczak, A., Manstead, A., & Darnon, C. (2021). Why lockdown and distance learning during the COVID-19 pandemic are likely to increase the social class achievement gap. *Nature Human Behaviour*, 5(10), 1273–1281. 10.1038/s41562-021-01212-734580440

Gundersen, C., & Ziliak, J. P. (2015). Food insecurity and health outcomes. *Health Affairs*, 34(11), 1830–1839. 10.1377/hlthaff.2015.064526526240

Haller, T., & Novita, S. (2021). Parents' perceptions of school support during COVID-19: What satisfies parents? *Frontiers in Education*, 6, 700441. 10.3389/feduc.2021.700441

Hampden-Thompson, G. (2013). Family policy, family structure, and children's educational achievement. *Social Science Research*, 42(3), 804–817. 10.1016/j.ssresearch.2013.01.00523521996

Härkönen, J., Bernardi, F., & Boertien, D. (2017). Family dynamics and child outcomes: An overview of research and open questions. *European Journal of Population*, 33(2), 163–184. 10.1007/s10680-017-9424-630976231

Harris, A., & Goodall, J. (2008). Do parents know they matter? Engaging all parents in learning. *Educational Research*, 50(3), 277–289. 10.1080/00131880802309424

Houtrow, A., Harris, D., Molinero, A., Levin-Decanini, T., & Robichaud, C. (2020). Children with disabilities in the United States and the COVID-19 pandemic. *Journal of Pediatric Rehabilitation Medicine*, 13(3), 415–424. 10.3233/PRM-20076933185616

Hung, M., Smith, W. A., Voss, M. W., Franklin, J. D., Gu, Y., & Bounsanga, J. (2020). Exploring student achievement gaps in school districts across the United States. *Education and Urban Society*, 52(2), 175–193. 10.1177/0013124519833442

Hunting, R. (2010). *Little people, big play and big mathematical ideas*. Conference report. *Mathematics Education Reference Group of Australasia*, 33, 725–730.

Lee, S. J., Ward, K. P., Chang, O. D., & Downing, K. M. (2021). Parenting activities and the transition to home-based education during the COVID-19 pandemic. *Children and Youth Services Review*, 122, 105585. 10.1016/j.childyouth.2020.10558533071407

McNeely, C., Chang, H. N., & Gee, K. A. (2023). *Disparities in Unexcused Absences across California Schools*. Policy Analysis for California Education (PACE).

Moreland, A., Herlihy, C., Tynan, M. A., Sunshine, G., McCord, R. F., Hilton, C., & Popoola, A. (2020). Timing of state and territorial COVID-19 stay-at-home orders and changes in population movement, United States, March 1-May 31, 2020. *MMWR. Morbidity and Mortality Weekly Report*, 69(35), 1198–1203. 10.15585/mmwr.mm6935a232881851

Patrick, S. W., Henkhaus, L. E., Zickafoose, J. S., Lovell, K., Halvorson, A., Loch, S., & Davis, M. M. (2020). Well-being of parents and children during the COVID-19 pandemic: A national survey. *Pediatrics*, 146(4), e2020016824. 10.1542/peds.2020-01682432709738

Piasta, S. B. (2016). Current understandings of what works to support the development of emergent literacy in early childhood classrooms. *Child Development Perspectives*, 10(4), 234–239. 10.1111/cdep.12188

Porter, A. (2007). Rethinking the achievement gap. *PennGSE: A Review of Research*, 5(1), 1.

Ren, J., Li, X., Chen, S., Chen, S., & Nie, Y. (2020). The influence of factors such as parenting stress and social support on the state anxiety in parents of special needs children during the COVID-19 epidemic. *Frontiers in Psychology*, 11, 565393. 10.3389/fpsyg.2020.56539333362628

Roy, A. K., Breaux, R., Sciberras, E., Patel, P., Ferrara, E., Shroff, D. M., Cash, A. R., Dvorsky, M. R., Langberg, J. M., Quach, J., Melvin, G., Jackson, A., & Becker, S. P. (2022). A preliminary examination of key strategies, challenges, and benefits of remote learning expressed by parents during the COVID-19 pandemic. *School Psychology*, 37(2), 147–159. 10.1037/spq000046535266770

Siracusano, M., Riccioni, A., Gialloreti, L. E., Segatori, E., Arturi, L., Vasta, M., Porfirio, M. C., Terribili, M., Galasso, C., & Mazzone, L. (2021). Parental stress and disability in offspring: A snapshot during the COVID-19 pandemic. *Brain Sciences*, 11(8), 1040. 10.3390/brainsci1108104034439660

Timmons, K. (2018). Educator expectations in full-day kindergarten: Comparing the factors that contribute to the formation of early childhood educator and teacher expectations. *Early Childhood Education Journal*, 46(6), 613–628. 10.1007/s10643-018-0891-0

Timmons, K., Cooper, A., Bozek, E., & Braund, H. (2021). The impacts of COVID-19 on early childhood education: Capturing the unique challenges associated with remote teaching and learning in K-2. *Early Childhood Education Journal*, 49(5), 887–901. 10.1007/s10643-021-01207-z34007140

Yamamura, E., & Tsustsui, Y. (2021). The impact of closing schools on working from home during the COVID-19 pandemic: Evidence using panel data from Japan. *Review of Economics of the Household*, 19(1), 41–60. 10.1007/s11150-020-09536-533456424

Zhang, Q., Sauval, M., & Jenkins, J. M. (2023). Impacts of the COVID-19 pandemic on the childcare sector: Evidence from North Carolina. *Early Childhood Research Quarterly*, 62, 17–30. 10.1016/j.ecresq.2022.07.00335999900

Chapter 3
Wait, We Have to Do What?
How Teachers Entering the COVID-19 Shutdown Paved New Pathways for Education

Jamie Sassano
https://orcid.org/0009-0005-4607-6523
Lacey Township School District, USA

ABSTRACT

This chapter delves into the multifaceted challenges faced by educators and during the the COVID-19 crisis, examining the emergent issues, experiences, and solutions in navigating remote teaching and learning. From technological constraints to the emotional toll of isolation, educators grappled with unprecedented challenges in adapting to online instruction while striving to maintain meaningful connections with students. Despite these challenges, the pandemic also spurred the emergence of new instructional techniques born out of necessity. Educators worldwide innovated in real-time, leveraging digital platforms and creative approaches to engage students and foster learning. Success stories highlight the resilience and adaptability of educators, as well as the transformative potential of technology-enhanced teaching practices. Looking ahead, the chapter explores the outlook for future teachers and educational systems, emphasizing the importance of integrating lessons learned from the pandemic into long-term contingency planning.

DOI: 10.4018/979-8-3693-1507-1.ch003

Copyright © 2024, IGI Global. Copying or distributing in print or electronic forms without written permission of IGI Global is prohibited.

INTRODUCTION

This chapter will explore the stories of educators and the challenges they faced with a range of students, while also connecting some of these insights into the current research that was developed during this unprecedented time in our shared living history. In February of 2020, the World Health Organization (WHO) declared a world-wide pandemic which shut down almost the entire world at once and our lives took a traumatic shift almost instantaneously (WHO, 2020). Specifically, in New Jersey, it remained a hotspot for COVID-19 through the Spring of 2020 and forced leaders to come face to face with the limited resources available to large populations of the state (Shamburg et al., 2022). Statistically, "at the beginning of April 2020, the number of students not attending school stood at 1.16 billion in 194 countries" (Blass, 2020). Some educators were just trying to figure out how to personally navigate an online classroom environment because they have never even participated in an online meeting. Others signed into an online class with thirty 7-year-old children and had to creatively keep them engaged on the screen, while trying to teach them basic sight words. Students who regularly received accommodations while in school were now in an unfamiliar, isolated environment with the rest of the class, but still separated in so many ways. The disparity of our families and students true real-world connections became explosively apparent when we were all locked down and asked to begin educating our students online; many of whom didn't even have the means to explain to a teacher that they didn't have Wi-Fi access, they just remained absent each day. How can one educator on a screen reach each student like they did in the classroom face-to-face? Teachers had to find clever ways to make these accommodations possible; it was teachers who were able to continue to make learning possible, even when it seemed inconceivable.

Lack of Technology and Connection

According to the United Nation's (2015) Sustainable Development Goal 4, "achieving inclusive and quality education for all reaffirms the belief that education is one of the most powerful and proven vehicles for sustainable development" (United Nations, 2015). Any meaningful effort toward this goal must rely to an extent on a collaboration between the government and the private sector. Of course, it can be easy for many to accept that rural areas in America just simply have less Wi-Fi access then those perhaps in cities or near the coastlines. These areas are less populated; there is so much land it is likely harder to create infrastructure in the middle of nowhere. However, this should not be the excuse. It is primarily because of these reasons that the governing leaders should have moved more quickly in education to connect these areas to online access in schools. The students and teachers in rural America were missing out on a world of information while the rest of the schools were pulling ahead. These areas were faced with a digital divide that became immediately apparent to the world when it shut down in the face of a worldwide pandemic. A digital divide describes an area, including rural and exurban areas, that have limited access to broadband connection (Aguliera & Nightengale-Lee, 2020).

The digital divide has been a major concern in equity for over 20 years. In the mid-1990s, Internet Service Providers (ISPs) such as America Online (AOL) and CompuServe provided the infrastructure for private use of the internet to the public. As the use of ISPs began to spread across private, home-use, and the academic sector, the phrase "digital divide" was adopted in both economic and political discussions over peoples' access to the internet and educational computing. However, the "digital divide"–the disparity between individuals who maintain knowledge of and access to technology and those who do not–still endures. (Shamburg et al., 2022)

Even more, it is not just rural areas that were suffering from technology blackout. Rural areas, by nature, are usually in remote areas far from communication towers leaving them with little to no connectivity at all. However, there are also many urban areas that suffered from a lack of connectivity as well. A digital divide existed due to a financial constraint from the ability to own or financially support new devices or broadband access (Aguliera & Nightengale-Lee, 2020). While there have been many strides in the past decade to get schools access to some kind of connectivity, whether it be handheld devices, smart boards in the classroom, or a 1:1 initiative, there was no preparation for what was about to happen to the world when the COVID-19 pandemic caused us all to remain indoors and disconnected from one another.

In June 2020, the NJ Department of Education conducted a compulsory survey to public and charter schools and "found that 231, 176 students of the approximately 1.4 million K-12 pupils in the Garden State lacked access to a device and the connectivity tools to access educational resources online" (Shamburg et al., 2022). In March 2020, NJ teachers and students were home and told to use whatever they had available to implement ERT [emergency remote teaching], an indefinite shift to fully remote teaching due to a crisis situation (Shamburg et al., 2022). However, as the schools remained closed, using devices such as smartphones were no longer feasible for teachers and students to reliably access educational materials (Shamburg et al., 2022). Because of the access difficulties, it led many students to avoid ERT altogether.

While those in rural areas found themselves isolated geographically, many urban residents were isolated financially. Bianca Nightengale-Lee, a leader in the Department of Curriculum, Culture, and Educational Inquiry at the Florida Atlantic

University College of Education, recalls a professional moment (experience) surrounding the COVID-19 crisis and her team in her publication regarding emergency remote teaching (ERT) in urban and rural contexts:

> *When the crisis first hit, I was working closely with upper administration in the department of curriculum and instruction from the local school district. I actually went to visit the school district building, and while there were warnings that people should be staying home, and while my university just closed its doors to protect people from the further spread of the virus, school district leaders and staff were bustling around the office, diligently strategizing an ERT plan to support the needs of over 195,000 students and their families. They were having multiple in-person meetings to consider how to "do school" in a digital format. From what I understood, much of their conversation was about creating weekly lessons that teachers could access through a digital repository to support distance learning. (Aguliera & Nightengale-Lee, 2020)*

This experience is not isolated by any means; figuring out how to "do school" seemed to be the hot button issue that was being reported each day on television, among other things. New pedagogy that was emerging was inspired by a mix of traditional pencils and paper with a blended learning paradigm because of the lack of any other protocols in place for such an emergency. The instructors had to teach the content they know how to teach in an entirely different way while each one of them was learning how to do it in real time.

Inequities Among Regions/Populations

In 2017, online education was not working for most students who chose to enroll in online classes. What is interesting is that the students who stated they were not prepared (Goodman et al., 2019), were the same students who at this time, were already using some kind of technology on a daily basis both in and out of the classroom. Educators were also being pushed into a new online learning environment and were finding their own challenges as they moved forward while trying to deliver lessons to a screen of faces, instead of a room of actual students.

Students enrolled in online courses, instead of in-person, increased the probability of dropping out of school (Cole et al., 2017). Analyses in this study also proved that "students in online courses perform substantially worse than students in traditional in-person courses." Moreover, this experience impacted their perception and future performance in online classes. It was also noted in this study that "the negative effects of online course-taking are far stronger for students with lower prior GPA" (Cole et al., 2017). There was a performance gap between online and face-to-face courses and the "strongest declines were males, younger students, Black students, and students with lower grade point averages" (Xu & Jaggars, 2014). In the back half of 2018 educators and students were still trying to successfully navigate this new educational environment together, but in 2019, nature forced our educators to figure it out quickly, and figure it out they did.

When COVID-19 hit the already struggling populations and regions in America learned very quickly that the solutions that were working for many, were not working for them. The existing educational inequities were not only highlighted but exasperated because of school closures and the abrupt shift to emergency remote teaching (ERT). Regarding access to technology, there was a large disparity between affluent and non-affluent communities. More affluent schools were already investing in technology, so when schools shifted to remote learning, these communities were more successful than poorer schools that lacked funding and digital resources (Shamburg et al., 2022).

The stunning shutdown of our country exposed the inability of many educational leaders to guide us through the next steps because they were completely unprepared for such an historical natural disaster (Omodon, 2020).

UL2: ...because most of the universities in question, including ours are still engaged in the conventional method of teaching, most of them are still struggling with the changes in the modern world, especially teaching with or through the use of internet. Rural campuses, even in my school do not have enough capacity to support and provide computer labs to sustain all students; now that it is a stay-at-home thing, with insufficient basic services, they don't all own laptops to view content and are unable to access the amount of data necessary to engage on course work. (Omodon, 2020)

Another problem faced in New Jersey was that the available technology couldn't supplement the current curriculum because it was written with materials and environments that required traditional classroom settings. Preparing and delivering the same lessons proved difficult and sometimes impossible. Teachers had to spend hours locating materials online that were remotely accessible to all of their students (Shamburg et al., 2022).

UM1: The students' smartphones may not have enough space to accommodate all of the downloadable materials. Students' access to data may also be another problem. Some of the students rely on internet access in open spaces such as libraries. These places are currently also observing the lockdown period. It becomes difficult for students to access these spaces. (Omodon, 2020)

Three Main Challenges

Unreliability of Technology

The responses of educational institutions to COVID-19 have been almost as jarring as the societal shifts influenced by the pandemic itself. While decisions at the state, district, and school-level may have been grounded in the best of intentions, these decisions may not fully respond to the everyday realities of teachers, parents, caregivers, and students living within historically marginalized communities. In addition to evidence-based and pragmatic approaches to ERT, there is also a need to understand the lived experiences of students and families living in urbanized and rural contexts, who in light of existing educational inequities, are being further exposed to inequitable access due to school closures and the abrupt shift to ERT.

One of the biggest difficulties we faced in our school was that most of our students did not have the necessary resources to work online whether it's a smart phone, a tablet, a computer, or even access to the Internet. It was decided that to reach out to children that did not have technology to elaborate booklets, for the expected learning was developed briefly, and with activities that could be useful for putting the learning into practice. Also, since there were some children that could work online, it was decided to offer them activities out of the ordinary, and then this way, for example, we organized ourselves with the Spanish Academy and elaborated a literary coffee, where we all had to attend in our pajamas, and they were presented with texts that they loved, and wish they could hardly approach in the future. In the future, these digital tools should continue to be used because they could be useful in the unfortunate case that a situation like the one we are still living is to be repeated or use them differently. If the students cannot attend the class they can communicate with their students through these tools: Leonard - teacher, Mexico. (UNESCO.org, 2022)

Teacher and Learner Lack of Skills

The lack of training in emergency remote learning for both teachers and students became a central problem, causing an inability to connect remotely for school. Teaching in the virtual classroom requires distinct skills and characteristics compared to face-to-face instruction. These include managing the online classroom, adapting instruction for virtual platforms, engaging and motivating online students, designing effective online instruction, and fostering social and learner presence in the virtual setting (Dolighan & Owen, 2021).

Elementary teachers recognized the children's inexperience using technology, they also recognized the parents' lack of experience using online resources (Shamburg et al., 2022). One teacher stated, "the biggest difficulty for me was not having the hands-on training and being expected to do things we were never taught how to do" (Shamburg et al., 2022). Teachers were doing more at home remotely than they were ever asked to do in the past for less and less compensation. Another middle school teacher stated that, "the biggest challenge I've had is managing my schedule. I find myself working late into the evening most days. It becomes impossible for me to just 'turn it off' and it's taking a toll on me" (Shamburg et al., 2022).

UL3: Swift transition will not be easy because as much as the students will for the first time be trying this online thing and unfortunately, we are going to come across a lot of hiccups, whereas if we already started with blended learning approaches, it would be easier because we would be familiar with the platforms that we are expected to use now. (Omodon, 2020)

Because there was a lack of consistent online learning in some form in the world, including much of America, the instructors and learners were expected to learn in real time. The stresses that came from this were immense. While the teachers were trying to find creative ways to deliver instruction to the students, they were also trying to navigate all of the setbacks that came along with new online platforms that completely foreign to them, and the usual hiccups that we as a population normally tolerate when dealing with technology and internet access.

UL3: I think the problem with rural [schools] is that they are still very reliant on the traditional way of teaching and learning. Innovation is very scarce, and academics are not encouraged to use innovative teaching and learning methods. I am currently doing a study on the use of the flipped classroom as a teaching and learning approach, and I struggled to find lecturers who used the approach in their classes because people are stuck with the teacher-centered way of teaching. (Omodon, 2020)

Teachers were stressed and connecting and engaging with students were at the top of their problems. Teacher stress and burnout was researched and documented prior to the global epidemic so this was not surprising (Shamburg et al., 2022). Teachers were becoming so frustrated with trying to help students with their device malfunctions, while class was in session for learning that it became simply unmanageable (Shamburg et al., 2022). Let us also not negate the fact that many students exploited these issues in order to avoid being held accountable for any work during the emergency, remote learning. Even more defeating, teachers were expected to hold their students accountable for their work, while their family may be dealing with sickness, job, loss, or even worse…death (Shamburg et al., 2022).

Despite the absence of external accountability measures such as standardized tests during school closures, Francois & Weiner's (2020) study suggests that teachers and principals maintained high expectations for student learning. Principals consistently engaged in dialogue with their staff regarding strategies to support student learning, encourage participation and attendance, and address challenges faced by struggling students. Schools implemented proactive measures, including clear communication of attendance expectations to parents, as well as reactive strategies based on observed patterns of participation. Principals leveraged established school routines to collectively identify, plan for, and support absent students in remote learning environments. Additionally, findings indicated that principals outlined expectations for grading students within the context of remote learning (Francois & Weiner, 2020). There was clearly inconsistencies among school districts for the sake of achieving what the community felt as its most important goals.

Moreover, there is discussion about presenting new accountability protocols our of what was learned about the student learning experience during the COVID-19 shutdown. The COVID-19 pandemic offers a unique opportunity to refine existing state accountability systems. This crisis underscores the imperative for accountability frameworks to adapt in several key areas. Firstly, there is a need to shift focus towards assessing individual students' mastery of content, moving away from traditional reliance solely on grade-level standards and average scores. There is a pressing need to address the complex challenges that schools face in achieving equitable outcomes and measure their effectiveness in overcoming these hurdles. Furthermore, mechanisms should be devised to accommodate varying learning experiences among students within the same school, considering factors such as fully virtual versus live instruction participation and addressing specific needs for students with disabilities while in online learning sessions. Lastly, there is a necessity to evaluate the effectiveness of COVID-19 response innovations, such as learning pods, tutoring initiatives, and small-group online instruction, utilizing appropriate assessment methodologies (Lake & Worthen, 2021).

Lack of Human Intimacy, Space, and Support

Educators are the facilitators that drive the academic programs and educational practices that promote social and emotional learning each and every day. In the past, these practices may have been an opening greeting activity to learn about the moods and statuses of their students. But in this new online environment that was forced upon us, these interactions between the teachers and students became more impersonal and slowly, or all at once, decreased any personal connection already established. A large focus had to be placed on SEL not only by the districts, but even more, the educators themselves. Social and emotional learning (SEL) is a developmental process that commences from birth and continues throughout one's lifespan. It encompasses the acquisition of skills essential for fostering healthy development and relationships among children, adolescents, and adults. These skills, pertinent to both adults and students, include self-awareness, self-management, social awareness, relationship skills, and responsible decision-making (Dusenbury et al., 2015).

SEL allows the teacher to connect with the students and at the very least, let them know that they were present and there to teach for the short time they were allotted online. Classrooms with these warm social-emotional relationships support deeper learning. However, it also seemed as though teachers' were poorly managing their own social and emotional well-being, which in turn could also cause students' behavior and academics to suffer (Schonert-Reichl, 2017). But what were the protocols? What curriculum were the teachers supposed to follow? There was an emergency preparedness graphic manual created by the CDC in case of a Zombie Apocalypse (Centers for Disease Control and Prevention (U.S.), 2011)—what about us? Where was our teacher manual about how to manage this educational crisis amid a global pandemic?

Educators have always had to pivot and adjust on the fly because that is simply the nature of effective teaching. The problem that educators faced in this unprecedented situation was that they had no control over the actual mode of delivery for that most-needed assistance with instruction. In full-lockdown, no one could find alternative forms of stimulation outside of the house, whether that was physical, mental, or emotional. In addition, that lack of stimulation was met with a paradox while being isolated at home; entire families were home together for twenty-four hours a day with the lingering uncertainty of what the future held (Blass, 2020).

Even so, the most immediate and logical path to instruct and educate the students of the world was to immediately move to a remote teaching model which was atypical for most of the population. It's true that classrooms with sincere teacher-student relationships promote positive social emotional growth and learning. But when the teaching part of SEL isn't managed well, the students' academic and social behaviors suffer (Schonert-Reichl, 2017).

A sixth grade English language arts and social studies teacher described her lack of connection with students: "My experience has been 'detached'... as I don't have connections with some students who learn best by one-on-one support, and

I don't feel as if I have my finger on the pulse of the students during learning." (Shamburg et al., 2022)

Classrooms with warm teacher-child relationships support deep learning and positive social and emotional development among students but when teachers poorly mange the social and emotional demands of teaching, students' academic achievement and behavior both suffer. We've learned that teachers can promote students' social and emotional competence, and that doing so increases not only the students' SEL skills, but also their academic achievement." (Schonert-Reichl, 2017)

While educational leaders were working toward a paradigm of instilling balanced teacher-student workplace environments and relationships, there were barriers because of lack of training, education, and funding in spite of the research showing the importance of implementing this instructional design into everyday curriculum.

Experiences During

During this unprecedented time, teachers, students, and parents had to adapt to unfamiliar learning methods. Online instructors encountered difficulties in communication, technology use, and organizing sessions, exacerbated by the emergency situation caused by COVID-19. Emergency Remote Teaching (ERT) differs from planned online learning, posing unique challenges. Operating amid a global pandemic requires flexibility from school leaders and educators. Prioritizing short and long-term needs, adapting policies, and fostering collaboration within online communities for support were key priorities that needed to be addressed, but how to do that effectively was unclear.

Ms. Young, a teacher surveyed from Douglas County, CO recalls that during classes, neither student attendance nor her absence was predictable. A "hold harmless" grading policy was implemented during the transition to remote instruction, ensuring students' grades would not decrease from pre-pandemic levels, allowing for grade improvements. Despite this policy, only half of the students consistently completed their work, with approximately 10% attending classes via Google Meets (Love & Marshall, 2022).

Everybody was doing something different. There [were] no real guidelines other than you can't do things like require [students] to turn on their cameras. You can't count any of the work that you're doing from here on out against them. You must accept late work...Even at that point I wasn't sure whether we should use Zoom, or Google, or just post things. I know teachers that were emailing kids their assignments...People were on Zoom. People were trying Google and a variety of things...FaceTime. Everybody was on any platform you could imagine. It was just chaos(Love & Marshall, 2022).

While the teacher perceived administrative support, they found it lacking in practical assistance. Some teachers operated independently with grading practices, resulting in a lack of accountability. Following the school year, a survey led to adjustments in learning formats, incorporating both asynchronous and synchronous learning based on student preferences. This resulted in teachers adopting a hybrid teaching approach, with some students attending classes in person while others remained remote, often with their cameras off.

Staff members consistently exceeded their formal responsibilities, demonstrating dedication to student well-being, fostering strong student relationships, engaging with families, and supporting colleagues. Whether driven by personal initiative or directives from the principal, teachers undertook numerous additional tasks benefiting the school community, sometimes at personal risk. For instance, teachers willingly facilitated the transition to remote learning, procuring and delivering technology, troubleshooting online issues, and creating instructional materials, despite these tasks falling beyond their formal duties and without additional compensation. Additionally, staff members prioritized maintaining relationships during school closures, with principals highlighting instances of teachers conducting home visits to offer support or counseling to students and families, exemplifying their commitment to community welfare (Hodges et al., 2020).

Teachers' beliefs—about their own teaching efficacy was a large stress factor because some began to doubt whether or not they could "do the job." While teachers were spending their days supporting and teaching students, they were also home with families, and worries, and even sickness. "Although the term social emotional learning has been around for 20 years, we recently seen a rapid surge in interest in SEL among parents, educators, and policymakers" (Jones & Doolittle, 2017). The pandemic inadvertently highlighted the usually ignored stressors that educators face each day because parents became an active participant in their child's education whether they liked it or not. The community as a whole began to realize the importance for support in the education system.

Take the case of teacher autonomy: among people in professional occupations, teachers rank lowest in believing they have a say in what happens in the workplace. Work-related stress encompasses the detrimental physical and emotional responses that arise from a mismatch between a job's requirements and a worker's capabilities, resources, and/or needs. (Schonert-Reichl, 2017)

Wait, We Have to Do What?

The COVID-19 pandemic worsened teacher frustration and burnout, compounding existing issues of dissatisfaction and disengagement in the U.S. education system. According to Anderson et al. (2021), there has been a long-standing problem of teacher shortage, aggravated by declines in teacher preparation programs. Even before the pandemic, a significant number of teachers were actively seeking alternative employment, as reported in a 2014 Gallup poll. The stress on educators was evident, with 61% reporting high stress levels in a 2017 survey by the American Federation of Teachers (Shamburg et al., 2022).

Despite the crucial role teachers play in children's development, addressing burnout has been a persistent challenge. The COVID-19 response introduced additional stressors, with sudden shifts to remote learning, socially distanced classrooms, and hybrid teaching. Teachers, already burdened, faced heightened demands and struggled to adapt. The closure of schools during the pandemic left many teachers feeling uncertain about their roles, unprepared for remote teaching, and disconnected from students. Significant factors that contributed to teacher burnout included anxiety, concerns about communication with parents, and issues with administrative support. There is a need for attention to these stressors to preserve the crucial teaching workforce (Aguliera & Nightengale-Lee, 2020).

Specifically, when teachers lacked key ingredients for teaching ranging from basic resource to such as paper and pencils and heat to child friendly furnishings and computers, students exhibited higher levels of externalizing problems for example trouble expressing emotions and resolving conflicts and internalizing problems such as anxiety, sadness, and low self-esteem (Aguliera & Nightengale-Lee, 2020). How much of this was exasperated by COVID-19? Imagine the obstacles that we were trying to navigate years before this hit and now there are little protocols in place, little training and teachers are being asked to do their best with what they have to work with.

During this crisis, I also had the opportunity to chat with teachers, to get their perspective of how the crisis is impacting student learning. I had the opportunity to chat with teachers who taught in affluent and marginalized school settings. Their responses were not necessarily surprising, and align with trends we see across these two educational settings. The Title I school teachers complained that kids were not showing up for class, and that parents were not making them do their work. There seemed to be much frustration from the teachers, and a lack of knowing how to further facilitate engagement from "reluctant" students. One teacher said that she had not even heard from her own principal to see if she was doing OK. Other instructional coaches said that they were inundated with teaching the teachers the functionality of using collaborative online programs, which took them away from their intended purpose of supporting students through curricular and instructional development. (Aguliera & Nightengale-Lee, 2020)

Several participants from New Jersey overtly pointed out that this shutdown was exacerbating the existing gaps in student success. Consistently, the responses referring to special education and ELLs described dramatic problems. An elementary special education teacher in an urban elementary school wrote: "I have had limited communication with my students. I don't feel as a special education teacher that their needs are really being met. The work is not modified the way it should be. Packets of work going home are not enough. The kids are missing out on so much socialization and interaction. It saddens me" (Shamburg et al., 2022). Similarly, a high school math and science teacher who also teaches advanced placement (AP) classes expressed concern, "Students with special needs (IEP/504) and ELL are not receiving the supports needed to be successful in many cases" (Shamburg et al., 2022). The shutdown had a disproportionately damaging effect on students who were already vulnerable; however, there were noteworthy exceptions that will be described later.

Emergence of New Instructional Techniques Out of Necessity

Explicitly promoting SEL in preservice teacher education is a must. There should be a comprehensive course about compassion that encompasses equity and kindness, and patience. It should be considered to be equally as important than the traditional instructional course work to better prepare our new teachers for the unknown circumstances that could arise in the world (Schonert-Reichl, 2017). Instead of looking back at this shared experience in an isolated manner, educators and leaders must use what was learned to forge ahead maintaining these same connective strategies and bring them back into the classroom pioneering a new way of educating. It is time to discuss a coherent online learning strategy for future emergencies or other unknown disasters moving forward and give our educators tools for success should another arrive (Ferri et al., 2020). Immediately stopping online learning in some way is not an option.

This wasn't a discussion about whether or not teachers can teach "online." This term was normally attributed to perhaps a student who was ill, bed-bound, in the hospital and unable to attend, or perhaps socially or mentally unable to be present. The COVID-19 Crisis was not that; it was an entirely new thing. There wasn't an established curriculum in place that was available to all parties that needed it. According to Audrey Azoulay, the Director-General at UNESCO, there was nothing in place to monitor learning and assure the continuity of learning for all students and they were working with other countries to find solutions to this emerging problem

(UNESCO, 2020). Our teachers and students have traumatically pivoted from teaching in the only way they knew person-to-person, and to try and undue the progress already made until now would just be naïve. It was a forced opportunity for many to be connected and finally have a reach into the world.

Because we were able to manage this situation in a different way as for the teaching in which we had to search for ways to go after the student not to leave any student behind regarding their studies, we had to invent methods and strategies for teaching in a very different way than usual using social networks we were there, but the strategy was not very good, because not every student participated as they should happen we did not have control over the totality of the students and I believe that if a pandemic. Returning, the students would already be more committed. They would already be more prepared for the situation, and I believe the strategy to be used in this case would be the best because everybody since the pandemic started to know better social networks in the communication platforms. In the end, it would be one of the best ways to teach a class and one of the best ways to create social, effective teacher-student bonds: Buta – teacher, Angola.(UNESCO, 2020)

In the framework of the IDL Design Framework [Interest-designed Learning], "usefulness" refers to the application of knowledge or skills beyond the educational setting. It pertains specifically to the learner's belief that they can utilize acquired knowledge or skills to achieve goals outside of the educational system, excluding motivations related to gaining approval or advancement within the educational system itself. This definition aligns with the concept of "value beyond school" in authentic pedagogy. Usefulness encompasses both personal and adopted utility. Personal usefulness pertains to goals held by students outside the learning environment, while adopted usefulness reflects roles assumed within the educational setting. Both forms of usefulness contribute to learner motivation, encompassing factors such as pleasure, concern, identity formation, life goals, and curiosity (Edelson & Joseph, 2012).

In a discussion about the importance of exploring the basic needs of students in order to encourage motivation while learning, different methods were explored. Instructors attempt to design lessons that are challenging, solutions-driven, and problem-based in order to celebrate learning for the sake of learning and gain a reward of self-success. Teachers that promote autonomously supportive classroom atmospheres tend to have autonomously motivated students (Sassano, 2022). Like project-based science, all of the innovative approaches to designing learning activities mentioned above incorporate strategies for establishing relevance -- making learning objectives instrumental to learners' interests (Edelson & Joseph, 2012).

Should remote learning be viewed and utilized as a reasonable substitute to in-person education, allowing for a smooth transition between each learning environment when necessary? Or should we begin to see this as a permanent possibility that emerged out of necessity and permit teachers and students to continue to access online educational materials in places there was no connection prior to the pandemic? Both are beneficial perspectives, but creating curriculum through each lens would produce slightly different results. A great use of the available cost-free online modalities could be used effectively if the learning goals were adjusted to meet the "new needs" of our learners. Features that are available, such as: jamboards, surveys, polls, whiteboards, interactive games, and quick formative assessments such as a quick thumbs up, are available in real time on platforms such as Google Meet, Zoom, Edmodo, and many more (Mukhtar et al., 2020).

When working with the range of students, many teachers found more success in delivering online instruction and, in turn, receiving effective results, from elementary-aged students rather than secondary students. This was large in part because of established routines where the younger students were more adept to follow and continue to perform in the same manner (Shamburg et al., 2022). This can be a positive, influential factor when reflecting on what worked across the board for most students, regardless of the grade-level or content area.

These established routines could also be in the form of open-schedules. For instance, in some cases, the teachers were able to pre-record their lessons so that the students could access them at any time of the day and engage in their school work uninterrupted. This was especially helpful for older, more experienced learners who may have struggled with having the entire family home at once trying to work and go to school all at once. Asynchronous learning could happen and online help could be available via email or a live class board that other students were also a part of. This can also be considered established routine interactions that the students could rely on, even if it was not always in real time. Parents were helping younger students while working online and perhaps there were not enough devices to share at home. A limitation of this mode of instructional delivery is the absence of immediate feedback and personal interaction. However, the future implications of implementing an asynchronous learning curriculum could positively benefit many teachers and learners in a future scenario.

For example, a physics teacher in an urban high school described her routine this way: I am posting daily assignments to our LMS, each assignment has the date in the title. I send out weekly announcements explaining that week's work. I hold a Google Meet every day, every period, for students to attend and ask questions. (UNESCO, 2020)

A pre-K teacher in an urban district described her routine: "I use a Google Site to post remote learning activities. I use multiple communication tools to keep in touch with parents and families. I conduct daily recorded videos and weekly Google Meets with students."(UNESCO, 2020)

An urban elementary teacher acknowledged that consistency has been key in having students complete their work and that consistency was based on "getting a routine."(UNESCO, 2020)

Effective routines tailored to the constraints of remote learning, coupled with a keen awareness of students and subjects, emerged as key contributors to success across various grades and subjects. These success stories encompassed enhanced academic performance, particularly among previously underachieving students, and improved professional practices marked by increased collaboration, community engagement, and parent involvement. Notably, the online environment proved conducive to specific learners, particularly those who struggled in traditional school settings due to social pressures.

A middle school social studies teacher highlighted the positive impact on a previously struggling student, citing the student's newfound comfort in the remote environment, leading to significant progress. Logistical benefits, such as improved organization and self-management, were also noted by participants. Educators reported personal and professional growth, with innovations in teaching practices often tied to the use of educational technology. The transformative nature of these changes was evident in comments about exploring new resources, reaching out in different ways, and creating stronger connections with families (UNESCO, 2020).

Increased collaboration and a sense of community were observed, with technologically adept participants expressing satisfaction in assisting their colleagues. This collaborative spirit extended beyond the teaching community to encompass advocacy for students, particularly those from lower socioeconomic backgrounds. The supportive atmosphere extended to teachers, as noted by a fifth-grade teacher who highlighted the public's positive attitude toward educators. Furthermore, educators reported strengthened connections with parents, students, and families, going beyond crisis management to establish new and meaningful relationships (Shamburg et al., 2022).

Moving Forward – Outlooks for Future Teachers – What's Working? What's Not?

Educators, must be inclined to ask, "now that we have emerged out of the other end of this pandemic experience, how can we take what we learned and use it to better prepare for the next unforeseen circumstances and put a viable contingency plan in place?" Looking at what you have done with each lesson, examining how they felt during the instructional process, and identifying areas of strengths and weaknesses in that lesson are going to be instrumental in educators' professional and personal growth. It is also going to allow us to integrate these new technologies and methodologies in education with ease because value is being placed on the lessons that were so foreign to many just a few years ago.

Since the last year, our class started to work with journalists and create a new newspaper for school, what we did was to create a debate around misinformation during the COVID-19 pandemic, kids worked on fake news by creating and simulating to be reporters they had to follow the lead rules, journalistic ways of writing the news and it ended up to be an activity that became part of the national campaign, so we really would like to continue to develop themes related to media literacy projects: Filipa, teacher, Portugal.(UNESCO.org, 2022)

Leaders and educators will stop thinking about online, blended, and remote learning as a space to relocate our current lessons by copy and pasting the same design on a computer screen. "The HundrED and the OECD have called for schools to not simply to look at technology during the COVID-19 shutdown as a short-term fix, but as a vehicle for substantive change (Shamburg et al., 2022). What is most important when examining and evaluating all of the programs and modalities available, is making sure we have the ability to edit the curriculum to make sure the modes of instructional delivery are effective, streamlined, and purposeful for the teachers and learners equally. The indefinite transition to ERT became a socio-educational experiment which examined whether or not a full or part-time transition to remote teaching and learning was a future paradigm shift in educational instruction (Blass, 2020).

Keeping students organized is a key instructional practice and should be the hallmark when establishing curriculum for emergency remote teaching (Shamburg et al., 2022). In addition, time must be taken to establish these routines and behaviors of a more self-directed learning approach in our in-person learning, so it can easily transfer to the students when they are not in the classroom for a number of reasons, sickness, personal loss, travel, and of course, unforeseen circumstances or disasters (Mukhtar et al., 2020). For example, conducting a Socratic Seminar in class that is completely reliant on students participation, can be just as effective in an online forum with careful planning and a structured lesson. The participants remain the same, it is only the environment that changes.

Educational policymakers should consider co-creating good practices, methodologies, and common goals necessary to consistency, learning, and achievement. The curriculum should be as universally accessible as possible and inclusive to all stakeholders. Training must be innovative and productive rather than recycled from past years. Finally, ongoing monitoring of these new initiatives must be considered to evaluate the effectiveness of the mode of delivery and should be considered when making decisions to improve, manipulate, or simply eliminate some protocols on a regular fluid basis without discrimination (Vlachopoulos, 2020).

In a qualitative study focused on teacher experiences during the COVID-19 teaching experience, accountability among administration, teachers, and students was addressed (Love & Marshall, 2022). Most notably, the study reveals that teachers generally experienced the transition to remote instruction similarly. Despite 96% of surveyed teachers coming from schools where online learning was integrated into the transition during the spring semester of 2019-2020, an equal proportion indicated having no prior online teaching experience before the COVID-19 pandemic (Love & Marshall, 2022). Open-ended comments suggest minimal training provided by schools or districts during the transition period. Despite this, almost half (49%) of surveyed teachers felt somewhat prepared for remote instruction (Love & Marshall, 2022).

A study conducted by Vidergor (2023) courses offered on utilizing distance learning (DL) for teaching influenced teachers' actual teaching practices and DL self-efficacy. This may be attributed to the focus of the professional development (PD) course on technical aspects, presenting options for DL usage without encouraging innovation tailored to individual classrooms and student needs. While the practical course fulfilled its objectives, it did not stimulate participants to explore and apply their own ideas about technology-enhanced teaching. Professional development must be focused on enhancing teachers' established practices using online tools and not a complete shift to solely using online tools and platforms (Vidergor, 2023). Other recommendations advocate for dedicated digital learning days to enhance comfort levels among students, teachers, and families. Additionally, it was suggested that remote teaching plans should address daily graded work, regular check-ins, and effective communication with staff and parents, especially within lower-income families. Furthermore, strategies tailored for elementary age children and students with special needs are deemed essential (Love & Marshall, 2022).

This study proposes three key recommendations. Firstly, prioritize the mental health of educators and students in both immediate and long-term educational policies, addressing the pre-existing frustration and burnout that were heightened by the pandemic. Secondly, acknowledge the nuanced challenges of the digital divide, recognizing that possessing a device and connection may not suffice to bridge disparities. Lastly, focus on identifying the beneficial aspects of online learning that students excelled in during the pandemic, particularly the reduction of social pressures and the promotion of a sense of independence.

The abrupt shift to remote learning during the COVID-19 school shutdown in 2020 posed unprecedented challenges for New Jersey educators. While many felt supported by administrations and believed students had improved technological resources, frustration lingered, especially regarding difficulties in reaching students. The study emphasizes the need to address technology access, cater to the needs of special education and English Language Learners (ELLs), and acknowledge the vital role of parents. Despite challenges, some positive outcomes emerged, such as students excelling in the remote environment and educators reporting enhanced professional practice, fostering innovation, community, and improved connections with students and their families. These positive developments, though not universally reported, serve as valuable starting points for exploring improved teaching methods and professional growth within the constraints of disrupted educational norms.

Solutions and new frameworks for remote teaching and learning will permit a future with a safe and seamless entry into ERT without any restrictions (Blass, 2020). Practicing with new technologies and instructional strategies will only improve the educational experience. The key to any mode of delivery is use what works and discard the rest that will become ineffective. Using new found tools wisely will empower educators with a feeling of self-efficacy, can increase their professional skills, and can even upgrade their professional status with in their district. In addition, it has been shown to increase professional autonomy among teachers developing confidence in their ability to learn new content and shift approaches on the fly. It leads to a wide variety of approaches and lesson plans which diversify any teacher's classroom experience (Blass, 2020). In the same conversation, we must also address the fact that the remote experience will never replace the kind of interpersonal contact that both educators and learners have in a traditional setting, but creating a more comfortable routine by doing it consistently will create open passages for communication, not close doors.

Teacher education and professional development must prioritize online instructional skills and the design of virtual learning environments. This entails equipping pre-service and in-service teachers with the necessary resources and training for online teaching. Providing access to virtual technical support and ongoing guidance in utilizing Learning Management Systems (LMS) is essential. Moreover, professional development initiatives should focus on long-term goals, empowering teachers to craft meaningful and engaging online learning experiences. Researchers emphasize the importance of specific preparation in online pedagogy and student support strategies. They advocate for longitudinal studies to assess the effectiveness of pre-service training for K-12 online learning programs (Dolighan & Owen, 2021). Given the imperative to create effective online learning environments, teacher professional development must evolve to meet the demands of this new reality.

Anchoring remote teaching as an integral part of the teachers' work will only continue to improve and empower the teachers and create fluent online learners. There are many schools who incorporate specific study periods or test days into their regular weekly schedule to increase the face-to-face learning time and encourage interactions that are meaningful and helpful. Including a remote learning day perhaps once a week will normalize remote learning so in the case of any unforeseen circumstance, the change will be nothing more than their usual educational experience, just extended.

REFERENCES

Aguliera, E., & Nightengale-Lee, B. (2020). Emergency remote teaching across urban and rural contexts: Perspectives on educational equity. *Information and Learning Science*, 121(5/6), 471–478. 10.1108/ILS-04-2020-0100

Blass, N. (2020). *Opportunities and risks to the education system in the time of the coronavirus: An overview.* Taub Center for Social Policies in Israel.

Centers for Disease Control and Prevention (U.S.). Office of Public Health Preparedness and Response. (2011). Preparedness 101: zombie pandemic. Author.

Cole, D. A., Nick, E. A., Zelkowitz, R. L., Roeder, K. M., & Spinelli, T. (2017). Online social support for young people: Does it recapitulate in-person social support; can it help? *Computers in Human Behavior*, 68, 456–464. 10.1016/j.chb.2016.11.05828993715

Dolighan, T., & Owen, M. (2021). Teacher efficacy for online teaching during the COVID-19 pandemic. *Brock Education Journal*, 30(1), 95–95. 10.26522/brocked.v30i1.851

Dusenbury, L., Calin, S., Domitrovich, C., & Weissberg, R. P. (2015). *What does evidence-based instruction in social and emotional learning actually look like in practice? A Brief on findings from CASEL's program reviews.* Collaborative for Academic, Social, and Emotional Learning.

Edelson, D. C., & Joseph, D. M. (2012). The interest-driven learning design framework: motivating learning through usefulness. In *Embracing Diversity in the Learning Sciences* (pp. 166–173). Routledge.

Ferri, F., Grifoni, P., & Guzzo, T. (2020). Online learning and emergency remote teaching: Opportunities and challenges in emergency situations. *Societies (Basel, Switzerland)*, 10(4), 86. 10.3390/soc10040086

Francois, C., & Weiner, J. (2020). Accountability during school closures: moving from external to internal. CPRE Policy Briefs. Retrieved from https://repository.upenn.edu/cpre_policybriefs/91

Goodman, J., Melkers, J., & Pallais, A. (2019). Can online delivery increase access to education? *Journal of Labor Economics*, 37(1), 1–34. 10.1086/698895

Hodges, C. B., Moore, S., Lockee, B. B., Trust, T., & Bond, M. A. (2020). The difference between emergency remote teaching and online learning. https://er.educause.edu/articles/2020/3/the-difference-between-emergency-remote-teaching-and-online-learning

Jones, S. M., & Doolittle, E. J. (2017). Social and Emotional Learning: Introducing the Issue. *The Future of Children*, 27(1), 3–11. https://www.jstor.org/stable/44219018. 10.1353/foc.2017.0000

Lake, R., & Worthen, M. (2021). *State Accountability Systems in the COVID Era and Beyond*. Center on Reinventing Public Education.

Love, S. M., & Marshall, D. T. (2022). Teacher experience during COVID-19. *COVID-19 and the classroom: How schools navigated the great disruption*, 21-65.

Mukhtar, K., Javed, K., Arooj, M., & Sethi, A. (2020). Advantages, Limitations and Recommendations for online learning during COVID-19 pandemic era. *Pakistan Journal of Medical Sciences, 36*(S4), S27.

Omodon, B. I. (2020). The Vindication of decoloniality and the reality of COVID-19 as an emergency of unknown in rural universities, *International Journal of Sociology of Education*. 10.17583/rise.2020.5495

Sassano, J. M. (2022). Student satisfaction outcomes for autonomy, competency, and relatedness in different learning environments (29257205) Doctoral dissertation, Grand Canyon University. ProQuest.

Schonert-Reichl, K. A. (2017). Social and emotional learning and teachers. *The Future of Children*, 27(1), 137–155. 10.1353/foc.2017.0007

Shamburg, C., Amerman, T., Zieger, L., & Bahna, S. (2022). When school bells last rung: New Jersey schools and the reaction to COVID-19. *Education and Information Technologies*, 27(1), 23–44. 10.1007/s10639-021-10598-w34226818

UNESCO. COVID-19 Educational Disruption and Response. (2020). The impact of COVID-19 on student voice: Testimonies from students and teachers. https://en.unesco.org/covid19 (accessed on 29 October 2023).

UNESCO.org. (2022, July 7). https://www.unesco.org/en/articles/impact-COVID-19-student-voice-testimonies-students-and-teachers

United Nations. (2015). United Nations Sustainable Development Goals. https://sdgs.un.org/goals/goal4

Vidergor, H. E. (2023). The effect of teachers' self-innovativeness on accountability, distance learning self-efficacy, and teaching practices. *Computers & Education*, 199, 104777. 10.1016/j.compedu.2023.10477736919161

Vlachopoulos, D. (2020). COVID-19: Threat or opportunity for online education? *Higher Learning Research Communications*, 10(1), 16–19. 10.18870/hlrc.v10i1.1179

WHO. (2020). Pneumonia of an Unknown Cause – China. https://www.who.int/emergencies/disease-outbreak-news/item/2020-DON229

Xu, D., & Jaggars, S. S. (2014). Performance gaps between online and face-to-face courses: Differences across types of students and academic subject areas. *The Journal of Higher Education*, 85(5), 633–659. 10.1080/00221546.2014.11777343

Chapter 4
COVID-19 and Mathematics Students at a Suburban New Jersey Middle School

Kaitlyn M. Sorochka
https://orcid.org/0000-0001-9249-5482
Monmouth University, USA

ABSTRACT

School closures in response to the COVID-19 pandemic caused students to experience new and different learning environments in public schools. This chapter focuses on the experiences of mathematics students in a large suburban middle school in New Jersey from 2019 through 2023. These perspectives elucidate the state of middle school mathematics achievement in the present day. Each pandemic school year is reviewed individually throughout the chapter for the school of study, highlighting several key factors, such as the student learning environment, instructional modalities, pandemic variables impacting student education, technology utilized, student success, and the overall student school-based experience. Student achievement data highlights the impacts of student learning experiences from the pandemic years on their knowledge attainment. The chapter concludes with a summary of the key details and the needs moving forward for middle-grade mathematics general and special education following the end of the pandemic.

DOI: 10.4018/979-8-3693-1507-1.ch004

Copyright © 2024, IGI Global. Copying or distributing in print or electronic forms without written permission of IGI Global is prohibited.

INTRODUCTION

From 2018 to 2023, the author of this chapter worked as a middle school mathematics and special education teacher in a large suburban New Jersey school district. She educated about 540 general and special education students during this time, about 430 of whom have had their education impacted by the COVID-19 pandemic. Mathematics achievement is a well-researched area of education, and it is documented that middle school mathematics achievement determines which mathematics courses students can take during high school, college, and beyond. Differing achievement sets students on differing paths through their academic careers and lives (Byun et al., 2015; Dougherty et al., 2015; Trotman et al., 2006). Due to this, it is important that students are enrolled in advanced courses in which they are prepared to find success and that students are being supported to ensure they succeed in those courses. Prior to the pandemic, mathematics achievement disparities existed in the school of study between grade-level middle school mathematics students and their same-aged peers taking above-grade-level courses (New Jersey Department of Education—NJ DOE, 2023). The pandemic has exacerbated this disparity (NJ DOE, 2023) in part due to the educational challenges experienced over the first three years of extreme change and disruption of student learning. The effects of the pandemic are still impacting students across the K–12 setting today.

There was a learning curve for school communities all over the world on the remote, online, and virtual learning that occurred rapidly and impacted student educational experiences indefinitely. Teacher knowledge of best practices for online learning for middle school mathematics students and the application of that knowledge impacted the student experience each year. Each new year posed near challenges for education that forced continued exponential growth.

This chapter presents educational experiences during the COVID-19 pandemic and provides insight to how the chosen instructional methods came to be in her middle school mathematics general and special education classrooms. The experiences are broken down by year, with a focus on the 2019–2020 school year, as this was where the greatest changes rapidly occurred having a ripple effect on the school for years to come. The chapter begins by providing demographic details on the school of study, presents the problem preceding the COVID-19 pandemic with middle school mathematics achievement, and then discusses in depth the experiences of students in the school of study each year during the pandemic. During the initial year the author was running an online learning program that provides student insight into online learning, which is briefly shared. There is also a focus on the author's experiences for best practices for educating middle school mathematics students with and without special needs in an online environment. This enriches the student experience by providing an analysis of how the student experience was formed during this period of experimentation and pedagogical growth. The chapter concludes with a summary of the key aspects of the student experience and suggestions on how to help increase student achievement moving forward.

Demographics for The School of Study

During the times specified in this chapter the author taught at a large suburban middle school in New Jersey serving students in Grades 6–8. According to the NJ DOE's school performance report (2023), the most recent demographic data available documents changes in the school of study's demographic data over the time-period of the COVID-19 pandemic. Table 1 compares the year of the onset of the pandemic, 2019–2020, to the most current data available, the 2021–2022 school year (pandemic School Year 3). As noted in Table 1, there was an overall decrease in student enrollment over the course of the pandemic in the school of study, but there is an increase in the percentage of both economically disadvantaged students (+3.8%) and students with learning disabilities (+2.2%) while there is a decrease in the percentage of students who speak English at home (-6.5%; NJ DOE, 2023).

Table 1. Demographic Data for the Middle School of Study

School year	Number of students	Economically disadvantaged	Learning disabilities	Speak English at home	White	Hispanic	Black/African American	Asian	Other*
	1,121	20.2%	16.5%	93.3%	77.2%	12.8%	5.0%	3.2%	1.8%
	1,013	24.0%	18.7%	86.8%	67.3%	20.8%	5.2%	3.8%	2.8%

*Other includes Native Hawaiian or Pacific Islander, American Indian or Alaska Native, and two or more races (NJDOE, 2023).

These changes could have been induced by the pandemic as its impact was widespread across the world. While there were great impacts on schools, all institutions underwent great periods of change and uncertainty. Despite most of the school not being economically disadvantaged or having learning disabilities there was a pre-existing low-level of mathematics achievement among grade-level learners. The following section will review this data and explain the relevance and new connection to the COVID-19 pandemic.

Middle School Mathematics Achievement

Even prior to the beginning of the COVID-19 pandemic, many middle-grade students struggled with standardized test performance in mathematics across the United States (National Center for Education Statistics, 2011). As seen in Table 2, in the school of study most middle school *grade-level students* (meaning students learning a grade-level curriculum) were not meeting nor exceeding the state expectations on the New Jersey Student Learning Assessment (NJSLA) prior to the pandemic (2018–2019; NJ DOE, 2023). Unsurprisingly, following the academic disruptions of the COVID-19 pandemic, student NJSLA scores dropped in the school of study (NJ DOE, 2023). Table 2 demonstrates that the final year of standardized testing prior to the onset of the COVID-19 pandemic in 2019–2020 the percentage of students meeting, or exceeding expectations was higher for each grade level in the school of study (+11.5% for sixth grade, +6.1% for seventh grade, and +24.3% in eighth grade) than in the first-year standardized testing resumed (2021–2022) after the initial cancellation due to the pandemic in the spring of 2020.

Table 2. Middle-School Math NJSLA Perfect of Test Takes Meeting or Exceeding Expectations in the School of Study (NJ DOE, 2023)

Year	Sixth Grade	Seventh Grade	Eighth Grade
2018–2019	47%	54%	41%
2021–2022	35.5%	47.9%	16.7%

Two years of spring testing were canceled between the 2018–2019 NJSLA and the 2021–2022 NJSLA (NJ DOE, 2021). The below sections will explain the learning modalities utilized during these years and the pandemic-induced learning circumstances. Finding ways to increase the success of middle school mathematics students learning grade level curriculum has become more important than ever following the pandemic due to the drop in student success. The following section will briefly explain an intervention model for middle grades mathematics students and their perspectives of program participation during the spring of 2020.

AN INTERVENTION MODEL FOR MIDDLE GRADES MATHEMATICS

When the author first began trying to address the inequities in achievement in 2019 before the COVID-19 pandemic began, research had well documented that technology could have positive impacts for students in the middle school math environment (Bellaver, 2016; Causey, 2014; Franklin & Peng, 2008; Gulley, 2009) and the author was determined to investigate if this could be further applied to enhance students' mathematical knowledge in the school of study. In part with her doctoral dissertation, the author designed, created, and ran (despite the interruption of the pandemic) a screencast-based independent virtual learning program during the spring of 2020 to investigate the possible impact of independent virtual learning on standardized testing scores for students enrolled in grade-level mathematics courses in the school of study.

The students viewed weekly custom-made screencasts (the 12-week curriculum was created from the 2018–2019 NJSLA evidence statements and solicited teacher feedback) and completed a corresponding Google Forms practice assignment. It was hoped that participation in the independent virtual program could help students meet or exceed expectations on the NJSLA in mathematics and subsequentially, possibly alter the course of their lives for the better. Unfortunately, this program was altered by the COVID-19 pandemic, as was the rest of education.

The pandemic began during week eight of the twelve weeks of the program. This disruption led to a low number of study participants and eliminated the possibility of analyzing state testing data (due to the cancelation of the NJSLA in 2019–2020). However, it did show unique student perspectives of virtual learning during the 2019–2020 school year when the independent virtual program happened to coincide with the emergency remote learning. During student interviews conducted via Google Hangouts during the spring of 2020, one study participant stated:

Student 2: I was very motivated because I had an opportunity to get better, so I would obviously want to do the work.
Interviewer: Is that important to you that your mathematical skills increased?
Student 2: Yes, I want to have as much knowledge as I can so, yeah.

The above interview exchange provides an example of an eighth-grade grade-level student who was intrinsically motivated to learn mathematics and was completing the independent online learning despite facing the COVID-19 induced emergency remote learning. Another student expressed their greatest source of motivation when completing the post-survey as follows:

The greatest source of motivation for me was the screencasts because I knew I could do most of the problems, but if I didn't the screencast was there for me to look back at.

Overall, I didn't have difficulties completing the program. (Student 2, Post-Survey)

This statement provides a student perspective that screencasts are helping learning tools for middle grades mathematics students that they are willing to utilize to try and increase mathematics achievement. These student statements cannot be generalized to all learners but provide a unique student perspective from an independent, virtual learning program in the school of study. However, Dung (2020) found that higher education students perceive motivation to be a key factor for success in virtual learning as well. While this program provides student insight into the student experience of the spring of 2020, there is more to explore for the school of study outside of the intervention program as well. The next section details the 2019–2020 school year and the school closures beginning in the spring of 2020. It also shares an in-depth analysis of best practices learned through experience by the author for teaching middle school mathematics to general and special education students online. This analysis explains the reasoning for how the student experience in middle grades mathematics came to be for the remainder of the pandemic years and beyond and can lend insight into the changing levels of student mathematics achievement on the NJSLA when state testing returned in the spring of 2022.

THE 2019–2020 SCHOOL YEAR: A YEAR LIKE NO OTHER

As mentioned, the 2019–2020 school year began in a traditional format but was the first to be impacted by the COVID-19 pandemic when schools worldwide were forced to close their doors to accommodate the need for social distancing. As of March 16, 2020, the school of study was closed for in-person learning due to the COVID-19 pandemic. Students, staff, and school leaders believed the closure would last for two weeks before they would return to normal. As such, the school leaders instructed the teachers to provide students with review work for this two-week period. In the mathematics department the review work was selected by administration. This was the first curricular disruption to student learning because of the pandemic.

Not all students had access to the Internet at home at this time, but all had a school-issued Chromebook. Students without Internet access were sent home on Friday, March 13, 2020, with packets of work to complete for two weeks that they would have been expected to turn in upon their return to the classroom. Students with Internet access were told to access the review packets after teachers posted them in Google Classroom, and to submit pictures of their work to the teacher on Google Classroom or via email. At this time students were faced with the largest educational equity issue of the pandemic: Internet access. Without the Internet, students could not receive feedback on work, as they could not submit their work. Also, students and teachers needed email or Google Classroom to initiate contact, which means that students without the Internet had to hope their teacher would call home to check in. If not, they could not access any assistance with their learning. When the two weeks concluded and the state showed no signs of reopening schools for in-person learning, students and teachers had to continue to adapt to these new conditions of learning.

At this time administrators communicated to teachers that new middle school mathematics lessons needed to resume in the new emergency remote learning format. Teachers were instructed to provide 20–30 minutes of mathematics lessons (moving forward with the curriculum) daily. These lessons could be screencasts, YouTube videos, written instructions, or any other method by which instruction could be delivered via Google Classroom or the teacher's district class page. Students were to be graded based on effort during this time and no one was to fail, even if work was not submitted. It was planned for this phase to last for the eight days remaining prior to spring break and the end of the marking period. The administration emphasized teachers trying to connect with students via email and phone calls to ensure students knew the school was still here to provide support and ensure their overall educational and general well-being. School administrators also worked to get students in need Internet access on their school issued devices, which was an effort to promote equity among the students.

During this time students began to reach out more frequently to teachers via email, concerned about their grades and trying to forge through new mathematical content on their own for the first time in their educational careers. Teachers were granted access to hold Google Hangout sessions with one another and students to both check in and try to provide academic support. Many teachers and students did not utilize this option at this time as it was unfamiliar. The technology was intimidating to many, which lent to a lack of connection between the teachers and students.

At the end of April, Governor Murphy announced that public schools would remain closed for in-person learning until at least May 15, 2020. The school district of study announced to the community that the current plan for remote learning would remain in effect for the duration of this time. Students and teachers had limited interactions and students were learning a limited amount of new curriculum asynchronously from the provided resources. While interactions between students and teachers were limited as compared to the traditional in-person learning environment, they were beginning to increase with longer phone calls to explain concepts and the use of Google Hangouts. Students seemed grateful to have the help of their teacher while engaging with mathematics. It was challenging to assist students in this way initially, but with experience and new technological tools (e.g., Google Hangouts and interactive online whiteboards), instructional needs began to be met.

Student learning experiences varied during this time due to the different levels of online access and teacher experience with online learning. Thankfully, due to the school closures and health guidelines the state of New Jersey canceled standardized testing for the 2019–2020 school year. This came as a relief to students and teachers due to the pandemic induced changes to the learning environment and resulting curricular disruptions. Due to the school closures, student activities experiences changed as well.

During the spring of 2020 student activities came to a halt initially, which was disappointing for students who had been active in clubs and diligently preparing for competitions and sporting events all year. Once the initial two-week period passed, administration instructed sports coaches and club advisors to provide students with the meaningful online connections and activities that related to the clubs and sports which could be completed in the safety of their homes. Students were open to these activities, as demonstrated by their video and photo submissions of completed activities. Toward the end of April, students also began to use Google Hangouts to connect with their peers and advisors or coaches for sports and other activities.

At the end of April 2020, the governor announced that public school in New Jersey would remain closed to in-person learning through the end of the 2019–2020 school year (Official Site for the State of New Jersey, 2020). This was unimaginable prior to the pandemic beginning and was eye opening to the need to find effective strategies to educate middle school mathematics students in the virtual learning environment. The subsection will review what the author learned about teaching mathematics virtually for both special education and general education middle grades students during the 2019–2020 school year. This is important to share with the student facing perspective, as this knowledge shaped instruction during the forthcoming virtual learning of the 2020–2021 school year and beyond.

Learned Teaching Methods for the Virtual Middle School Mathematics Environment

As the emergency slowed and the pandemic progressed, the remote learning environment became a virtual learning environment, where students were met with a higher level of online learning delivery. After self-reflecting upon her remote and virtual learning teaching experiences in the spring of 2020 and running the independent online intervention program described above, the author identified four key factors that contributed to student success with virtual learning: access to technology and its meaningful usage, addressing the needs of the students and staff with rapid change, finding creative ways to promote student engagement, and equity. This section reviews these challenges with a special focus on students with special needs and promote the importance of adapting to change as an institution for the virtual learning environment, increasing communication between virtual and school and home, promoting student engagement in online learning environments, using different tools and instructional modalities (i.e., interactive whiteboards and screencasts), and the role of equity in the virtual learning environment.

Addressing Students With Special Needs in the Virtual Environment

In addition to delivering effective mathematics instruction in the virtual learning environment was also the need to meet the legal requirement to follow individualized education plans (IEPs). IEPs were written to address the special needs of students while learning in the traditional classroom setting. Yet, special educators were still required to meet the special needs of learners outlined within their IEPs in the online learning environment.

Similar to general education students, learners with special needs struggled both to practice content that was considered *prior knowledge* and to learn new content in middle school mathematics. It quickly became clear to the author that daily interaction was necessary between teachers and middle grades mathematics students to find success with virtual learning, especially students with special needs. Many special education teachers focused upon strategies that closely mimicked the traditional learning environment: the closer to the traditional classroom, the easier it was to follow the IEP. The author met IEP requirements by creating a virtual classroom that mimicked the traditional classroom setting by providing frequent real-time, virtual face-to-face instruction, and by creating customized screencasts for students to reference as needed. Meeting their IEP requirements was difficult, but in most cases was not impossible.

Oftentimes IEPs include accommodations for assisting with focus, engagement, scheduling, organization, modeling, and hands on instruction. Students with these accommodations require communication with how their needs will be met. The school needed to adopt remote and virtual learning special education guidelines and policies and then communicate these to staff and families. Due to the heavy reliance on technology to meet accommodations and modifications, communication was required of both staff and families to help students feel supported and to be successful with their learning. Teachers, students, administrators, and parents all needed to understand how and when to communicate and when and where assignments would be posted with clear timeframes for completion. For this communication to be effective, students needed to have clearly communicated guidelines for the procedures for accessing class materials, guidelines for work completion and submission, and on how to access their accommodations and modifications to address their learning needs. Sharing these guidelines also help students and families understand that the IEP is being followed, which in turn can help the school avoid a legal issue.

Within the virtual schooling guidelines was the need for a consistent routine with lessons, assignments, and additional help materials. While this is often in a student's IEP, the consistency also helped general education students find success while learning independently online. Students with special needs often rely heavily on assistance from paraprofessionals and teachers with organization and time management during the school day. In the remote setting, it was effective for teachers to develop a remote class routine and then follow it each day. For example, one effective practice was to create a student online planner for the week. The planner included the date and day of the week, scheduled Google Hangouts, daily assignments, and linked videos and notes to assist with the work. The planner also clearly stated where to find an assignment (or hyperlinked to it when appropriate), when the assignment was due, and how to submit the assignment when complete.

Having established virtual schooling norms would lessen the burden teachers faced with communication and would ease the frustration felt by all when unsure of how to gain access to important information. Additionally, following a consistent routine and helping to organize the students even in the online setting benefits all students, especially learners with special needs, and allows for organization and routine aspects of IEPs to be followed in the remote learning environment.

Virtual Real-Time Instruction

A missing element during the initial remote learning period was a face-to-face connection between the students and their teachers. With these interactions students can receive immediate feedback that is valuable to learning mathematics. Google Hangouts provided a school-approved platform for teachers and students to virtually interact face-to-face. In order for students and teachers to conduct the Google Hangout the school needed to provide the necessary technology, i.e., laptops with cameras and microphones, which were not in everyone's possession at the start of the remote learning period. Once equipped, a shift was made where teachers began using the casual check-in to teach lessons as a full class or in small groups in real-time. Having a platform where an entire class could be online at the same time as the teacher and have conversations, ask questions, and interact improved the types of instruction that could be provided without being in the school building. Using Google Hangouts to provide virtual real-time teaching made it possible for students with special needs to receive the accommodations and modifications needed for success.

Interactive Online Whiteboard

The author also found that for mathematics online instruction with Google Hangouts there was a need for a platform that would allow for the teacher and students to discuss and show their mathematical thinking simultaneously. The use of an interactive online whiteboard (IOW) that could be shared on both the teacher's and students' screens during a Google Hangout allowed for this connection to be possible. Free platforms at the time such as Whiteboard.fi and the Google Jam Board provided this experience.

During whole class, small group, and parent approved one-on-one Google Hangouts the teacher could set up a class on the IOW and share their screens on Google Hangouts to display the whiteboard. Students seemed to benefit from these interactions and attendance and participation were high for Google Hangout sessions. The use of the IOW allowed for the author to follow a more traditional style of direct instruction; she would explain and show the math to the students simultaneously. From a special education standpoint, it was beneficial to also be able to utilize multiple colors to help coordinate and show students how different text matched parts of the problem. There are some concepts that are easier to display on the IOW than others, but this also depends on the level of tech savviness of the teacher. For example, algebra concepts were easy to simply write out and solve on the IOW. Geometry concepts, such as the volume of three-dimensional figures, required more skills with drawing electronically on the online whiteboard. Hopefully this will change as IOW platforms progress.

Teaching with the IOW during the Google Hangouts session also increased the teacher's ability to meet the needs outlined in student IEPs. The teacher was able to provide visuals, hands on instruction, immediate feedback, breaks as needed during the lesson, and provide guided instruction. The teacher was also able to quickly see what students were writing down and redirect as needed when students would hold their notebook up to the camera. Following the real-time virtual direct instruction on the IOW, the virtual-special education teacher then used the student responses to questions to determine the next step of the lesson, just as they would have done in the traditional classroom. The teacher was able to better assess student understanding while the students were able to ask questions and receive immediate feedback as well.

The seventh and eighth grade mathematics students with special needs had very positive feedback to the combination of Google Hangouts and the IOW and were appreciative of their teacher's time and efforts. The students reported feeling very supported during these online sessions and that learning became easier in the remote learning setting.

Custom Made Screencasts for Independent Learning

In addition to the virtual and real-time online instruction, students needed additional supports in place while completing mathematics work. At the beginning of the remote learning the seventh and eighth grade mathematics students with special needs (and some without) reported difficulty learning from outside videos such as Khan academy, as the instructional delivery was unfamiliar. Just as students with special needs thrive on a consistent routine, they also learn best when the presentation of the information is familiar. Therefore, these supports needed to mimic the additional help that teachers could not provide in the moment.

One solution to this was having the teachers individually create custom made screencasts geared toward student needs, with their exact style of instruction. This allowed for a more personalized approach to remote instruction during the moments the teacher could not be on Google Hangouts. Additionally, the supplemental use of screencasts allowed for the students to learn at their own pace; having the ability to pause instruction and rewind as needed allows the students to move at a pace that is comfortable. Hearing their teacher's voice added a level of familiarity to the screencasts that helps to make the students more comfortable as well.

Students with special needs often have in their IEPs that the teacher needs to chunk information and draw attention to different aspects of the lesson. The user-friendless of the app allowed for the teacher to make these accommodations, and therefore provided another aspect of legally meeting student needs as outlined in their IEPs. It was possible to use multiple colors and different features, such as highlighting, which helped with attention and engagement in addition to meeting IEP accommodations.

For this practice to be implemented on a broader scale, the school districts would need to have the ability to provide teachers with the appropriate technology and corresponding training. While this is an avenue, it was highly beneficial and would greatly benefit all students, but especially those with special needs when learning online or as an intervention model.

Summary

Due to the COVID-19 pandemic special education underwent many rapid changes to instructional delivery while simultaneously meeting the standards of IEPs written for the traditional school setting. It became necessary to establish remote school norms along with effective remote and virtual teaching practices and supplemental instruction. The use of Google Hangouts with the IOW was a great substitute for in-person instruction under the needed guidelines and allowed for special education teachers to meet many accommodations and modifications outlined in IEPs. The use of custom-made screencasts allowed for students to learn from their teacher on their own time and provided a sense of familiarity with teaching style. The teacher could also customize the screencasts to meet specific student needs: which videos and screencasts produced by other educators may not consider. The lessons learned from March of 2020 through June of 2020 were invaluable to the path forward through the pandemic induced online learning environments. The next section details the first full school year impacted by the COVID-19 pandemic.

THE 2020–2021 SCHOOL YEAR: IN, OUT, AND ALL ABOUT?

The 2020–2021 school year was pivotal in the pandemic, as schools were finally given health guidelines that made it possible to move forward from the emergency remote learning model the closures forced (Official Site for the State of New Jersey, 2020). This was a key move as the previous model was developed in a reactionary manner to the public health emergency, and as mentioned, did not allow for the full learning of the mathematics curriculum. The summer months allowed for administration to create a robust plan that aligned with ever-evolving government mandated health guidelines. With this, there was also time for teachers to seek professional development about online teaching models and improving their practice. In the district of study, the school was able to prioritize creating the safest possible space for in-person learning (through a hybrid learning model) while also meeting the possible need of staff and students for virtual learning (by creating a separate online learning academy). This section documents student experiences as they reentered the school in the Hybrid Learning Program, or, as they chose to remain at home and become a part of the Remote Learning Academy for the duration of the school year. A return to school activities and sports began this year as well, although with different requirements and some virtual components.

Hybrid Learning Model

In the school of study, a hybrid instruction model was implemented to allow for in-person learning to resume in the Fall of 2020. The school was split into two groups to minimize the number of people in the building and meet the public health guidelines put in place by the NJ DOE. The main variables that were challenging to meet and required the students to attend school on alternating days were the requirements to remain six feet apart and masked over the nose and mouth whenever they were not. To have the space in classrooms and the lunchroom the only option for in-person learning was to split the school into two groups that attended on alternate days. The school day was run on the shortened-day schedule to allow for the Google Meet session (a larger platform for meeting than Google Hangouts) to be run for the at-home groups daily during the last two hours of the school day. After-school help, normally available daily for half an hour after school, was conducted during the final 30 minutes using Google Meet. Students sometimes utilized this option, but not as often as they had in-person help in previous school years.

This was an incredibly different in-person experience for students than they had ever been a part of before, and there was much uncertainty about how to feel and act during this time. Most students were very quiet during the day (possibly due to wearing the mask), and there many different opinions they needed to navigate around mask wearing, cleaning precautions, and social distancing. There were mandated quarantines for staff and students for two weeks following exposure to a positive COVID-19 case, which created large disruptions to the learning environment and student knowledge attainment. During December of this year the school district of study had to close to in-person learning for two weeks due to a shortage of bus drivers due to cases of COVID-19 and exposure quarantines. When students were quarantined during the year, they were not allowed to attend in-person classes for two weeks, but instead would log into class on the Google Meet if they felt well. In the building students needed to be seated in the same seat with social distancing measures in place to monitor their proximity to suspected or positive COVID-19 cases, which severely limited their abilities to complete any group or partner work, which had a negative impact on learning.

Instructionally the hybrid model was meeting student needs better than remote learning as they did have in-person instruction every other day, with daily synchronous meetings via Google Meet for about 20 minutes with the whole class. On the days students were at home they were expected to complete assigned lessons and assignments before attending the Google Meet. The meeting time was meant to field questions and provide any needed reinforcement of the lessons. The strategies the author began using in 2020 were utilized throughout this year as well: providing students with screencasts, IOW in Google Meet, organizational online planners, and strong communication between school and home. Students were able to control their own engagement in Google Meet: They were more engaged when their camera was on and the meeting required their active participation. A higher level of engagement led to a greater level of understanding. This model did not allow for instruction to be on pace with the district curriculum as the students were receiving reduced instructional time. On a positive note, students were receiving more face-to-face instructional time than they did spring of 2020.

Due to the challenges faced from March 2020 on, the state of New Jersey again decided to cancel standardized testing in the spring of 2021. This was a decision that was well received by students but provided no data to document student progress during this period of great change in education. During this school year, sports teams were allowed to resume which had a positive impact on the student experience. Sports resuming was challenging for coaches, athletes, and families as there were many requirements for maintaining compliance with the health guidelines. Masks were worn even at outdoor sporting events, even by the athletes who were playing. There was an equity issue with participation as participation required parents provide transportation to and from the school for all practices and competitions due to the shortened school day. Another equity issue was that clubs and activities did not resume until later in the fall, using Google Meet. Eventually, toward the end of the year students were in the school building daily but still without in person clubs and activities and masked at sports. Fighting through the curriculum with a variety of learning strategies and environments while accommodating quarantines was incredibly challenging for students and teachers. Recall that the other option for learning was the remote learning academy, which is described in the following subsection.

Remote Learning Academy

Six months after the pandemic began, in September 2020, many were not ready to make a return to in-person learning for various reasons, such as personal or family health concerns and fear. The school district of study met this need by forming its first ever official remote learning academy. Families were able to opt out of the in-person learning hybrid model, and into this fully virtual option. Students were enrolled in their classes the same way they would be in the hybrid model, but each class was fully held on Google Meet, following the same shortened day schedule, with the option for additional support in the second of the day, still on Google Meet. The author taught one middle school mathematics class in the remote academy and witnessed the student experience.

Students were encouraged to be engaged with the same techniques described above (IOWs, guided notes during the Google Meet, using the provided support materials). During the meeting, similar behaviors were witnessed as during the meets for the hybrid model, where students could choose to engage or to turn off their camera and microphone and disengage, despite teacher prompting. Students were more engaged when information was presented clearly and concisely, and they could have their questions answered in a manner that made sense to them.

Summary

The 2020–2021 school year was unlike any preceding year. Students were able to engage with one another and their teachers more than they could in the spring of 2020. However, due to COVID-19 induced health guidelines, the delivery of instruction and curriculum was impacted and limited. Thankfully, in late 2020 and early 2021, the COVID-19 vaccine began to be distributed which began to alter health guidelines again and create new opportunities for students.

THE 2021–2022 SCHOOL YEAR: FULL SCHOOL DAYS AND THE RETURN OF STATE TESTING

The 2021–2022 school year was the first time since early March of 2020 that students and staff were all back in the building for a full school day of in-person learning in the district of study. Every student was scheduled to be in the building daily within this format. This was a great improvement to the learning environments of the prior year and mimicked the traditional school environment prior to the COVID-19 pandemic. Students were more engaged with learning than they had been in years. However, restrictions were still in place in the school. During the year many students and staff were subject to periods of quarantine due to COVID-19 cases and exposures, and masks were still required daily. During quarantines students could choose to keep up with class either synchronously or asynchronously. There was also one school-wide closing due to COVID-19 following the December holiday break in January, when the week following New Year's Day had synchronous virtual instruction with Google Meet during class times. This was a minor disruption to student experience but is worth noting. Due to seating requirements group work was still limited, so much of what could be done was independent practice.

The in-person learning environment allowed for students and teachers to have a higher level of engagement with one another than the previous school year. Students were able to move through the curriculum at a pace like years prior to the pandemic but with difficulty due to the learning loss resulting from the learning conditions during the prior year and half. Students had the option of in-person after school help to supplement their learning on two days per week.

In the spring of 2022, the NJSLA resumed, and student achievement was documented officially for the first time since the pandemic began. As seen in Table 2, students in the school of study saw a decrease in scores from the last year of testing prior to the pandemic, which exacerbated the issue of middle school mathematics achievement. Instruction had been disrupted in multiple ways (as described above) for over two full school years, which impacted student performance on the assessment. While school engagement was higher during the 2021–2022 school year than the year and a half prior, the disruptions still had an impact on student learning as evidenced by the NJSLA scores.

School engagement was higher for learning and for extra-curricular activities, which positively impacted the student experience. During this year school clubs and activities were able to resume in-person and sports continued with increased ease on health precautions as the year progressed. This involvement created an important connection to the school, which had been missing during the pandemic. The following section will introduce our new normal in education as of the 2022–2023 school year following the end of the public health emergency.

A NEW BEGINNING: THE 2022–2023 SCHOOL YEAR

The 2022–2023 school year was the first traditional school year since March of 2020. Everything was back to normal with no school closures or extended quarantines and full school extracurricular activities, clubs, and sports. Mask-wearing and social distancing were no longer required. With this being the first stable year since the beginning of the COVID-19 pandemic for the in person learning environment, more implications of this time became present than ever before. Students struggled

COVID-19 and Mathematics Students

in various ways, teachers struggled to assist students, administrators struggled to assist students and teachers alike. The demand for intervention overtook resources, mental health concerns were more prevalent than ever, and the delivery of mathematical content was different than ever before. Students spent the year re-learning how to be students in a new educational landscape.

With all that was learned about online learning the mathematics teachers in the school of study continued with meaningful integration of technology for mathematics education, such as programs like IXL. These were used to help identify and address gaps in learning, as more intervention was needed than ever before. The students were also met with conceptual learning initiatives in mathematics, using hands on models and group work to try and increase foundational skills and knowledge. NJSLA testing data for this school year will help to determine if the in-person instructional and supplemental interventions were effective in increasing student achievement post-pandemic.

The COVID-19 pandemic disrupted learning more than any other event in recent times. Students and teachers are still working through the effects of the pandemic in the 2023–2024 school year, despite the continuation of the normalcy brought by the 2022–2023 school year. Student experiences need to be documented and analyzed to aide educators in their efforts to propel the education system forward and continue promoting positive student learning outcomes.

CONCLUSION

The COVID-19 pandemic caused a great disruption and shift in how middle grades mathematics instruction is delivered. Student experiences throughout the course of the pandemic have impacted current levels of achievement, as demonstrated from state testing data. Students need a reconnection to school and learning to increase knowledge gains. It is imperative that educators continue to move forward in education to adapt to the changing needs of students, while being sensitive to the lived experiences of the pandemic. As virtual learning is now a familiar learning model for middle grades students, it is imperative that educational researchers continue to explore the best virtual learning practices for middle grades mathematics students. This model offers potential for providing much needed intervention and change to help middle grades mathematics students increase their achievement, and thereby improve the trajectory of their lives.

REFERENCES

Bellaver, C. M. (2016). *A study to determine a relationship between a response to intervention math program and standardized math assessments* (Publication No. 3746431). [Doctoral dissertation, Capella University]. ProQuest Dissertations & Theses Global. (1760153044).

Byun, S., Irvin, M. J., & Bell, B. A. (2015). Advanced math course taking: Effects on math achievement and college enrollment. *Journal of Experimental Education*, 83(4), 439–468. 10.1080/00220973.2014.919957026508803

Causey, C. J. (2014). *Measuring the effects of computer-assisted instruction on teacher confidence and student achievement in 8th grade math* (Publication No. 3630384). [Doctoral dissertation, Trevecca Navarene University]. ProQuest Dissertations & Theses Global.

Dougherty, S. M., Goodman, J. S., Hill, D. V., Litke, E. G., & Page, L. C. (2015). Middle school math acceleration and equitable access to eighth-grade algebra: Evidence from the wake county public school system. *Educational Evaluation and Policy Analysis*, 37(1_suppl, 1S), 80S–101S. 10.3102/0162373715576076

Dung, D. T. H. (2020). The advantages and disadvantages of virtual learning. *IOSR Journal of Research & Method in Education*, 10(3), 45–48. 10.9790/7388-1003054548

Franklin, T., & Peng, L. (2008). Mobile math: Math educators and students engage in mobile learning. *Journal of Computing in Higher Education*, 20(2), 69–80. 10.1007/s12528-008-9005-0

Gulley, B. (2009). A computer based education (CBE) program for middle school mathematics intervention. *Journal of Computers in Mathematics and Science Teaching*, 28(4), 381–404.

National Center for Education Statistics. (2011). *Findings in brief: Reading and mathematics 2011—National assessment of educational progress at Grades 4 and 8*. https://nces.ed.gov/nationsreportcard/pdf/main2011/2012459.pdf

New Jersey Department of Education. (2021, April 14). *USED's determination regarding NJ's requirements to administer 2020-2021 statewide assessments*. https://www.nj.gov/education/broadcasts/2021/april/USEDsDeterminationRegardingNJsRequirementstoAdminister2020-2021StatewideAssessments.pdf

New Jersey Department of Education. (2023). *NJ school performance report*.

Official Site for the State of New Jersey. (2020, June 26). *Murphy administration announces reopening guidance for New Jersey schools.* https://nj.gov/governor/news/news/562020/approved/20200626b.shtml

Official Site for the State of New Jersey. (2020, May 4). *Governor murphy announces that schools will remain closed through the end of the academic year.* https://www.nj.gov/governor/news/news/562020/20200504a.shtml#:~:text=TRENTON%20%E2%80%93%20Citing%20the%20need%20to,the%202019%2D2020%20academic%20year

Trotman Reid, P., & Roberts, S. K. (2006). Gaining options: A mathematics program for potentially talented at-risk adolescent girls. *Merrill-Palmer Quarterly*, 52(2), 288–304. 10.1353/mpq.2006.0019

Chapter 5
Laboratory at Home:
Science Instruction During COVID-19

Kyle Seiverd
Ocean County Vocational Technical Schools, USA

Jennifer Huey
Toms River Regional School District, USA

ABSTRACT

Every course has elements that make it special. These special qualities can be due to the personality of the teacher, atmosphere of the school, set up of the class, or more. Science classes are one of the only courses to provide students with laboratory activities. These activities are often hands-on and done under teacher supervision. However, when COVID-19 forced learning to go virtual, providing laboratory activities to students became one of the biggest challenges. This chapter will provide an overview on the purpose of laboratory activities, how labs were changed to accommodate virtual learning, and the challenges educators faced when making these changes.

INTRODUCTION

The outbreak of COVID-19 in March of 2020 was a wakeup call to education. News about COVID-19 was changing and schools were trying to stem its transmission. The high population-density of classrooms made it ideal for disease transmission. To slow the spread, health officials called for the temporary suspension of in-person learning. The rapid transition to online learning was something many educators never foresaw. Nonetheless, teachers rose to the call when tasked

DOI: 10.4018/979-8-3693-1507-1.ch005

Laboratory at Home

with reinventing their classes to a virtual environment. Science teachers were in a unique position, compared to other subject area teachers. Science classes have the distinction of providing students with hands-on laboratory experiments. Not only do labs enrich learning, they are mandated by the curriculum. COVID-19 fueled the resourcefulness of science teachers to still provide laboratory experiences while students were at home.

The challenges educators faced during the COVID-19 pandemic were daunting. Each teacher overcame obstacles via collaboration, grit, and patience. Some of these obstacles included masking, virtual learning, social distancing, and quarantine. During the onset of the pandemic, all students were restricted to virtual learning. Their home environment became a cafeteria, gym, classroom, and science lab.

Science is taught like most classes, however the style depends on the subject matter and instructor. Most courses have four main elements; lecture, group assignments, independent work, and laboratory activities/experiments (Table 1). Lecture is also known as direct instruction. In this style, the teacher presents a topic while students play a passive role in the learning experience. During lecture, students typically participate by writing down key material presented, either by filling in guided-notes or free-choice writing. Group work is student-centered and collaborative. Often, the teacher provides a prompt and students work together to develop an answer. Independent work includes assignments such as tests, homework, and quizzes. Students work by themselves to demonstrate knowledge of a particular area. Laboratory work lessens the teacher-centered focus of lecture, while also providing the opportunity for group collaboration. Students are provided guidelines and background material by the teacher, and it is the students task to complete the laboratory experiment following the guidelines. Either working independently or as a group, students perform a laboratory experiment and analyze data. The most effective teaching-styling incorporates a mixed-methods approach. A mixed-methods approach provides students with differing learning styles and the opportunity to learn in multiple ways (Roots of Holistic Education, 2020).

Table 1. Four Main Elements of a Science Class

Element	Teacher-Centered	Student-Centered	Examples	Learning Style
Lecture	X		Powerpoint presentation, video recording	Visual and Auditory
Laboratory	X	X		Physical and Logistic
Group Work	X	X	Debate, POGIL©, Projects	Verbal and Social
Independent		X	Test, Quizzes, homework	Logistic and Solitary

When learning went virtual, science teachers needed to think about what materials at home could supplement authentic science instruments. Reflecting on the elements of a science laboratory, the most commonly used tools include a bunsen burner for heat, beakers for measurement, and thermometers to measure temperature. Each of these laboratory instruments had an analogous tool commonly found in the home (Table 2). These tools served as the foundation to build an at-home laboratory program. In addition to laboratory tools, the two other essential aspects of a home laboratory are chemicals and safety. Some labs are only possible at school because proper safety gear is needed. Common safety gear includes goggles, tongs, fume hood, fire blanket, and more. The importance of safety made some labs undoable at home. When these situations arose, the teacher performed the lab at school and recorded himself/herself or gave a digital version of the lab. In rare cases, the experiment was eliminated. It may be tempting to allow safety guidelines to slide in order to still conduct the lab, however safety should never be compromised. Compromising safety is a risk to the student and a liability to the teacher.

Table 2. Common Household Objects That can be Supplemented as Scientific Instruments

Scientific Instrument	Household Object
Beaker	Measuring cup
Bunsen burner	Microwave/oven
Hot hands/gloves	Oven mitts
Scale	Bakers scale
Timer	Kitchen timer

Many districts require that students be taught and assessed on lab safety. In a traditional classroom, teachers may present students with actual science equipment and show them where the fire extinguisher, safety blanket, and eye wash are located. This had to be modified due to virtual learning. The Google Suite offers numerous tools that make modifying safety protocol to a virtual environment seamless.

Adapting the paper safety contract to a digital platform was done using Google Forms. Students were required to read the safety rules then sign a Google Form acknowledging that they had read and understood all aspects of laboratory safety. In some school districts, students are also required to be assessed and demonstrate mastery of laboratory safety before partaking in a lab. Using Google Forms, a safety quiz was made. The safety quiz consisted of 20 multiple choice questions, with each question containing one correct answer. The lab safety Google Form was posted on Google Classroom and given as a quiz. Using Google Classroom as an instructional hub allowed the teacher to communicate, assess, and post resources to the students.

Laboratory at Home

    Students had to complete the quiz during the class period. To reduce cheating, the safety quiz was posted on 'lockdown mode'. This option prevents students from opening other tabs while completing a Google Form. Grading the quiz was up to teacher discretion. Many science teachers had the quiz count as a lab or homework grade, and considered a student score of 80% or higher to earn full credit. If a student earned less than an 80%, they were given the option to retake the quiz. For a student to participate in a lab, a signed safety contract and completed safety quiz of 80% or higher was required. Few students earned scores less than 80% on the safety quiz.

    In many instances science teachers modified their labs so that students would be able to have hands-on experiences using items commonly found at home. Participating in hands-on laboratory exercises increases learning and generates authentic experiences that can inspire. Students experience what it is truly like for scientists in the field, by reading a procedure and trying to replicate that procedure, possibly failing or getting a different result, and then trying again. Students gather an understanding of the scientific process when they are given the opportunity to experiment with materials. The preparation work involved in modifying these science labs took up a bulk of the science teachers' time. As educators, one understands the work that must be done in order to form those connections between lecture and content. In order to achieve the "ah ha moment" that usually happened in a classroom, surrounded by their peers with their teacher as a guide, students had to work through the process themselves and learn to ask questions or approach situations differently. To ensure those learning moments still happened and in the safety of a student's home, science educators reflected and modified labs.

    Science instruction is guided by learning standards. In the United States, it is the state's right to determine what is taught in public schools. For example, New Jersey has generated a list of student learning standards (SLS) for high school based on the Next Generation Science Standards (NGSS). These standards are grouped into three categories; earth science, biology, and physical science. For a student to receive a high school diploma, they must demonstrate mastery of these standards. It is up to the school district to determine how these standards will be taught. Most school districts offer SLS embedded in specific courses. By taking all the required courses, students will have been taught and assessed on each SLS the state has mandated.

    Across all science classes, scientific design, methodology, and engineering is covered as an introductory part of class. Each teacher may have their own style of how they expect laboratory reports or notebooks, however the process tends to be uniform. All scientific inquiry begins with making observations and asking questions. These questions must be based on the natural world and be testable. Philosophical or theological questions can be appropriate in certain situations, however the traditional science class is not the place to try and generate data to answer these questions.

Science teachers that engage in these style questions often find themselves in hot water with administration and/or parents/guardians.

Science inquiry is a process that students engage in. The style of science inquiry is dependent on the teacher. Background information can be mined before or after asking questions. Some teachers prefer to have their students propose a question then research and refine their thoughts. Others have students research and build a foundation before asking questions. Either way, students will design an experiment using background knowledge.

Scientific Inquiry is broken down into a series of steps that help guide students and scientists to a conclusion. Students are given a summary of these steps in every science course they take. Using background knowledge or research, students generate a hypothesis. In order to conduct an experiment, their hypothesis needs to be testable. Since students are taught about scientific inquiry throughout their science education careers, they should be well acquainted with the rules of generating a hypothesis. From there, students will design an experiment that can help prove or disprove the hypothesis. An experiment can have a variety of approaches, techniques, and appearances. When most students think about a laboratory experiment they envision a scene out of a science-fiction movie, but an experiment can be conducted in the comfort of their home or outside in the environment. A traditional experiment has independent, dependent, and controlled variables. The independent variable is what the students or experimenters are manipulating. There is only one independent variable in an experiment. For example: If a student's hypothesis was about dogs choosing blue toys over red toys, the independent variable would be a red colored toy. The dependent variable is the variable being measured. Dependent variables can be collected using quantitative (numerical) or qualitative (physical characteristics) data. Sticking with the previous example, the dependent variable would be the number of times the red dog toy was or was not picked by the dog. Controlled variables are what needs to remain the same during each trail. An experiment should have numerous controlled variables to increase the confidence that the result is the effect of the independent variable. Reflecting back on the example listed above, using the same shaped toy, is an example of a controlled variable. By only changing the color of the toy, it remains consistent with the student's hypothesis, that the dog is choosing the color blue, and is not choosing the toy based on something else, like its shape.

Once the variables have been identified and the materials gathered, the experiment can begin. Students will collect and record their data to determine whether their hypothesis was supported or rejected. Documenting every step of scientific inquiry is essential. Students and scientists need to account for each decision they make. This is especially true during data collection and interpretation. Data in an experiment is crucial. It will be used to support a scientist's conclusion. When the trials from the experiment are over, the data is graphed and analyzed. Students are shown a variety of different ways to present their data in the form of graphs (pie, line, or bar) and how to conduct statistical analyses. This information allows students and scientists to revisit their initial hypothesis and make a determination whether the data supports their claim.

When students and scientists make a determination based on their data, they are drawing a conclusion. This is one of the last steps of scientific inquiry. Students must be able to think critically to determine what their results are telling them. Sometimes the data gathered does not support their hypothesis, in this step students reflect back to see if there was anything they could have done differently that could have produced a different outcome. Oftentimes teachers have questions prepared at the end of a lab assignment that prompt the students to work through drawing a conclusion and explain how they might have done something wrong or suggest improvements. With virtual learning, to reflect on methodology and error, students would have to meet synchronously to discuss their experiments. In the classroom, students would be able to circulate around the room and visibly see other students' data and conclusions. As long as there was an exchange of ideas and peer review, students could feel what it is like to have others assess their work.

SCIENCE DURING VIRTUAL INSTRUCTION

Science answers questions about the universe. The answers to these questions are guided by scientific laws and theories. What is warming our planet? How much energy is contained in a loaf of bread? Why does the sun rise in the east? All these questions have a scientific answer. The ubiquity of science is one of the reasons why it is a mandatory part of education. In the United States, formal science instruction begins in elementary school. The amount of time and the content presented varies depending on the state and school district. Generally students receive greater science instruction as they progress from elementary, to middle, and ultimately to high school. The number of science classes/credits a student needs in high school to graduate depends on the state.

The most common requirement is for students to complete 3 years of science in order to graduate high school (Education Commission of the States, 2019). The specific science courses needed to graduate varies, however most states require students to take biology. Other science courses include earth science, chemistry, physics, and environmental science. The sequence and pacing of these courses is determined by the district, following recommendations by the state department of education (Figure 1).

Figure 1. Recommended Course Sequence for Secondary Science Classes by the State of New Jersey (2023).

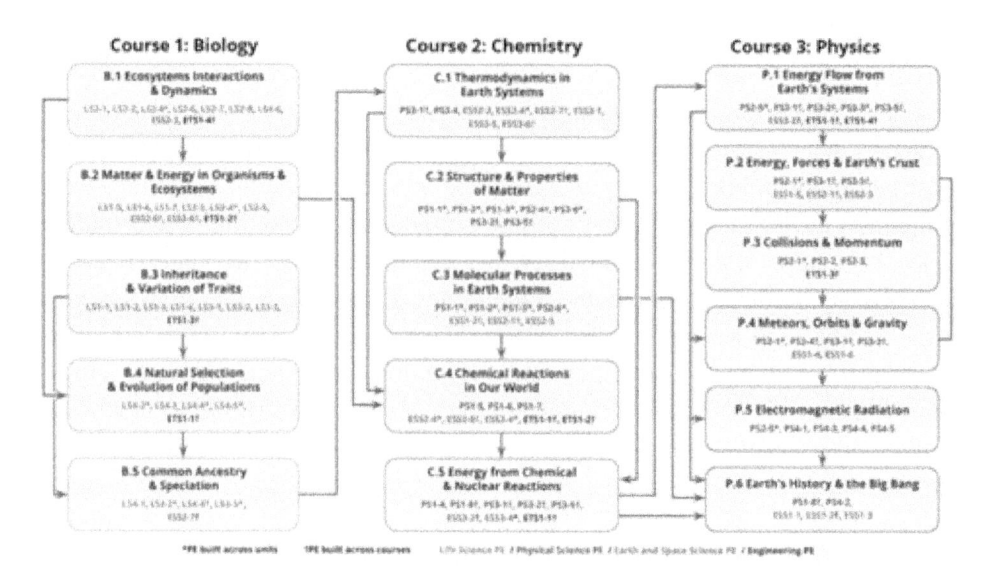

Often students take earth science their freshman year. The logic behind this is that earth science tends to be the most concrete science. Students are more familiar with earth science concepts and terminology, such as parts of the water cycle and plate tectonics. Chemistry and physics are often at the end of the science sequence, usually being offered to students in their junior or senior year of high school. Topics in chemistry and physics often are abstract and require a foundation in math. Some of these topics include balancing redox reactions, periodic trends, optics, and electrical forces. Students may also take additional science classes outside of the traditional sequence and scope, such as anatomy and physiology or forensic science. This is not mandatory, however a student's interest may lead them to want to take more science courses.

ENVIRONMENTAL SCIENCE: BACKYARD BIODIVERSITY SCAVENGER HUNT

Environmental science is often a science elective for students in their junior or senior year of high school. This class centers on how humans are impacting the environment. A traditional environmental science class incorporates outdoor lessons and field trips. With virtual learning, these experiences had to be tailored, so students

Laboratory at Home

could still acquire real-world knowledge of the natural world. One laboratory activity done in the class was the 'Backyard Scavenger Hunt'. This lesson has students use content knowledge to identify biotic and abiotic factors, succession, symbiosis, and human interactions around the school. However with students at home, this lesson was changed so students could still experience the lab.

For the 'Backyard Scavenger Hunt', students were asked to explore the environment around their home. Students were given the option to go to a local park, but were advised to follow all COVID safety protocols. This lab had students use their cellphones or a device that took photos to document species and species interactions. Students also had to identify what species they saw. Identifying species can be taxing, even to the trained biologist. Luckily, there are two apps that can be downloaded to smartphones that will do the identification for the user. These apps are called Seek and iNaturalist. Both of these apps are free to download from the app store. Once downloaded, these apps use artificial intelligence to identify the species of tree, animal, or fungus the user has the camera focused on. Once the app identifies the species, it will record it in the app's catalog and allow the user to identify more species. Sometimes the apps are unable to identify the photo down to the species level, and stop at the genus or family level. In this situation, the narrowest identification was accepted for credit. If students did not have access to a smartphone, they were allowed to use the internet or a species identification key for assistance.

The lab is set up following the 5E model (engage, explore, explain, elaborate, and extend), rather than traditional scientific inquiry. Each section is designed to build on a different aspect of learning. In the 'engage' section, students are asked to think about their home biome. They had to research the biome they live in, describe it, and list major threats to it. For example, central New Jersey is located in the temperate forest. The major threats to this area of New Jersey are deforestation, development, and wildfires. Students may not know the information about this section. If they do not know, they could use the internet or a textbook to find out.

The second part of this activity is 'explore'. This section begins with students selecting a location to do their scavenger hunt. The exact area varies pending what is feasible and accessible to the students. Some students chose to walk down the street in front of their home/apartment, while others went to a local park. Either way, all locations provide students with the opportunity to fulfill the requirements of the assignment. Students had to take a photo and describe the location. In the description, students were required to use terminology learned in class. Key terms included biotic and abiotic factors, symbioses, anthropogenic, and natural. By observing their chosen location, students needed to describe the predominant vegetation. This may have been trees, grasses, marsh grass, etc. The predominant vegetation was location dependent. To examine the relationship between flora and abiotic factors, students needed to examine the soil. Soil features vary depending on the location and human influences. Some soils are rich in organic matter and appear dark in color while other soils can be rich in clay and look reddish. By including soil into the 'explore' section, it opens the conversation of what plants can be supported by different soils. Soils that are rich in sand do not hold water long and may support very few plants compared to soils rich in silt and clay. One of the most surprising findings from this activity was how few students knew the closest body of water to their chosen location. Students who selected their home frequently did not know that the closest body of water was a stream or bay. Often the students listed the ocean as their answer. This was a learning opportunity to explain how pollution near their home enters the ocean via tributaries and streams that ultimately flow into the ocean.

To help organize the information acquired in the 'explore' section, two tables were provided. One table had students input the photos of the species they photographed along with their identification and trophic level. The second table focused on succession. Students had to put photos of their natural environment and put the stage of succession that photo was in. This provided an opportunity for students to take content learned in class and apply it to real-life situations. These tables were used as a reference for the last three sections.

Section three was 'explain'. This section was a combination of recalling background information as well as building on information acquired during the 'engage' and 'explore' sections. It began by having students recall key terminology when describing an environment. This included terms such as richness, evenness, and anthropogenic. By having students initially focus on terminology, it primed their thinking to use these words in the questions that followed. From there, students were asked to 'identify' and 'describe' various aspects of the environment. The action verbs were bolded to guide students in their responses. If the question was 'identify', the response could be as short as one sentence. Questions that used 'describe' needed at least a two sentence explanation. Students needed to describe species interactions and nutrient cycling in their selected environments. They could use photos to support their answers. Students were also asked to identify pioneer species and stages of ecological succession. This is when students would refer back to the tables under the 'explore' section to support their answer. To build on the complexity of the 'identify' questions, a 'describe' subquestion was added. This pushed the question into higher order thinking and provided greater richness in their response.

The fourth section had students 'elaborate'. This section had students think about what they observed, and built upon it. This is the highest order of questioning so far in the lab. Students needed to explain the importance of biodiversity in their ecosystem and list and describe ecosystem services they observed directly or indirectly. Ecosystem services include pollination, nutrient cycling, aesthetic beauty, and more. Students were then given a diagram of the stages of succession and asked to explain each. The last question had students recall the two types of succession and

Laboratory at Home

explain which happens faster and why. This section was one of the shorter sections with few students incorrectly answering questions.

The last section was 'extend'. This section provided students the opportunity to take what they had learned and apply it to new situations. For this part, the extension focused on the effects of climate change. Depending on the geographic region, this part can be modified to be about increasing industrationalization, a wildlife outbreak, land presentation, etc. Each scenario requires students to have a foundational understanding of the extension prompt, and apply it to their selected environment. This is the highest order of thinking in this lab. Because of the complexity of the 'extend' section, student answers had the greatest variation. Scoring for this section was the most lenient due to the complexity of the answers.

When students were finished, they submitted the assignment on Google Classroom. Students were given 3 days to complete the assignment. Having multiple days gave students an opportunity to ask the teacher questions, troubleshoot technology issues, or wait for ideal weather conditions. If students did not have access to a camera phone or their laptop did not have a camera, hand-drawn pictures were accepted. In this situation, students were allowed to submit fewer photos since drawing takes more time. Because this assignment had multiple sections, it usually took the teacher a few days to grade and return it. As detailed as this assignment was, it had students reflect and possibly see their local environment differently.

ENVIRONMENTAL SCIENCE: SOIL LAB

Advanced Placement Environmental Science (APES) is a course high school students can take during their sophomore, junior, or senior year. In most school districts, the prerequisite for Advanced Placement Environmental Science is chemistry. Students can take chemistry and APES concurrently or wait until after they have completed chemistry to take the course. Advanced Placement Environmental Science is a course developed and overseen through College Board. In order to teach this course, the teacher must take a preparation course to understand the depth and rigor required to ensure that students are equipped with the knowledge they need to pass the final Advanced Placement (AP) Exam in the spring. There are nine units that students must learn for the AP exam in May. The premise of Advanced Placement Environmental Science is how humans are impacting the environment and the solutions needed to fix these problems. The nine units go into detail about the problems that the human race are facing and the units end by discussing the solutions. On the advanced placement exam, students are presented with an environmental problem, and their task is to design a solution. One of the tasks required by the advanced placement teacher is to help students mentally prepare for the critical thinking required to do well on the exam. Depending on the score the students earn, and the college or university they want to attend, students will be given college credits. In essence, AP courses are like taking a college course while in high school. During the COVID pandemic, Advanced Placement courses still gave their final exams and hoped that students were doing their part on their virtual side to prepare for the exam.

Environment-Earth Science is a hybridization between earth and environmental science. This course unifies key elements of earth science, but eliminates rocks from the curriculum and adds renewable energy. Environmental-earth science would usually be assigned in a student's freshman year. This course is used as an introductory high school science course because the concepts are easier for students to visualize. According to the Next Generation Science Standards, Environmental-Earth Science should cover space science, climate change, earth systems, history of earth, and human sustainability. There are some overlapping areas in the Advanced Placement Environmental Science course and the Environmental-Earth Science course. However, the complexity is where the courses truly differs, but the Soil Lab can be used in both courses.

In unit four of Advanced Placement Environmental Science, the first few sections are about plate tectonics, soil properties, and soil composition. Environmental-earth science also discusses plate tectonics and soil composition. The standard addressed in the Soil Lab is Next Generation Science Standard HS-ESS1-6 that states: Apply scientific reasoning and evidence from ancient Earth materials to construct an account of Earth's formation and early history (NGSS, 2013). In the Soil lab, students determine the composition of their soil by using the "Jar Method." Students work through some of the steps of scientific inquiry to make a conclusion about the properties and composition of their soil. In order for this lab to be successful, students needed the following materials that can usually be found in every household. They needed a straight edged jar (like a tomato sauce jar) with the label removed, a soil sample from around their residence, a powdered dish or laundry detergent pod, marker, ruler or tape measurer, spade, paper towels, scissors, and a colander.

Students need prior knowledge about the different types of soil textures, their properties, as well as, how to read a soil texture pyramid. Once the students have that background information, they are prompted to hypothesize what type of soil they have in their own yard. Students are asked to observe their surroundings and make a prediction as to what type of soil texture they might find in their area. For example: for a student that lives by a body of water, such as the ocean or bay, he/she may expect to have a higher sand percentage in their soil sample.

Once the student has made a hypothesis, they start the experimental process. Students needed to gather the supplies listed above before collecting their sample. The straight edge jar should be prepped with the label removed because after the detergent is mixed with the soil, the Soil Jar must remain undisturbed for 48 hours.

Laboratory at Home

With the supplies gathered and prepped, students needed to go outside and find an easy place to dig with loose soil. Students can use a spade, if available, or their glass jar to help them dig about a few inches down before collecting their sample. Students need about a cup of soil to ensure that distinct layers form. Next, the students either use a colander or their fingers to remove any debris, such as twigs or large rocks from their sample. A colander would make easy work of this step, to ensure the sample is strictly soil. Students should also crush any lumps of soil in their sample.

Making sure that the straight edge jar is cleaned and prepped, students fill their jar about one quarter of the way. Using scissors, students cut open the powdered laundry or dish detergent pod and add it to their soil jar. The students then add water to their soil/detergent jar until the water reaches the top of their jar. Securing the lid and making sure that it does not leak, students shake the mixture vigorously for about 2-3 minutes. After that, the soil jar should be placed in an area that will not be disturbed for 24-48 hours. After the jar has sat undisturbed for about 24 hours, students can return and gather data. Students should see about three different layers in their soil jar. Figure 2 is a student submission of a soil jar. From looking at Figure 2, one can see the different layers vary in thicknesses and color.

Figure 2. Soil Jar Example with Layering

Laboratory at Home

Sand being the biggest and heaviest of the soil particles, it settles to the bottom the quickest. A student may have two layers of sand depending on the coarseness. Thicker coarse sand will be at the bottom and finer coarse sand will sit on top. The silt layer will be the next. Silt tends to form a layer on top of the sand, after about two hours. The last layer, and the longest to settle out is clay. The reason why students need to use a powdered laundry or a dish detergent pod, is to help the clay sink faster. If after 48 hours, students do not see a layer of clay, students can assume that their soil sample is 5% clay. When the students' water is clear, and can see their soil layers, it is time to take their measurements and record their data. Using a marker, students should mark on their jar where they see each layer end. The first recorded measurement should be the total depth of their soil. Students should record all measurements in millimeters. From there, students should measure the thickness of each of their soil layers using the marks they made on their jar and record them for percent calculations. To calculate the percent of each soil layer, students will use the number they recorded for that layer's thickness, divide it by the total (the first number they wrote down) and multiply by 100. For example, if a student's total depth of soil in their jar is 50 mm, and their measurements were 20 mm of sand, 17 mm of silt, and 13 mm of clay at the top. The percentages would be 40% sand (20mm/50mm x 100), 34% silt (17mm/50mm x 100) and 26% (13mm/50mm x 100) clay. These numbers will vary based on the soil found in each student's area. With the percentages of each soil layer calculated, the experimental part of scientific inquiry is complete, and students will use their data to form a conclusion.

Using the Soil Texture Pyramid (Figure 3) students will be able to determine the soil texture of the area sampled, and either accept or reject their hypothesis. Using the prior knowledge discussed earlier about how to use a Soil Texture Pyramid (Figure 3), students will find where their percent of sand, silt, and clay intersect. Using the information listed above, the percentage of sand for the example was 40%, students should locate 40% sand, on the bottom of the triangle and note the direction in which the numbers are slanted. Students should place one of their fingers where the 40% is located, or if students printed the lab, they can highlight the line in the same direction the 40% is slated. The slant of the numbers tells the reader what line to follow. The silt percentage from the example was 34%, students will need to locate the 34% on the right hand side of the triangle, and note the direction in which the number is slanted and place a second finger or trace the line for 34%. Finally, with a third finger or traced line in the direction the numbers are oriented, students will locate where 26% clay is found. Using their three placed fingers and following the slant of each number, students will bring their fingers together and identify what soil texture all three percentages land in. With the proposed percentages, Loam is the soil texture for this area. Students will form a conclusion about their soil texture and accept or reject their hypothesis. To differentiate between the advanced placement course and environmental-earth science course, additional questions and scenarios should be given to the advanced placement classes. Recall that advanced placement students need practice thinking critically, and generate solutions to environmental problems, for they will have to perform the same task during the Free Response section of their advanced placement exam. An advanced placement scenario question can look like this: Pretend you are a soil scientist. Someone brings you a sample of soil that is 70% clay, 20% sand, and 10% silt. Using the soil texture triangle, how would the soil be classified? What suggestions would you give that person to help their soil drain better? Advanced placement students should be given a few of these scenarios in order to prepare for the exam.

Figure 3. Soil Pyramid (Terry, 2004)

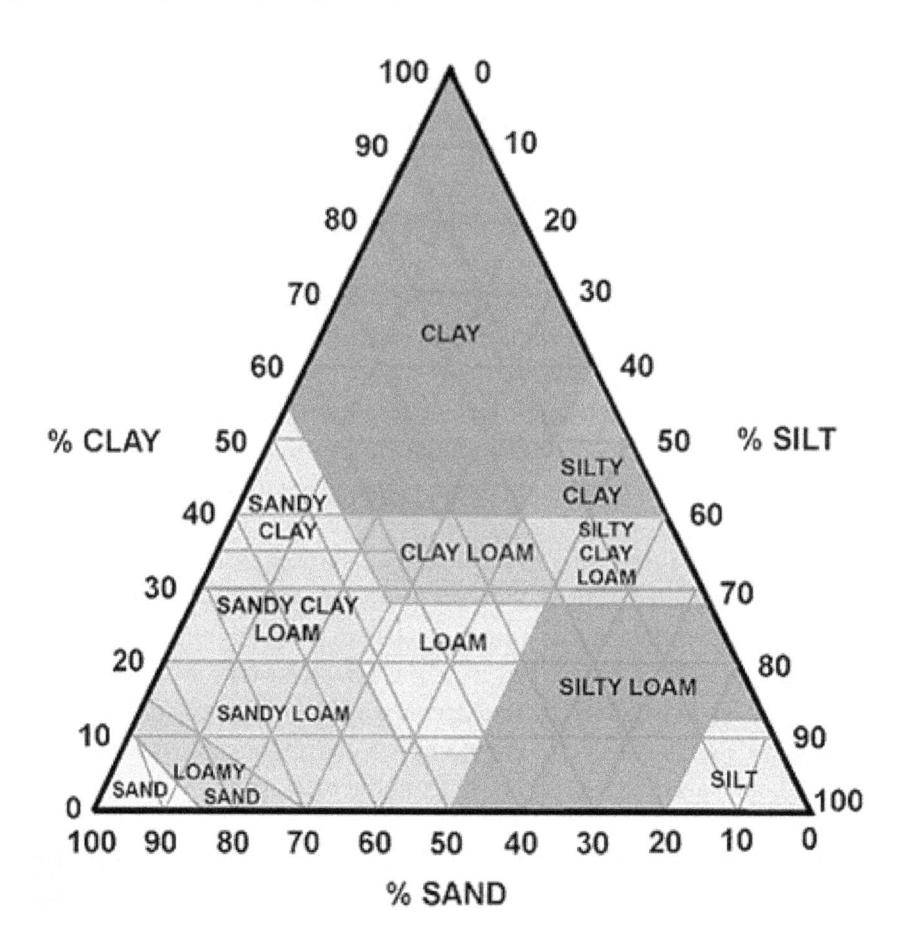

Laboratory at Home

The final step of scientific inquiry is to communicate your findings to be peer reviewed. In the virtual world of COVID, students did not have the opportunity to look at one another's soil jars and make their own measurements and conclusions about each other's soil texture. To ensure the last step on scientific inquiry was completed, students were required to take a picture of their soil jars and place them in the class/period's Google slide presentation. Students had to insert a picture, type their initials in the presenter note section, and on the slide identify what type of soil texture they concluded that they had. From there, each student, to the best of their ability, would choose two students' jar pictures and measure their classmates' soil layers to agree or disagree about what soil texture they had. Each student would write a discussion for the teacher to read, about what student's jar they choose and if they accept or reject their classmate's conclusion and the reasons why.

Once the students have completed each step of scientific inquiry involved in the Soil Lab, they were to turn in their lab via Google Classroom. In total, students were given four days for this assignment. Day one students should gather materials, soil sample, and complete the first part of the procedure up to where it says to leave the jar undisturbed for 24-48 hours. Even if students did not start on day one, they still had enough time for a layer to form and make calculations. Day two and three were devoted to having the layers fully develop. Day four should be spent measuring and calculating the percentages, drawing conclusions, and reflecting on their peer's submissions. This lab can be graded for completion or for correctness, it is up to the teacher's discretion. Advanced placements students were given scenarios which have correct answers, teachers can choose whether they want to make sure students are understanding the concepts, and are generating the correct solutions to the problems presented, or use the lab as an opportunity to see what the teacher needs to review more going forward. The purpose of this Soil Lab is to have students think critically, work through the steps of scientific inquiry like practicing scientists do on a daily basis, and show that there is more to Earth's soil than meets the eye.

WHAT ABOUT PHYSICS?

Of the three key strands of science, physics is the most challenging to find instructors. As a result, many districts have incorporated physics into their environmental-earth science classes. This allows instructors with biology certifications to teach selected aspects of physics. One example of this includes the infusion of Kepler's Laws and the Doppler Effect into environmental-earth science classes. Online simulations provided students the opportunity to explore the Doppler Effect, as well as other physics concepts. However, neither authors teach physics, so when physical science was covered, it was strictly the basics of those concepts. There are many online resources that provide teachers and students with instructional materials and simulations that can be implemented virtually. Physics is a subject area with opportunities to develop additional resources. This can be attributed to the shortage of physics teachers, thus limiting the output of teacher-developed instructional materials compared to the other science courses.

SUMMARY

The idea of virtual learning and instruction may trigger nightmares for students, teachers, parents, and more. However, this different learning style offered educators the opportunity to reflect on classroom practice and reinvent their traditional routine. Historically, science courses mostly focused on providing students hands-on experiences while in the classroom and reinforcement activities, such as worksheets at home. This no longer has to be the scenario for science education. Teachers can adopt a 'flipped classroom' approach, allowing students to explore authentic science experiments at home. Flipping some assignments to be done at home, creates an opportunity for more time in the classroom reinforcing skills and covering content. While some labs and lessons require in-person instruction, out of classroom experiences can also be used to enhance learning.

Flipping traditional in-person instruction to virtual instruction is not easy. Relying on your teacher community for support is vital. Depending on your situation, your teacher community may be coworkers in your building, in another district, or online. When districts flipped to virtual instruction, subject area teachers formed teams to support each other. Groups of biology teachers shared digital worksheets, strategies, lab, and tools on how to stitch together a virtual classroom. The limited time to implement these changes, and minimal training, added to the stress, however depending on an educational community reduced that burden.

Online teaching communities are a valuable resource to help guide educators on what works best for virtual instruction. Resources for virtual instruction may be found on sites such as Teachers Pay Teachers, AP Community, Facebook groups, and more. Many of these resources are free or come with a minimal fee. Using these resources can save teachers hours of work. Teachers will find that some things are adaptable to virtual learning, while others need in-person instruction. Even if the material is not usable for virtual learning, it may provide a resource to teach a concept in the classroom.

COVID also showed those working in education the value of in-person learning. Some things are taught better in-person rather than online. Perhaps the most valuable lesson learned during lockdown was not what could be learned at home, but the value of being together. Science education and in-person laboratory experiences are

Laboratory at Home

more than just learning content. It gives instructors and students an opportunity to interact and develop a deeper relationship that virtual learning lacks. To maximize the learning experience, virtual learning needs to tie in relationship building with the content. This can be a challenge, but the greatest learning occurs when there is human connection behind the content.

REFERENCES

Education Commission of the States. (2019). *High School Graduation Requirements: 50 state comparison*. Education commission of the States: Your education policy team. https://c0arw235.caspio.com/dp/b7f930000e16e10a822c47b3baa2

Mayo Clinic Staff. (2020). *Severe acute respiratory syndrome (SARS)*. Mayo Clinic. https://www.mayoclinic.org/diseases-conditions/sars/symptoms-causes/syc-20351765

Next Generation Science Standards. (2013). http://www.nextgenscience.org/next-generation-science-standards

Roots of Holistic Education. (2020). *Holistic Application of Google Platform to Education*. Googlesites.

Sarikas, C. (2020). *The High School Science Classes You Should Take*. Prepscholar. https://blog.prepscholar.com/the-high-school-science-classes-you-should-take https://www.nj.gov/education/standards/science/Sci9-12.shtml

Terry, S. (2004). *Soil Triangle Diagram*. Media Storehouse. https://www.mediastorehouse.com/science-photo-library/soil-triangle-diagram-6342015.html

Chapter 6
Secondary School Learners' Experiences During COVID-19 in Africa and Beyond:
A Systematic Review

Daniel L. Mpolomoka
https://orcid.org/0000-0002-2479-2693
UNICAF University, Zambia

Petronella Mwaka
Zambian Open University, Zambia

Joseph Mandyata
https://orcid.org/0009-0007-9755-4809
University of Zambia, Zambia

ABSTRACT

This chapter is informed by findings of a study that explored the lived experiences of learners who survived COVID-19 in secondary schools of Kasama District. The study emanated from the backdrop that while these experiences by COVID-19 survivors in their communities and society at large are well documented, little is known about such experiences involving learners as COVID-19 survivors in school environments which are much more vulnerable and delicate communities. A Systematic Literature Review (SR) was conducted on the subject. Specific search engines were employed with a distinct inclusivity and exclusivity criterion applied. Findings indicate that schools recorded COVID-19 cases among the learners more especially during the time when schools were in session. Literature abounds that confirms that schools

DOI: 10.4018/979-8-3693-1507-1.ch006

Copyright © 2024, IGI Global. Copying or distributing in print or electronic forms without written permission of IGI Global is prohibited.

had learners who experienced and survived the ills of the COVID-19 who required support system from their teachers, peers, and the school within the school community for the experience that they went through with COVID-19.

INTRODUCTION

This chapter provides a systematic literature review of Secondary School Learners' Experiences during CoviD 19. It is arranged in several sections of literature that is of concern. The first three sections of the chapter focus on literature that is related to the three objectives of the study hence the sections draw attention to literature on adverse emotional experiences of COVID 19 in survivors, experiences of academic nature of COVID 19 survivors and coping strategies of COVID 19 survivors to undesirable experiences. These sections are then followed by global studies on the experiences of COVID 19 survivors and African studies on the experiences of COVID 19 survivors. Thereafter, Zambian literature on COVID 19 in schools follows, and then a research gap in the reviewed literature is presented.

Rationale

The chapter may be beneficial to both the school management as well as education policy makers by shedding more light on the experiences of learners who survived COVID-19 in secondary schools. This may in turn aid school management teams and policy makers in designing strategies to control and manage the adverse experiences of learners that have survived COVID-19 in school environments especially that, at the turn of the year 2023, the Ministry of Health and Council offices countrywide record increases in COVID-19 cases. Thus, the findings of the study may be vital in the creation and implementation of safety approaches and longer-term planning for control and management of COVID-19 survivors' adverse experiences in school communities. The effective control and management of adverse COVID-19 experiences in schools may in turn make the school environment safe and accommodative for the survivors of COVID-19 both in future COVID-19 outbreaks and even in future outbreaks of other similar pandemics.

Considering that COVID-19 is a cross cutting issue in various sectors, the findings of the study may also be useful to other institutions and organizations in other sectors apart from just the education sector. Other institutions can also benefit from this study by gaining insight into the experiences of COVID-19 survivors which can aid them to create strategies to cope and counteract the experiences for an all-encompassing and accommodating work environment that safely accommodates COVID-19 survivors too. As a result, other institutions across sectors may find

Secondary School Learners' Experiences

the best strategies to employ and place a policy which they can use to counter the adverse experiences of COVID-19 survivors if and when such experiences occur in their institutions and organizations.

This chapter may also be helpful to the health practitioners. From the experiences of the learners that have survived COVID-19, the health practitioners may also gain access to experiences that are of concern to their work. Given the ambiguity in the time of the disease eradication and its continuing course, a deep understanding of the COVID-19 survivors' experiences may help health practitioners to make appropriate decisions and take measures to assess and identify adverse experiences that may affect the health of survivors. In so doing, the health practitioners may design interventions to improve and manage the COVID-19 survivors' health.

Emotional Experiences of COVID 19 Survivors

Discrimination Against COVID 19 Survivors

According to literature (Adom et al., 2021, Atinga et al., 2022; Dar et al., 2020, Okonofua et al., 2022, Rillo, et al., 2021; Romulo and Urbano, 2022; Silwal, et al, 2021), there have been several emotional experiences of COVID-19 that included stigma, discrimination, and social exclusion among others. In fact, Rillo et al (2021:36) asserted that "stigma and discrimination described the survivors' experiences about the social stigma that the COVID-19 pandemic has caused." According to literature, discrimination against the survivors of COVID-19 was noted in various parts of the world. In Nepal for instance, Silwal et al (2021) revealed that discrimination was faced by the COVID-19 survivors in various environments including family (home) and workplace environments. These environments included discrimination against COVID-19 survivors in their work places, health care institutions and even in their societies in the context of Nepal (Silwal et al, 2021). Discrimination was too, revealed among COVID-19 survivors where COVID-19 survivors were found to have suffered more from the implications of discrimination than from the disease's physiological effects in the Philippines (Romulo and Urbano, 2022). COVID-19 survivors were also found to be discriminated against in society by being rejected or avoided, being denied as well as by being physically of verbally abused as a result of having been COVID-19 positive, a situation that was experienced in Philippines (Rillo et al, 2022).

Literature has also revealed that the discrimination against the COVID-19 survivors was similar even in the African context (Atinga et al., 2022, Okonofua et al., 2022; Peprah and Gyasi, 2021). Peprah and Gyasi (2021) echoed that there was rising discriminatory behaviors against COVID-19 survivors in the sub-Saharan Africa. Similar echoes were heard particularly from Nigeria, Ghana, and Zimbabwe. In

117

Nigeria, Okonofua et al (2022) established reports of discriminatory encounters of both direct and indirect nature in a study of lived experiences of recovered COVID-19 persons. In Ghana, narratives of Ghanaian COVID-19 survivors in a study by Atinga et al (2022) revealed intense themes of discrimination against COVID-19 survivors. According to Atinga et al. (2022), COVID-19 survivors experienced discrimination both directed towards their families and discrimination from within their families towards them as COVID-19 survivors that was exhibit through poor attention given to survivors, discriminatory behaviours of family members towards the survivors as well as literal victimization of survivors for having been infected with COVID-19. Other discriminatory trends against COVID-19 survivors in Ghana were those from the community and discrimination from the workplace environment through unwelcoming attitudes, mood changes towards COVID-19 survivors and unfair treatment from the supervisors in the work place (Atinga et al., 2022).

Stigmatization Against COVID 19 Survivors

Literature has also revealed Stigmatization against the survivors of COVID-19 as another emotional experience of COVID-19 survivors. Actually, Dar et al (2020) asserted that approximately 98% of COVID-19 survivors have experienced a form of stigmatization after their recovery. As a matter of fact, it was revealed that stigmatization was a common unpleasant experience of COVID-19 survivors (Rillo et al, 2022). According to literature, the stigmatization of COVID-19 survivors was experienced in different societies of the world and was thus a worldwide experience. This stigmatization of COVID-19 survivors was revealed in various studies in different parts of the world including those by Silwal et al (2021) in Nepal, Romulo and Urbano (2022) in the Philippines, Dar et al (2020) in India, Okonofua et al (2022) in Nigeria as well as Adom et al (2021) and Atinga et al (20220 in Ghana. In India, it was revealed that at least 98% of the COVID-19 survivors had suffered some form of stigmatization in their communities.

In Nepal, Romulo and Urbano et al (2022) also observed various traits of stigmatization against COVID-19 survivors and even against their families in communities, public places and even in workplaces. Similarly in Philippines, Romulo and Urbano (2022) and Rillo et al (2022) all revealed stigmatization trends against survivors of COVID-19. Actually, Rillo et al (2022) suggested that COVID-19 stigma was still present and experienced among the COVID-19 survivors even after surviving the infection and declared COVID-19 negative and that this stigma creates psychosocial effects in survivors that persist long after the COVID-19 infection (Rillo, et al, 2022). Stigma against COVID-19 survivors was also experienced in China (Liu et al, 2020; Li and Guo, 2022; Yuan, et al, 2021). While Yuan et al (2021) noted stigma in form of social rejection, internalized shame and social isolation were noted, Liu et al (2020) noted experiences mental health problems in form of anxiety, depression, and PTSD among the COVID-19 survivors whose main predictor was perceived stigma and discrimination.

In the African experience, literature revealed stigmatization trends against COVID-19 survivors in Ghana for instance, that were exhibited through behaviours that were labeling the COVID-19 survivors as well as stigma against their families and relatives (Atinga et al, 2022). These stigmatization trends in the context of Ghana were seen in the prejudices, stereotyping and status undermining that the COVID-19 survivors went through at the hands of society in their communities (Atinga et al, 2022).Other forms of stigmatization established by literature were forms such as stereotyping and mockery targeted against COVID-19 victims (Adom et al, 2021).

COVID-19 survivors were often stigmatized by not only their communities but also by their own friends after their release from COVID-19 isolation centres (Adom, et al, 2021; Silwal, 2021). This supports the earlier various sources of literature that have argued for the stigmatization of COVID-19 survivors from all around their environments including their communities, families and even friends. In other cases, not only were the COVID-19 survivors the only target of stigma but also their families as well (Adom et al, 2021; Atinga, et al, 2022; Silwal, 2021). This view was noted among others by Adom et al, 2021) who asserted that the families of COVID-19 survivors and even victims were in one way or the other stigmatized against by having their homes labeled as COVID-19 infected homes, while others victimize the families by calling them names and despising them. In fact, this stigmatization was not only for Ghanaian COVID-19 survivors but also from Ghanaian isolation centres but also for Ghanaian returnees and foreigners from COVID-19 hotspot countries (Adom et al, 2021). The COVID-19 foreign survivors from COVID-19 hotspot countries such as such as Korea, UK, USA and more especially from the Asian countries where COVID-19 is believed to have originated, were also stigmatized by the general populace in Ghana (Adom, et al, 2021). This was so because the general populace believed that COVID-19 is mainly for white skinned people and their associates especially of Asian origin (Adom, et al, 2021).

Social Exclusion of COVID 19 Survivors

Reviewed literature posits that social exclusion of COVID 19 survivors from social environments was also another emotional experience of COVID 19 survivors. COVID 19 survivors have also experienced social seclusion from the people, communities and even from public institutions (Adom et al, 2021; Atinga et al, 2022, Dar et al, 2020; Rillo et al, 2022). In fact, social barriers were created to limit the access and control of COVID 19 survivors from many social spaces including religious, sport, traditional and even children' playing spaces (Atinga et al, 2022).

COVID 19 survivors found themselves denied access to public facilities such as recreational facilities, markets and even other shopping areas (Adom et al, 2021; Atinga et al, 2022). In Ghana, for instance, Atinga et al (2022) found out that there social exclusion and social avoidance of persons that have survived COVID 19 as well as through Barriers to social adjustments towards COVID 19 survivors.

There is empirical evidence that other COVID-19 survivors were socially excluded through denial to retail shops and markets as owners of businesses refuse to sale to COVID-19 survivors and their families for having been infected with COVID-19 (Adom et al, 2021; Atinga et al, 2022; Mushibwe, Mpolomoka, Mwelwa, Mushima & Kakoma, 2024). As a matter of fact, the social exclusion of COVID-19 survivors and even their families from the shopping spaces in some African countries was at times under the claim that the money that was from COVID-19 survivors and their families has been infected with COVID-19 even though the survivors had fully recovered and tested negative for COVID-19 (Adom et al 2021). This simply showed the lack of understanding of COVID-19 in terms of its spread, contraction, infection and recovery which facilitated fear and anxiety towards the COVID-19 survivors. This scenario was seen in Philippines where there was fear and even anxiety towards the COVID-19 survivors (Rillo et al, 2022).

Mental Health Problems in COVID 19 Survivors

Mental health problems were also one of the lived experiences that COVID 19 survivors went through. For example, mental health experiences of depression and stress, anxiety and even PTSD were revealed to be experienced by COVID 19 survivors (Liu et al, 2020; Olufadewa et al, 2020). Mental illness was for instance experienced among COVID 19 survivors in China's Wuhan City where COVID 19 began.

According to Liu et al (2020), COVID-19 survivors in Wuhan experienced mental illnesses in the form of anxiety, depression and PTSD. Liu et al (2020) further revealed that in the case of China's Wuhan City, stigmatization and discrimination against the COVID-19 survivors mainly facilitated these mental illnesses severely and significantly as indicated by statistical tests through multivariate logistic regression. Similar mental health problems were experienced among COVID-19 survivors in the context of Nigeria (Olufadewa et al., 2020). Thus, it is on record that COVID-19 survivors in Nigeria suffered negative mental problems such as anxiety and paranoia.

Experiences of Academic Nature of COVID 19 Survivors

Literature has also shown that there is an indication of a negative experience of COVID 19 survivors on their academic performance. For instance, Taunan et al (2021) established that those who had COVID 19 had a severe effect on their mental health and sometimes experienced mental instability and struggled to be productive which resulted in an effect in some on their academic performances. This study is one of the rare studies that have been reviewed on the learners who have survived COVID 19 with regard to their experiences in school academic activities.

We can postulate that the literature reviewed has indicated a severe lack of literature on the experiences of academic nature of learners that have survived COVID 9 in schools. Much of what studies have focused on with regard to COVID-19 in schools and education in general, has been on the impact of COVID-19 on school performance and school activities. This is one subject that has been extensively researched with regard to COVID-19 and education. Such studies have undoubtedly revealed that the outbreak of COVID-19 affected greatly almost all the educational levels in different contexts across the globe (Oyinloye, 2020; UNHCR, 2020; UNESCO, 2020). Other areas of focus have been on learner performance (Hapompwe et al, 2020; Sintema, 2020), COVID-19 safety measures in schools (UN-OCHA, 2020; UNESCO et al 2020; Honickman, 2023), effect of the school closures and confinements on learners (Gonzalez, et al, 2020; ILO, 2020; TUAC-OECD, 2020), remote learning during to COVID-19 (Mhlanga and Moloi, 2020; UN, 2020; UNHCR, 2020; Saiz-Gonzalez, Fernández-Río & Iglesias, 2023) among many other related topics. While massive literature exists on the impact of COVID-19 in school performance and generally in education, extremely scanty information exists regarding the learners who survived COVID-19 and how their experiences regarding school academic activities have been, hence, the necessity of this study.

Coping Strategies to Undesirable Experiences of COVID 19 Survivors

Literature has unearthed various strategies that the COVID 19 survivors used to cope with the negative experiences that they suffered on the basis of having tested positive to COVID 19. One such coping strategy according to literature was the use of prayer in the context of Africa to gain strength and faith that whatever experiences they were passing through was only but a phase that would pass with time. The use of prayers as a coping strategy to negative experiences of COVID 19 survivors was supported by Atinga et al (2022) in Ghana.

According to literature, other coping strategies to avoid undesirable behaviours against COVID 19 survivors were those that involved dealing with the safety of the survivors to prevent the reoccurrence of COVID 19 having undergone adverse experiences as COVID 19 survivors. Such measures included proper handwashing, wearing masks and avoiding crowds were the best ways to prevent from getting the infection (Silwal, et al, 2021; Mushibwe, Mpolomoka, Botha and Machaka, 2020). In a study by Silwal et al (2021) in Nepal, COVID 19 survivors still used safety measures like masks, Hand washing in friend circles and patient care, maintaining distance and being less exposed in crowded areas as coping mechanisms to COVID 19. Additionally, the COVID 19 survivors' used coping strategies with the aim of preventing of reoccurrence of the contraction of COVID 19 which included the use of home remedies, mainly comprised of ginger, garlic and lemon as well as the use of eucalyptus and tsunami which were added to water for steaming (Munsaka and Rukweze, 2021).

International Studies on Lived Experiences of COVID 19 Survivors

Here, China, Philippines, Nepal are discussed.

In China, Liu et al (2020) carried out a study on the risk factors associated with mental illness in hospital discharge patients infected with COVID-19 in Wuhan City which was the starting point of the COVID-19. The study found out that the COVID-19 survivors experienced adverse mental health problems which included anxiety, depression, and PTSD which were evident after their discharge from hospitals. The study further established that perceived stigma and discrimination were a major predictor of mental illness in form of anxiety, depression and PTSD in COVID-19 survivors. In fact, the study's findings emphasize the vital role of stigma and discrimination in intensifying the emotional impact of COVID-19 as established by the importance score analysis and multivariate logistic regression which indicated that perceived discrimination was linked to clinically significant symptoms of PTSD, severe anxiety and severe depression.

Similarly in China, Li and Guo (2022) focused on how pandemic precautions result in lingering discrimination among COVID-19 survivors. The study was an examination of whether COVID-19 survivors experience discrimination which was carried out during the lockdown in Xi'an with over 3, 000 participants. The study found out that COVID-19 survivors suffered social discrimination and prejudice and there was significantly lower willingness to socialize with COVID-19 survivors. The discrimination effect of COVID-19 survivors was prominent among those with high levels of education, social status and social capital partially due to limited knowledge among the public on COVID-19 recovery, a situation that aggravated the fear of infection in social relations hence limited social interactions with COVID-19 survivors.

In Philippines, Rillo et al (2022) conducted a qualitative interpretative phenomenological study on the lived experiences of hospitalized COVID-19 survivors or quarantine victims. The study was aimed at exploring the experiences of COVID-19 survivors during and after their admission to the COVID-19 facilities. The study established the lived experiences of hospitalized COVID-19 survivors after the infection that included stigma and discrimination against them In this case, the COVID-19 survivors experienced prejudices, rejections and even self-isolation.

In Nepal, Silwal et al (2021) conducted a phenomenological analysis of lived experiences of COVID-19 survivors. The study focused on a phenomenological qualitative research of ten (10) COVID-19 survivors. The study revealed social stigma and discrimination towards COVID-19 survivors in workplaces and even in health facilities by health workers and recommended adequate counseling to address physical and psychological concerns among the survivors.

African Studies on Lived Experiences of COVID 19 Survivors

Here, Ghana, Nigeria and Zimbabwe are discussed.

In Ghana, Atinga et al (2021) carried out a study entitled "Recovered but constrained: Narratives of Ghanaian COVID-19 survivors- Experiences and Coping Strategies of Sigma, Discrimination, Social Exclusion and their Sequels." The study focused on the lived experiences of people who recovered and were discharged after being clinically diagnosed positive of COVID-19 and were admitted into a designated therapy treatment facility (Atinga et al, 2021). The findings of the study established that the everyday lived experiences of participants were disrupted with indirect stigmatization both against relatives and family members of COVID-19 survivors (Atinga et al, 2021). The study further revealed that there was "direct stigmatization (labelling, prejudices and stereotyping), barriers to realizing full social life and discriminatory behaviours across socio-ecological structures [such as] workplace, community, family, and social institutions" (Atinga et al, 2021: 1801). The study further revealed coping strategies of participants to the adverse lived experiences which included prayers of supplication, self-social withdraw, aggressive and self-assertive behaviour, supporting counseling belief in self and reliance on family for support (Atinga et al, 2021). The sequels of the adverse experiences of the COVID-19 survivors were according to the study found to include reduced happiness, reduced morale, low self-confidence, insomnia, loneliness and fear, distress and frustrations (Atinga et al, 2010).

Another Ghanaian study by Adom et al (2021) was carried out on the psychological distress and mental health disorders from COVID-19 stigmatization. The study's purpose was to investigate the cases of COVID-19 related stigma and discrimination against health workers, suspected persons with COVID-19, Asians and persons with travel history from COVID-19 hotspot countries as well as against COVID-19 recovered patients, who are of particular importance to the study. The study's findings were that victims of COVID-19 have encountered a variety of stigma and discrimination which included stereotyping, social exclusion, mockery, finger pointing and insults.

In Nigeria, Uzobo et al (2022) investigated the lived experiences of COVID-19 survivors in South-Western Nigeria with specific attention on the "existing social practices with regard to stigmatization and discrimination against COVID-19 survivors" (Uzobo et al, 2022:211). This phenomenological qualitative study of 25 participants pointed out that the COVID-19 survivors were a subject of stigmatization and discrimination in the form of hostility, mockery and social exclusion which were in nature psychological. The study further indicated that COVID-19 survivors reacted to stigma and discrimination in a manner that manifested in unpleasant emotions such as suicidal thoughts and emotional outbursts.

In Zimbabwe, a study was carried out by Munsaka and Rukweza (2021) on the lived experiences of survivors of COVID-19 in Hwange. The study employed a phenomenological approach with 15 participants who recovered from COVID-19 and were either employees of Hwange Colliery Company Limited or their dependent and all residents of Hwange Colliery Concession Area. The study found out that the experiences of COVID-19 survivors included fear and self-isolation coupled with family support while church and neighbor support was viewed rare. Additionally, the study established the survivors' coping strategies to include the use of home remedies, mainly comprised of ginger, garlic and lemon as well as the use of eucalyptus which were added to water for steaming.

Zambian Studies on COVID 19 in Schools

Studies in the Zambian context with regards to COVID 19 in schools have been carried out in different parts of the country although not necessary on lived experiences of learners in schools after surviving COVID 19. These studies include among others a study by Luchembe (2021) on the preventive measures against the spread of COVID 19 in an exploration of policy responses in selected primary schools in Lusaka District. This study's findings were that there was the introduction of new operational policies for schools with key preventive measures against the spread of COVID 19 being masking, physical distancing and the observation of good hygiene and sanitation standards. The study also revealed major challenges experienced in the policy responses to COVID 19 to include parents' unwillingness to allow their children to return to school after a COVID 19 school closure, lack of adherence to physical distancing among pupils as well as loss of learning time due to the split of large classes to allow physical distancing (Muvombo, Mpolomoka, Kabungo, Banda, Chikopela & Mayamba, 2023; Muvombo, Mpolomoka, Kabungo, Banda, Chikopela & Mayamba, 2023).

Sintema (2020) also did a study on the effect of COVID-19 on the performance of Grade 12 students with specific focus on the implications on STEM education at a public secondary school in Chipata Eastern Zambia. The findings of the study had revealed a likelihood of a reduction in the percentage pass rate of secondary school students for the 2020 national examinations in the absence of the containment of COVID-19 in the shortest possible time. The study further revealed that the reduced pass percentage may also be especially since the school calendar was suddenly disturbed by the early and untimely closure of all schools countrywide.

A study conducted in Zambia by USAID (2021) on the resilience in return to learning during COVID-19. The study's purpose was to describe the alignment of response with the USAID Return to Learning (RtL) framework's five priorities for primary and secondary education levels. The study case further described the challenges and opportunities contributing to the resilience of returning to learning during theCOVID-19 responses. This Zambian case study showed that much of the return to learning framework may be adopted in the initial phases of the COVID-19 crisis response so as to absorb shock but guaranteeing a continued learning during the closure of schools was challenging. According to the finding of the case study indicated that all priority areas of the USAID RtL were in fact relevant to the MoGE COVID-19 response planning for both distance learning and return to learning in the course of the COVID-19 pandemic. These relevant USAID RtL priority areas included learner re-engagement, education re-opening plans, instructional time, curricular learning supports, examinations and promotions as well as educators and the learning space.

Another study by Hapompwe et al (2020) was carried out in Lusaka to establish E-learning issues in Zambia's 2020 General Education Examination candidates' academic performance. The study revealed a great negative impact on both the quality of general education and on the average academic performance in public schools. While the study revealed the presence of remote learning for the learners while on school closures due to COVID-19, it however revealed that the established *Edu.tv* broadcast programmes for remote learning had several challenges. These challenges according to the study included the lack of access to internet for online learning materials, power interruptions through power load shedding and challenges to do with accessibility due to lack of access to devices such as television sets for many learners.

In-Depth Assessment of the Long-Term Impact of COVID-19 on Education

A cross section of literature has systematically documented varying short, medium and long-term impacts of CoviD 19 on education. For example, from the education stakeholders' perspectives, ADEA & APHRC (2023) posit that the long-term impacts of COVID-19 on education in Africa are projected to manifest in three main ways. First is on learners, which includes learning loss, school dropout, and psychological well-being. Second is the impact on teachers, reflected in teacher truancy and well-being. Third is the impact on the school system, entailing the institutionalization of information and communication technology (ICT); integration of water, sanitation, and hygiene (WASH); and school resource constraints. Such revelations call for the need by individual ministries of education, schools, NGOs, communities, individuals with keen interest in education to invest in mitigating and putting up resilience mechanisms, knowing that CoviD 19 is still being recorded in some countries, though at a small scale.

This chapter has shown how schools should continue adapting curricula to suit various disasters and teaching-learning needs, put in place health wellness measure for both learners and teachers, create healthy, inclusive and least restrictive learning environments. There is need for government and all stakeholders to increase resource allocation and mobilization to help schools become resilient to CoviD 19 and survive the post era. In fact, educational resource mobilization is one of the cornerstones of education that has never been in surplus (Banda & Mpolomoka, 2023).

Thus far, this chapter has equipped you with relevant information as parents, teachers, administrators, schools, teachers, governments to enable you undertake actionable practices regarding post CoviD 19 instances. One striking take home for citizenry is the call to trust in government as disasters and pandemics occur. In a study sample of 12,758 individuals from 34 countries, Karakulak, Tepe, Dimitrova, et al. (2023) established that trust in government moderates the association between fear of COVID-19 as well as empathic concern and preventive behaviour.

Oppong, Appiah, Hapunda & Kheswa (2023) posit that Africa-based researchers and practitioners should work towards adapting or generating context-responsive assessment tools, show preference for validated versions of tools, and contribute to culturally appropriate guidelines and testing practices in Africa and the Global South.

Research Gaps in Literature Reviewed

With regard to Zambia, there seems to be lack of studies too focusing on the lived experiences COVID 19 survivors in the school communities. The reviewed studies have focused on other subjects, policy responses to COVID 19 during in schools (Luchembe, 2021), remote learning during COVID 19 (Hapompwe et al, 2020), effects of COVID 19 on the performance of students in school (Hapompwe et al, 2020; Sintema, 2020) and response resilience to COVID 19 in schools (USAID, 2020). All these studies may have focused on COVID 19 issues in schools but have neglected the school lived experiences of learners who survived COVID 19, a gap that this study has filled. Oppong, Appiah, Hapunda & Kheswa (2023) provided evidence about the efforts by African researchers and practitioners at generating new tools, validating existing ones, and adapting the practices of assessment before, during, and after the COVID-19 pandemic in Africa through a collection of reports of original research, systematic reviews, and comprehensive narrative reviews.

CONCLUSION

Drawing strength from gaps in literature, this chapter highlighted findings of a study that deployed qualitative phenomenological methods to explore the lived experiences learners who survived COVID 19 of Kasama District with specific attention to the adverse experiences and their coping strategies as well as their academic experiences in school communities.

The chapter first focused on literature revealing emotional experiences of COVID-19 survivors that included stigma and discrimination in families, communities and workplaces as well as social exclusion and mental health problems. The second section of the literature covered experiences, academic in nature of COVID-19 survivors in their school communities. Literature reviewed indicated both improved and declined experiences of academic performance among COVID-19 survivors. The third section of literature covered coping strategies of COVID-19 survivors to undesirable experiences revealed strategies such as aggressive behaviour, counseling and prayers, society and organizational withdraw, reliance of social support systems, self-belief and assertiveness. Other coping strategies according to the reviewed literature focused on ensuring that COVID-19 survivors do not re-contract COVID-19 and so for such survivors, hand washing, masking, sanitizing, steaming and physical distancing were important coping strategies.

The third and fourth main sections of the chapter presented literature on the experiences of COVID-19 survivors at the global level where literature showed various experiences of COVID-19 survivors in different parts of the world. These included adverse health problems such as depression, anxiety and PTSD as well as social discrimination and prejudices in China, stigma and discrimination in form of rejection, prejudices and self-isolation in Philippines as well as stigma and discrimination in workplaces in Nepal. Then came literature reviewed from African countries including Ghana, Nigeria and Zimbabwe. These African studies revealed experiences of direct stigma and discrimination in form of labelling, stereotyping and prejudices in Ghana, social exclusion, hostility and insults in Nigeria as well as fear, and self-isolation in Zimbabwe as experiences of COVID survivors. Zambian studies on COVID-19 in schools were uncovered too, which revealed remote learning due to school closures as a result of COVID-19, impact of COVID-19 on student performance in schools and response resilience to COVID-19 in schools. The final section of this chapter was the research gap in the literature reviewed which attempted to fix the neglect of the experiences of learners who survived COVID-19 in schools in the Zambian context. Literature showed that while COVID-19 in schools is a widely researched subject despite having been in existence for three (3) year now, no such research has been dedicated to the lived experiences of learners who survived COVID-19 in schools.

REFERENCES

ADEA & APHRC. (2023). *The Long-Term Impact of COVID-19 on Educational Systems in Africa: Perspectives of Education Stakeholders from sub-Saharan Africa.* Association for the Development of Education in Africa & African Population and Health Research Center.

Adom, D., Mensa, J. A., & Osei, M. (2021). The Psychological Distress and Mental Health Disorders from COVID-19 Stigmatization in Ghana. *Social Sciences & Humanities Open*, 4(1), 1–10. 10.1016/j.ssaho.2021.10018634250461

Banda, A., & Mpolomoka, D. L. (2023). A Critique of the Southern African Development Community's Protocol on Education and Training. In *Sustaining Higher Education Through Resource Allocation, Learning Design Models, and Academic Development*. IGI Global. 10.4018/978-1-6684-7059-6.ch009

Banda, S., Mpolomoka, D. L., Mbono, D., & Sampa, R. L. (2017). Use of Questions in Qualitative Research: How Questions guided Our Study. *International Journal of Developmental Research*, 7(12).

Braun, V., & Clarke, V. (2012). Thematic Analysis. *APA Handbook of Research Methods in Psychology*, 2, 57-71 10.1037/13620-004

Campbell, S., Greenwood, M., Prior, S., Shearer, T., Walkem, K., Young, S., Bywaters, D., & Walker, K. (2020). Purposive Sampling: Complex or Simple? Research Case Examples. *Journal of Research in Nursing*, 25(8), 652–661. 10.1177/17449 8712092720634394687

Dar, S. A., Khurshid, S. Q., Wani, Z. A., Khanam, A., Haq, I., Shah, N. N., Shahnawaz, M., & Mustafa, H. (2020). 'Stigma in Coronavirus Disease-19 Survivors in Kashmir, India: A Cross-Sectional Exploratory Study'. *PLoS One*, 15(12), e0244715. 10.1371/journal.pone.024471533362246

Devi, P. B. (2008). *Content Analysis: A Method of Social Science Research*. Sage.

Di Gennaro, F., Pizzol, D., Marotta, C., Antunes, M., Racalbuto, V., Veronese, N., & Smith, L. (2020). 'Coronavirus Diseases (COVID-19) Current Status and Future Perspectives: A Narrative Review.'. *International Journal of Environmental Research and Public Health*, 17(2690), 1–11. 10.3390/ijerph1708269032295188

Di Pietro, G., Biagi, F., Costa, P., Karpinski, Z., & Mazza, J. (2020). *The likely Impact of COVID-19 on Education: Reflections based on the existing Literature and Recent International Datasets. European Union and JRC Technical Report, EUR 30272*. European Union.

Gentles, S. J., Charles, C., Ploeg, J., & McKibbon, K. N. (2015). Sampling in Qualitative research: Insights from an overview of the methods literature. *The Qualitative Report*, 20(11), 1777–1789. 10.46743/2160-3715/2015.2373

Gonzalez, T., De la Rubia, M. A., Hincz, K. P., Comas-Lopez, M., Subirats, L., Fort, S., & Sacha, G. M. (2020). Influence of COVID-19 Confinement on Students' Performance in Higher Education. *PLoS One*, 15(10), e0239490. 10.1371/journal.pone.023949033035228

GRZ. (2020). *Statement by His Excellency, Dr. Edgar Chagwa Lungu, President of the Republic of Zambia, on the COVID-19 Pandemic, 25th March, 2020.* GRZ.

Hallgarten, J. (2020). Evidence on Efforts to Mitigate the Negative Educational Impact of Past Disease Outbreak. *KD4 Helpdesk Report No. 793.* Education Development Trust.

Hapompwe, C. C., Kukano, C., & Siwale, J. (2020). Impact of COVID-19 on Zambia's 2020 General Education Examination Candidates' Academic Performance in Lusaka: E-Learning Issues. *International Journal of Scientific and Research Publications*, 10(5), 647–654. 10.29322/IJSRP.10.05.2020.p10175

Harnett, B. M. (2015). *The value of Content Analysis as a Qualitative Research Method: Research Proposal.* The British University in Dubai.

Honickman, T. K. (2023). *A qualitative study using ecological systems theory to understand the lived experience of students with academic risks during the return to in-person classrooms following the COVID-19 pandemic.* Available from ProQuest One Academic. (2843777412). Retrieved from https://www.proquest.com/dissertations-theses/qualitative-study-using-ecological-systems-theory/docview/2843777412/se-2

ILO. (2020). *Terms of Reference for an Assessment on the Impact of COVID-19 on the Informal Sector in Zambia.*

Jabareen, Y. (2008). Building a Conceptual Framework: Philosophy, Definitions and Procedure. International Journal of Qualitative Methods, 8(4), 49-62. doi:10.1177/160940690900406

Karakulak, A., Tepe, B., Dimitrova, R., Abdelrahman, M., Akaliyski, P., Alaseel, R., Alkamali, Y. A., Amin, A., Lizarzaburu Aguinaga, D. A., Andres, A., Aruta, J. J. B. R., Assiotis, M., Avanesyan, H., Ayub, N., Bacikova-Sleskova, M., Baikanova, R., Bakkar, B., Bartoluci, S., Benitez, D., & Rudnev, M. (2023). Trust in government moderates the association between fear of COVID-19 as well as empathic concern and preventive behaviour. *Communications Psychology*, 1(43), 1–16. 10.1038/s44271-023-00046-5

Kinfu, Y., Alamu, U., & Achoki, T. (2020). COVID-19 Pandemic in the African Continent: Forecasts of Cumulative Cases, New Infections and Mortality. MedRxiv: *Preprint Server for Health Sciences*.10.1101/2020.04.09.20059154

Kumah, D., Malviya, R., & Sharma, P. K. (2020). Corona Virus: A Review of COVID-19 History and Origin. *EJMO*, 4(1), 8–25.

Li, X., & Guo, X. (2022). COVID-19 *Survivors: How Pandemic Precautions Result in Lingering Discrimination in China.*10.21203/rs.3.rs-2336680/v1

Liu, D., Baumeister, R. F., Veilleux, J. C., Chen, C., Liu, W., Yue, Y., & Zhang, S. (2020). Risk Factors associated with Mental Illness in Hospital Discharged Patients infected with COVID-19 in Wuhan, China. *Psychiatry Research*, 292, 1–9. 10.1016/j.psychres.2020.11329732707218

Lopez, K. A., & Willis, D. G. (2004). Descriptive Versus Interpretive Phenomenology: Their Contributions to Nursing Knowledge. *Qualitative Health Research*, 14(5), 726–235. 10.1177/1049732304263638151071 74

Luchembe, M. (2021). Preventive Measures against the Spread of COVID-19: Exploring Policy Responses in Selected Primary Schools in Lusaka, Zambia. *Kokusai Kyoiku Kyoryoku Ronshu*, 24(2), 97–111.

Mhlanga, D., & Moloi, T. (2020). COVID-19 and the Digital Transformation of Education: What are we learning on 4IR in South Africa? *Education Science,* 10(180), 1-11. Available on https://bmjopen.bmj.com/

Miles, M. B., Huberman, A. M., & Saldana, J. (2014). *Qualitative Data Analysis: A Methods Sourcebook* (3rd ed.). SAGE Publishers.

MoE. (2020a). Education Contingency Plan for Novel Coronavirus. Lusaka: GRZ.

MoE. (2020b). *Ministry Statement on Re-opening of Schools*. GRZ.

MoE. (2021c). *Ministerial Statement on Re-Opening of Schools*. GRZ.

MoH. (2020). *Updates*. Lusaka: MOH.

MoH. (2021). *Updates*. Lusaka: MOH.

Mpolomoka, D. L., Banda, A. M., Mushibwe, M., Banda, S., Nherera, S., Muvombo, M., Mainde, D., & Shawa, R. (2023). *Promoting Health and Well-Being of Secondary School Students in Chibombo District*. Paper presented at the International Conference on Making Sense of Educational Systems for Sustainable Development, Kibaha Kwa Mfipa, Tanzania.

Munsaka, J., & Rukweza, J. (2021). Lived Experiences of Survivors of COVID-19 Disease at Hwange Hospital, Zimbabwe. *European Journal of Medical and Health Sciences*, 3(6), 95–100. 10.24018/ejmed.2021.3.6.1084

Mushibwe, C. P., Mpolomoka, D. L., Mwelwa, A., Mushima, M., & Kakoma, M. (2024). Socio-Economic Implications of COVID-19 in Densely Populated Compounds (Komboni) in Lusaka, Zambia. *Journal of Culture. Social Development*, 73, 45–59. 10.7176/JCSD/73-05

Muvombo, M., Mpolomoka, D. L., Kabungo, C. J., Banda, A. M., Chikopela, R., & Mayamba, S. (2023). *Narratives by parents of what early childhood learners were doing during CoviD 19 in communities in Western and Eastern Provinces, Zambia: A Post-mortem and Binoculars lens*. Paper presented at the International Conference on Making Sense of Educational Systems for Sustainable Development, Kibaha Kwa Mfipa, Tanzania.

Northall, T., Chang, E., Hatcher, D., & Nicholls, D. (2020). The Application and Tailoring of Colaizzi's Phenomenological Approach to a Hospital Setting. *Nurse Researcher*, 28(2), 20–25. Advance online publication. 10.7748/nr.2020.e170032309916

Okonofua, F., Ntoimo, L. F. C., Onoh, V. I., Omonkhua, A. A., Alex-Ojei, C. A., & Balogun, J. (2022). Lived Experiences of Recovered COVID-19 Persons in Nigeria: A Phenomenological Study. *PLoS One*, 17(8), e0268109. 10.1371/journal.pone.026810935969603

Olufadewa, I. I., Adesina, M. A., Oladokun, B., Baru, A., Oladele, R. I., Iyanda, T. O., Ajibade, O. J., & Abudu, F. (2020). I Was Scared I Might Die Alone: A Qualitative Study of the Physiological and Psychological Experience of COVID-19 Survivors and the Quality of Care Received at Health Facilities. *International Journal of Travel Medicine and Global Health*, 8(2), 51–57. 10.34172/ijtmgh.2020.09

Oppong, S., Appiah, R., Hapunda, G., & Kheswa, J. G. (2023). Editorial: Contextualizing psychological assessment in Africa: COVID-19 and beyond. *Frontiers in Psychology*, 14, 1150387. 10.3389/fpsyg.2023.115038736895746

Oyinloye, O. (2020). The Possible Impact of COVID-19 on Senior Secondary School Students' Performance in Science Education in Nigeria. *Journal of Pedagogical and Psychology*, 2(2), 80–85. 10.33902/JPSP.2020263901

Peprah, P., & Gyasi, R. M. (2021). Stigma and COVID-19 Crisis: A Wake-Up Call. *The International Journal of Health Planning and Management, 36*(1), 215-218.10.1002/hpm.3065

Rillo, J. A., Uy, T. M. E., Macapagal, C. D., Mariano, C. R., Melosantos, M. F., Villena, C. M. D., Flores, E. A., & Catabona, Z. B. (2022). Quarantine Victors: Lived Experiences of Hospitalized COVID-19 Survivors. *Proceeding Series on Health and Medical Sciences: Proceedings of the 2nd International Nursing and Health Sciences,* 2, 21-41. Available on https://conferenceproceedings.ump.ac.id/index.php/pshms.issue/view/10

Romulo, S. G., & Urbano, R. C. (2022). *Separation and Discrimination: The Lived Experiences of COVID19 Survivors in Philippine Isolation Centres*. Sage Publication Journals.

Saiz-Gonzalez, P., Fernández-Río, J. & Iglesias, D. (2023). Lessons from COVID's social distancing in the physical education class. *Apunts. Educació Física i Esports*, (154), 52-60. https://doi.org/.(2023/4).154.05 10.5672/apunts.2014-0983.es

Silwal, S., Khadgi, D., Mahato, A., Basnet, S., Thapa, S., & Niraula, A. (2021). 'Lived Experiences of COVID-19 Survivors in Nepal: A Phenomenological Analysis'. *JCMS Nepal*, 17(4), 298–307. 10.3126/jcmsn.v17i4.41887

Sintema, E. J. (2020). Effects of COVID-19 on the Performance of Grade 12 Students: Implications for STEM Education. *Eurasia Journal of Mathematics, Science and Technology Education*, 16(7), 1–6. 10.29333/ejmste/7893

Sundler, A. J., Lindberg, E., Nilsson, C., & Palmer, L. (2019). Qualitative Thematic Analysis based on Descriptive Phenomenology. *Nursing Open*, 6(3), 1–7. 10.1002/nop2.27531367394

Taunan, M., Domingo Barcelona, S. R., Sandoval, R. N. P., & Flaviano, R. L. (2021). Lived Experiences of the Senior High School Learners at Goshen of Technology and Humanities During the COVID-19 Pandemic. *International Journal of Multidisciplinary: Applied Business and Education Research*, 2(6), 679–484. 10.11594/ijmaber.02.06.03

TUAC-OECD. (2020). *Impact and Implications of the COVID-19 Crisis on Education Systems and Households. TUAC Secretariat Briefing*. TUAC.

UN. (2020). *Policy Brief: Education during COVID-19 and Beyond*. New York: UN.

UN OCHA. (2020). Zambia Cluster Status: Education. *Situation Report.* Retrieved from: https://reports.unocha.org/en/country/zambia/

UNESCO, *WHO, & UNICEF.* (2020). *Considerations for School-related Public Health Measures in the Context of COVID-19.* WHO, UNESCO and UNICEF.

UNHCR. (2020). Supporting continued Access to Education during COVID-19. *Emerging Promising Practices.* Copehagen: UNHCR.

Uzobo, E., Nwanwene, I., & Ojo, T. F. (2022). The Lived Social Experiences of COVID-19 Survivors in Southwestern Nigeria. *Journal of Social, Behavioral and Health Sciences*, 6(1), 211–225. 10.5590/JSBHS.2022.16.1.15

White, C. J. (2005). *Research: a practical guide.* Ithuthuko Investment.

WHO. (2020a). *Coronavirus Disease 2019 (COVID-19) Situation Report – 41.* WHO.

WHO. (2020b). *Coronavirus Disease 2019 (COVID-19) Situation Report – 94.* WHO.

Wirihana, L., Welch, A., Williamsin, M., Christensen, M., Bakon, S., & Craft, J. (2018). Using Colaizzi's Method of Data Analysis to Explore the Experiences of Nurse Academics Teaching on Satellite Campuses. *Nurse Researcher*, 25(4), 30–34. 10.7748/nr.2018.e151629546965

Wojnar, D. M., & Swanson, K. M. (2007). 'Phenomenology: An exploration'. *Journal of Holistic Nursing*, 25(3), 172–180. 10.1177/089801010629517217724386

Yuan, Y., Zhao, Y. J., Zhang, Q. E., Zhang, L., Cheung, T., Jackson, T., Jiang, G. Q., & Xiang, Y. T. (2021). COVID-19 'Related Stigma and its Socio-demographic Correlate: A Comparative Study'. *Globalization and Health*, 17(1), 17–54. 10.1186/s12992-021-00705-433962651

Zezima, K., Craig, T., Wan, W., & Sonmez, F. (2020). *Coronavirus Now a Global Pandemic as U.S., World Scramble to Control Outbreak.* Washington, DC: The Washington Post.

Zhu, H., Wei, L., & Niu, P. (2020). The Novel Coronavirus Outbreak in Wuhan, China. *Global Health Research and Policy*, 5(1), 1–3. 10.1186/s41256-020-00135-632226823

Chapter 7
Leading Through Uncertainty:
Stakeholder Dynamics in PK-12 Education During the COVID-19 Pandemic

Silvana Zircher
Monmouth University, USA

Ryan J. Eckert
https://orcid.org/0009-0001-5818-096X
Monmouth University, USA

ABSTRACT

This chapter delves into the transformative effects of the COVID-19 pandemic on PK-12 education, emphasizing the adaptive leadership and stakeholder dynamics that emerged. It begins by highlighting early challenges faced by educational leaders in ensuring continuity and equity in learning amidst the shift to remote education. The narrative then transitions to the evolution of educational practices, underscoring the integration of technology and the reimagining of pedagogical approaches. Central to this discussion is the focus on the digital divide and the efforts to bridge disparities in access and digital literacy. It further explores the collaborative dialogues between educational leaders and community stakeholders, crucial in formulating effective, inclusive responses. Concluding with reflections on the lessons learned and future implications, it not only recounts historical events but also provides insights and strategies for managing future crises in education, underlining the importance of resilient, adaptive leadership and community engagement.

DOI: 10.4018/979-8-3693-1507-1.ch007

INTRODUCTION

The COVID-19 crisis undeniably served as a catalyst for transformation within the realm of PK-12 education. The onset of the pandemic thrust school districts into a labyrinth of complexity, demanding swift and decisive action amidst the turbulence of unforeseen challenges and a very real sense of urgency from stakeholders. Difficult issues presented themselves ranging from logistical hurdles to the emotional and psychological well-being of students and staff alike (Cipriano & Brackett, 2020). This moment was further intensified by a widespread fear of the unknown, combined with a feeling of helplessness regarding personal health and community safety. It is within this context that reflecting upon the experiences of school leaders offers us models of resilience and resourcefulness, providing valuable insights for steering future educational trajectories.

The evolution of educational leadership during this period was marked by a remarkable display of agility and innovation. Leaders were compelled to reinterpret and reimagine their strategies to maintain the continuity of education. They embraced adaptive measures, integrating technology and remote learning platforms. The transition was not merely technological but pedagogical and philosophical, as educators sought to preserve the essence of scholastic interaction in a virtual realm (Harris & Jones, 2020).

Educational leaders faced a multifaceted dilemma encompassing not only the immediate imperative of adapting to remote learning modalities but also the long-term implications for educational policy and equity. Districts grappled with the digital divide, striving to ensure that every child had access to the tools necessary for remote learning. The challenge extended beyond hardware to the realms of connectivity and digital literacy, where disparities in access and proficiency threatened to exacerbate pre-existing educational inequities (Reich et al., 2020).

The tales of district leaders during these tumultuous times are emblematic of a steadfast dedication to the principles of education. They signify an unwavering commitment to student welfare and academic progression, even as the traditional models of schooling were upended. The narratives of these leaders underscore the adaptability and creativity that came to the fore in addressing the demands of the moment (Kraft et al., 2021; Tanner-Smith & Fisher, 2020).

The ensuing dialogue between district leaders and the broader community was instrumental in sculpting a unified response to the pandemic. Collaborative efforts with public health officials, parents, and other stakeholders were vital in formulating policies that were both responsive to the public health crisis and tailored to the educational needs of students (Haller & Novita, 2021; Roy et al., 2022).

Leading Through Uncertainty

This chapter is structured to sequentially navigate through the various dimensions of the educational landscape altered by the pandemic. It begins with the initial responses to the crisis, explores the evolution of educational practices during the height of the pandemic, and concludes with reflections on the lessons learned and the implications for the future of PK-12 education. Each section is punctuated with firsthand accounts from district leaders, providing a vivid portrayal of the challenges faced and the strategies employed to overcome them.

In essence, this chapter aims to provide a nuanced examination of a pivotal moment in educational history. It endeavors to honor the experiences of those at the helm of PK-12 education during a period that upended traditional educational paradigms. Through this exploration, the chapter seeks to contribute to the ongoing discourse on educational leadership, policymaking, and the pursuit of student success in the face of adversity. In that sense, the reflections encapsulated in this chapter are not mere historical accounts but may serve as useful future resources. These narratives of endurance and ingenuity provide a blueprint for navigating future crises, highlighting the efficacy of adaptive leadership and the importance of community engagement in the educational sphere. They serve as a reminder of the resilience inherent in the human spirit and the capacity of dedicated individuals to transcend the constraints of their circumstances.

THE INITIAL IMPACT OF THE PANDEMIC

As the world awoke to the reality of the COVID-19 pandemic, the impact on PK-12 education was immediate and profound. The initial response from PK-12 school districts was a blend of urgency and uncertainty, as educators and administrators sought to comprehend the breadth of the crisis. This section delineates the initial reactions of school districts, the early hurdles encountered by educational stakeholders, the preliminary strategies deployed by leaders, and the varied economic and cultural factors that influenced the crisis management (CDC, 2020).

The onset of the pandemic triggered an educational emergency of unprecedented scale. Schools were ordered to close their doors, not as a mere precaution, but as a necessary act to curb the spread of the virus. This abrupt shift left educators, students, and parents in a state of disarray. The fabric of daily life, once woven around the structure of school schedules, was unraveled (Gee et al., 2023).

Educators found themselves struggling with the logistics of remote instruction, a concept that was novel to many and characterized with both technical and pedagogical challenges. Students, on the other hand, faced the daunting prospect of isolation and unfamiliar learning expectations. Parents were suddenly forced to balance work commitments with the new reality of facilitating their children's education from home. Districts encountered the task of ensuring that students had the necessary technology for distance learning. This was not merely a logistical issue but one of equity, as the digital divide became glaringly apparent. Many households lacked reliable internet access and/or the necessary devices needed to engage in online learning, a disparity that disproportionately affected students from lower socioeconomic backgrounds (Gee et al., 2023).

Additionally, educators had to rapidly develop new curricula tailored to virtual platforms. This process required not only technical proficiency, but also a willingness to adapt and evolve new teaching methodologies suitable for an online format. The spectrum of technical knowledge among teachers varied greatly, with some possessing advanced skills and others starting from a beginner level. The readiness to embrace new technologies and adapt to change also differed among educators. Some viewed the transition as an opportunity to innovate and experiment with new teaching methods, while others approached the change with trepidation.

The first reactions of district leaders were critical in setting the tone for the crisis response. These measures, although implemented rapidly, were designed to mitigate the immediate impacts of the school closures. They sought to balance the urgency of continuing education with the health and well-being of students and staff.

This critical work began with a redesign of department and school level leadership roles. District leadership conducted a thorough audit of individuals' strengths and background expertise. It quickly became apparent that anyone with a health related background could serve as a district liaison to the Department of Health or an internal advisor. Technology experts were needed for the transition to online instruction. School districts also became dependent on those leaders with strong ties to the community who could assist in leveraging local resources.

Using and understanding virtual communication and social media became priorities. School leaders soon realized that the best form of communication was through electronic means. Of course, the increasing reliance on virtual connectivity also highlighted gaps in technology access. The distribution of laptop devices and hotspots for Wi-Fi became a priority. This necessitated the reallocation of funds for the acquisition of devices and hotspots, as well as navigating issues of availability and demand.

The cultural contexts also influenced communications and response strategies, as leaders had to consider the linguistic and cultural needs of their diverse student populations when developing communication materials and support services. Multilingual communication was always a consideration for school districts, but now effective communication was directly linked to the health and wellbeing of the community. Addressing multilingual barriers was no longer a preference or a goal to strive for, but instead a necessity. Resources such as the use of translation devices, professional translation services, and multilingual staff were used to ensure everyone accessed messaging about testing, vaccination, and protection.

The response of district leaders was, of course, influenced by the economic and cultural contexts of the larger community. Wealthier districts may have had the resources to promptly distribute technology and launch sophisticated online platforms. In contrast, districts in economically challenged areas, who under normal circumstances often relied on public resources, now had an even more drastic need. This required schools to be responsive.

The economic well-being of families emerged as a major worry for schools amid the pandemic, with the loss of income and job prospects affecting many. Schools found themselves taking on broader community roles, particularly in ensuring access to nutritious food and meals. The state department offered opportunities for food and meal distribution, but these had to be managed through local school systems. This approach was new to school districts, necessitating adaptation, creative planning, and effective leadership. Coordination was needed for schools to safely distribute food during a time of high contamination. Once again, partnerships with local food service agencies, the health department, community food banks, and local police were needed to establish the necessary systems for food preparation, deliveries, and distribution. In effect, district schools transformed into community hubs, distributing not only educational materials but also essential supplies to families in need (Haller & Novita, 2021).

Another important area of focus was on mental health support, recognizing the profound psychological impact the pandemic had on students and families. The strategies employed were a testament to the innovative spirit and adaptability of district leaders who, despite facing an unparalleled crisis, remained steadfast in their commitment to education. District leaders turned to mental health experts to plan accordingly. A combination of school-based services and contracted supports provided a balanced and comprehensive approach. School counselors and psychologists were made available to provide virtual support sessions for students and parents, while an employee assistance program addressed the mental health needs of teachers and staff. Many classroom teachers found themselves struggling with changing their methods, practices, and delivery of instruction, while simultaneously managing their own personal fears and struggles related to the pandemic. Virtual calming and therapeutic "spaces" were set up for students, parents, and teachers to visit regularly. Recommendations and tips were sent to parents to help them manage virtual instruction at home. Google classrooms were used to post updates, field questions, and share a variety of support resources.

As the pandemic unfolded, the experiences of educators, students, and parents continued to evolve. The resilience of communities, the ingenuity of educators in delivering instruction, and the resourcefulness of students in adapting to new modes of learning began to emerge as cornerstones of the narrative. It was a time that underscored the importance of leadership, community engagement, and the collective endeavor to ensure that education could persevere in the face of adversity.

BALANCING HEALTH AND EDUCATION

Educational leadership during the COVID-19 crisis is largely a story of the need to balance the return to in-person instruction with the imperative to protect the health of students and staff. The decision to reopen schools was not merely a logistical challenge but a complex moral and ethical one, as it involved weighing the educational needs of students against the potential health risks of resuming traditional classroom settings (Patrick et al., 2020).

This dilemma was evident in the varying responses from school districts. Some opted for a hybrid model, combining both remote and in-person instruction, aiming to minimize the number of individuals in the school at any given time. Others delayed the reopening of physical classrooms, extending remote learning despite concerns about the effectiveness of online instruction and the impact on students' social and emotional development.

Many educators expressed anxiety about exposure to the virus, particularly those with underlying health conditions or vulnerable family members at home. Some teachers, however, were eager to return to the classroom, highlighting the challenges of engaging students through a screen and the pedagogical limitations of remote instruction. Administrators, too, struggled with these decisions. Leaders found themselves having to be not just decision-makers but also communicators and counselors, offering reassurance and support to their staff and community. They had to build consensus where possible and make tough calls when consensus was out of reach, all while maintaining the focus on the educational mission.

The role of local, state, and federal guidelines were pivotal in these decision-making processes. Leaders relied heavily on the Centers for Disease Control and Prevention (CDC) recommendations, state health departments, and local health officials to inform their strategies. These guidelines, however, were often confusing and sometimes contradictory. The ever-evolving nature of the pandemic meant that these guidelines were subject to frequent updates, requiring leaders to remain agile and responsive to new information. The interpretation of these guidelines also varied, with some districts adopting a more conservative approach than others, reflecting the diverse risk tolerances and community values.

Without expertise in epidemiology, district leaders were left to make decisions that, while grounded in guidelines, were based largely on their own instincts and propensity to manage emergent and rapidly changing environments. Quite often,

Leading Through Uncertainty

leaders relied on each other for support, feedback, and inspiration. They shared communication documents, updated policies, and continually-evolving procedures. Regional school district leaders met often, and created tools such as monitoring spreadsheets and virtual platforms to share information and artifacts. It was a time to come together and provide fellow colleagues perspective, sympathy and emotional support. In essence, the pandemic unified district leaders in the spirit of perseverance and survival.

The leadership quandary of balancing health and education during the pandemic presented a multifaceted challenge. This required making decisions which were seldom straightforward, with administrators often having to weigh conflicting interests and opinions. Successfully leading through this time required empathy, consensus-building, collegiality, and a principled yet flexible approach.

ADAPTING TO VIRTUAL LEARNING: CHALLENGES AND INNOVATIONS

The abrupt shift to virtual learning ushered in by the COVID-19 pandemic forced school districts to reimagine the delivery of education. Administrators and educators were tasked with evaluating the effectiveness of virtual instruction and its limitations, all while navigating the complexities of new teaching methods and the realities of the digital divide. In response to these challenges, districts adopted a range of innovations. Synchronous and asynchronous learning became commonplace terms. Teachers leveraged video conferencing tools to create interactive lessons and used online platforms that allowed for collaborative projects and discussions. Some districts developed their own virtual learning environments, complete with resources and supports tailored to their students' needs.

Virtual instruction was a double-edged sword. On one hand, it offered a means to continue education when traditional classrooms were inaccessible. On the other hand, it presented significant challenges. Students faced difficulties with self-motivation, and the lack of face-to-face interaction made it harder to maintain engagement. Educators had to rethink assessment methods, moving away from traditional testing to more creative ways of measuring student understanding.

This abrupt transition necessitated the rapid development of new curricula designed for online platforms. This shift required educators to exhibit not just technical proficiency but also adaptability and a forward-thinking approach to teaching. Teachers' familiarity with technology spanned a broad range, from those with sophisticated expertise to individuals at the initial stages of digital literacy. Similarly, educators' attitudes towards adopting new technological tools and methods varied considerably. While some embraced the shift as a chance to explore and apply innovative instructional techniques, others felt apprehensive, questioning the effectiveness of online teaching and worrying about diminishing the rapport they had established with their students in a traditional classroom setting. Educators with greater training in technology became invaluable resources, often assisting colleagues in navigating new tools and platforms. Professional development played a crucial role during this time, with districts offering workshops and training sessions to upskill their teaching staff. Collaboration became a cornerstone of curricular development, with teachers sharing resources and best practices on how to engage students through screens (Roy et al., 2022).

The development of new curricula was not simply a matter of transferring existing materials online. It required a thoughtful reimagining of instructional delivery. Teachers worked to maintain interactivity and personalization in their teaching, employing a variety of online tools such as discussion forums, virtual breakout rooms, and multimedia resources to create a more engaging learning environment.

Engaging students in learning has always been a priority for teachers, but during the pandemic, student engagement became a critical ingredient for effective virtual instructional delivery. Teachers used approaches such as setting up one-on-one or small group instructional sessions with students who needed individualized attention. They helped students minimize physical and environmental distractions by helping them set up a dedicated learning area in their home. In essence, part of the instructional period was devoted to teaching students how to become effective virtual learners. Teachers leveraged the internet's nearly-infinite array of audio and video resources to enhance instruction. To encourage students to maintain an element of socialization, many formerly independent assignments were replaced with partner- or small group-based activities. Clear expectations and updated classroom rules, including the requirement to keep cameras on, were carefully defined. Innovative systems were implemented to effectively monitor and enhance student participation. In addition to academic support, targeted interventions were introduced to assist students in overcoming challenges related to managing essential technology.

Making connections with students also became an important engagement strategy. For the first time ever, teachers had a first row seat to students' family situation and homelife. In turn, students engaged in learning while their teacher held their infant or pet on their lap. While virtual instruction was isolating in many ways, in some regards it also enabled new connections that were never considered before.

Educators also had to consider the pace and structure of lessons, recognizing that the attention span and dynamics of a virtual classroom differed from in-person settings. This often led to shorter instructional periods, interspersed with interactive activities or assignments that students could engage with asynchronously. The attitudes toward embracing this change were critical in shaping the virtual learning experience. Educators who adopted a growth mindset and were willing to experiment found creative ways to overcome the barriers of remote instruction. They used the crisis as a catalyst for growth and innovation in their teaching practices.

However, teachers who were hesitant, prompted by a variety of reasons, required additional support from district administrators and peers alike. Those teachers who had been reluctant to incorporate technology in their regular classroom environment were now left with no choice. Some were self-taught, while others relied on expert colleagues for assistance and support. Peer mentorship and supportive leadership provided the encouragement needed for these educators to step out of their comfort zones and adapt to the new normal. Technology teams developed in-house hubs to access their own tutorials and resources. Good leaders provided teachers with the necessary professional development along with adequate time to learn these new skills, enabling teachers to become comfortable with one aspect of virtual learning at a time. As responses to the crisis transitioned from an originally-predicted short term fix to an extended adaptation to new reality, teachers became more comfortable and proficient in virtual instructional practices.

The transition to virtual learning during the pandemic was a significant undertaking that pushed the boundaries of traditional pedagogy. It called upon educators to embrace change, adapt their instructional methods, and develop new curricula suited to the online format. The varied technical skills and attitudes toward change among teachers underscored the importance of support systems and professional development in ensuring the successful adoption of these new approaches. The collective efforts of educators during this period have left a lasting impact on teaching and learning practices, likely influencing educational strategies well into the future

Virtual Learning and The Digital Divide

Not all students had access to reliable internet or devices, which led to a gap in educational opportunities. School districts, in partnership with local governments and organizations, undertook significant efforts to bridge this divide. This included distributing laptops and tablets, setting up Wi-Fi hotspots, and even creating internet-accessible spaces within the community. Districts engaged in connectivity assessments to better understand accessibility barriers. First, a focus was placed on those students with chronic absenteeism or other significant attendance issues. Leaders relied on inputs from teachers and counseling staff to help identify students with connectivity barriers. State and Federal grants, made much more easily accessible due to the pandemic, were key sources of funding to provide and distribute laptops and wifi access points to community members in need.

The feedback from students and families was varied. Many appreciated the flexibility that virtual learning provided, allowing students to learn at their own pace and schedule. However, others struggled with the lack of structure and social interaction. Parents found themselves in the role of co-educators, a position for which many felt unprepared and unsupported. Despite the diligent efforts of educators, it was clear that virtual instruction could not fully replicate the in-person experience. The nuanced social learning, the hands-on activities, and the personalized support that students received from teachers were difficult to translate into a virtual format (Roy et al., 2022). Administrators felt the pressure from state authorities to return to in-person instruction, a stance supported by growing evidence of the importance of physical classroom environments. The American Academy of Pediatrics, among others, advocated for the return to in-person schooling, citing the critical role it plays in child and adolescent development, not just academically but also socially and emotionally.

In this complex landscape, school districts had to balance the immediate need to provide effective virtual learning with the longer-term goal of returning safely to in-person instruction. They had to listen to and address the concerns of families, meet the requirements of state and local authorities, and consider the educational and health implications of every decision.

The experiences during this period highlighted the resilience of the educational system and its ability to adapt to unprecedented circumstances. They also emphasized the need for continued investment in technology and training to ensure that all students have equitable access to high-quality education, whether in the classroom or through a computer screen.

STRATEGIC LEADERSHIP: COMMUNICATION AND CONSENSUS-BUILDING

Leading during the pandemic required a delicate approach toward the intricate dynamics of stakeholder interests. Achieving consensus between the concerned parties required strategic efforts to articulate and communicate the rationale behind the decisions, while making individual stakeholder cohorts feel as though their voices were heard.

Leaders adapted, synthesized, and forged new connections. Through this period, administrators adopted innovative strategies, fostering partnerships and open dialogues with community leaders to create synergy in their approach to the numerous challenges at hand (Kraft et al., 2021).

Central to this leadership was the process of stakeholder consultation and engagement. Achieving consensus among diverse groups—parents, students, teachers, staff, and the wider community—necessitated an inclusive approach that honored the multiplicity of perspectives. Leaders had to employ a delicate touch in managing the intricate dynamics of stakeholder interests, ensuring that each group felt their concerns were acknowledged and addressed.

To facilitate this, techniques for effective communication were paramount. Leaders leaned on multiple platforms, from traditional emails and letters to virtual town halls and social media, to disseminate information and gather feedback. They used clear, consistent messaging to outline the steps being taken and the reasons behind them. This approach was key in creating a shared understanding of the challenges and the measures implemented to address them.

The process by which consensus was reached—or the difficulties faced when it was not—are telling of the pandemic's complexity. In instances where consensus was achieved, it often came about through iterative dialogue, where proposals were refined through feedback loops with stakeholders.

Many districts held virtual update meetings and Q&A sessions This allowed stakeholders to better understand the process used for decision making, but also provided a forum for feedback. Sometimes multiple stakeholder groups interacted with one another for the first time in these sorts of virtual forums, allowing each to be exposed to the varied perspectives of their fellow community members. The varying priorities and interests became apparent, helped each interest group better understand the others' point of view. Alternatively, other occasions saw individual interest groups meet with district leadership directly. For example, some sessions were reserved for teachers and staff only, so they could share freely and openly the challenges they were facing.

One of the most novel elements of this period was the newly emerged phenomenon of virtually-held Board of Education meetings. Attendance was never greater than at these meetings, due not only to the important matters of discussion but also the availability and convenience of a virtual forum. Transparency and empathy emerged as cornerstones of effective communication between Boards and school administrators. Leaders who were transparent about the uncertainties and complexities of the situation fostered greater trust. The most effective dynamics were established by leaders who were honest about what they knew, what they didn't know, and how they were making decisions. Empathy was equally important. Openly acknowledging the fears, frustrations, and challenges faced by each group helped to build emotional connections and demonstrate to community members that their leaders were attuned to their experiences.

Effective strategic leadership during this period also meant recognizing the need for flexibility. Decisions might need to change as new information came to light, and leaders had to communicate these shifts without diminishing stakeholders' confidence. This required a careful balance of confidence and humility—projecting a sense of direction while being open to learning and adjusting along the way. One approach to communication was adopted that emphasized transparency and adaptability. This strategy involved delivering information in segmented, manageable parts, always accompanied by a "subject to change" disclaimer to set the expectation that the situation was fluid and plans might evolve. Emphasizing honesty and being upfront in messaging was a key component, ensuring that the community was kept informed with the most current and accurate information. It acknowledged the need to pivot or reconsider plans, demonstrating a proactive stance in handling changes. Although this method led to some frustration among community members, there was a general understanding of its necessity. This need for flexibility mirrored the broader societal changes happening outside of just school matters. By framing the approach within the context of these wider shifts, it helped normalize the need for adaptability, mitigate parent frustration, and foster a greater sense of cooperation and understanding within the community.

The leadership narratives from this time reflect a commitment to creating educational environments that could thrive even under the most challenging circumstances. Administrators who succeeded in building consensus did so by creating partnerships and fostering open dialogues, not just within the school community but with public health officials, local governments, and other community leaders. This collective approach helped to address the myriad of challenges, from the logistics of virtual learning to the emotional well-being of students and staff. The process of building consensus, while fraught with challenges, was essential in a period of unprecedented upheaval, underscoring the importance of communication that is transparent, inclusive, and adaptive.

DATA-DRIVEN DECISIONS: UTILIZING INFORMATION TO GUIDE ACTIONS

In the heart of the pandemic, data-driven decision-making became a critical component of educational leadership. Infection rates, vaccination data, and other health metrics were closely monitored by district leaders, providing a quantitative foundation upon which to base operational decisions. These data points were instrumental in assessing the risk levels associated with various instructional models and informed the timing and manner of school reopenings. The creation and use of COVID-19 data dashboards became a widespread practice among school districts. These dashboards provided a transparent and accessible way for all stakeholders to understand the current state of the pandemic within their community. They included not only infection and vaccination rates but also metrics such as school attendance numbers, the status of in-school transmission, and local hospital capacity. The regular updating and availability of this data allowed for a dynamic response to the evolving situation, facilitating timely decisions regarding school operations.

However, balancing the quantitative nature of data with the qualitative human element of trust and confidence presented a unique challenge. While data dashboards and charts provided a clear picture of trends and informed decision-making, they were not a panacea for the anxiety and fear experienced by the school community. For many educators and families, the risks of returning to in-person instruction were not merely statistical probabilities but real concerns about their health and safety.

Leaders recognized that numbers and trends needed to be contextualized with empathy and transparency to be truly effective in building trust. Communication strategies included not just sharing the data but also explaining what the data meant for the daily lives of students, staff, and families. Like always, the most effective communications were conducted through personal conversations and connections. The virtual world did not replace this concept, but rather provided enhanced opportunities to forge new interpersonal connections. During the pandemic, many working parents were suddenly available during school hours to meet virtually with principals, teachers, and guidance counselors. While students engaged in learning at home, parents experienced a glimpse of their child's classroom experience, academic progress, and social behavior. As a result, a new sort of parental involvement became an unprecedented but positive side effect of the pandemic.

Leaders grappled with the realization that data and information, while crucial, was not the sole driver of confidence. The human element – understanding the community's emotional landscape, acknowledging fears, and building relationships – was equally important. The most effective leaders were those who could integrate data into a broader strategy of community engagement and support, ensuring that decisions were made not just with the mind but also with the heart. Data-driven decisions during the pandemic provided a model for sound practices to adopt even during times of relative calm. Fundamentally, this period demonstrated that making good decisions requires a balance between the empirical and the emotional.

RESOURCE MANAGEMENT: RESPONDING TO NEW DEMANDS

The COVID-19 pandemic led to an extraordinary reallocation of resources, compelling educational leaders to navigate a landscape radically altered by new demands (Moreland et al., 2020). The swift assessment and redistribution of these resources were pivotal in addressing the dual imperatives of health and education.

This new role for schools required a rapid rethinking of resource allocation. Schools, traditionally centers of learning and community life, expanded their roles significantly during the pandemic. They transformed into community hubs, providing not only educational resources but also critical health services and information. This dual function was essential as healthcare systems were overwhelmed, and communities sought reliable information and support.

Quite often, and especially in rapidly-emerging, dynamic crisis situations, public schools become the hub for community services and support. During the pandemic this became evident as schools transitioned from institutions of learning to community centers for meal distribution, device and hotspot pick up, and COVID-19 testing and vaccination sites. As supplies such as tests and vaccines became high in demand but low in availability, schools were able to leverage an assortment of state and federal grant programs to effectively obtain them. In the interest of decreasing the spread of COVID-19 and returning to educational and social normalcy, schools were directly invested in playing whatever part they could in minimizing and eradicating the pandemic.

The shift to digital learning resources was one of the most pronounced changes in resource allocation. Textbooks, physical handouts, and face-to-face instruction gave way to virtual classrooms, online textbooks, and digital assignments. This transition was not seamless; it required substantial investment in technology and training for educators and students alike. School districts leveraged federal funding, grants, and partnerships with technology companies to ensure that students had the necessary devices and internet access to engage in remote learning. These innovative approaches not only addressed immediate needs but also laid the groundwork for more equitable access to technology in the future.

Yet, these shifts were not without their challenges. The rapid move to digital resources highlighted and sometimes deepened disparities among students. Leaders had to be mindful of the digital divide and work tirelessly to ensure that resources were allocated equitably. This often meant prioritizing the most vulnerable students for resource distribution and creating new support systems for students and families navigating the digital landscape for the first time. Lessons learned in resource reallocation during the pandemic were numerous.

Flexibility and swift decision-making emerged as critical leadership qualities. The ability to reassess and redirect resources in real-time showed adaptability and resilience. Leaders who communicated clearly and effectively with their stakeholders, explaining the changes and the reasoning behind them, were able to maintain community support and trust. The narrative of resource management illustrates a moment in time when educational leaders were called upon to provide more than learning—they became key actors in the public health response, advocates for equity, and architects of a new educational model.

COOPERATION WITH TEACHERS' UNIONS

The interplay between school districts and teachers' unions took center stage as the pandemic unfolded, highlighting the complex nature of labor relations during a time of crisis. Negotiations became more frequent and intense, with the stakes higher than ever as they directly impacted the health and safety of educators and students alike.

Teachers' unions, advocating for their members, often found themselves at odds with district leaders pressured to resume in-person instruction. The concerns raised by teachers included not only the obvious risks of COVID-19 transmission but also the adequacy of safety measures in schools, the quality of ventilation systems, the feasibility of social distancing in classrooms, and access to personal protective equipment. Moreover, many educators were also parents themselves, facing the same childcare challenges as other working parents during school closures.

To address these concerns, leaders had to write policy, develop procedures, and work with the teachers' union to reach a compromise on these matters. While typical negotiations are usually centered on salary and compensation, these conversations were related to working conditions and health. Despite this shift in focus, effective leaders used familiar negotiation tactics, but with an empathetic and patient ear. Some demands, such as providing protective gear, were somewhat easy to accommodate when resources were available. Others, such as a total continuation of virtual instruction, were not. Mutual agreements were achieved through compromises, including the adoption of half-day schedules and a four-day week, allowing for a dedicated day of thorough cleaning. Feedback from both union leadership and members was actively embraced, and whenever feasible, carefully considered and implemented to foster a collaborative and inclusive decision-making process.

Perhaps the most challenging aspect of negotiation during this time was emotionally charged nature of conversations between staff and leadership. The fear of potential illness and the stark global statistics, conveyed through media and health department updates, injected an unprecedented level of tension into already-agitated negotiation discussions. In certain instances, this heightened anxiety translated into frustration, manifesting as anger and insult. Leaders had reach inward, draw upon their inner resilience, and refrain from taking these emotional moments personally. Recognizing the unique context of the current situation and the dynamic nature of the challenges at hand, leaders worked towards a deeper understanding and fostered an environment conducive to constructive dialogue. In essence, leaders had to employ deescalating tactics before they could consider presenting local data and defending both their approach and decision-making.

Ultimately, these negotiations played a critical role in establishing safety protocols that would allow for the resumption of in-person learning. The long-term implications for district-union relations post-pandemic are yet to be fully understood. However, the intensity and frequency of negotiations during the pandemic have likely reshaped the dynamics between the two entities. The shared experience of navigating the crisis could potentially lead to stronger collaborative relationships in the future, as both sides have had to work closely under difficult circumstances. On the other hand, some districts could find that the contentious nature of the negotiations may have sown seeds of mistrust that could take time to heal. Either way, it demonstrated that when it comes to the well-being of educators and the students they teach, there is a vital need for cooperative and constructive negotiations.

Expanding the Scope of Negotiations

The pandemic also necessitated a reevaluation of teachers' roles and responsibilities from a labor standpoint. Teachers had to rapidly adapt to online teaching, often without prior experience or adequate training; this shift not only impacted their teaching methods but also their work-life balance, as they navigated the challenges of remote education while managing their personal responsibilities. Union negotiations thus also had to address professional development and support for teachers in this new digital landscape. Training sessions, technical support, and resources for online teaching became crucial points of discussion.

Furthermore, the mental health and well-being of teachers emerged as a significant concern. The stress of adapting to a new mode of teaching, coupled with concerns about their own and their students' health, took a toll on many educators. Unions advocated for mental health support, including counseling services and additional days off for mental health, recognizing that educators' well-being is intrinsically linked to their ability to teach effectively.

In addition to these new areas of focus, the pandemic brought forth an increased need for transparent and timely communication between district leaders and union representatives. Regular updates, open forums for discussion, and clear channels for feedback became essential in maintaining trust and ensuring that all voices were heard. This enhanced communication not only facilitated negotiations but also helped in disseminating accurate information to dispel rumors and alleviate fears among educators.

In sum, the pandemic expanded the scope of what will soon become regular talking points in union negotiations going forward, encompassing aspects of digital literacy, mental health, and transparent communication. These expanded dialogues could serve as a blueprint for future interactions between school districts and teachers' unions, potentially leading to more holistic approaches to addressing educators' needs in a rapidly evolving educational landscape.

THE HUMAN ELEMENT: LEADERSHIP AND EMPATHY IN ACTION

The COVID-19 pandemic was instrumental in assessing the legitimacy, skill, and adaptability of school leaders. Throughout the pandemic it became obvious that leaders would have to take on additional roles to their already multifaceted functions. The pressure of making decisions that could potentially impact the health and wellbeing of the community was a heavy weight on the shoulders of leaders. Moreover, school leaders had to leverage the expertise of others while also becoming knowledgeable of the science of the pandemic. This became critical in order to address issues in an informed manner that engendered the trust of others.

Many stories of desperate moments during this period are accompanied with thoughts of abandoning their position or throwing up hands in despair. But out of the devastation came this acknowledgement that no task is too arduous, and no situation would stop school leaders from persevering in the name of the best interest of children and their education. The pandemic served as a catalyst for leaders to gain profound insights into their strengths, fostering creative thinking and tapping into their deepest reservoirs of grit and determination. School leaders emerged as a stabilizing force amid chaos, adept at resolving intricate problems and offering much-needed guidance and support during critical junctures. This challenging period not only revealed leaders' personal resilience but also highlighted their pivotal role in navigating complexity and uncertainty with a steady and reassuring presence.

Leaders played a crucial role in re-establishing a sense of normalcy while acknowledging the profound changes the pandemic had brought about. This included revisiting and revising school policies, updating health and safety protocols, and implementing new educational strategies to address learning gaps caused by the pandemic. The emphasis was on fostering a resilient school culture, one that could withstand future crises while maintaining a focus on holistic development.

Moreover, leaders had to be conscious of equity issues that became more pronounced during the pandemic. Ensuring equal access to resources, supporting marginalized and disadvantaged groups, and addressing digital divides were essential components of the recovery strategy. The pandemic underscored the need for inclusive and equitable educational practices, challenging leaders to rethink and restructure their approaches to meet these needs.

Much of the emotional heavy lifting came during the recovery phase of the pandemic. This is when leaders had the opportunity to reflect, to consider, and in some cases to forgive. The recovery phase post-pandemic offered a unique opportunity for school leaders to engage in introspection and reconciliation. Leaders were tasked with rebuilding not just the physical aspects of schooling, but also the emotional and psychological well-being of the school community. They had to address the lingering effects of the pandemic, such as trauma, grief, and anxiety among students and staff. The challenge was to create an environment that was not only safe but also nurturing and conducive to learning and growth.

The crisis and the fears it generated brought out some of the worst behaviors and actions in school community members, and leaders had to consider how to move forward in a non-judgmental way. This "reconstruction" process shaped the success of subsequent recovery efforts and set the foundation for successful transitions back to traditional school environments. The manner in which districts reconstructed after returning to school will undoubtedly be a subject of future study and analysis. The lessons learned from this period of rebuilding will offer valuable insights for leaders, with their full extrapolation still unfolding. The resilience and adaptability demonstrated during this phase will serve as a rich source of knowledge for future leaders grappling with unforeseen challenges and disruptions.

CONCLUSION: LESSONS FOR THE FUTURE

The pandemic posed unprecedented challenges for school leaders, with circumstances demanding ingenuity, resourcefulness, and grit. Amidst a changing landscape, school leaders felt a greater responsibility than ever before in being tasked with high stakes decision making that potentially impacted not only student learning, but the health and wellbeing of the entire community. Navigating the demands of meeting the diverse needs of all school community members during this health crisis proved to be a transformative experience for school leaders. The challenges encountered spurred the development and enhancement of their skills, prompting the creation of innovative approaches that extend beyond the confines of the current emergency. These lessons learned and creative strategies devised during the crisis now serve as valuable assets, poised to be applied in both emergent and non-emergent situations in the future. The adaptability and ingenuity cultivated during this period have equipped school leaders with an updated toolkit for addressing a spectrum of challenges that may arise, fostering an even more proactive and forward-thinking approach to leadership.

The ability to transition an entire curriculum and instructional approach helped teachers and school leaders understand the importance of flexible and individualized learning. The experience underscored the positive impact of integrating technology into education, shedding light on the challenges and nuances inherent in adopting a strategic and purposeful approach. Schools also learned what it means to become a community hub for social services and resources, clearly highlighting the direct correlation between these elements and student learning outcomes. This realization emphasized the need for a holistic approach to education that extends beyond traditional academic realms, acknowledging the intricate interplay between community support, social services, and learning environments.

Communication forums underwent a significant transformation, adopting new avenues such as the expanded use of social media, virtual meetings, podcasts, and data dashboards. These innovative approaches, initially forced upon leadership as a necessary response to the challenges of the pandemic, have evolved and become integrated into best practices for effective communication today. Beyond the mediums themselves, there has been a fundamental shift in how messages are presented and received. There is now a heightened emphasis on cultivating an empathetic ear and a deeper understanding of individuals' family dynamics, playing a pivotal role in school messaging and the distribution of information. This shift has fostered a more inclusive and nuanced communication style that recognizes and respects varied points of view, contributing to a more cohesive and understanding school community.

The experiences and decisions made during the post-pandemic recovery phase are likely to redefine educational leadership. The insights gained and the strategies developed during this period will be invaluable for future educational leaders. They provide a blueprint for dealing with disruptions and highlight the importance of empathetic, resilient, and inclusive leadership in the face of adversity.

The COVID-19 pandemic, despite being one of the most exhausting and challenging periods for school leaders, has catalyzed the emergence of best practices that have fundamentally reshaped the educational landscape. Innovation and problem-solving were pivotal, and adaptability became the new normal. The lessons gleaned from this transformative period not only fortified educators' abilities to navigate crises but also positioned them to proactively shape the future of education with resilience and foresight. Undeniably, the pandemic resulted in experiential learning that refined and strengthened the skills and competencies of leaders.

REFERENCES

Bryant, J. (2020, November 9). The pandemic is a crisis for students with special needs. *The Atlantic*. https://www.theatlantic.com/politics/archive/2020/11/pandemic-crisis-students-special-needs/616808/

Centers for Disease Control and Prevention. (2020). *Interim guidance for administrators of US K–12 schools and childcare programs: Plan, prepare, and respond to coronavirus disease (COVID-19)*. Centers for Disease Control and Prevention.

Cipriano, C., & Brackett, M. (2020). *Teacher interrupted: Leaning into the social-emotional learning crisis amid the COVID-19 crisis*. EdSurge News.

Darling-Hammond, L., Schachner, A., & Edgerton, A. K. (2020). *Restarting and reinventing school: Learning in the time of COVID-19 and beyond*. Learning Policy Institute.

Gee, K. A., Asmundson, V., & Vang, T. (2023). Educational impacts of the COVID-19 pandemic in the United States: Inequities by race, ethnicity, and socioeconomic status. *Current Opinion in Psychology*, 52, 101643. 10.1016/j.copsyc.2023.10164337442079

Goldstein, D. (2020, April 6). When can we go to school? *The New York Times*. https://www.nytimes.com/2020/04/06/us/coronavirus-schools-reopen.html

Haller, T., & Novita, S. (2021). Parents' perceptions of school support during COVID-19: What satisfies parents? *Frontiers in Education*, 6, 700441. 10.3389/feduc.2021.700441

Kraft, M. A., Simon, N. S., & Lyon, M. A. (2021). Sustaining a sense of success: The importance of teacher working conditions during the COVID-19-19 pandemic. *Journal of Research on Educational Effectiveness*, 14(4), 727–769. 10.1080/19345747.2021.1938314

Moreland, A., Herlihy, C., Tynan, M. A., Sunshine, G., McCord, R. F., Hilton, C., & Popoola, A. (2020). Timing of state and territorial COVID-19 stay-at-home orders and changes in population movement, United States, March 1-May 31, 2020. *MMWR. Morbidity and Mortality Weekly Report*, 69(35), 1198–1203. 10.15585/mmwr.mm6935a232881851

Patrick, S. W., Henkhaus, L. E., Zickafoose, J. S., Lovell, K., Halvorson, A., Loch, S., & Davis, M. M. (2020). Well-being of parents and children during the COVID-19 pandemic: A national survey. *Pediatrics*, 146(4), e2020016824. 10.1542/peds.2020-01682432709738

Roy, A. K., Breaux, R., Sciberras, E., Patel, P., Ferrara, E., Shroff, D. M., & Becker, S. P. (2022). A preliminary examination of key strategies, challenges, and benefits of remote learning expressed by parents during the COVID-19 pandemic. *School Psychology*, 37(2), 147–159. 10.1037/spq000046535266770

Tanner-Smith, E. E., & Fisher, B. W. (2020). Open schools, COVID-19, and child and teacher morbidity in Sweden. *The New England Journal of Medicine*, 383(15), 1484–1485.

Chapter 8
Challenges in Online Education During the COVID-19 Pandemic:
A Case Study in Higher Education Institutes of Rural Areas of Birbhum District of West Bengal, India

Tirthankar Mandal
https://orcid.org/0000-0002-5815-0381
Krishna Chandra College, India

ABSTRACT

COVID-19 has had a serious impact on all aspects of society, all citizens, and all institutes around the country. In India, educational institutions have compulsorily changed their traditional teaching methods to an online platform. The transition to online mode has been an abrupt one due to the unprecedented lockdown imposed to manage COVID-19, and all the educational institutes did not have time to design and adopt the course contents for an online delivery system. Several obstacles like infrastructure, internet service, e-resources, communication gap, rural-urban gap, financial constraints, social and family burden, etc. have made the education and learning system far behind the previous system. The present study has tried to find out the difficulties students face to continue smooth learning such that a skilled and technologically efficient generation will arise soon.

DOI: 10.4018/979-8-3693-1507-1.ch008

INTRODUCTION

The World Health Organization (WHO) declared COVID-19 as a global public health emergency on 30th January 2020 as well as a pandemic on 11th March 2020. COVID-19 has had a serious impact on all aspects of society, all citizens, and all institutes around the globe (M. Adnan, 2020). Educational institutions in India have also made a transition to an online teaching environment soon after Union Government decided to impose a nationwide lock-down for 21 days from 25th March 2020 which was later extended for 19 more days. In India, the system of online education has never been tried compulsory for all. The shift to online mode has been an abrupt one due to unprecedented lockdown imposed to manage the COVID-19, and the institutes did not have time to design and adopt the course contents for online mode (T. Muthuprasad et al., 2021). The shift of teaching and learning to an online delivery mode obliged by the Pandemic COVID-19 has become an integral part of the education system in the world. However, the levels and methods of using them to achieve quality education are varied and depended upon the various factors associated with Information and Communication Technology (ICT) policy and their practices in education (P. Paudel, 2021). Since March 2020 the traditional education system has been stopped and a new system of online education became compulsory for all students at colleges and university levels to achieve degrees. Apart from some premium educational institutes, almost every institute faced a severe crisis to continue learning in online mode. There are several issues like infrastructure, internet service, e-resources, communication gap, rural-urban gap, financial constraints, social and family burden, etc. all the obstacles made education and learning system far behind than the previous system.

The current chapter meticulously examines specific challenges within the state of West Bengal, India. It will focus intensively on delineating the disparities between rural and urban institutions concerning infrastructure, technological proficiency, financial support, and various social concerns. To what extent has online education achieved success within the parameters of varied caste, gender, economic status, and various subject streams in the higher education institutes of West Bengal? This query necessitates a thorough exploration of the effectiveness of digital learning platforms across diverse demographic segments and academic disciplines, assessing the equitable access, engagement, and outcomes facilitated by such educational modalities. The primary challenges are to demonstrate the lack of proper education and learning imparted by most of the institutions as there is no mechanism to measure the exact outcome of teaching-learning process during the pandemic. There appears to be a deficiency of sufficient engagement from the Government's perspective, while some issues may originate from the institution's end. Most of the higher educational institutes belong to the rural area, they have no support from the institute as well as infrastructure and social constraints. Besides this few urban institutes run their online education without having a proper ICT framework for both teacher and student. Most of the institutes have no e-contents or e-resources to carry on online education smoothly. Thechapter tries to highlight the success and failure of online education and generating skills by comparing different kinds of stakeholders, institutes, and finally the role of Government as well as society.

Before the COVID-19 pandemic, the Indian educational landscape was predominantly offline, characterized by traditional classroom settings across levels from primary to higher education. This preference for in-person learning was shaped by cultural, infrastructural, and policy factors that emphasized face-to-face interaction as the cornerstone of education. Prior to the pandemic, the digital infrastructure in India's educational sector was not uniformly developed, especially in rural and semi-urban areas. According to the Annual Status of Education Report (ASER) 2018, only a fraction of schools had access to computers and an internet connection. The report highlighted that in rural India, only about 44% of schools had electricity, a prerequisite for digital education. These infrastructural limitations significantly constrained the capacity for online education, making offline education the most feasible option for most institutions.

The current research primarily investigates the enhancement of student skills within a higher education context, specifically through online learning modalities during the COVID-19 pandemic. The geographical focus of this study is on higher educational institutions situated in both rural and urban sectors of the Birbhum district, West Bengal, India. Within this framework, the survey encompassed 159 undergraduate students from diverse academic disciplines and subjects residing in the Birbhum district. To establish a correlation between online education and gender, a non-parametric statistical test was employed. The availability of internet service, significantly influenced by the students' residence, emerged as a critical factor. Notably, in many rural locales of the Birbhum district, consistent and uninterrupted internet service remains elusive. The findings unequivocally reveal a pronounced disparity in the ability of rural and urban students to engage with the online educational framework, with rural areas facing a pronounced internet connectivity crisis that hampers streaming of video content or participation in live classes. This discrepancy poses a notable disadvantage for rural students in comparison to their urban counterparts. Moreover, the occupational status of students' guardians/parents, along with stakeholders' monthly income, caste and creed, and the social milieu, were identified as significant determinants of online educational efficacy in Birbhum, West Bengal, India. The inaugural instance of COVID-19 in West Bengal was documented on March 17, 2020. In response to the escalating threat of the Novel Coronavirus (COVID-19), all educational institutions within the Indian state of West Bengal were preemptively closed on March 16, 2020, as

Challenges in Online Education During the COVID-19 Pandemic

a measure to mitigate the virus's spread. Subsequently, after a hiatus extending to 20 months, schools and colleges in West Bengal resumed in-person instruction on November 16, 2021.This chapter is dedicated to a comparative analysis of student performance across various streams, genders, and residential backgrounds in the context of online learning during the COVID-19 pandemic, spanning from March 2020 to November 2021, in West Bengal, India.

LITERATURE REVIEW

According to a study by Bhattacharya and Sharma (2020), rural areas in West Bengal and other parts of India face significant challenges due to inadequate internet connectivity and lack of access to digital devices. This issue is compounded by the digital divide between urban and rural areas, with the latter lagging in terms of broadband internet penetration and the availability of digital learning tools.The research conducted by S. Sen, S. Chatterje, A. Das (2020) elucidated that within South Bengal, the prevalence of inadequate internet connectivity, coupled with restricted access thereto and frequent link failures, emerged as paramount concerns. Furthermore, the severity of these issues disproportionately impacted students to a greater extent than educators. According to B. Sarkar, N. Islam, R. Roy, and others (2023), the cessation of school operations has profoundly affected primary education. This investigation delves into the repercussions of school shutdowns on the continuum of teaching and learning activities within government and private primary schools in West Bengal, highlighting the disparity in educational opportunities during the COVID-19 pandemic within formal and non-formal education frameworks. Employing a structured questionnaire, the research was orchestrated through an online survey across West Bengal. The authors' evaluation elucidated significant variations in the availability of teaching and learning opportunities. Moreover, the study uncovered a distinct divide between government and private primary educational institutions. It was observed that students residing in urban locales benefited from greater access to online educational resources compared to their counterparts in rural settings.

N. Kapasia, P. Paul, A. Roy, and others (2020) undertook a study to evaluate the repercussions of the COVID-19 lockdown on undergraduate and postgraduate students across various colleges and universities in West Bengal. An online survey was conducted from May 1 to May 8, 2020, to gather data. To facilitate this, a structural questionnaire was disseminated via 'Google form' links sent through WhatsApp and E-mail to the students. A group of 232 students furnished comprehensive responses to the survey. The analysis employed simple percentage distribution to assess the learning status among the participants. Findings indicate that during the lockdown, approximately 70% of learners engaged in e-learning, predominantly through android mobile devices. The study participants reported encountering several challenges, including depression, anxiety, inadequate internet services, and suboptimal study environments at home. Particularly, students hailing from remote areas and marginalized communities encountered significant obstacles in their educational pursuits amidst the pandemic. The study advocates for targeted interventions aimed at fostering a conducive study environment for students from socio-economically vulnerable sections. There is an urgent need for strategies to fortify the resilience of the education system within the state, ensuring the development of skills crucial for employability and enhancing the productivity of young minds.

The research conducted by S.K. Behera, M.S. Ansary, S. Roy (2022) focuses on examining the attitudes of undergraduate (UG) students towards online education at Sidho-Kano-Birsha University located in the Purulia District of West Bengal, India. Motivated by the technological advancements and the compelling circumstances necessitating the adoption of online educational strategies, this study endeavors to ascertain the implications of this educational shift. Utilizing a survey-based quantitative methodology, the study sampled a modest group (n=100) of university students. To gauge students' perceptions of online education, a self-developed online perception scale was employed. The analysis of the collected data involved statistical methods, including the calculation of mean, standard deviation, and the application of t-tests and F-tests. The findings suggest that undergraduate students in the Purulia District hold a moderate perception of online education. Interestingly, the study indicates no significant perceptual differences based on the students' gender, geographical location (rural vs. urban), or caste (General, OBC, SC, ST). However, significant variations in perception were observed with respect to the students' academic semester (fourth to sixth) and their field of study (arts, science, commerce), suggesting that these factors play a crucial role in shaping students' attitudes towards online learning.

In **Parashar Banerjee's 2020** study, it is articulated that most higher education institutions in West Bengal find themselves ill-equipped to deploy online teaching and learning platforms. This inadequacy is attributed to a dual set of challenges: on one front, there is a palpable lack of necessary infrastructure; on the other, a significant proportion of students residing in rural and semi-urban areas of Bengal are devoid of access to essential technological tools such as Android smartphones, laptops, or desktop computers. Furthermore, private college administrations are encountering resistance from students' guardians regarding tuition fees, an issue that has become a recurrent theme in both print and broadcast media. Students on the verge of completing their education are engulfed in anxiety concerning their immediate professional futures, especially about internships and placements. Companies that had previously extended job offers to final-year students are now postponing the final stages of recruitment. Additionally, the pandemic has precipitated a marked decline in the global mobility of students, suggesting long-term impacts on international educational exchanges.

T. Muthuprasad et.al (2021) made a study on an agriculture institute in India and found that due to the unprecedented lockdown of COVID-19 the institute had not sufficient time to incorporate online courses and infrastructure properly. But they are preparing online e-contents and shifting their course curriculum. Most of the students preferred online classes but they avoided long-duration classes and preferred a break between two classes. This is because of physical stress caused using electronic gadgets long time. Masduki Asbari et al (2020) studied to understand the influence of hard skills and soft skills on teachers' innovation capability and the influence of organizational learning on it. They found that hard skills sharing had a positive and significant influence on teacher innovation capability. Hard skills and soft skills had a positive and significant influence on organizational learning. The better the hard skills and soft skills possessed by teachers, the more positive the formation and development of organizational learning and the teacher innovation capability of individuals in a school will also increase. In a study, Sir John Daniel (2020) pointed out the role of guidance to teachers, institutional heads, and officials in this pandemic situation. He questioned the preparations should institutions make in a short time and how do they address students' needs by level and field of study. Reassuring students and parents is a vital element of institutional response. Schools and colleges should take advantage of asynchronous learning, which works best in digital formats. Dr. Wahab Ali (2020) in a study intended to examine how teaching and learning can continue during these unprecedented times. He also raises some challenges and benefits of online learning. He recommended that higher institutions need to have basic ICT infrastructure to take online learning effectively. All staff need ICT tools and should have access to applications and learning platforms. Staff also need to have the capacity to use ICT effectively. Ibrahim Doyumğaç et al (2021) again raised the issues supporting and strengthening online education and barrier, problems complicating students, academicians, and teachers in this context. Their study found that online education did not provide equal opportunities, students were exposed to the lack of technology and access limitations in online education, and the parents were not well-informed about online education. Not only those students and educator also experienced psychological and social problems. To achieve better and timely solutions in distance learning education Aras Bozkurt and Ramesh C. Sharma (2020) suggested a collaboration with different shareholders like psychologists, sociologists, therapists, etc. We have to keep in mind that students will remember not the educational content delivered, but how they felt during these hard times. Francesca Gallè et al (2020) carried out a survey among Italian undergraduates to explore their level of knowledge about the epidemic and the behaviors they adopted during the lockdown. They found that science students have a good level of knowledge about pandemics and their control. They clearly established life science students have better information than other courses students and female students have a better knowledge about the epidemic and its control. A study by Ratna S. Putri et al (2020) identifiedthe constraints of the online teaching and learning process at home as a result of the unprecedented situation with the pandemic COVID-19. They studied over 15 teachers and parents of two primary schools in Indonesia. The main challenges were limited communication and socializing among students. Parents saw the problem was more related to a lack of learning discipline at home, more time spent to assist their children's learning at home. On the school's side, teachers are struggling with the drastic change causing an interruption in learning and teaching. At home, not all parents are not ready with what is required to facilitate home learning.

The theme of the book, *Challenges and Transitions in Education in Times of Crisis*, is closely aligned with the content of the chapter detailing the trials faced by higher education institutes in the rural areas of Birbhum District, West Bengal, India, during the COVID-19 pandemic. This alignment is evident as the chapter focuses on a critical examination of the abrupt shift from traditional to online education, spotlighting the myriad obstacles encountered in this transition, which is central to understanding educational challenges in crisis times. The chapter not only explores the tangible challenges such as infrastructural inadequacies, limited internet services, and lack of e-resources, but also delves into the socio-economic disparities between rural and urban educational institutes, highlighting the financial constraints and social burdens that exacerbate educational inequalities. By providing a case study from West Bengal, the chapter enriches the broader theme of the book with specific instances of how crises, like the COVID-19 pandemic, can amplify existing educational disparities and necessitate immediate, yet sustainable, adaptations. Furthermore, it underscores the necessity for resilience and innovation in education systems, particularly in under-resourced areas, to ensure continuity of learning and to foster a generation that is both skilled and technologically proficient. This chapter, therefore, not only contributes to the thematic exploration of educational challenges during crises but also offers insights into potential pathways for overcoming these obstacles, making it an indispensable part of the dialogue initiated by the book.

Objectives

The present work focuses mainly on the skill development of students in a higher educational institute in the context of online education during COVID-19 situation. The study area is higher educational institutes, belonging to rural and urban areas in the district of Birbhum, West Bengal, India. The main objectives are as follows.

Challenges in Online Education During the COVID-19 Pandemic

- To make a comparative study regarding the performance of all students from different stream, gender, and residence through online learning during COVID-19 pandemic situation.
- To identify the gap between rural and urban students, science and literature, or social science students to learn through an online platform.
- To measure financial support and obstacles faced by all stakeholders to assist afford the burden of online education.
- Finally, to analyze the role of society and family to support online learning.

Hypothesis

H1: It is hypothesized that the gender gap is significantly playing the role in the teaching-learning process through online platforms.

H2: It is hypothesized that the rural-urban gap is widened further during the pandemic time owning to better access to infrastructure in urban areas.

H3: It is hypothesized that the subject & stream of students is significantly playing the role in the teaching-learning process through online platforms.

H4: It is hypothesized that the occupation and economic conditions of stakeholders are significantly playing the role in the teaching-learning process through online platforms.

H5: It is hypothesized that the socio–economic status of students is significantly playing the role in the teaching-learning process through online platforms.

Methodology

The primary data was collected with the help of a structured questionnaire covering the villages, major urban centers of the Birbhum district of West Bengal. Some questions are based on 7-point Likert Scale and some are on absolute values. According to our objective the dependent variable (X_i) is 'Online education'. At first, a composite mean score has been calculated based on all questionnaire related to dependent variable. The basic questions regarding the online education were daily attendance of class, availability of laptop or smart phone, internet availability and affordability, daily uses of internet, understanding the theoretical and practical subjects, teacher – student communication, evaluation method and performance etc. etc.

Since the data set does not follow normal distribution hence, we apply non parametric test to check the significance of our hypothesis. We use two independent samples tests which compares two groups of cases on one variable. The most popular of the two-independent samples tests is the Mann-Whitney U test, which tests if two sampled populations are equivalent. For several independent samples the procedure to compare two or more groups of cases on one variable the Kruskal-Wallis test has been applied. These tests determine whether one can reject the null hypothesis that two or more independent samples come from the same population distribution.

We follow a simple regression equation to establish our hypothesis as follows;

$$X_i = a + b_1 Y_i + u$$

Where, X_i is dependent variable and in this study it is 'Online Education'. Y_i is independent variable. Several parameters are considered as independent variable like;

1. Gender (0 for female, 1 for male)
2. Residence (0 for rural, 1 for urban)
3. Subject Stream (0 for Arts & Literature, 1 for Social Science, 2 for Science)
4. Occupation (0 for wage labour, 1 for farmer, 2 for business, 3 for Government service)
5. Monthly Income (0 for below Rs 5000, 1 for Rs 5001 – 10000, 2 for Rs 10001 - 20000, 3 for Rs 20001- 40000, 4 for Rs 40000 and above)
6. Social Category (0 for general cast, 1 for schedule cast, 2 for schedule tribe, 3 for other backward class)

Mann-Whitney U test:

$$U = R - \frac{n(n-1)}{2}$$

R is the sum of ranks, n is the number of items in the sample

Kruskal-Wallis test:

$$H = \frac{12}{N(N+1)} \sum_{i=1}^{k} \frac{R_i^2}{n_i} - 3(N+1)$$

Where N is the total sample size, k is the number of groups we are comparing, R_i is the sum of ranks for group i, and n_i is the sample size of group i.

If the null hypothesis becomes true after analyzing the significance of non parametric test, a Post hoc Analysis has been applied to identify exactly which groups differ from each other and which parameter is most significant.

RESULTS AND DISCUSSION

A. Online Education and Gender

A non-parametric test has been conducted to determine a relation between online education and gender. From table 1 it has been found that there is a significant gap between male and female student in performing the online education system. It has been clearly indicating that during COVID-19 situation all students did not attain equally their regular classes and other academic activities. Both male and female students are not equally efficient and availed proper facilities to study.

The table 1 accepts our null hypothesis that there is a significant gender gap in online learning system. Now to find out the category for which the above results become significant a post hoc analysis has been conducted. Since there are less than three different categories, a one-way ANOVA has been applied. It is clear from the table 2 that the test of homogeneity between male and female student is not significant (0.111), and the difference between groups is significant (.000). The pair wise differences are also significant according to Bonferroni test at 5% level of significance (table 3). The result clearly indicates that female students have attained and performed better online education than male students. Figure 1 shows the marginal mean difference between male and female students. The reason behind the fact is the engagement of male student in daily earning. During COVID-19 situation the normal earning opportunities for all families except government's service person became hamper and daily earning became very volatile. The need of education becomes secondary than earning money. But the scenario was opposite for female student. They are comparatively less worried about earning money. The main work for female students was to take care of their internal family work. That is why female students managed more time and scope to attain online class and other activities regularly.

Table 1. Independent Variable = Gender (N = 159)

		N	Mean Rank	Sum of Ranks
Online Education	Female (0)	69	93.91	6480.00
	Male (1)	90	69.33	6240.00
	Grouping Variable: Gender			
	Mann-Whitney U			2145.00
	Wilcoxon W			6240.00
	Z			-3.340
	Asymp. Sig. (2-tailed)			**.001**

Table 2. Test of Homogeneity of Variances

Levene Statistic	df1	df2	Sig.
2.573	1	157	.111

Table 3. Pairwise Comparisons

(I) Gender	(J) Gender	Mean Difference (I-J)	Std. Error	95% Confidence Interval for Difference[a] Lower Bound	95% Confidence Interval for Difference[a] Upper Bound
Female	Male	.392*	.102	.190	.594
Male	Female	-.392*	.102	-.594	-.190

Based on estimated marginal means

*. The mean difference is significant at the .05 level.

a. Adjustment for multiple comparisons: Bonferroni.

Table 4. Univariate Tests

	Sum of Squares	df	Mean Square	F	Sig.	Partial Eta Squared
Contrast	6.004	1	6.004	14.751	.000	.086
Error	63.906	157	.407			

The F tests the effect of Gender. This test is based on the linearly independent pairwise comparisons among the estimated marginal means.

Figure 1. Estimated Marginal Means of Online Education with Respect to Gender

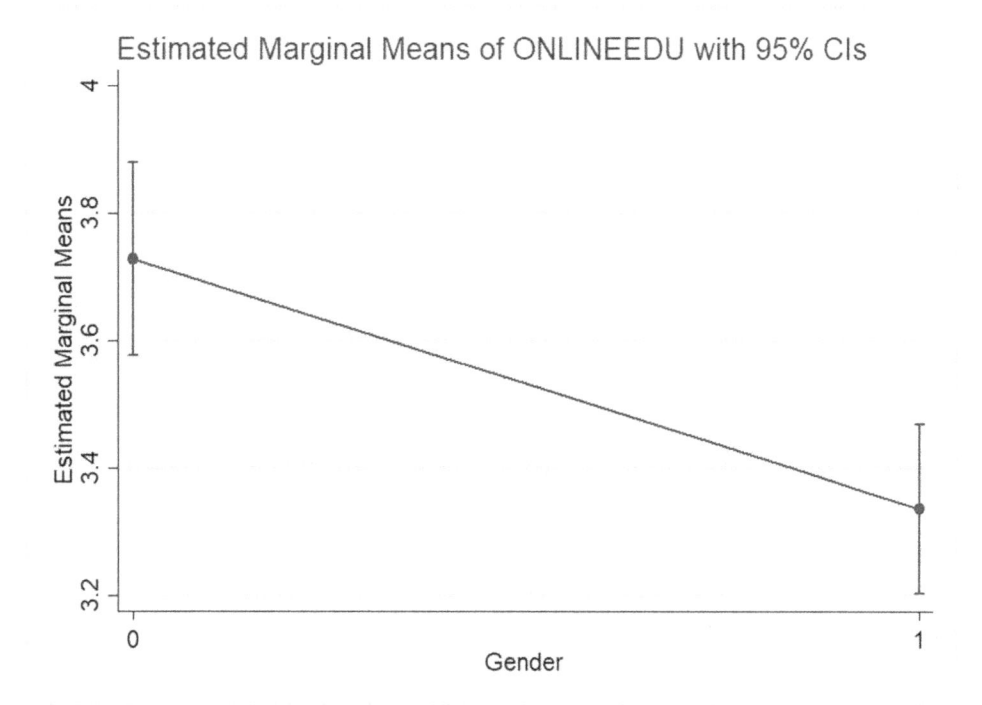

[Figure: Estimated Marginal Means of ONLINEEDU with 95% CIs, plotting Estimated Marginal Means (y-axis, ~3.2 to 4) against Gender (x-axis, 0 and 1). Value at 0 ≈ 3.73; value at 1 ≈ 3.34.]

B. Online Education and Residence

Residence is an important factor to determine the accessibility of internet service. In most of the rural area of Birbhum district, it is very common that a smooth and uninterrupted internet service is not always available. Table 5 clearly indicates that there is a significant gap between rural and urban students to perform the online education system. There is a crisis of internet in rural area particularly to run any buffering video or any live class. This might be a serious drawback for rural student as compare to urban students. The null hypothesis regarding this issue is accepted and the rural-urban gap is widened further during the pandemic time owing to better access to infrastructure in urban areas. Table 6 shows one way ANOVA between rural and urban group and the result is significant. The pair wise differences are also significant according to Bonferroni test at 5% level of significance (table 7). The marginal mean difference between rural and urban area is shown in figure 2. From this analysis it is very clear that urban students accessed more internet services than rural students and also urban students attained more online classes and assignments than rural counterpart.

Table 5. Independent Variable = Residence (N = 159)

		N	Mean Rank	Sum of Ranks
Online Learning	Village (0)	131	74.16	9714.50
	City (1)	28	107.34	3005.50
	Grouping Variable: Residence			
	Mann-Whitney U			1068.500
	Wilcoxon W			9714.500
	Z			-3.465
	Asymp. Sig. (2-tailed)			.001

Table 6. ANOVA

	Sum of Squares	df	Mean Square	F	Sig.
Between Groups	7.570	1	7.570	19.066	.000
Within Groups	62.339	157	.397		
Total	69.910	158			

Table 7. Pairwise Comparisons

Dependent Variable: ONLINEDUCATION

(I) Residence	(J) Residence	Mean Difference (I-J)	Std. Error	95% Confidence Interval for Difference[a] Lower Bound	Upper Bound
Village	City	-.573*	.131	-.832	-.314
City	Village	.573*	.131	.314	.832

Based on estimated marginal means

*. The mean difference is significant at the .05 level.

a. Adjustment for multiple comparisons: Bonferroni.

Table 8. Univariate Tests

	Sum of Squares	df	Mean Square	F	Sig.	Partial Eta Squared
Contrast	7.570	1	7.570	19.066	.000	.108

continued on following page

Table 8. Continued

	Sum of Squares	df	Mean Square	F	Sig.	Partial Eta Squared
Error	62.339	157	.397			

The F tests the effect of Residence. This test is based on the linearly independent pairwise comparisons among the estimated marginal means.

Figure 2. Estimated Marginal Means of Online Education with Respect to Residence

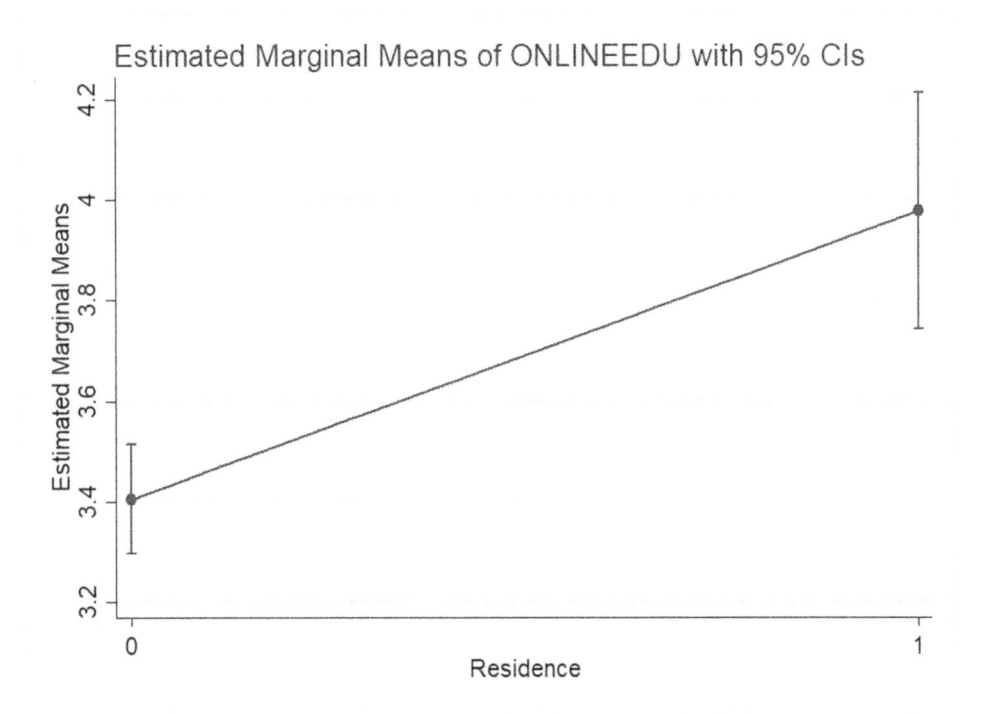

C. Online Education and Subject Stream

In the present study, 159 students of Birbhum district have been asked in the survey. All students are undergraduate students of different stream and subject. In case of science students no technical students or medical students or engineering students have been considered. Only general degree course students of main stream subjects are considered here. In this survey 92 students belong to Arts and Literature stream, 61 students belong to Science stream and only 6 students from Social Science stream. The table 9 shows a significant result about the distinction among the stream. Since there are more than two groups to compare, a Post hoc analysis has been exercised.

The pair wise difference among three groups is significant according to Bonferroni test at 5% level of significance (table 11, 12). Among all three pairs of comparison only a single pair becomes significant. There is a difference between Social Science stream and Arts & Literature stream. It cannot be strongly concluded about the significance if the result since the sample size of Social Science students was very small (only 6). Yet, one can easily find the difference between Arts & Literature students with other group in most of the educational institutes in Birbhum. Social Science and Science students are much aware and technically efficient than arts & literature students. The marginal mean difference is plotted in figure 3.

Table 9. Independent Variable = Stream (N = 159)

		N	Mean Rank
Online Learning	Arts & Literature (0)	92	73.16
	Social Science (1)	6	119.00
	Science (2)	61	86.48
	Kruskal Wallis Test; Grouping Variable: STREAM	
	Chi-Square		7.555
	df		2
	Asymp. Sig.		**.023**

Table 10. Levene's Test of Equality of Error Variances[a]

F	df1	df2	Sig.
3.403	2	156	.036

Tests the null hypothesis that the error variance of the dependent variable is equal across groups.
a. Design: Intercept + Stream

Table 11. Univariate Tests

	Sum of Squares	df	Mean Square	F	Sig.	Partial Eta Squared
Contrast	3.810	2	1.905	4.496	.013	.055
Error	66.099	156	.424			

The F tests the effect of Stream. This test is based on the linearly independent pairwise comparisons among the estimated marginal means.

Post Hoc Tests

Table 12. Multiple Comparisons

(I) Stream	(J) Stream	Mean Difference (I-J)	Std. Error	95% Confidence Interval Lower Bound	95% Confidence Interval Upper Bound
Arts & Literature	Social_Science	-.7244*	.27427	-1.3734	-.0754
	Science	-.1951	.10748	-.4495	.0592
Social_Science	Arts & Literature	.7244*	.27427	.0754	1.3734
	Science	.5292	.27851	-.1298	1.1882
Science	Arts & Literature	.1951	.10748	-.0592	.4495
	Social_Science	-.5292	.27851	-1.1882	.1298

Based on observed means.
The error term is Mean Square(Error) = .424.

*. The mean difference is significant at the .05 level.

Homogeneous Subsets

Table 13. Tukey HSD

Stream	N	Subset 1	Subset 2
Arts&Literature	92	3.4038	
Science	61	3.5990	3.5990
Social_Science	6		4.1282
Sig.		.683	.064

Means for groups in homogeneous subsets are displayed.
Based on observed means.
The error term is Mean Square(Error) = .424.

Figure 3. Estimated Marginal Means of Online Education with Respect to Stream

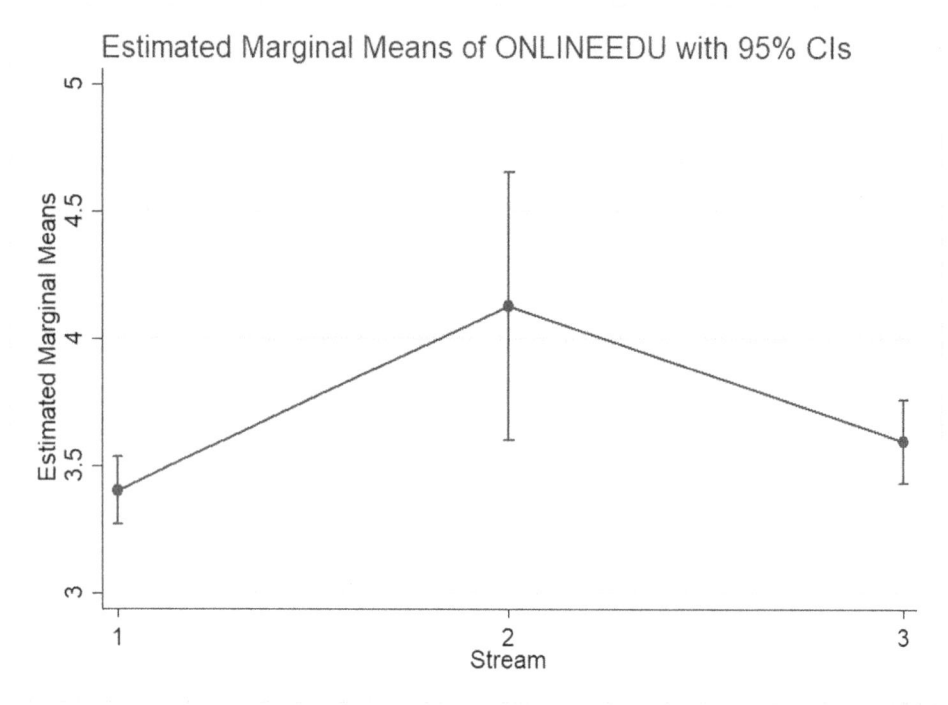

D. Online Education and Occupation

Occupation plays a crucial role in determining the performance of online education. It is obvious that an assured monthly income from any service or from established business helpsguardians to sustain education through online mode using ICT infrastructure during COVID-19 pandemic. Table 14 indicates the difference exist in online education system. The parents having any secure government service are significantly different from others. During pandemic situation it was very difficult to find any suitable work for wage labour either any agricultural field or any industry or elsewhere. Therefore, the earning opportunities became challenging for them to survive daily life. The consequences highly impact on education system of their children. We accept null hypothesis and apply Post hoc analysis to find out the particular occupation group for which the result becomes significant. The Post hoc analysis shows the pair wise difference among groups is significant according to Bonferroni test at 5% level of significance (table 16, 17). The stakeholders belongs to service sector are significantly different from wage labour and farmer. Figure 4 shows the marginal mean difference among the different occupation.

Table 14. Independent Variable = Occupation (N = 159)

		N	Mean Rank
Online Learning	Wage Labour (0)	27	70.44
	Farmer (1)	76	74.55
	Business (2)	37	83.36
	Service (3)	19	108.84
	Kruskal Wallis Test; Grouping Variable: Occupation	
	Chi-Square		9.902
	df		3
	Asymp. Sig.		**.019**

Table 15. Univariate Tests

	Sum of Squares	df	Mean Square	F	Sig.	Partial Eta Squared
Contrast	5.250	3	1.750	4.195	.007	.075
Error	64.659	155	.417			

The F tests the effect of FamilyOccupation. This test is based on the linearly independent pairwise comparisons among the estimated marginal means.

Post Hoc Tests

Table 16. Multiple Comparisons

Tukey HSD

(I) FamilyOccupation	(J) FamilyOccupation	Mean Difference (I-J)	Std. Error	95% Confidence Interval Lower Bound	95% Confidence Interval Upper Bound
Wage_labour	Farmer	-.0871	.14470	-.4629	.2887
	Businessman	-.2202	.16348	-.6448	.2043
	Serviceman	-.6205*	.19341	-1.1228	-.1182
Farmer	Wage_labour	.0871	.14470	-.2887	.4629
	Businessman	-.1331	.12947	-.4694	.2031
	Serviceman	-.5334*	.16566	-.9637	-.1032

continued on following page

Challenges in Online Education During the COVID-19 Pandemic

Table 16. Continued

<table>
<tr><td colspan="7">Tukey HSD</td></tr>
<tr><td rowspan="2">(I) FamilyOccupation</td><td rowspan="2">(J) FamilyOccupation</td><td rowspan="2">Mean Difference (I-J)</td><td rowspan="2">Std. Error</td><td></td><td colspan="2">95% Confidence Interval</td></tr>
<tr><td></td><td>Lower Bound</td><td>Upper Bound</td></tr>
<tr><td rowspan="3">Businessman</td><td>Wage_labour</td><td>.2202</td><td>.16348</td><td></td><td>-.2043</td><td>.6448</td></tr>
<tr><td>Farmer</td><td>.1331</td><td>.12947</td><td></td><td>-.2031</td><td>.4694</td></tr>
<tr><td>Serviceman</td><td>-.4003</td><td>.18229</td><td></td><td>-.8737</td><td>.0732</td></tr>
<tr><td rowspan="3">Serviceman</td><td>Wage_labour</td><td>.6205*</td><td>.19341</td><td></td><td>.1182</td><td>1.1228</td></tr>
<tr><td>Farmer</td><td>.5334*</td><td>.16566</td><td></td><td>.1032</td><td>.9637</td></tr>
<tr><td>Businessman</td><td>.4003</td><td>.18229</td><td></td><td>-.0732</td><td>.8737</td></tr>
<tr><td colspan="4">Based on observed means.
The error term is Mean Square(Error) = .417.</td><td></td><td></td><td></td></tr>
<tr><td colspan="4">*. The mean difference is significant at the .05 level.</td><td></td><td></td><td></td></tr>
</table>

Homogeneous Subsets

Table 17. Tukey HSD

<table>
<tr><td rowspan="2">FamilyOccupation</td><td rowspan="2">N</td><td colspan="2">Subset</td></tr>
<tr><td>1</td><td>2</td></tr>
<tr><td>Wage_labour</td><td>27</td><td>3.3390</td><td></td></tr>
<tr><td>Farmer</td><td>76</td><td>3.4261</td><td></td></tr>
<tr><td>Businessman</td><td>37</td><td>3.5593</td><td>3.5593</td></tr>
<tr><td>Serviceman</td><td>19</td><td></td><td>3.9595</td></tr>
<tr><td>Sig.</td><td></td><td>.540</td><td>.075</td></tr>
</table>

Means for groups in homogeneous subsets are displayed.
Based on observed means.
The error term is Mean Square(Error) = .417.

Figure 4. Estimated Marginal Means of Online Education with Respect to Occupation

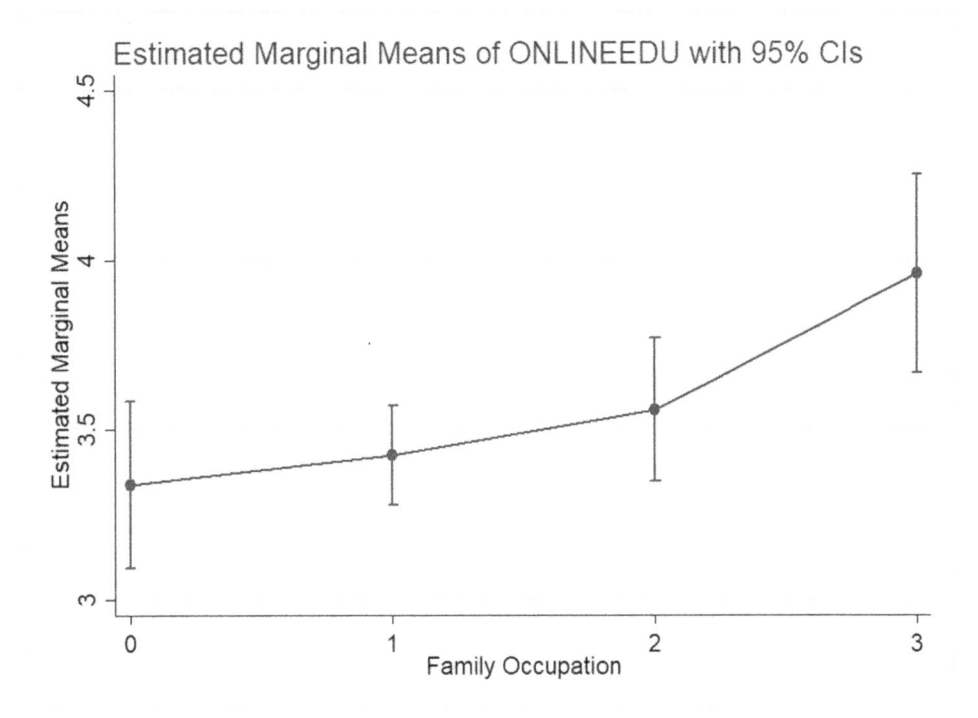

E. Online Education and Monthly Income

The role of stakeholder's monthly income is similar to their family occupation as discussed above. If occupation assures a secure monthly income then during pandemic situation then affordability and accessibility of internet services and other ICT tools to attain online classes becomes easier. The students with high and secure monthly income of parents was more regular and attentive in online education platform than other students. Table 18 shows that the difference exist significantly. The Post hoc analysis clearly indicates that the difference is for a high income group (table 19, 20). Stakeholders having monthly income of Rupees. 40000 above plays dominant role in online education system than any lower income group. Out of 159 students only 6 have their own laptop, and incidentally they belong to high monthly income group of above Rupees 40000 per month. And, only 16 students enjoy more than 2 GB or unlimited internet data service. Therefore a stable, secure, and high monthly income group plays significant role in education system during pandemic. Figure 5 shows the marginal mean difference among the different group of monthly income.

Challenges in Online Education During the COVID-19 Pandemic

Table 18. Independent Variable = Monthly Income (N = 159)

		N	Mean Rank
Online Learning	Below Rs. 5000 (0)	74	69.96
	Rs. 5000 - 10000 (1)	50	81.81
	Rs. 10001 - 20000 (2)	14	88.50
	Rs. 20001 - 40000 (3)	9	68.67
	Above Rs. 40000 (4)	12	132.96
	Kruskal Wallis Test; Grouping Variable: Monthly Income		
	Chi-Square		20.535
	df		4
	Asymp. Sig.		**.000**

Table 19. Levene's Test of Equality of Error Variances[a]

F	df1	df2	Sig.
.749	4	154	.560

Tests the null hypothesis that the error variance of the dependent variable is equal across groups.
a. Design: Intercept + Monthlyincome

Table 20. Univariate Tests

	Sum of Squares	df	Mean Square	F	Sig.	Partial Eta Squared
Contrast	11.603	4	2.901	7.661	.000	.166
Error	58.307	154	.379			

The F tests the effect of Monthlyincome. This test is based on the linearly independent pairwise comparisons among the estimated marginal means.

continued on following page

Challenges in Online Education During the COVID-19 Pandemic

Table 21. Continued
Post Hoc Tests

Table 21. Multiple Comparisons

Tukey HSD						
					95% Confidence Interval	
(I) Monthlyincome	(J) Monthlyincome	Mean Difference (I-J)	Std. Error	Sig.	Lower Bound	Upper Bound
Below_5K	5K-10K	-.1176	.11264	.834	-.4285	.1934
	10K-20K	-.1873	.17933	.834	-.6823	.3078
	20K-40K	-.0029	.21722		-.6025	.5967
	Above_40K	-1.0499*	.19149	.000	-1.5785	-.5213
5K-10K	Below_5K	.1176	.11264	.834	-.1934	.4285
	10K-20K	-.0697	.18605	.996	-.5832	.4439
	20K-40K	.1147	.22280	.986	-.5003	.7297
	Above_40K	-.9323*	.19780	.000	-1.4783	-.3863
10K-20K	Below_5K	.1873	.17933	.834	-.3078	.6823
	5K-10K	.0697	.18605	.996	-.4439	.5832
	20K-40K	.1844	.26289	.956	-.5413	.9101
	Above_40K	-.8626*	.24207	.004	-1.5308	-.1944
20K-40K	Below_5K	.0029	.21722		-.5967	.6025
	5K-10K	-.1147	.22280	.986	-.7297	.5003
	10K-20K	-.1844	.26289	.956	-.9101	.5413
	Above_40K	-1.0470*	.27133	.002	-1.7960	-.2980
Above_40K	Below_5K	1.0499*	.19149	.000	.5213	1.5785
	5K-10K	.9323*	.19780	.000	.3863	1.4783
	10K-20K	.8626*	.24207	.004	.1944	1.5308
	20K-40K	1.0470*	.27133	.002	.2980	1.7960
Based on observed means. The error term is Mean Square(Error) = .379.						
*. The mean difference is significant at the .05 level.						

continued on following page

Table 22. Continued
Homogeneous Subsets

Table 22. Tukey HSD

Monthlyincome	N	Subset 1	Subset 2
Below_5K	74	3.3732	
20K-40K	9	3.3761	
5K-10K	50	3.4908	
10K-20K	14	3.5604	
Above_40K	12		4.4231
Sig.		.904	1.000

Means for groups in homogeneous subsets are displayed.
Based on observed means.
The error term is Mean Square(Error) = .379.

Figure 5. Estimated Marginal Means of Online Education with Respect to Income

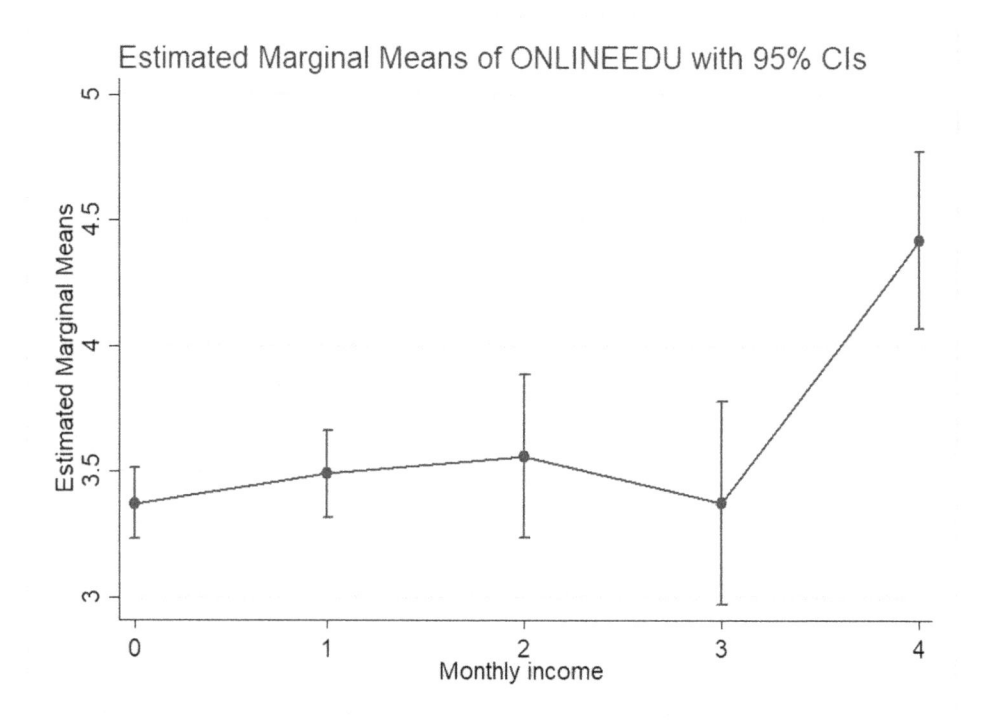

F. Online education and Social Category

In 21st century, caste& creed, social environment till now play a dominant role in every sector of society especially in rural part of India. Education sector is not the exceptional. The present work tried to find out the role of society in performing online education during pandemic. Table 23 shows that there is a significant difference among all groups of caste performing online education. The null hypothesis is again true and to find out which community accessed most the online education; Post hoc analysis applied. Table 26, 27 show the pair wise difference among different groups of caste. General caste students are in a superior position than other backward class students. The marginal mean difference is plotted in figure 6. Therefore, the results clearly conclude that learning opportunities and scope are not for same for all class of people in our society.

Table 23. Independent Variable = Category (N = 159)

		N	Mean Rank
Online Learning	General Caste (0)	82	90.62
	Schedule Caste (1)	24	82.12
	Schedule Tribe (2)	3	74.50
	Other Backward Class (3)	50	61.89
	Kruskal Wallis Test; Grouping Variable: Category		
	Chi-Square		12.218
	df		3
	Asymp. Sig.		**.007**

Table 24. Levene's Test of Equality of Error Variances^a

F	df1	df2	Sig.
3.870	3	155	.011

Tests the null hypothesis that the error variance of the dependent variable is equal across groups.
a. Design: Intercept + Category

Table 25. Univariate Tests

	Sum of Squares	df	Mean Square	F	Sig.	Partial Eta Squared
Contrast	6.005	3	2.002	4.855	.003	.086
Error	63.905	155	.412			

The F tests the effect of Category. This test is based on the linearly independent pairwise comparisons among the estimated marginal means.

Post Hoc Tests

Table 26. Multiple Comparisons

Tukey HSD						
(I) Category	(J) Category	Mean Difference (I-J)	Std. Error	Sig.	95% Confidence Interval	
					Lower Bound	Upper Bound
General_Caste	Schedule_Caste	.1879	.14902	.589	-.1992	.5749
	Schedule_Tribe	.3962	.37744	.720	-.5841	1.3764
	Other_Backward_Class	.4336*	.11521	.001	.1344	.7328
Schedule_Caste	General_Caste	-.1879	.14902	.589	-.5749	.1992
	Schedule_Tribe	.2083	.39320	.952	-.8129	1.2295
	Other_Backward_Class	.2458	.15945	.415	-.1683	.6599
Schedule_Tribe	General_Caste	-.3962	.37744	.720	-1.3764	.5841
	Schedule_Caste	-.2083	.39320	.952	-1.2295	.8129
	Other_Backward_Class	.0374	.38167		-.9538	1.0287
Other_Backward_Class	General_Caste	-.4336*	.11521	.001	-.7328	-.1344
	Schedule_Caste	-.2458	.15945	.415	-.6599	.1683
	Schedule_Tribe	-.0374	.38167		-1.0287	.9538

Based on observed means.
The error term is Mean Square(Error) = .412.
*. The mean difference is significant at the .05 level.

Homogeneous Subsets

Table 27. **Tukey HSD**

Category	N	Subset
		1
Other_Backward_Class	50	3.2446
Schedule_Tribe	3	3.2821
Schedule_Caste	24	3.4904
General_Caste	82	3.6782
Sig.		.442

Means for groups in homogeneous subsets are displayed.
Based on observed means.
The error term is Mean Square(Error) = .412.

Figure 6. Estimated Marginal Means of Online Education with Respect to Social Category

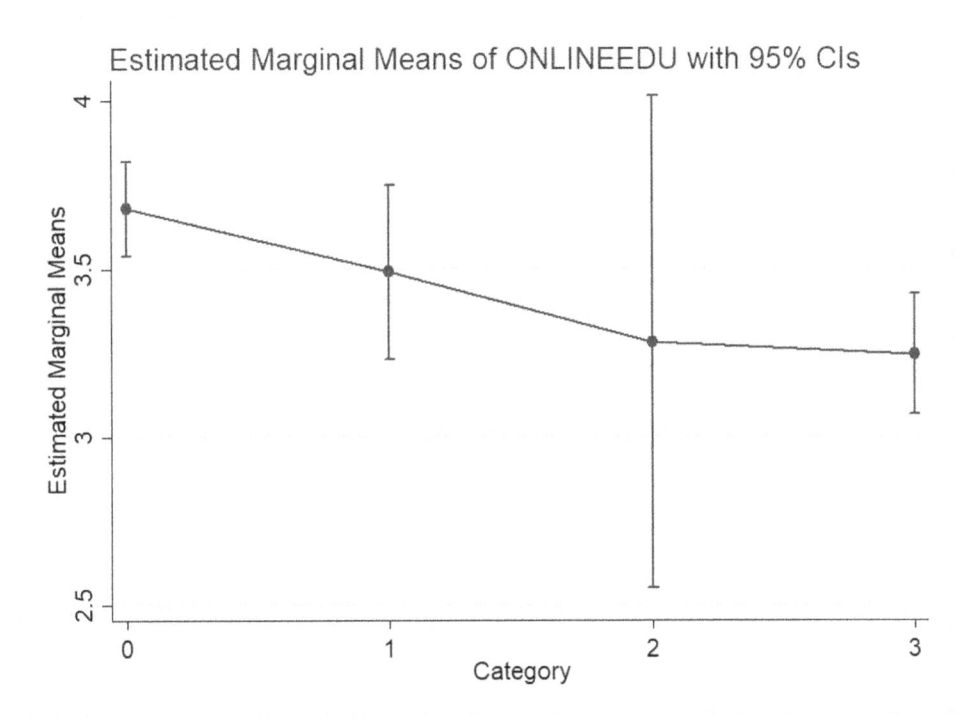

CONCLUSION AND POLICY IMPLICATION

The impact of COVID-19 had very serious on all aspects of society, all citizens, and all institutes around the globe. Educational institutions in India have also made a transition to an online teaching environment. The shift of teaching and learning to an online delivery mode obliged by the pandemic COVID-19 has become an integral part of the education system in the world. However, the levels and methods of using them to achieve quality education are varied and depended upon the various factors associated with Information and Communication Technology (ICT) policy and their practices in education. To produce a skilled and technologically efficient generation we need to modify our online education system from the grass-roots level. India, a developing nation, follows several traditional methods and spirits in every field of the economy. More than 70 percent population belongs to the rural and semi-urban areas where the education system runs by the conventional method or structure prepared by higher authorities. A sudden shift of the education system toward online mode pushes all citizens towards an unprecedented future. The efficacy of online education, alongside the challenges and barriers encountered by students and educators within the Indian higher education sector, is significantly hampered by a paucity of internet facilities, insufficient interaction and engagement with students, and a deficiency in technological proficiency. The abrupt transition to online learning modalities has posed considerable difficulties for both students and teachers. Furthermore, online education has failed to furnish equitable opportunities, leaving students vulnerable to technological inadequacies and access constraints inherent in online learning environments. Additionally, there exists a notable gap in parental awareness and understanding of online educational platforms and methodologies.

REFERENCES

Anne, Y., Starkey, L., Egerton, B., & Flueggen, F. (2020). High school students' experience of online learning during COVID-19: The influence of technology and pedagogy. *Technology, Pedagogy and Education*, 01(30), 59–73.

Asbari, M., Purwanto, A., Fayzhall, M., Purnamasari, D., & Firdaus, R. A. (2020). Hard Skills or Soft Skills: Which are More Important for Indonesian Teachers Innovation. *International Journal of Control and Automation*, 13(02).

Banerjee, P. (2020). The Impact of COVID-19 in Higher Education: An Empirical Study from West Bengal. *Research & Exploration*, 116–122.

Behera, S. K., Ansary, M. S., & Roy, S. (2022). Perception of Undergraduate Students on Online Education during COVID-19 Pandemic in Purulia District of West Bengal. In *Digital Innovation for Pandemics* (pp. 113–134). Auerbach Publications. 10.1201/9781003328438-6

Bozkurt, C., & Sharma, R. (2020). Emergency remote teaching in a time of global crisis due to Corona Virus pandemic. *Asian Journal of Distance Education*, 15(1).

Daniel, S. J. (2020). Education and the COVID-19 pandemic. *Prospects*, 49(1-2), 91–96. 10.1007/s11125-020-09464-332313309

Datta, M., & Bhattacharya, S. (2022). Factors Affecting Undergraduate Medical Students' Perception of Online Education During the COVID Pandemic at a Teaching Hospital in Eastern India. *Journal of Medical Education*, 21(1). Advance online publication. 10.5812/jme-122541

Doyumğaç, A., Tanhan, A., & Kiymaz, M. S. (2021). Understanding the Most Important Facilitators and Barriers for Online Education during COVID-19 through Online Photovoice Methodology. *International Journal of Higher Education*, 10(1), 166. 10.5430/ijhe.v10n1p166

Gallè, E., Sabella, E. A., Da Molin, G., De Giglio, O., Caggiano, G., Di Onofrio, V., Ferracuti, S., Montagna, M. T., Liguori, G., Orsi, G. B., & Napoli, C. (2020). Understanding Knowledge and Behaviors Related to CoVID–19 Epidemic in Italian Undergraduate Students: The EPICO Study. *International Journal of Environmental Research and Public Health*, 17(10), 3481. 10.3390/ijerph1710348132429432

Kapasia, N., Paul, P., Roy, A., Saha, J., Zaveri, A., Mallick, R., Barman, B., Das, P., & Chouhan, P. (2020). Impact of lockdown on learning status of undergraduate and postgraduate students during COVID-19 pandemic in West Bengal, India. *Children and Youth Services Review*, 116, 105194. 10.1016/j.childyouth.2020.10519432834270

Muthuprasad, T., Aiswarya, S., Aditya, K. S., & Jha, G. K. (2021). Students' perception and preference for online education in India during COVID -19 pandemic. *Social Sciences & Humanities Open*, 3(1), 100101. 10.1016/j.ssaho.2020.10010134173507

Putri, R. S., Purwanto, A., Pramono, R., Asbari, M., Wijayanti, L. M., & Hyun, C. C. (2020). Impact of the COVID-19 Pandemic on Online Home Learning: An Explorative Study of Primary Schools in Indonesia. *International Journal of Advanced Science and Technology*, 29(5), 4809–4818.

Sarkar, B., Islam, N., Das, P., Miraj, A., Dakua, M., Debnath, M., & Roy, R. (2023). Digital learning and the lopsidedness of the education in government and private primary schools during the COVID-19 pandemic in West Bengal, India. *E-Learning and Digital Media*, 20(5), 473–497. 10.1177/20427530221117327

Sen, S., Chatterje, S., & Das, A. (2020). Problem of online education system in South Bengal during the COVID-19 pandemic: An appraisal. *IOSR J. Humanit. Soc. Sci*, 25(10), 7-20.

Wahab. (2020). Online and Remote Learning in Higher Education Institutes: A Necessity in light of COVID-19 Pandemic. *Higher Education Studies, 10*(3).

Chapter 9
Online Education and Its Commercial Viability With Reference to the COVID-19 Pandemic

Kapil Kumar Aggarwal
https://orcid.org/0000-0002-2752-9495
Chandigarh University, India

Satakshi Agrawal
Ajay Kumar Garg Institute of Management, India

ABSTRACT

Over the past few years, online education has been an exciting research topic. Many educationists are working on the future and the scope of online education. Due to the COVID-19 outbreak, it has become a significant source of imparting knowledge among the youth, keeping in mind the health and safety of the children. While talking about EdTech, internet connectivity and the lecturer play a crucial role in defining the effectiveness of online education. The chapter mainly focuses on online education as a new emerging business in the country. The chapter also discusses its growing role and increasing contribution to GDP during the COVID-19 pandemic. Earlier, there was less awareness and trend of online learning; however, it is interesting to know that the pandemic has highlighted the importance of online learning, and it has emerged as a rare business that has shown an upward trend in crises. Online learning has emerged as an affordable, convenient and time-efficient method of gaining knowledge.

DOI: 10.4018/979-8-3693-1507-1.ch009

INTRODUCTION

Education plays a significant role in the overall development of an individual. It has become one of the most important social as well as commercial sectors nowadays. Traditionally in India, education was imparted in brick-and-mortar form. From ancient times the "Gurukul" was a kind of form wherein teachers and students lived in the same or nearby locality which was considered for imparting spiritual knowledge to the individuals. Children used to give regard to there "Guru" (teachers) in the form "Gurudakshina" and this "Gurudakshina" could be in any form either in monetary terms or in the form of accomplishing a task as directed by their Guru.

As time changed, the school was introduced as the source of imparting knowledge to the students. In this mode of education, students need to pay fees in monetary terms to gain knowledge. In this form, students from various backgrounds and regions come together and gain knowledge.

In the modern era, a new type of education mode came into existence which is the online way of education also known as an e-learning program. This is a very innovative way to connect with students from various places, cities and even countries. People can connect and get an education from world-class teachers. Students can now connect to any institute or teacher and gain knowledge. There are no boundaries left as there were in the traditional system of education. Various online certification courses are available and are gaining importance day by day. Many companies even encourage their employees to get such type of certification course done. Online education is becoming a new trend of education and even the government of India is working diligently for the development in this direction. MOOC courses relating to NIOS (grades 9 to 12 of open schooling) are launched by the government and are also uploaded on the SWAYAM portal. Around 92 courses have been launched on this portal. Radio broadcasting system is also used as a means of providing education to students in remote areas who do not have access to online sources. DTH channels using sign language have been launched for children having listening impairment. NCERT has launched e-textbooks in different languages namely English, Hindi, Urdu and Sanskrit. The launching of E-Pathshala by NCERT and CIET has enabled the availability of the NECRT textbooks, audio-visual material issued by NCERT, teaching and non-teaching modules and various printed and non-printed items.

Online education was earlier not considered by many people in India. However, it became popularized due to the outbreak of the COVID-19 pandemic, during which the health and safety of children became the priority. Many reputable institutes are now providing online classes and degrees for the orderly operations of their education systems, while ensuring the safety of social distancing norms.

Online Education and Its Commercial Viability

The pandemic has changed the pattern of doing the businesses, and this includes education. Most of the focus has been shifted to the online mode of working, or "working from home". Many offices have announced work from home and many schools and colleges have shifted to online platforms for providing education. This has increased the number of people using online services.

COVID-19 is one of the latest examples, it was a very fast-spreading virus and in the beginning, there was no vaccination available. Social distancing was seen as the only way to prevent it from spreading. Even after months of lockdown, with minimal situational change, an online platform had to be adopted as the means for conducting uninterrupted work and education in India.

During the pandemic many traditional tuition classes were shifted online, providing convenience to the students. Also many online education businesses like Byjus, Vendantu, Unacademy, Toppr, etc. had a marked a rapid rise in their business. Many students who did not have access to quality education earlier were able to connect with world-class teachers, improving their skills and capabilities.

During this time, the Indian government played a crucial role in promoting online education. The government announced initiatives to provide internet services in every village by 2022 under the "National Broadband Mission". This mission enabled equal internet access to all, especially the rural areas and will reduce the problem of the "digital divide".

The online learning sector has witnessed significant expansion and triumph, propelled by technological breakthroughs and a movement in preferences towards adaptable and easily accessible instruction. The worldwide e-learning industry, with an estimated worth of over $144 billion in 2019, is expected to grow significantly and reach $374.3 billion by 2026, indicating its fast rise. The COVID-19 pandemic greatly expedited the use of online learning, with around 98% of institutions currently providing online courses, which is a huge rise compared to the period before the pandemic. This transition has resulted in a consistent rise in online registration, especially among adult students who are looking to manage their education alongside other responsibilities.

Online education has become a crucial tool for educating and developing employees in the corporate sector. Approximately 90% of organizations employ various types of online learning, which is a significant increase from just 4% in 1995. The use of online training is motivated by its efficiency and efficacy, enabling employees to acquire five times more knowledge without extending the duration of training. Companies claim significant advantages, such as a 218% rise in revenue per employee and a 24% boost in profit margins.

Moreover, online learning has enhanced the availability of education, allowing individuals from many backgrounds to gain new expertise and credentials. The increase in educational technology is backed by substantial investments, approximately worth $18.7 billion in 2019. The online learning business is expected to continue growing due to the increasing demand for flexible and high-quality education. This sector is reshaping the global delivery of education and professional training.

REVIEW OF LITERATURE

This review of literature will first analyse the past studies on this topic. Our research is based on the study of online education as the new emerging business strategy and its exceptional performance during the pandemic.

The literature shows how online learning has provided support to the students during pandemic. Studies have shown mixed reviews about the effectiveness and its psychological impact on students. However some studies state that online learning can be as effective as the traditional classroom education system (Poonam & Aggarwal, 2023). Past research has shown that quality is very important in online teaching platforms. Second, being the subject matter expert and planning about how to impart the skills through online mode is very important with providing lectures on the online platform. Technical support and the training of the faculty to use video graphical tools are important in making online education interesting. Lederman (2020) argued that the arrival of the COVID-19 pandemic has pushed education to the online mode that has compelled students and teachers to have the digital platform experience as the result of the online-learning process. The role of the teachers is different in the online mode than in the face-to-face traditional mode and they also need to get training to use the technology efficiently. DQ Institute (2019) teachers can easily cater to the students to the digital skills of the students who are most prone to cyber risk in educational opportunities and achieve success in the era where education has shifted to the online platform. It was found that there has been increasing demand for online learning, especially in the case of higher education and many institutions have already opted for the blended mode of learning. However, it has also been seen that many institutes still superfluously provide traditional education over online learning due to many different reasons. There are findings where it was observed that there is a growing trend in online certification courses and various skill development programs. Some literature has addressed the growing need for online education amid the COVID-19 pandemic and how the EdTech platform acted as the backbone of the education system of various countries. The coronavirus was spreading at such a fast pace that it had changed the lives of many people (EdSource, 2020) and had endangered the current structure of the education system has caused the system to convert to online mode. E-learning is seen as one of the cheap and convenient sources of gaining knowledge. Working online has reduced the requirement of papers as now everything can be maintained in softcopies which has helped save our environment. The designing of online courses is a very critical and time-consuming task. It requires fulfilling the needs of most of the students keeping in mind the problem of the digital divide.

The growing Information and Communication Technology has enabled various businesses to opt for online modules. Many businesses like Ola, Uber, Amazon, Olx, Flipkart, MakeMyTrip and many more operate online, emerging as a low-cost and high-revenue business model. Smartphones, apps and internet connectivity play a vital role in supporting the online platform.

Electronic Books

The idea of E-learning was already present in foreign countries however it is a relatively new concept in India. It is observed that the contribution of online platforms to the economy has been increasing continuously in the US. The rate of employment and the quality of services are on continuous improvement. It has been observed that E-books require various hardware and software to access them as against the traditional books and the constant improvement and huge supply of gadgets has made it quite affordable. The handling and organisation of E-books is much easier than that of traditional books. These books are accessible anytime and anywhere. There has been increasing competition in the market of E-books however the success of the E-books will depend upon the content, applicability, accessibility and affordability of it. Some studies have described new techniques by integrating internet and cloud-based methods to digitally enhance the classical study group used by final-year residents studying for the Royal College of Physicians and Surgeons of Canada examination. It has also been seen that the online learning satisfaction derived by an individual also depends upon the person's perception regarding the online platform. It is believed that differences in technology, and characteristics of teachers and students would have a bearing on the level of satisfaction among the students.

Telehealth

Since Coronavirus is a communicable disease, it has increased the burden on hospitals and various healthcare institutes, so healthcare services have also shifted online to provide free pre-screening of the health condition of the patient. The new development and quick access to telehealth services have enabled people all over the world to react quickly to their deteriorating condition. There have been studies where the experience of parents and their struggles have been surveyed concerning the closure of schools and shifting to remote learning during the pandemic. It was found that most of the parents were in favour of the closure of schools to ensure the safety of their children. This version of parents supports "Maslow's Need hierarchy theory" wherein he states that first the basic and safety needs to be satisfied to move on to the higher-level order needs. Keeping the children safe and secure was recognised as the most important need by the parents which led to the shifting of education online and gave way to new business modules. Some findings in the literature point towards the mental status of students, and parents and their growing needs however the studies lack its commercial viability and don't provide insight to see it as an emerging business module.

OBJECTIVES OF THE STUDY

1. To analyse the role of online learning during the COVID-19 pandemic.
2. To study online education as a new emerging business.
3. To study the transition from the traditional education process to the online mode of education.
4. To study the impact of lockdown on the economy and the contribution of EdTech to GDP and "K" shape GDP recovery curve.

ROLE OF ONLINE LEARNING DURING COVID-19 PANDEMIC

The coronavirus pandemic crisis was one of the situations that has arisen for the first time. It was a very dangerous virus and has resulted in a huge number of deaths across the globe. As the long-duration closure had hampered the education system and the work, so online mode is only seen as an option. Teachers, students and all others had to shift to the online mode for imparted education.

Teachers were using various online platforms like Google Meet, Zoom, WebEx, Microsoft Teams and many more that are very new to them for imparting education amid this COVID-19 pandemic. Parents also find that mode safe for their children to carry on their education while remaining safe against the virus. Educators could share the study material in PDF, Word, PPTs, and audio-visual formats that could be communicated in seconds through e-mail, WhatsApp, college website etc. with the students. It also enabled the students to become more technologically savvy and made them more aware of the new ways of acquiring education. The IT sector has emerged as a major source for enabling modern education. It facilitated the use of information and communication technology for the smooth interaction between the teacher and the students.

ONLINE EDUCATION AS NEW EMERGING BUSINESS

Online education was seen as the new interest of the investors as many investors had invested huge money in these EdTech companies during the COVID-19 pandemic. It was seen as an innovative source of earnings as its valuation has increased 3X in India. Since the trend of online education was now increasing due to the spread of the coronavirus many new potential students were turned into actual students leading to an increase in demand for online education and skilled teachers.

During the time of lockdown imposed due to the pandemic, Byjus added over 25 million new students to its app. At that time, Byjus had more than 70 million students that are registered with it and 4.5 million had annual paid subscriptions. With 220 percent growth and more than 2 million students attending live online classes, Vednatu is another Edtech company that has shown remarkable growth. From 150,000 students in January 2020 to more than 1 million students studying every month on the platform, Unacademy had 30 million registered users and has recorded more than 350,000 paid subscribers. Due to the growing success of EdTech companies, many funding companies have shown their interest in investing in these EdTech companies.

The investors to Byjus include US investors the world's largest asset manager, BlackRock, Sands Capital and Alkeon Capital, a hedge fund. At one point, it has raised $500 million in funding from these companies.

The investors to Vedantu include WestBridge Capital, TAL, Omidyar Network, Accel Partners and Tiger Global Management. Investors to Unacademy include Blume Ventures, Steadview Capital, Sequoia India and Nexus Venture Partners. Financers to TopPro include Dubai-based investment firm Foundation Holdings, and Kaizen Private Equity which had raised to around Rs 350 crore.

According to the reports the leading EdTech platform Byjus had reported FY 18-19 its revenue as 1,480 crores and during the pandemic according to news they had earned revenue of 2,800 crore as reported on 27 May 2020 in FY20 which is approximately double from the previous year. As per reports due to the lockdown, students were using Byjus daily and were spending an average of 100 minutes per day. Another EdTech Vedantu had claimed that more than one million students had attended live online classes in one month and the total watch time of those video classes stands at a staggering 1 billion minutes. Its revenue grew by 80% which is the highest in the last 2.5 years. Unacademy claimed an 82% increase in its revenue in April 2020 as compared to April 2019.

CONTRIBUTION TO GDP AND "K" SHAPE RECOVERY CURVE

Gross Domestic Product (GDP) is the worth of the ultimate goods and services produced by a country within its geographical boundaries during the specified period. It is the indicator of the economic performance of a country. The higher GDP of a country indicates economic strength whereas the lower GDP indicates economic weakness.

Since the pandemic has occurred, many businesses faced difficulties to remain open to the public and functioning. Many traditional businesses which were earning profits earlier had to face losses due to the pandemic. Various industries like tourism, hospitality, clothing, laundry and personal services, schools, colleges, book industries and many more were negatively impacted by Coronavirus. India had recorded a decline in GDP rate by 23.9% in quarter one; it was the largest rate of contraction in GDP in the history of India, as the government announced the lockdown on 25 March 2020 and only essential services were allowed.

Many budgeted schools with no fees had already shut down. Schools were under pressure to receive no fees and provide salaries to their staff which made their survival very difficult. Providing education online was seen as the only way to carry on education, or "business," as well as protect the future of children. Introduction of the students to the online platform ultimately has provided these students with exposure to a new, convenient and affordable way of learning.

Online education is a business which has seen an upward trend during lockdown. It enabled asynchronous learning through recorded lectures. It also enhanced the understanding among the students by using videos, graphics and 3D effects. Various companies like Byjus, Vedantu, Unacademy, Topper, and Extramarks earned huge revenue during this lockdown period. They have seen an upward trend in their business. When most of the businesses were suffering and may have been on the verge of closing, these EdTech companies were performing exceptionally well and were earning profits. The investment in education technology start-ups had increased nearly four times from $409 million in 2019 to $1.5 billion in 2020 according to the data from "Venture Intelligence".

As some of the industries were making losses while the business of some of the industries like EdTech had increased drastically, India seems to have experienced "K" shape recovery curve. Under "K" shape recovery curve some sectors gained even more from their past situation and some sectors declined from their past conditions.

Under the COVID-19 pandemic, professionals in IT sectors, Pharmacy, EdTech, FMCG sector etc were experiencing growth. They had booked profit more than their past business. In contrast, some industries, like those involving books, aviation, tourism, real estate, etc., had noted losses. So, it was expected that some sectors would move upward and would emerge as a new business boom whereas some traditional businesses would be abolished and the contribution of all these sectors together would form this combined contribution to GDP. This is why economists had forecasted the "K" shape GDP recovery curve in India.

Therefore, the COVID-19 pandemic changed the general style, model of running business in India; it also has affected the consumer preference for goods and services. Customers are now seeking websites like Amazon, Flipkart, and Tata Cliq as the new way of convenient, online shopping.

Figure 1. It represents the condition of businesses before lockdown and how after lockdown some entities became profitable and some started to decline and became a loss-making entity

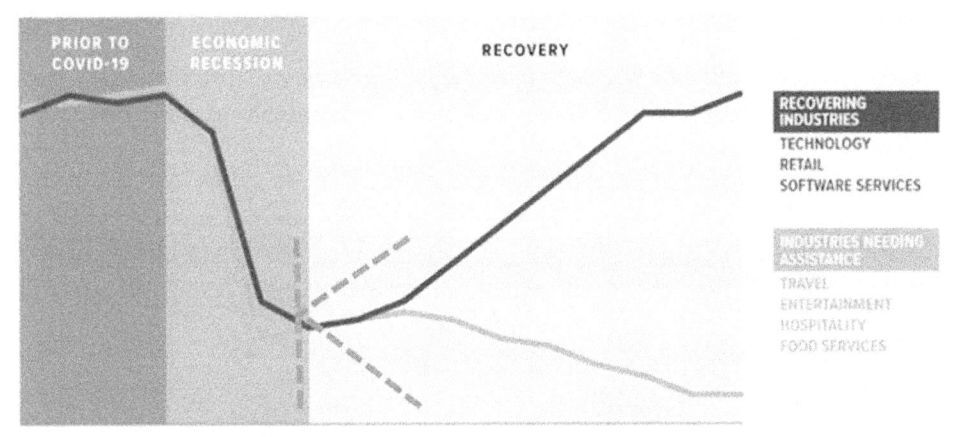

Source: U.S. Chamber of Commerce.

FINDINGS AND DISCUSSION

By analysing and studying the trend of online education it was found that the valuation of many EdTech companies had increased twofold.

According to Red Seer, across grades 1 to 12, the EdTech market was estimated to be of $1.7 billion while the market for grades above 12 was estimated to become $1.8 billion by 2022. In the post-K-12 grades especially in higher education wider growth of about 60% market share was expected which would include a 19% share of technical skills, a 14% share for preparation of government jobs and test preparation for other professions will comprise only a 7% share. Experts believe that such immense growth in the EdTech sector is supported by low-cost phones, the

Online Education and Its Commercial Viability

availability of inexpensive data packs, affordable and convenient electronic payment infrastructure and the growth of vernacular language apps.

The online platform has also been seen as the new source of employment in various fields like marketing, call centre services etc. It could also be a good source of employment for retired teachers and professors who did not get a pension and need money to run their houses. There is evidence to prove that during COVID-19 when many sectors were severely impacted, the EdTech sector grew drastically and showed an exceptional upward trend. This provided support to both the education sector as well as the economy. Many central universities like the University of Delhi and Banaras Hindu University have resorted to issuing online degrees due to the pandemic which has also reduced the requirement of papers and thus saving our environment.

Figure 2. It represents the increase in traffic, average time spent, movement from traditional offline tuitions to EdTech, and increase in number of users from 2019 to 2020

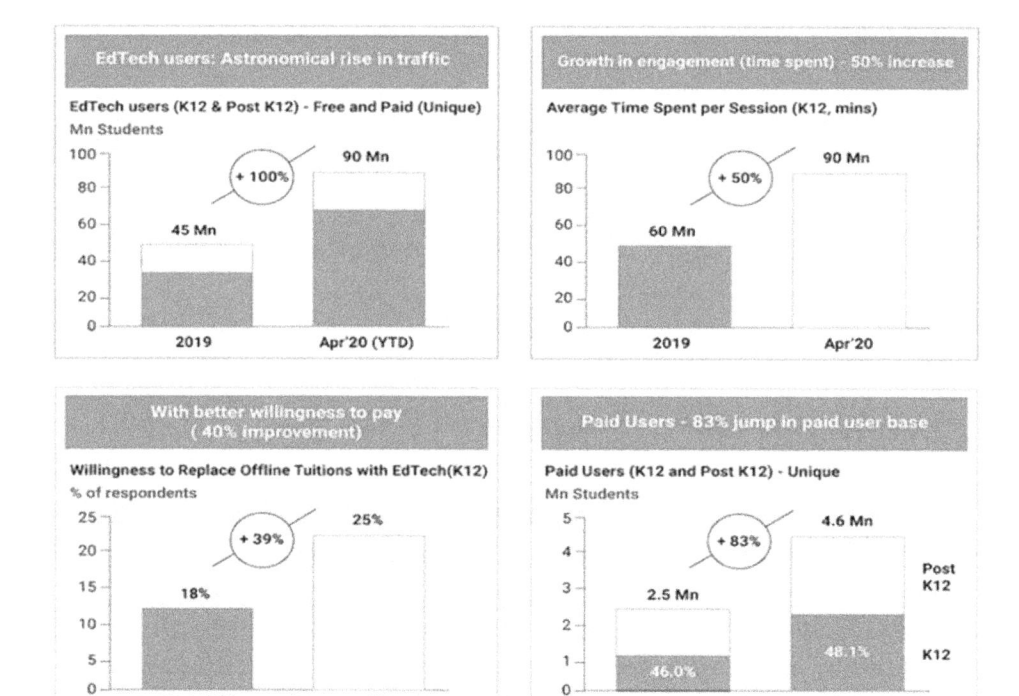

Source: RedSeer and Omidyar Network Edtech Report

CONCLUSION

It can be concluded that with the support of technology and growing infrastructure education from any part of the world at any time has become possible. With the large-scale users, the cost of technology has been reduced which has enabled the affordability of online education to the various sections of the society. Many retired teachers/professors are getting employment in these EdTech companies that will help in providing support to their families. Students can get knowledge from the world class teachers at their convenience enabling students to manage both jobs and studies simultaneously. The use of emails, links, and PDFs has reduced the use of paper, thus ensuring the protection of the environment. This sector has provided exceptionally strong support to the GDP of India during the time of crisis through contributions in taxes, employment, and increased use of technology. EdTech has emerged as the future business model a way "to learn and earn" and has brought a transformation in the traditional methods of imparting education.

REFERENCES

Allen, I.E. & Seaman, J. (2006). Growing by degrees: Online education in the United States, 2005. Sloan Consortium (NJ1).

EdSource. (2020). Coronavirus: Highlighting strategies for student success. Retrieved from https://edsource.org/topic/coronavirus

Farrell, D., & Greig, F. 2017. The online platform economy: Has growth peaked? Available at *SSRN* 2911194. 10.2139/ssrn.2911194

Garbe, A., Ogurlu, U., Logan, N., & Cook, P. (2020). COVID-19 and remote learning: Experiences of parents with children during the pandemic. *American Journal of Qualitative Research*, 4(3), 45–65.

DQ Institute (2019). Outsmart the Cyber-pandemic: Empower every child with digital intelligence by 2020. Retrieved from file:///D:/COVID/DQEveryChild%20DQ%20Institute.html.

Lederman, D. (2020). (March 18, Will shift to remote teaching be boon or bane for inline learning? Inside Higher Ed. Retrieved from file:///D:/COVID/Most%20teaching%20is%20going%20remote.%20Will%20that%20help%20or%20hurt%20online%20learning.html

Poonam & Aggarwal, K. K. (2023). Analysis of the impact of COVID-19 on the stock market and capability of investing strategies. *AIP Conference Proceedings, 2782*. 10.1063/5.0154174

Ramsetty, A., & Adams, C. (2020). Impact of the digital divide in the age of COVID-19. *Journal of the American Medical Informatics Association : JAMIA*, 27(7), 1147–1148. 10.1093/jamia/ocaa07832343813

Soni, V. D. 2020. Global Impact of E-learning during COVID 19. Available at *SSRN* 3630073. 10.2139/ssrn.3630073

Chapter 10
Fostering and Maintaining Student Communities:
Persistence of Business Students Through COVID-19

Jenna Cook
https://orcid.org/0009-0005-9822-0283
Gabelli School of Business, Fordham University, USA

Marisa Villani
Gabelli School of Business, Fordham University, USA

ABSTRACT

The purpose of this mixed-methods study was to understand how the Gabelli School of Business at Fordham University's academic and co-curricular interventions that led to a remote, virtual, and hybrid experience during the period of the COVID-19 Pandemic (March 2020 to May 2022) impacted student academic persistence and experience. Built on the Interpretative Phenomenological Awareness qualitative methodology, this chapter examined how the perceived student experience and student persistence were impacted by the pandemic in four specific areas: academic experience, community and social experience, academic persistence, and academic support resources. Students who were enrolled from May 2020 to March 2023 were invited to participate. The researchers found that enrollment and retention rates were maintained and identified three main takeaways from the qualitative responses: Community and engagement are critical, intentionality in building academic experiences matter, and student support systems need to connect in more meaningful ways to the institution.

DOI: 10.4018/979-8-3693-1507-1.ch010

The Coronavirus Disease of 2019, or COVID-19, pandemic inevitably and unequivocally altered education as a whole. In doing so, it created a platform for innovation to take the forefront in the development of new and engaging educational programs and models. The Gabelli School of Business at Fordham University, a Jesuit university in New York, offers a prime example of how pivoting in a time of need can profoundly impact the establishment of a sense of community among students during an inherently stressful period—the transition from high school to college and beyond. Yukhymenko-Lescroart and Sharma (2023) noted that student attrition, especially among first-year students, has always been a concern for institutions of higher education. The Gabelli School is no different. It prides itself on its rigorous academic curriculum, community-based and innovative learning experiences, and industry connections that assist with career placement for its students. The pandemic strengthened these commitments, but not without reflection on ways to improve itself for its students and the assessment of the effectiveness of existing initiatives.

In March 2020, the United States introduced new laws and regulations in an attempt to stop the spread of the virus, one of which was physical location closures (Fauci et al., 2020). The disease spreads most quickly in densely populated, high-volume areas. New York City, the city that Fordham University calls home, was the first in the nation to face acute and urgent challenges related to the crisis. Fordham often found itself well-prepared, as demonstrated by its response to an early 2000s H1N1 outbreak. However, previous preparation did not offer enough experience and insight into the impact of a global pandemic and how profoundly it would disrupt the core of Fordham's identity—its vibrant, engaged student community.

Though the exploration of educational technology has been a focus and a high-growth area, with domestic investments of over 17 billion dollars in 2019, universal standards on academic delivery or assessment have not been established (El Said, 2021). Innovations were taking shape on campuses across the country. Customer relationship management systems (CRMs) were introduced as tools to support and enhance student engagement. Improved data collection and analysis enabled higher education institutions to focus more precisely on retention and persistence efforts. While community and classroom engagement used to be limited to in-person interactions, communities now benefit from technological advancements that facilitate increased, broad, and meaningful programs and events. Yet, there is hesitancy. Laumer and Eckhardt (2012) state that resistance to technologies occurs due to a perceived inability for the technology to enhance job performance as well as ease of use. Siegel et al. (2017) conducted a research study to determine the effectiveness of the technology acceptance model (TAM) and found that rewards for technological implementation and praise for use were driving factors amongst faculty. However, implementing TAM and rewards systems in higher education take time and changes unfold slowly as resources and buy-in are allowed.

Fostering and Maintaining Student Communities

In March 2020, as the world started to shut down, institutions of higher learning experienced an unprecedented and immediate shift. Institutions were no longer able to conscientiously make slow changes. Students and staff across all education sectors were asked not only to continue learning but also to quickly adapt to remote learning and student support without the possibility of face-to-face interactions. Lane (2007) stated that there is a level of conservatism among professors. This is attributed to the fact that their research, students, and teaching practices are generally under their control. "Because of the long prevailing paradigms in both content and pedagogy, faculty members are often teaching as they were taught, and any challenge to the method may be perceived as challenging the credibility of their own training and their previous teaching efforts" (Lane, 2007, p. 87). Organizational changes can disrupt this dynamic and create instability, fear, and a loss of autonomy for an individual. The pandemic, a sudden catalyst for nationwide change, has created a high level of uncertainty for all stakeholders. Chandler (2013) also recognized that higher education institutions "are steeped in history, with unchanging traditions and members with long tenures" (p. 2).

The pandemic challenged universities to find new ways to connect with their students. A recent study of the most effective change management models indicates five steps to effectively implementing change: (1) Communicate about change; (2) Involve stakeholders; (3) Focus on organizational culture; (4) Consider the organization's mission and vision; and (5) Provide encouragement and incentives for change (Phillips, 2023). Communication, buy-in, and understanding of the mission are critical factors in successful change management. Institute of Electrical and Electronics Engineers (IEEE) recent study on the factors of success and failure in change management indicates that failure occurs when institutions resist change, apply a one-size-fits-all approach, and have a short-term vantage point on change management (Dempsey et al., 2022). During a crisis characterized by high levels of uncertainty and difficulties in communication, positioning an institution in a way that allows them to identify change and apply the five key steps fosters innovation.

The Gabelli School adopted a completely remote modality for its course administration until the fall of 2020. Even though a hybrid modality was adopted in the 2020–2021 academic year, the university found itself more inclined to teach in remote, synchronous settings due to pocket outbreaks and strict exposure mandates imposed by New York State. Community engagement programs and persistent support programs, such as academic advising, adhere to the same rigid guidelines that apply in the classroom setting.

Before the pandemic, engagement and persistent support systems were widely implemented in in-person individual, small, and large group settings. The pandemic severely negatively impacted the Gabelli School's ability to rapidly and meaningfully connect in the successful ways it was accustomed to. Face-to-face conversations shifted to one-sided video calls at times. Large group meetings have transitioned into webinars. Students were no longer able to walk into an office with a quick question. Common in-person student interventions related to academic, professional, and personal growth came to a screeching halt. Yet, as time went on, administrators and faculty navigated this uncharted territory. The disruption spurred a new level of support that allowed the Gabelli School to examine its existing programs, innovate in strategic student support areas, and maintain retention and graduation rates. This study will examine three specific research questions.

Research Questions

1. How did the institution's approach to developing and implementing crisis intervention plans influence students' perceived experiences and academic persistence?
2. How were the students' academic experiences and social/co-curricular experiences impacted by the COVID-19 pandemic?
3. How was student persistence impacted by the COVID-19 pandemic?

Building on the Interpretative Phenomenological Awareness qualitative methodology, this chapter will examine how the perceived student experience and student persistence were impacted by the pandemic in four specific areas: academic experience, community and social experience, academic persistence, and academic support resources.

LITERATURE REVIEW

Student (or academic) persistence refers to the effort, behavior, and motivation that a student displays in college to advance toward degree completion (Tinto, 2017; Villani, 2022). A student demonstrates persistence by advancing in the traditional avenues that lead to course completion, such as turning in assignments, completing exams, and attending class. Additionally, they exhibit persistence by engaging with their campus community, peers, faculty, and administrators. Oftentimes, colleges and universities place an extended focus on retention, which refers to the ability of the institution to maintain student enrollment and prevent student withdrawals (Tinto, 2017). Institutions of higher learning should prioritize supporting students' motivation to persist in college. One way to promote persistence is to increase the programmatic interactions of academic and social experiences within the educational environment. This allows a student to learn deeply and more comprehensively (Tinto, 1997).

For the Gabelli School, traditional avenues and delivery methods of programs and services were at the forefront of day-to-day operations. Additionally, the undergraduate program enrolls almost exclusively traditional students. As defined by Adams and Corbett (2010), traditional college students, like those enrolled in the undergraduate program at the Gabelli School, are people aged 18–22 who attend college immediately after completing high school. Traditional students are typically enrolled in a full-time course load, ranging from 12 to 18 credit hours of study. Courses generally require students to dedicate double the number of credit hours to studying outside the classroom, making the total hours spent on academics equivalent to a full-time job. This is a drastic shift from high school time commitments.

In addition to a more rigorous academic curriculum, students find themselves in a new environment where they may not know anyone. "Mattering" is a feeling that an individual makes a difference and fits in with a community (Rayle & Chung, 2007); Rayle and Chung (2007) specifically noted that first-year traditional students going through a life transition are less likely to feel that they matter compared to their already established upperclassmen. This can lead to feelings of isolation or alienation. Further, the resulting self-consciousness may directly affect students' abilities to perform up to their academic capabilities, resulting in lower academic success and greater academic stress (Sand et al., 2005; Rayle & Chung, 2007, p. 22).

To mitigate these stressors, higher education institutions have developed a multitude of student support programs for both academic and social engagement. Student support programs and academic interventions at the Gabelli School's undergraduate program are based, in part, on Chickering's Student Development Theory. Traditional college-aged students integrate into college by building individual and meaningful relationships with faculty, administrators, and their peers (Chickering, 1981; Chickering & Reisser, 1993; Schelbe et al., 2019). Villani (2022) dissected Tinto's (2017) research, stating that psychosocial and holistic support for students creates a better environment to foster academic persistence among the students broadly and provides intentional opportunities for them to develop into well-rounded individuals. Not all advising is created equal, and there are specific criteria that influence the strength and impact of a successful advising program. White (2015) explained that academic advising is "the single most underestimated characteristic of a successful college experience" (p. 81).

There is a strong connection between advising and retention. This connection is especially significant because the relationships developed within advising can often uncover student dissatisfaction before a student decides to withdraw from a university (Baker & Griffin, 2010; White, 2015). The effectiveness of support programs is crucial, particularly during times of crisis. Generally, programs foster community and academic confidence, while targeted approaches for specific class years and designated populations, such as first-generation college students and transfer students, help support persistence. As shown in Table 1, there are a variety of modern advising programs implemented on college campuses. Habley, in Kuhn (2008), offers an overview of modern advising programs. The models discussed include:

- a faculty-only model with no formal advising office;
- a supplementary model where faculty provide instructional advising in conjunction with an advising office; a split model where professional advisors support undecided/undeclared students while faculty advise declared students;
- a dual model where students receive concurrent advising from faculty and professional advisors; a total intake model where a professional advisor offers support until transitioning to a faculty advisor;
- a satellite model where each division within the institution offers its style of advising;
- and a self-contained model with a centralized advisor office throughout the student's academic experience.

Table 1. Habley's Analysis of Advising Programs

Model	Description
Faculty-only	Relies purely on faculty to serve as academic advisors with no centralized advising office.
Supplementary	Students are paired with faculty advisors and also have access to an advising office that offers advising and student resource support.
Split	Assigns only specific students to advisors within the advising office, such as students enrolled in education opportunity programs, with all students being assigned faculty advisors.
Dual	Students are assigned two advisors; one advisor is a faculty advisor and provides counseling related to the student's academic interest, and the second advisor is often professional staff and advises the student on academic policy and requirements.
Total in-take	A layered approach to advising. Students begin college with professional advisors until a specific academic milestone, at which point the student transitions to a faculty advisor.
Satellite	The advising approach of a university with multiple colleges is part of its system. Within this model, each college or division may take a different approach to academic advising.
Self-contained	Describes an academic counseling approach that keeps advising within a centralized office throughout the college career of the student.

Note. This table details different advising models colleges and universities may use.

Administratively, the Gabelli School follows a professional advising, self-contained model in which each class year is supported by one advising dean. This self-contained approach allows for a hyper-focused academic advising experience (Kuhn, 2008). Each class dean is explicitly responsible for supporting academic persistence for their portfolio of students from one academic year to the next through small and large group advising, periodic check-ins during high-risk times (e.g., add/drops, registration, midterms, and finals), and degree auditing to ensure students are on track to graduate. In addition to class deans who support academic advising based on class year, there is a select group of specialty advisors. This group includes a transfer student-specific advisor and an advisor who supports at-promise students facing various obstacles, such as academic-specific issues and mental health challenges. Specialized advisors can enhance academic support and provide holistic assistance to students due to their unique professional training. Classroom interactions and relationships with faculty are vital to student success. Student success is also significantly affected by an array of overlapping factors both inside and outside the classroom (Young-Jones et al., 2013).

Creating support structures and facilitating student transitions presented challenges before the pandemic but became significantly more difficult at the onset and peak of it. Fruehwirth et al. (2021) acknowledged that even before the pandemic, campuses were reporting increased mental health struggles among their college students, noting a significant rise in reported case percentages. "In a national sample of universities, the rate of mental health treatment increased from 19% to 34% between 2007 and 2017. Among students seeking mental health treatment on campuses, anxiety and depression were the most frequent concerns" (Fruehwirth et al., 2021, p. 1). Some college students relied on attending school in person to receive mental health care from psychological service facilities (Schwartz et al., 2021). By transitioning to an online format with minimal physical interaction, colleges and universities faced challenges in engaging students and had concerns about student persistence.

Villani (2022) explained that academic persistence research places a heavy focus on first-year experiences, including students' academic and social engagement, as well as intentional relationships. There is a need for students to engage with members of the school community, particularly faculty members, so they can feel invested and develop throughout their college career (Tinto, 1997). Anistranski and Brown (2023) noted that students who leave high school relationships behind may undergo emotional challenges when attempting to find a new social circle in college. To mediate this, Anistranski and Brown (2023) explained that social support structures in university settings can increase a student's sense of belonging, thereby increasing their likelihood of persistence. The Gabelli School firmly believes that it has developed a transitional support method that allows students to feel engaged with the community while also creating a safe space for them to develop a sense of belonging.

The overview of the Gabelli School advising program, coupled with its approach to persistence support, demonstrates an environment that is open to change.

METHODOLOGY

Foundationed upon the Interpretative Phenomenological Awareness qualitative methodology, this chapter examined how did the institution's approach to developing and implementing crisis intervention plans influence students' perceived experiences and academic persistence; how students' academic experiences and social/co-curricular experiences were impacted by the COVID-19 pandemic; and how student persistence was impacted by the COVID-19 pandemic. Interpretative Phenomenological Analysis (IPA) was the chosen method for this chapter because IPA is concerned with how study participants examine their lived experiences (Smith & Fieldsend, 2021). The case study method seeks to develop an in-depth understanding of a phenomenon and the contextual conditions related to that phenomenon. It allows for input from multiple levels and stakeholders regarding the same phenomenon, which sets it apart from other qualitative methods (Yin, 2018). The case study method identifies context and themes within a specific and bounded case that offer insight into larger societal issues (Merriam, 1998). This method differs from other qualitative research methods because it involves a holistic analysis specific to a social phenomenon that is bounded in the case (Creswell & Poth, 2018).

IPA also connects with existing research in phenomenology, the study of phenomena, and hermeneutics, a theory of interpretation (Blicharz, 2021). The key areas of IPA are experiences, idiography, and interpretations. Lived experiences encompass particular events that create meaning for a person, which can be interpreted as either important or irrelevant. For Gabelli School students living through the pandemic, there is a shared experience on a surface level, but there are idiographic and interpretative differences that influence student satisfaction and persistence. The researchers identified multiple data sources to ensure rich and robust data are available for analysis. Data sources often include qualitative methods such as interviewing, surveys, document analysis, and field observations (Creswell & Poth, 2018; Merriam, 1998). The case study approach offered the researcher the unique opportunity to conduct comprehensive research to address questions related to complex social phenomena (Yin, 2018). This research study was a single-case study; one institution was studied extensively.

In addition to the qualitative method of IPA, this chapter analyzed publicly available quantitative data from Fordham University. The institutional data included the total number of students who entered The Gabelli School during the research period, second-year retention rates, and demographic and longitudinal enrollment data. The researchers also reviewed COVID-19 pandemic messaging to examine themes and trends in community-wide outreach. It should be noted that the authors of this publication declare there are no competing interests. Additionally, this research received no specific grant from any funding agency in the public, commercial, or

Fostering and Maintaining Student Communities

not-for-profit sectors. Funding for this research was covered by the authors of the chapter.

The Gabelli School Overview

The Gabelli School was chosen as the pool for participants because it offered exceptional insight, thanks to its dual campuses and diverse student body. The Gabelli School is a top 20 high-ranking business school, according to Poets and Quants (2023). The Gabelli School has two primary campuses: Rose Hill in the Bronx, New York, and Lincoln Center in Manhattan. Additionally, it has satellite campuses in Westchester, New York, and London, England. The pandemic impacted campus operations early on in the global crisis, as New York City was the epicenter of the crisis in the United States at the beginning of the outbreak (COVID-19 outbreak, 2020). In 2023, the total undergraduate population was 2,742. It was composed of 60% male-identified students and 40% female-identified students. Fourteen percent of the Rose Hill students are listed as international students, while 22% of the Lincoln Center students are international. The overall first-year retention rate was 93.5%. Popular majors were, and remain, business administration, finance, and public accounting. At the heart of the Gabelli School's efforts to support student persistence is its mission, which is centered on fostering thought generation and innovation. Therefore, the researchers assumed that the mission is reflected in the crisis intervention planning.

Participants and Structure of the Case Study

The researchers identified 3,204 students who graduated from the classes of 2023, 2022, 2021, and 2020. The researchers invited all members—domestic, international, commuter, and resident—of the listed classes to participate. For this study, only students enrolled at the Rose Hill or Lincoln Center campuses were considered. The distinct components of the study supported data triangulation and offered multiple perspectives on data collection.

The 20- to 30-minute survey was created using Google Forms and distributed via email. An invitation to participate in a voluntary, private, and confidential qualitative survey was sent to all enrolled students. As a means of increasing response rates, the researchers conducted a raffle for two $25 Starbucks gift cards among randomly selected participants. These funds were not associated with the Gabelli School of Business. Survey questions were structured based on the following categories: academic experience, community and social experience, academic persistence, academic support resources, and a free-response section. The responses "offer each subject approximately the same stimulus," which allowed for the data to be consistent and more easily comparable (Berg & Lune, 2017, p. 67). Data analysis was conducted across (horizontal) and among (vertical) participants, and the individual answers of each participant were collected to ensure a more meaningful understanding of the breadth and depth of their experiences.

Qualitative Survey Questions

The first set of questions addressed the participants' academic, community, and social experiences before, during, and post-pandemic. The next set of questions asked participants to rate their academic performance before, during, and after the pandemic. Participants were also asked to rate the questions on a scale of one (very little effort) to five (significant effort). The set of final questions in the survey asked participants to rate their satisfaction with the support structures established by the Gabelli School. Participants were asked to rate their experience on a scale from one (not satisfied at all) to five (extremely satisfied).

Institutional Data Analysis

The researchers also analyzed the institutional documents and data available publicly through Fordham University's Office of Institutional Research and the Fordham Forward COVID-19 Response section of the university's website. The reviewed material included longitudinal enrollment trends, Gabelli School retention rates, and previous COVID-19 university-wide messages shared with students and families.

Limitations

Qualitative research has limitations related to researcher bias and validity because of its focus on human behavior and experiences (Creswell & Poth, 2018; Yin, 2018). These concerns are mitigated through the application of the IPA methodology. Additional limitations exist in the breadth of research available through the case study method. To address this challenge, the researchers designed a study that enables comprehensive data collection, allowing for both breadth and depth, which ensures expansive data analysis. Further triangulation occurred through the interpretation of institutional reports and documentation. Researchers used their professional and academic experiences to ensure objective data collection and analysis. The authors of this publication declare that there are no competing interests, and the research was funded by the authors of the article.

FINDINGS

After distributing the survey to 3,204 eligible participants, 31 informed consent forms were returned. Out of those, 10 participants shared their experiences with the researchers. To protect the identities of the participants, each participant was listed alongside a randomly assigned uppercase letter. The survey was divided into five sections: academic experience, community and social experience, academic persistence, academic support resources, and a free-response section. After collecting the responses, the researchers categorized them into two or three common terms that were prevalent across all responses. The researchers also reviewed institutional data that is widely available. Specifically, the researchers analyzed the demographic and enrollment trends of the studied population, retention rates, and university-wide COVID-19 messages. With both sets of data, the researchers determined the answers to the research questions, which are explained below. This section will detail the institutional findings first, followed by the survey response data.

Institutional Data Research Findings

Retention Rates

The Gabelli School of Business maintained its overall enrollment and retention rates throughout the pandemic. The school's overall second-year retention rate increased from 89.4% in 2019 to 90.1% in 2021. In 2019, the retention rate for both campuses was 91%. In 2021, after crisis interventions were implemented for the pandemic, the second-year retention rate increased to 96.4%. The school maintained a somewhat consistent composition of the undergraduate student body, with similar distributions of students coming from a variety of national and international regions.

COVID-19 Messages

All reviewed COVID-19 messages connected to steps in change management theory and consistently focused on four specific themes: safety, health, community, and consistency. These themes were underscored regardless of the message sender. Messages were distributed on a large scale to students, families, and employees by the university president, other executive leaders at the university, and members of the COVID-19 Emergency Task Force (communicating the change). Messages all reinforced the university's desire to remain open and return to normal operations (involve stakeholders). In the March 9, 2020, message to the community, the University President, Joseph McShane, SJ, shared, "I am proud of the work ethic, dedication, and resiliency of the Fordham community, and I assure you we will get through this together." His community-centered messaging (focusing on organization culture) continued throughout the pandemic. In his message to extend remote learning through the remainder of the spring 2020 term, he concluded his message with:

... I must say here that I am deeply impressed by the spirit and dedication of the faculty who seamlessly continued to deliver classes on short notice; by the students who adapted quickly and with enthusiasm to the new model; and by the staff and administrators who continue to carry out the business of the University with dedication and élan, despite the trying circumstances. (McShane, 2020a)

Messages also emphasized the importance of health and safety to protect the community, ensuring its strength. Each message ended with appropriate protocols to remain healthy, and as university testing and reporting protocols developed, the message detailed on-campus resources. Finally, consistency was a direct theme throughout the messages. When possible, messages relied on what students and families could count on as consistent in an ever-changing environment. While messages commonly referenced COVID-19 policy pages and resources for health and academic support, they also included care for the overall well-being, personal, and spiritual aspects, which connects to one of the tenets of Jesuit education *cura personalis,* or "care for the whole person" (organizations missions and vision). The following example from April 2020 demonstrates a focus on care and connection with spirituality:

For those of you who are looking for ways to cope with loss, or to stay connected or reconnect with your spirituality, Campus Ministry has an excellent slate of resources to help you do so, including a virtual prayer wall. (McShane, 2020b)

As the pandemic advanced, the university introduced hybrid operations along with language to encourage the community to approach their engagement in a new way (providing encouragement for change):

We are currently planning our programming, including orientation programs, around in-person and virtual components. Student clubs and organizations are busy planning programs and events for you to engage with your peers, both in person and online. For commuter students: In addition to the library, the Student Involvement areas on each campus are planning for spaces in which commuter students can study and rest between classes and socialize in a safe manner. Our staff members and offices have continued to maintain active virtual meeting schedules with many of our standing committees, student leaders and students. We urge you to continue to remain engaged with us as much as your schedules allow, and to share your feedback with us. Please stay in touch and let us know how we can assist you. (Gray, 2020)

Qualitative Research Findings

Overall, the researchers identified seven key themes among qualitative responses: academic performance, academic support/resources, community, engagement, irregularity, mental health, and motivation. After reviewing the institutional data, researchers identified an increase in second-year retention rates between 2019 (before the onset of the pandemic) and 2021 (when the university transitioned to a hybrid learning model). This will be further discussed along with the quantitative findings for institutional research.

Academic Experience

This section focused on gathering information about the academic student experience before, during, and after the onset of the pandemic. As previously mentioned, the Gabelli School integrates business and liberal arts curricula to create an inclusive learning space for all students to thrive. Implementing collaborative learning opportunities in an ever-changing remote/hybrid learning environment was a challenge, especially when attempting to create collaborative spaces early in the pandemic.

The findings section of this chapter analyzed the prevalent themes by category of survey questions and then compared qualitative themes to themes presented in the institutional data analysis. Table 2 illustrates the themes and common terms associated with the academic experience questions in the survey. Community and student engagement were key priorities and motivators for the participants. Decreased engagement and lack of motivation were most notable during the onset and post-pandemic periods. At the outset of the pandemic, responses indicated that the variability of teaching styles and resources was directly connected to students' level of engagement within their classroom communities. There is a correlation between stability in the classroom and positive community engagement.

Table 2. Academic Experience | Questions and Common Terms

Question	Common Terms	Themes
1. Describe your academic experience prior to March 2020, when Fordham operations were fully in-person.	Challenged Engaged Connected	Community Engagement

continued on following page

Table 2. Continued

Question	Common Terms	Themes
2. How did you engage with academic support resources (such as meeting with your class deans and advisors) prior to the start of the pandemic?	In-person Engaged	Community Engagement
3. Please tell me about your academic experience in March 2020, when Fordham operations moved to fully remote.	Variety of experiences with the professor's ability to navigate technology Low morale/motivation Challenging	Irregularity Motivation
4. How was your personal learning style impacted by the transition to fully remote learning in March 2020?	Lack of accountability More difficult to learn Disconnected	Irregularity Motivation Engagement
5. Please describe how your learning experience changed from March 2020 to August 2020.	Slightly better remote experience Isolated Lack of motivation	Irregularity Motivation
6. How did your engagement with academic support resources change from March 2020 to August 2020?	Decreased use of resources Increased ease of access	Irregularity
7. As the pandemic continued (September 2020 to May 2022), did your learning experience remain consistent or change further?	Increased engagement Increased student expectations Selective motivation	Irregularity Motivation
8. How was your personal learning style impacted by the transition to hybrid (mix of in-person and virtual, synchronous and asynchronous) learning?	Positively impacted Negatively impacted Undefined impact	Irregularity

Note. This table lists the commonly noted phrases for each of the responses from Participants A through J.

Participants shared that their academic experience before March 2020 was filled with engagement, socialization, and connectedness. Participant F noted that while the workload was heavier than they had experienced before, they were more engaged in class because they had to pay attention. When asked how they engaged with academic support resources (such as meeting with class deans), all responses indicated that they met with academic support personnel in person. Participant B wrote, "I used to like visiting the writing center to fix my essays and go to my professors' office [hours]. It was easy to make [an] appointment and visiting the office in-person felt more intimate and effective." Participant G felt that it was "silly" to stay in their apartment when they could walk into Hughes Hall and connect with their deans and classmates.

In response to the shift to remote learning, six out of nine participants stated that one of the most challenging aspects of the transition was the varying levels of their professors' technological proficiency. Participant B shared:

All classes were moved suddenly online, and one of the classes I was taking did not go very well online. Since it was a math class, it was hard for the professor to show the solution for problems and [it] was also extremely hard to focus on class.

Participant C wrote:

Fostering and Maintaining Student Communities

Some of my professors were able to adjust to online school really well. Others did not at all. One of my professors told us just to pass/fail the class, and one was older and had absolutely no idea how to use the technology.

Among the survey responses, a connection was found between the themes of irregularity and community. Responses suggested that irregularities within the classroom or program lead to greater feelings of isolation or a lack of community.

Many participants indicated that there was a lack of motivation, which was another prevalent theme, to continue their studies. Participant H noted that even though it was their final semester, they did not feel engaged with their studies, nor did they feel like they could push themselves to perform at their best. This feeling also permeated the responses to several questions. When asked to reflect on their personal learning styles during the pandemic, three common responses emerged among participants: a lack of accountability in their studies, feeling disconnected from their studies and classroom, and a sense of not learning. Participant A stated that they had to create their own academic check-ins to ensure that they did not fall behind. Participant F expressed similar sentiments, mentioning that they found it challenging to "show up and do lessons without any checks." Participant I admitted, "found it more difficult to stay engaged and motivated, as [they] missed the in-person interactions and the structure of a physical classroom." It is worth noting that Participants E and I acknowledged the advantages of remote learning; however, the unexpected nature of the pandemic made them feel less passionate about their studies.

When asked to reflect on their learning experiences after remote learning settled, participants indicated that there was more consistency, which outweighed any irregularities. Participants A and I noted that their professors seemed to be more adept with virtual learning and were able to integrate technology into the classroom better than at the onset of the pandemic. However, seven out of the 10 participants felt that their learning experience was negatively impacted by the pandemic, even after the learning kinks had been worked out. These respondents noted that they felt isolated from their community and lacked motivation. Participant G mentioned that they were "less likely to go above and beyond given [they were] managing a time difference for [their] classes, and got more easily distracted in virtual classes." Participant H echoed this sentiment, stating that they were not as curious or idea-seeking as they had been when classes were in person. This trend of decreased engagement continued when participants were prompted to discuss their utilization of academic support resources. The responses overwhelmingly stated that the students decreased their use of resources; however, Participant I noted that there was newfound ease of access during the pandemic. Participant I commented:

My engagement with academic support resources during this period shifted to online platforms and virtual meetings with class deans and advisors. I actually found it easier to connect with members of the Dean's office virtually as sometimes it was challenging to go in person due to other commitments.

When asked about engagement levels during and after the pandemic, participants noted that their engagement levels had increased, but their motivation was more variable. Participant C noted that they did not return as the same students they were before the pandemic. They cited a lack of internal motivation as the key issue with this change. However, they also mentioned that having an engaging professor who can blend delivery methods makes them more likely to be engaged. Another notable trend that participants mentioned was the change in course workload and expectations for students. Participant B stated, "I definitely felt that workload for all classes were getting larger and I had to spent [*sic*] double, sometime even triple time just to finish the homework for a certain class."

The last question in the academic experience survey section asked participants to reflect on how their personal learning style was impacted during the transition to a hybrid model. Participants had mixed responses. Participants B, C, F, G, and J felt that hybrid learning was difficult and led to an increase in the workload assigned to students. Participant B felt that they were spending too much time on work outside of the classroom. Participant C expressed similar feelings, stating that they sped up the asynchronous learning videos to finish them faster. Participants A and I, however, felt that their personal learning styles were positively impacted by hybrid work. Participant A shared:

I feel like hybrid has improved my learning style as I sometimes benefit from completing work on my own time vs in-person lectures. Certain classes can be engaging, but others can feel like a waste of time where I do not learn. Therefore, hybrid helps me take advantage of my time and engage with materials that are better suited for learning.

Participant I noted that they appreciated the content created by some of the faculty because it was done with intentionality.

Overall, student responses indicated strong feelings of engagement before the pandemic, a lack of motivation and disconnectedness during the pandemic, and challenges in returning to pre-pandemic levels of motivation during the shift to hybrid learning.

Fostering and Maintaining Student Communities

Community and Social Experience

As mentioned in the literature review, building individual and meaningful relationships is imperative to create a sense of belonging and increase student persistence (Chickering, 1981; Chickering & Reisser, 1993; Schelbe et al., 2019). This section of the survey aimed to gather information on how respondents interacted with each other and the Fordham community before, during, and after the pandemic.

Table 3 demonstrates themes and common terms associated with community and student engagements. Responses in this section aligned with academic experience, and participants indicated that engagement and connectedness were key themes. They reported being engaged and connected with the community before the onset of the pandemic, then experiencing a decrease in engagement and a lack of motivation during and after the pandemic.

Table 3. Community and Social Experience | Questions and Common Terms

Question	Common Terms	Themes
9. Describe your community and social experiences prior to March 2020, when Fordham operations were fully in-person.	Active engagement Active social life	Engagement
10. How did you engage with the Fordham and Gabelli community at the start of the pandemic (March 2020)?	Active/virtual engagement No engagement	Engagement Irregularity
11. Please tell me about your community and social experiences in March 2020, when Fordham operations moved to fully remote.	Awkward No engagement	Engagement Irregularity
12. In what ways did you engage with the Fordham and Gabelli School community from March 2020 to August 2020?	Maintained person engagements Virtual engagement No engagement	Engagement Irregularity
13. In what ways did you engage with the Fordham and Gabelli School community from August 2020- May 2021?	Attended virtual events Used virtual resources	Academic support/ resources
14. In what ways did you engage with the Fordham and Gabelli School community from June 2021- May 2022?	In-person events Virtual events	Engagement
15. Describe the impact the pandemic had on your mental health.	Stress Anxiety Depression	Mental health
16. How did you engage with the Fordham and Gabelli community after May 2022, at the end of the pandemic?	Attended events	Engagement

Note. This table shares engagement types and overall themes students shared when discussing their community as a whole.

When asked to describe their experiences before the pandemic, all 10 responses stated that they were very satisfied with their community and social lives. Participant D stated that it was "nice" to attend a large school and meet new people. Participant H shared that they were involved in clubs, athletics, and various social activities. Participant F noted that although they were not engaged in on-campus activities, they spent time outside of class with their friends in social areas. When describing their engagement with Fordham during the pandemic, six out of the 10 participants stated that they did not engage at all. This is a significant decrease from the levels of engagement that the participants reported having in question nine. Participants shared that they attempted to engage in on-campus activities during virtual learning. However, there were still some respondents who did not engage at all. Participant J stated, "Not much, it was hard to engage with the community with so many clubs and events (like spring weekend and club fairs) shut down due to the pandemic."

Student engagement increased during hybrid learning. Participant J shared that "it was more enjoyable being in the classroom regardless of having to wear masks because we could see our classmates and be able to communicate/form bonds and friend groups like we would have pre-pandemic." Being back on campus, even in a limited capacity, assisted students in creating a new routine and reconnecting with their peers. Participant C credits some of their re-engagement to the honors career placement program, a highly competitive academic and career preparatory program that was initiated by the Personal and Professional Development Office, a business-student-focused career center for Gabelli students. Participant I shared that they enjoyed coming to campus for "smaller, socially distanced in-person events, which helped foster a sense of community while adhering to safety guidelines." Participant G, however, stated that they went to class but did not engage in anything outside of that, even though they noted that they were engaged prior to the start of the pandemic.

Responses for the community and social experience sections of the survey are similar to the responses that participants shared when asked about their mental health. All respondents indicated that their mental health was negatively impacted, and they experienced increases in stress, anxiety, and depression. Participant E shared that they "had a lot of anxiety (experienced [their] first panic attack), and even had to start therapy because [they were] unable to cope." Participants H and I also noted feeling without guidance and isolated from their community. Participant C felt as though they had been stripped of the traditional college experience. They wrote:

I know myself and I know I need in person interaction to stay sane and so just based on my personality I really struggled during that time. I became friends with people at Fordham post pandemic who I later realized were in my classes online and I never knew. I felt like a wasted opportunity to have had friends that I missed out on because of the pandemic.

Participant C noted that once operations were back in person, they tried to remain extremely involved and take on leadership roles to make the most of the time they had left in college. Participants B, E, I, and J did the same. Overall, participants felt that it was difficult to navigate engaging in a community where they were unsure of what the next day would hold. There was also a strong sense of loss evident in the participants' responses. Much like Participant C, it can be noted that all participants felt that they were unable to return to a fully traditional college experience.

Academic Persistence

As stated in the literature review, student persistence is the combination of effort, behavior, and motivation that a student showcases to progress toward degree completion (Tinto, 2017; Villani, 2022). In this section, participants were asked to reflect on and quantify their academic performance before, during, and after the pandemic. The researchers noted a high level of variability in this section's responses, which aligned with the varying student experiences highlighted in the previous two sections. Table 4 presents the questions that participants were asked, along with the common overall response and rating.

An overwhelming majority of participants stated that the grades they received during the pandemic were consistent with the grades they received prior to the pandemic. Two, however, felt that their grades were lower than pre-pandemic grades. Participant B stated that they utilized the pass/fail option for one of their courses. Pass/fail grading means that instead of receiving a letter grade that contributes numerically to the student's Grade Point Average (GPA), they will receive a P (pass) with credit hours or an F (fail). It should be noted that the grade of F will be factored into the student's GPA. Traditionally, the Gabelli School allows students to pass/fail one liberal arts elective per academic year. However, during Spring 2020, the pass/fail option was extended to all courses to accommodate the abrupt transition to remote learning. Participants who believe they will perform well in a course typically do not pass/fail it. Participant A felt that, despite maintaining consistent grades, they struggled to achieve the same level of academic excellence.

When asked if grades equated to the amount of effort put into a course, three participants reported that their grades did not reflect their effort; however, there is variability in why they felt this way. Participant B felt that they put much more effort into studying and classwork, which was not reflected in their final grades. Participant F felt that faculty were more lenient in grading, giving them the opportunity

Fostering and Maintaining Student Communities

to earn higher grades than they would have if they were in-person pre-pandemic. Participant J wrote:

Sometimes - for example, certain classes I feel that the effort put in should have resulted in a lower grade, but for example, in some classes that really challenged me, I feel as though the online format (with online office hours, no in person interaction, etc) attributed to a lesser understanding of the topic and thus a lower grade.

On the other hand, Participant D stated that they used similar study strategies before the pandemic and felt comfortable with their grades. Participant E shared, "There was really nothing else to do but study." Participant I felt that faculty were more understanding of deadlines and were able to work with students more than before the pandemic.

The next four questions asked participants to rate their satisfaction with the support structures established by the Gabelli School. Participants were asked to rate their experience on a scale from one (not satisfied at all) to five (extremely satisfied). Participants were very satisfied (4.2 out of 5) with their academic performance and effort before the pandemic. They were satisfied with their academic performance during (3.3 out of 5) and after (3.1 out of 5) the pandemic. Lastly, they were satisfied (3.5 out of 5) with the Gabelli School of Business's support of their academic persistence from the onset of the pandemic to their graduation/current academic standing.

Table 4. Academic Persistence | Questions and Rating

Question	Rating	Theme(s)
17. Were the grades you received prior to the pandemic consistent with the grades you received during the pandemic?	Eight responded consistent Two responded inconsistently	Irregularity
18. Do you feel that the grades you received during the pandemic reflected the academic effort you applied in your courses?	Five responded that their grades reflected their effort One responded that there was more effort than the grades reflected Four responded that grades did not equal effort	Irregularity
19. Rate your academic performance and effort before the onset of the pandemic (up to March 2020).	Average of 4.2	Academic performance
20. Rate your academic performance and effort during the pandemic (March 2020 to May 2022).	Average of 3.3	Academic performance
21. Rate your academic performance and effort post-pandemic (May 2022 – present).	Average of 3.1	Academic performance

continued on following page

Fostering and Maintaining Student Communities

Table 4. Continued

Question	Rating	Theme(s)
22. Rate overall satisfaction with the Gabelli School of Business support of your academic persistence from the onset of the pandemic to your graduation/current academic standing.	Average of 3.5	Academic performance

Note. This table uses both qualitative and quantitative methods to determine how students felt about their academic performance.

Academic Support Resources

As noted in the summary section, the Gabelli School applies a self-contained advising model where advising deans provide academic support to students. In addition to class deans, the Gabelli School has an academic support coordinator and the Office of Personal and Professional Development for career support. Participants were asked to reflect on which engagement strategies were most effective and what the biggest change they experienced was in these support services.

Table 5. Academic Support Resources | Questions and Common Terms

Question	Common Terms	Theme(s)
23. Through what engagement, programs, and initiatives did you feel supported in your academic experience during your period of remote learning? Why?	Academic advising Faculty office hours Peers	Academic support/ resources
24. How did your engagement with academic support resources change after May 2022, at the end of the named pandemic?	Mixed modalities	Academic support/ resources

Note. This table lists resources that made students feel supported and how they engaged with resources post-pandemic.

Five participants stated that they felt most supported by their class deans. Participants A and C commented that creating availability via Zoom was helpful as it allowed the deans to provide individualized academic support promptly. Participant J noted the integrated learning community (ILC), which was supported by an assistant dean. ILC for Global Business aimed to achieve several goals for incoming transfer students: experiential learning, insight into ethical business practices, and promotion of diversity within the community. Participant J noted that their dean "really tried to go above and beyond for a group of sophomores in order to bring us together and create a support system." During the sophomore year, students engage in an integrated cohort-style learning experience, where the same 35 students take seven business core curriculum courses together throughout the term. Cohort, therefore, refers to the student's academic program for the given semester. Participant B noted that their advising dean created a cohort for international students. They wrote:

For the Fall 2020 semester, which was my first semester for Sophomore year, GSB designed a cohort that would fit into Asian students' time zone. I was really grateful for that - although the workload was still heavy, at least I didn't have to stay up at 4 am every day.

Participants noted that after the pandemic, their engagement with academic support resources remained high, and the respondents appreciated the mixed modalities being offered to them. They could meet with these offices either virtually or in person. Participant A noted that while they favored online meetings for basic interactions, they preferred attending career-specific events in person. This connects back to one of the common phrases mentioned in Table 2: selective motivation. Overall, responses supported the quantitative ratings of support services; participants were satisfied with the levels of support they received from academic support resources before, during, and after the pandemic.

External Support Systems

Though understanding on-campus support and resources is imperative, the researchers wanted to gauge the level and types of support students received from outside the campus community. The common categories noted as support systems include family and friends. While advising deans is recognized as part of the campus community, multiple respondents also identified advising deans as part of their external support community. Participant B stated that their roommate invited them to live with the roommate's family so that Participant B could finish their degree before having to return to their home country. Participant E stated that they had "a lot of external support" through their family, therapist, neurologist, and friends.

Some participants shared that they struggled to stay connected to their support system due to their living situations and pandemic regulations. Participant J stated that their family lived far away from them, but they were able to talk often. Participant J also noted that it was difficult to maintain friendships because, even though they lived on the same campus, COVID-19 protocols restricted them from visiting each other's rooms. Additionally, it was challenging to meet outside during the colder months.

When asked if they felt any pressure from their support system to change their academic trajectory, an overwhelming majority of participants responded no. Participant J, however, stated that they felt pressure from their support system to change their minor since Participant J was unhappy with the academic curriculum.

Fostering and Maintaining Student Communities

Participant J felt that they needed a more hands-on learning experience that would provide opportunities to work closely with others. Their support system encouraged them to prioritize their needs.

Table 6. External Support Systems | Questions and Responses

Question	Common Terms	Theme(s)
25. Describe the external support systems, if any, that you had during the pandemic (family, friends, peers, etc.).	Family Friends Deans	Community
26. Was there a time in which you felt pressure from your support system to change your academic trajectory in any way (degree switch, career change, educational pause, continuing studying, etc.)?	Nine responded, "no" One responded, "yes"	Community
27. Has the pandemic changed your relationship with your support system? If so, please explain.	Two responded that relationships grew more meaningful Seven responded no changes occurred	Community
28. Describe the impact that your support system had on your academic performance.	Academic Support Mental Health Support	Community Academic support/ resources

Note. This table demonstrates no significant changes in support systems for the participants.

Table 6 shows that when asked about changes in their relationships with support systems, the majority of participants stated that they had no significant changes in the relationships they had with their group. Two respondents stated that the meaningfulness of their relationships increased. Participant I attribute this change to their ability to connect virtually and their reliance on virtual communication. Participant I also noted that "their [the support system] encouragement and emotional support helped [them] stay motivated and focused. They [the support system] provided a sense of stability and understanding during a period of uncertainty."

Free Response

Two participants shared additional information in the free-response section. Participant D noted that they were transfer students and only had one semester to experience Fordham pre-pandemic. They felt a sense of regret for not being able to experience what it would have been like to be a traditional college student. Participant E expressed a desire for reduced education costs, citing unfulfilled experiences. However, they appreciated Fordham's efforts to foster a sense of community during challenging times.

DISCUSSION

The researchers identified three key takeaways from the study: community and engagement are critical, especially in times of crisis; intentionality in building academic experiences matters; and student support systems need to connect in more meaningful ways to the institution.

Crisis Planning

At the Gabelli School of Business, crisis intervention planning supported both the perceived student experiences and the student's academic persistence. The themes identified from both qualitative research and institutional data analysis indicate that community and engagement are the underpinnings of the student experience at the Gabelli School of Business. More specifically, during times of crisis, community becomes even more important to both students and the institution as a whole. Therefore, at institutions of higher learning, more time and effort must be devoted to understanding how to develop a community. In times of crisis, resources (personnel, financial, and others) need to be allocated to ensure intentional community building to support academic interventions. After the immediate impact of the pandemic and the abrupt transition into a remote learning environment, participants experienced a sense of community in more meaningful ways through class dean engagement, co-curricular experiences, and clubs and events. Even in a hybrid and highly regulated environment with masks and testing required, community development had a significant impact on students. It supported better academic performance and mental health. Community and student engagement are some of the most significant factors in supporting consistency in times of crisis.

Academic and Social/Co-Curricular Experiences

At the onset of the pandemic, the student's academic and co-curricular experiences were negative. These experiences permeated students' academic performance and overall well-being. As the pandemic continued, the experiences became more positive, likely due to the increase in expertise in developing appropriate crisis interventions. Intentionality in building academic experiences is crucial. After the initial shock of the shift to online learning subsided, students started to benefit from creative responses to creating collaborative learning environments. This was specifically noted in the development of international cohorts to support students living abroad during the university's hybrid learning period. Faculty members have also been better equipped to support students in fully virtual and hybrid classroom settings. The researchers also discovered that a hybrid system to implement academic resources and provide advice was well-received by students. There are instances where students prefer virtual engagements with deans and advisors because it helps them manage their time for assignments, co-curricular activities, and internships.

Support Systems

Students' support systems are critical. Students shared that they were grateful that their relationships with their support systems did not drastically change during the pandemic. Outside of the regular pandemic messages to families, there were no intentional interactions between the Gabelli School and support systems. In times of crisis, the institution should seek to create pathways to connect with other members of the students' support systems. If support systems had access to information about student academic and mental health resources, students may be more encouraged to take advantage of these opportunities. In addition, it can provide better, more detailed insight into specific students' needs for deans and other advisors at the institution.

Continued Initiatives

Gabelli School Initiatives: Virtual Support

As previously mentioned, support programs for the Gabelli School were primarily conducted in person. This meant that students had to ensure they carved out time in their day to meet with a multitude of offices at both the academic and student engagement levels. With the ability for students to engage from anywhere, Zoom remained a viable option for students and staff alike. Students can schedule appointments with their advising dean and choose the modality. With hybrid work in effect, staff can change their availability to meet with students via Zoom. Staff meetings for deans and advisors are conducted via Zoom to ensure that all employees are present and engaged. Additionally, the Gabelli School can host events with partners who would not have been able to travel to the campus otherwise. Virtual support has ultimately become an integral part of the overall student experience due to its ease of access and will remain a staple in student support moving forward.

Gabelli School Initiatives: Incoming Freshman Advice

The Gabelli School's First-Year Advising Mentors (FAM) are exceptional upper-class students currently studying at the Gabelli School. FAM are leaders and role models for incoming first-years, helping new students navigate all aspects of their first year at Fordham. They are advised, trained, and supported by the first-year class dean. The program is structured so that one FAM is assigned a partner, and together, they mentor between 12 and 18 first-year students. FAM engages with their first-year mentees in many ways, including through leading orientation sessions, small group sessions, panels, and conducting one-on-one meetings throughout the year. FAM is responsible for communicating with their first-year mentees well before the academic year begins to answer any questions they may have before starting school in the fall. FAM is actively engaged in the Fordham community. FAM also builds on their own experiences and uses them to advise first-year students on how to succeed.

Like many of the Gabelli School's persistence programs, FAM met with their students primarily in person. When the pandemic suspended all in-person activities, the Gabelli School had to be creative in delivering meaningful content to its students in a digital space. Additionally, the first-year dean, who led the program, had to be especially considerate of the mental health and academic performance of the mentors. Like their mentees, the mentors were undergoing an entirely new educational experience.

Immediately after the onset of the pandemic, FAM engaged with the first-year dean in technology training, virtual engagement strategy sessions, and regular virtual personal check-ins. There was a sense of constant learning, growing, and connecting despite the physical distance that existed. As the early months of the pandemic passed, the program expanded through an innovative response to remote learning. The FAM program and first-year onboarding were strengthened by the GABELLI SMART program. The GABELLI SMART program was created in the spring of 2020 during the pandemic era when students, faculty, and staff were required to stay at home. During the program, a series of summer engagement and community-building events took place synchronously as first-year students awaited the start of their college experience. In addition, asynchronous materials were created to guide students in learning about policies and procedures, such as registration and academic integrity. In 2023, the FAM program delivered its support, mentoring, and resources through a variety of modalities that work best for the incoming students and the FAM.

One lesson learned from the pandemic, demonstrated in the new approach to first-year advising, is the desire to innovate regularly. This innovation and creativity are spurred by a variety of community members, including the first-year dean, the student leadership engaged in the program, and the students who participate in the program. Maintaining an open mindset and adopting a flexible approach to advising over 550 students is not always easy, but it is worth the challenges, especially when it comes to promoting increased engagement and support.

REFERENCES

Adams, J., & Corbett, A. (2010). Experiences of traditional and non-traditional college students. *Perspectives*, 2(1), 2.

Anistranski, J. A., & Brown, B. B. (2023). A little help from their friends? How social factors relate to students' sense of belonging at a large public university. *Journal of College Student Retention*, 25(2), 305–325. 10.1177/1521025120985107

Baker, V. L., & Griffin, K. A. (2010). Beyond mentoring and advising toward understanding the role of faculty 'developers' in student success. *About Campus: Enriching the Student Learning Experience*, 14(6), 2–8. 10.1002/abc.20002

Berg, B. L., & Lune, H. (2017). *Qualitative research methods for social sciences* (9th ed.). Pearson Education Limited.

Blicharz, J. (2021). *The perceptions of English language learners on their level of preparedness to complete college courses taught in English: An interpretative phenomenological analysis drawing upon culturally responsive pedagogy* [Doctoral dissertation, Saint John's University]. Theses and Dissertations. https://scholar.stjohns.edu/theses_dissertations/318

Chandler, N. (2013). Braced for turbulence: Understanding and managing resistance to change in the higher education sector. *Management*, 3(5), 243–251.

Chickering, A. (1981). *The modern American college: Responding to the new realities of diverse students and changing society*. Jossey-Bass, Inc.

Chickering, A., & Reisser, L. (1993). *Education and identity* (2nd ed.). Jossey-Bass, Inc.

Creswell, J., & Poth, C. N. (2018). *Qualitative inquiry and research design: Choosing among five traditions* (4th ed.). Sage Publications.

Dempsey, M., Geitner, L., Brennan, A., & McAvoy, J. (2022). A review of the success and failure factors for Change Management. *IEEE Engineering Management Review*, 50(1), 85–93. 10.1109/EMR.2021.3130989

El Said, G. R. (2021). How did the COVID-19 pandemic affect higher education learning experience? An empirical investigation of learners' academic performance at a university in a developing country. *Advances in Human-Computer Interaction*, 2021, 1–10. 10.1155/2021/6649524

Fauci, A. S., Lane, H. C., & Redfield, R. R. (2020). COVID-19—Navigating the uncharted. *The New England Journal of Medicine*, 382(13), 1268–1269. 10.1056/NEJMe200238732109011

Fruehwirth, J. C., Biswas, S., & Perreira, K. M. (2021). The COVID-19 pandemic and mental health of first-year college students: Examining the effect of COVID-19 stressors using longitudinal data. *PLoS One*, 16(3), e0247999. 10.1371/journal.pone.024799933667243

Gray, J. (2020, July 21). *Fordham fall opening plans and campus life update*. Fordham News. https://news.fordham.edu/university-news/fordham-fall-opening-plans-and-campus-life-update/

Kuhn, T. L. (2008). Historical foundations of academic advising. In Gordon, V. N., Habley, W. R., & Grites, T. J. (Eds.), *Academic advising: A comprehensive handbook* (pp. 3–16). Jossey-Bass.

Lane, I. F. (2007). Change in higher education: Understanding and responding to individual and organizational resistance. *Journal of Veterinary Medical Education*, 34(2), 85–92. 10.3138/jvme.34.2.8517446632

Laumer, S., & Eckhardt, A. (2012). Why do people reject technologies: A review of user resistance theories. *Information Systems Theory: Explaining and Predicting Our Digital Society*, 1, 63–86. 10.1007/978-1-4419-6108-2_4

McShane, J. (2020a, March 13). *University operations. Fordham forward*. Fordham News. https://news.fordham.edu/university-news/university-operations-update-march-13-2020-8-p-m/

McShane, J. (2020b, April 24). *University COVID-19 update*. Fordham News. https://news.fordham.edu/university-news/university-COVID-19-update-friday-april-24-2020/

Merriam, S. (1998). *Qualitative research and case study applications in education*. Jossey-Bass Publishers.

Phillips, J., & Klein, J. D. (2023). Change Management: From Theory to Practice. *TechTrends*, 67(1), 189–197. https://link.springer.com/article/10.1007/s11528-022-00775-0#citeas. 10.1007/s11528-022-00775-036105238

Rayle, A. D., & Chung, K.-Y. (2007). Revisiting first-year college students' mattering: Social support, academic stress, and the mattering experience. *Journal of College Student Retention*, 9(1), 21–37. 10.2190/X126-5606-4G36-8132

Schelbe, L., Becker, M. S., Spinelli, C., & McCray, D. (2019). First-generation college students' perceptions of an academic retention program. *The Journal of Scholarship of Teaching and Learning*, 19(5), 61–76. 10.14434/josotl.v19i5.24300

Schwartz, K. D., Exner-Cortens, D., McMorris, C. A., Makarenko, E., Arnold, P., Van Bavel, M., Williams, S., & Canfield, R. (2021). COVID-19 and student well-being: Stress and mental health during return-to-school. *Canadian Journal of School Psychology*, 36(2), 166–185. 10.1177/0829573521100165334040284

Siegel, D., Acharya, P., & Sivo, S. (2017). Extending the technology acceptance model to improve usage & decrease resistance toward a new technology by faculty in higher education. *The Journal of Technology Studies*, 43(2), 58–69. 10.21061/jots.v43i2.a.1

Smith, J. A., & Fieldsend, M. (2021). Interpretative phenomenological analysis. In Camic, P. M. (Ed.), *Qualitative research in psychology: Expanding perspectives in methodology and design* (2nd ed., pp. 147–166). American Psychological Association. 10.1037/0000252-008

Thompson, C. N., Baumgartner, J., Pichardo, C., Toro, B., Li, L., Arciuolo, R., Chan, P. Y., Chen, J., Culp, G., Davidson, A., Devinney, K., Dorsinville, A., Eddy, M., English, M., Fireteanu, A. M., Graf, L., Geevarughese, A., Greene, S. K., Guerra, K., & Fine, A. (2020). COVID-19 outbreak — New York city, February 29–June 1, 2020. *MMWR. Morbidity and Mortality Weekly Report*, 69(46), 1725–1729. 10.15585/mmwr.mm6946a233211680

Tinto, V. (1997). Classrooms as communities: Exploring the educational character of student persistence. *The Journal of Higher Education*, 68(6), 599–623. 10.1080/00221546.1997.11779003

Tinto, V. (2017). Reflections on student persistence. *Student Success*, 8(2), 1–8. 10.5204/ssj.v8i2.376

Villani, M. T. (2022). *First things first: Mission, relevancy and supporting persistence of first-generation college students* (Publication No. AAI28970073) [Doctoral dissertation, Fordham University]. ETD Collection for Fordham University. https://research.library.fordham.edu/dissertations/AAI28970073

Yin, R. K. (2018). *Case study research and applications* (Vol. 6). Sage.

Young-Jones, A. D., Burt, T. D., Dixon, S., & Hawthorne, M. J. (2013). Academic advising: Does it really impact student success? *Quality Assurance in Education*, 21(1), 7–19. 10.1108/09684881311293034

Yukhymenko-Lescroart, M. A., & Sharma, G. (2023). Sense of purpose and progress towards degree in freshman college students. *Journal of College Student Retention*, 25(1), 187–207. 10.1177/1521025120975134

KEY TERMS AND DEFINITIONS

Academic Advising: Formal insight and guidance for students directly related to academic program planning: major and minor selection; professional coaching; connecting curricular, personal, and/or co-curricular opportunities; and seeking counsel on financial, social, and personal matters (Villani, 2022).

Academic Advising Programs: Professional and faculty-based models that offer academic counseling, including one-on-one meetings, support for course and major selection, and resource connections to other units within the university setting (Villani, 2022).

Asynchronous Learning: Formal learning that takes place individually and not always at the same time among a group of learners and instructor, whether in an in-person, virtual, or hybrid setting.

Retention: Refers to a college or university's ability to keep students enrolled and prevent student withdrawal from the institution (Tinto, 2017).

Support Systems: A community of individuals and groups that provide personal and moral support for an individual.

Student Persistence: Student (or academic) persistence is the effort, behavior, and motivation that a student displays in college to make progress toward degree completion (Tinto, 2017; Villani, 2022).

Student Success: A term used in higher education that describes a student's academic achievement within their college career, namely, deriving purposeful and satisfactory educational progress that demonstrates academic growth and skill-based development and is a product of on-going academic persistence (Villani, 2022).

Student Support Programs: Programs developed and implemented by an institution to offer academic and persistence support for enrolled students.

Synchronous Learning: Formal learning that takes place among a group of learners and
   instructor in real-time: whether in an in-person, virtual, or hybrid setting.

Traditional College Students: As defined by Adams and Corbett (2010), traditional college students, like those who are enrolled in the undergraduate program at the Gabelli School, are people ages 18–22 who attend college immediately after high school.

Fostering and Maintaining Student Communities

Transfer Students: Students who started their college career at a separate institution and transferred to their current institution with earned credits. At many institutions, transfer students do not engage in the same onboarding as a student who begins college and remains at the same institution.

Chapter 11
Relationship Between Student Involvement, Leadership, and Belonging Before and During the Pandemic:
Points of Comparison and Differentiation

Dayna S. Weintraub
https://orcid.org/0000-0002-0399-2952
Rutgers University, New Brunswick, USA

Ralph A. Gigliotti
Rutgers University, New Brunswick, USA

Tori Glascock
Rutgers University, New Brunswick, USA

Gregory Dyer
Rutgers University, New Brunswick, USA

Salvador B. Mena
Rutgers University, New Brunswick, USA

ABSTRACT

The COVID-19 pandemic dramatically changed the college experience; however, it

DOI: 10.4018/979-8-3693-1507-1.ch011

Copyright © 2024, IGI Global. Copying or distributing in print or electronic forms without written permission of IGI Global is prohibited.

also provided an opportunity to engage with and support students differently. The COVID-19 pandemic dramatically changed the college experience; however, it also provided an opportunity to engage with and support students differently. Participation and leadership in college organizations at many institutions has traditionally been an in-person experience; however, during the first two years of the pandemic, this practice shifted to a fully or partially remote setting for many colleges and universities. This chapter compares two years of data from the Multi-Institutional Study of Leadership (MSL) in 2018 and 2021 and explores the pandemic's effect on the relationship between student involvement and leadership experiences and feelings of belonging. Results show slight declines in involvement and leadership experiences and decreased feelings of belonging during the pandemic. The chapter concludes with crucial questions for leaders in education to consider regarding the cultivation of student involvement and leadership in the aftermath of the pandemic.

THE COVID-19 PANDEMIC

The impact of the COVID-19 pandemic has been felt across organizations, sectors, and communities around the world. Within higher education, much has been written about the sudden shift to a fully online teaching and learning environment (Gigliotti, 2020; 2021; Khalil et al., 2020; Major, 2020; Ntsiful et al., 2022; Ramlo, 2021); the impact on student experiences and expectations (Aucejo et al., 2020); the disproportionate effect on students' health behavior, mental health, and emotional well-being (Reuter et al., 2021); and the potential long-term implications that the pandemic might have on a wide array of issues, including the future of work (Broady et al., 2020), online learning (Lockee, 2021), international education (Firang, 2020; Mok et al., 2021), and leadership education (Thwaite, 2022; Whitaker & Kniffin, 2022). Another important area of focus, yet one that has not been as widely explored to date in the scholarly literature, centers on the impact of COVID-19 on undergraduate student involvement and feelings of belonging, along with strategies that leaders in education might draw upon to help cultivate student belonging in a post-pandemic environment. This chapter examines the impact of the pandemic on student involvement, their experiences in pursuing student leadership opportunities, and their sense of belonging within the context of a large, research-intensive university with significant racial and economic diversity.

Cultivating Sense of Belonging on a College Campus

As we take a closer look at the undergraduate student experience and investigate the reverberations caused by the COVID-19 pandemic, the growing body of pandemic-related research highlights the short- and long-term impacts of the public health crisis on this population. Of the many outcome variables for undergraduate students that were impacted by COVID-19, college students' sense of belonging is an instrumental component of the undergraduate student experience. Sense of belonging is a universal desire and need to feel connected to the college and university community and an acknowledgement that one matters (Strayhorn, 2019).

In the higher education setting, sense of belonging is related to academic progress, academic achievement, and social acceptance (Freeman et al., 2007; Walton & Coben, 2007). Museus et al. (2017) affirm sense of belonging is related to academic progress, academic achievement, and social acceptance (citing Freeman et al., 2007 among others), suggesting that elements of the campus environment (i.e., environments that are relevant, familiar, and meaningful to students' cultural backgrounds and identities) are important indicators associated with sense of belonging. The Culturally Engaging Campus Environments (CECE) model of college success is a useful framework for explaining the connections between institutional environments, student success, and outcomes such as academic progress, academic achievement, and social acceptance. Involvement in clubs and organizations and participation in extracurricular and co-curricular programs, all of which experienced individuals survive, adapt, develop, and grow in a community setting (Hagerty et al., 1996; Strayhorn, 2019). Sense of belonging is of unique interest to the college setting because care, support, and validation in a community promote students' academic motivation, retention (Pedler et al., 2022), and overall well-being (Suhlmann et al., 2018). Furthermore, studies have validated decreases in sense of belonging, especially for racial-ethnic minorities (Barringer et al., 2022).

Active engagement in higher education allows students to develop a stronger sense of connection to the community and allows individuals to benefit from the support, care, and mentorship of others. For many colleges and universities, connection to community has been traditionally cultivated through meaningful in-person experiences. However, the pandemic and the resulting shift to a fully or partially remote environment provided a unique context for considering the impact on students' sense of belonging and the implications for a post-pandemic future.

The COVID-19 pandemic created voids in students' experiences and forced students to find alternate ways to connect with peers and others throughout the broader community. While research has acknowledged the impact of the pandemic on sense of belonging on campus (Potts, 2021), a deeper understanding of differences in student involvement and engagement in leadership opportunities raises important questions and implications for supporting students in the aftermath of the pandemic. In addition to the impact of sense of belonging on increased motivation and academic progress, one's sense of belonging also acts as a key protective factor for issues related to social isolation, anxiety, and depression among college students (Gopalan et al., 2022). Improving understanding of what impacts sense of belonging among college students can help to enable university administrators to provide a fulfilling experience that supports students more holistically.

Moving Forward

The reverberations of the COVID-19 pandemic will be felt across colleges and universities for years to come. Cultivating sense of belonging in a post-pandemic environment presents a unique opportunity to rethink which aspects of student involvement and leadership development are most critical, necessary, or advantageous—and to explore how to encourage student involvement and student leadership across in-person, hybrid, and virtual learning environments.

Variables that Impact Sense of Belonging

Several variables have the potential to impact sense of belonging. For example, one common approach to cultivating sense of belonging is through participation in on-campus engagement opportunities and work-study programs that provide paths for student involvement. As Holloway-Friesen (2018) found in their content analysis, commuter students who participated in campus employment opportunities reported an increased sense of belonging. A part-time job program for Latino students at the University of Texas-Brownsville was found to have a measurable impact on student degree completion (Stern, 2014).

College student leadership development can occur through participation in formal and informal programs and through engagement in leadership opportunities within student-led clubs and organizations. Participation in leadership education programs, paired with an activity that allows for the practice of newly acquired leadership skills, can lead to higher levels of socially responsible leadership among students (Martinez et al., 2020), and Dugan et al. (2012) found unique predictors of socially responsible leadership when disaggregating their analysis by race. Leadership education program participation also aids in the development of social perspective taking (Hemer et al., 2019). Social perspective taking (SPT) fosters empathy and understanding of others' thoughts and emotions, aligning with principles of self-awareness and relationship skills. Research indicates that social perspective taking is the process of infusing individual leadership values into group leadership values, emphasizing its role in promoting socially responsible leadership across various domains (Dugan, Bohle, & Woelker, 2019). Berger & Milem (1999) found that early peer involvement strengthens perceptions of institutional and social support. Students who have access to leadership opportunities are more likely to be highly involved on campus and feel a part of the community, while also gaining competence and self-efficacy (Young et al., 2019). Kodoma & Dugan (2013) found that holding formal leadership positions in university recognized organizations is an important way for Latino and multiracial students to develop leadership efficacy; and participating with leadership efficacy for African American, Asian American, and multiracial students. First-generation college students are less likely to hold formal leadership positions (Soria et al., 2014). On the contrary, early non-involvement results in students being less likely to perceive the institution or peers as supportive, ultimately leading to less integration and sense of belonging. Early involvement and methods like community service, exposure to diverse viewpoints, and intentional leadership training, are all examples of methods that can enhance social perspective taking, promoting individual and group leadership values and improving students' capacities for citizenship and effective leadership.

Connecting the learning in the classroom to life outside of academics can also enhance students' sense of belonging. For example, engagement in instructor-led group fitness or exercise classes, intramural sports, open recreation, outdoor adventure activities and/or trips, and sports clubs led to students feeling more connected to their institution (Soria et al, 2022). Additionally, high-impact practices such as participation in learning communities contributed to a greater sense of belonging in college (Ribera et al., 2017). These engagements require a great deal of time and effort, making them more potent experiences for students, and leading to meaningful interactions with people from diverse backgrounds. Peer and professional mentoring relationships can also increase sense of belonging for students (Liu et al, 2022; Holloway-Friesen, 2021; Apriceno et al, 2020). Students who engage in discussions that challenge their religious and political views develop a deeper awareness of their worldview and identities, while also building connections with students who hold different global perspectives, which can be attributed to a greater sense of belonging (Correia-Harker et al., 2019).

Demographic variables have also been found to impact student feelings of belonging during their time on campus. Duran et al. (2020) found differences in the relationship between cocurricular engagement and sense of belonging by race and generation status. In particular, Museus & Saelua (2017) emphasize the importance of affirming and culturally engaging environments to mitigate racial and economic differences in students' sense of belonging. First-generation college students confront additional challenges that involve family, cultural, social, and academic transitions that can lead to feeling less connected with their campus and lower feelings of belonging (Hsiao, 1992). First-generation college students who perceive their campus as having greater common ground, relevant learning opportunities, and collectivist orientations report a higher sense of belonging (Museus & Chang, 2021). Gillen-O'Neel, C. (2021) also found sense of belonging affected daily motivation and engagement for first-generation students. Race is also an important factor in students' sense of belonging, with African American and Black students reporting that environments that welcome cultural values and help affirm racial identity culminate in higher levels of sense of belonging (Hunter, Case, Harvey., 2019). Rosch et al. (2015) found Asian American students had lower motivations to lead, making the case for future studies to explore racial differences in how students engage and participate in leadership experiences.

Pre- and Post-Pandemic

Prior to the start of the pandemic, a sense of belonging was fostered through engagement in both academics and extracurricular activities. Clubs and student organization meetings provided spaces, typically in-person, for students to meet other individuals with similar interests. On-campus employment opportunities were available to students and provided a source of connection with the institution and financial support to students. Leadership development opportunities were available through student organizations and leadership education programming. Living learning communities enabled students to develop smaller communal groups in residential spaces, and study abroad experiences allowed students to engage in meaningful interactions with people from diverse backgrounds.

During the COVID-19 pandemic, on-campus student employment opportunities were limited, and many positions were eliminated due to a lack of work and budgetary constraints. While working on campus is traditionally a strong predictor for having a sense of belonging in previous research (Stern, 2014; Holloway-Friesen, 2018), this measure was not included in this study given that it was not applicable during the university's shift to remote instruction. Leadership development in student organizations continued in this virtual space; however, those engaged in such opportunities experienced challenges in adapting to technologies and ways of virtual engagement that were new to many students and university personnel. . When Rutgers University–New Brunswick closed most of their residence halls for the 2020-2021 academic year, learning communities pivoted to a virtual space for programming, but found that student engagement was minimal, and the different community populations decreased (A. Leget\, personal communication, October 26, 2023). Other experiences, which are primary forms of involvement and contributors to forming relationships and community for students, including study abroad experiences, were put on hold due to COVID-19 travel restrictions.

As the world returns to a sense of normalcy, some of these variables have remained at the pandemic level and others have returned to pre-COVID standards. Student organizations often meet both in-person and virtually, allowing for increased accessibility, such as for commuter students who may not be able to drive back to campus for evening meetings or students who are juggling other commitments that require them to engage in activities away from the physical campus . Although learning communities were once again available as students returned to an in-person learning environment, enrollment in living-learning communities continues to lag behind pre-pandemic levels focused on identities and shared cultural experiences are returning to their pre-pandemic numbers faster than the academic major-focused communities. Finally, study abroad experiences for students have reopened as travel restrictions were lifted.

METHOD

Site

Home to over 35,000 undergraduate students across its 12 schools and colleges, Rutgers University–New Brunswick is the flagship location for Rutgers, The State University of New Jersey. Like most other colleges and universities across the country, Rutgers University–New Brunswick was forced to adapt quickly in response to the public health crisis. The densely populated New York metro area was one of the initial sites with extensive spread of the virus. New Jersey Governor Phil Murphy issued executive order 104 on March 16, 2020, limiting gatherings to 50 individuals, closing non-essential businesses and schools, and suspending in-person instruction at higher education institutions within the state beginning March 18. In addition to staying online for the remainder of the 2020-2021 academic year, the university's telecommuting and virtual learning policy was extended throughout the 2021-2022 academic year amid the continuing pandemic.

A random sample of 4,000 undergraduate students at Rutgers University–New Brunswick was invited to complete the Multi-Institutional Study of Leadership (MSL) in 2018 and a separate sample was invited to complete the survey in 2021. The responses from these two samples—collected at two distinct points in time prior to and during the pandemic—provide comparative data for understanding potential shifts in student leadership perceptions during a period of profound disruption. The MSL is an international research program focused on understanding the influences of higher education in shaping socially responsible leadership capacity and other leadership related outcomes (e.g., efficacy, cognitive skills, resiliency) (Multi-Institutional Study of Leadership, n.d.). The validated tool allows for an examination of student leadership values at institutional and national levels with specific attention placed on campus experience factors that influence leadership development among college students (Multi-Institutional Study of Leadership, n.d.).

This chapter describes college students' perceptions of and experiences in formal leadership positions from 2018 and 2021 and any noticeable shifts in the responses that may be partially attributed to the COVID-19 pandemic and the abrupt shift to a fully online teaching and learning design. Building upon the existing literature regarding student leadership development and the impact of COVID-19 on the undergraduate student experience, and drawing upon the comparative MSL data from two points in time, this chapter explores the following research questions:

- To what extent did the experiences of COVID-19 impact the relationship between undergraduate student involvement and leadership experiences and sense of belonging?
- Do race and status as first-generation college student have a differential impact on the relationship between involvement and leadership experiences and sense of belonging?

Data Source

The MSL is a comprehensive survey measuring the leadership development of undergraduate students. Developed by researchers at the University of Maryland, the instrument is guided by Astin's (1993a, 1993b, 2011) "input-environment-output" (I-E-O) college impact model (Astin, 1993a, 1993b; Astin & Antonio, 2012) and the Social Change Model of Leadership Development (HERI, 1996). Since its first administration in 2006, the survey has expanded its theoretical framework to include more contemporary leadership concepts and research based in social psychology, human development, and principles of social justice (Multi-Institutional Study of Leadership, n.d.). For example, Durgan et al. (2008) used the social change model to study socially responsible leadership and concluded that African American and Black students scored higher on Consciousness of Self, Controversy with Civility, Citizenship, and Change. This is consistent with literature that talks about holding formal leadership positions as a way of contributing to society through advocacy. In 2022, the MSL changed its leadership structure and is now a collaboration between the following three distinct organizations: The Aspen Institute, SoundRocket, and Marquette University, and includes a research team of accomplished scholars in higher education. The instrument is administered annually to a comprehensive set of internationally represented colleges and universities ranging in institutional type and size and numerous studies are published on its findings. Recent studies that utilize the MSL instrument include research by Correi-Harker & Dugan (2020); Johnson & McClure (2022); Lewis (2020); Leupold, Lipina & Skloot (2020); Martinez et al. (2020); Soria et al. (2019); and Soria et al. (2022). Participating institutions receive a report of their survey findings, which are used to evaluate how a single institution's results compare to peer institutions and to inform the development and improvement of curricular and co-curricular programs related to leadership development.

The theoretical framework of the MSL is organized around the Social Change Model of Leadership Development (HERI, 1996). This model highlights seven dimensions or values—consciousness of self, congruence, commitment, common purpose, controversy with civility, collaboration, and citizenship—all of which are manifested in and work together to accomplish change. The MSL also reflects I-E-O (Inputs-Environment-Outcomes) College Impact Model (Astin, 1993a, 1993b; Astin & Antonio, 2012), with a focus on inputs, such as students' pre-college characteristics (e.g., demographics, high school achievement); the programs, experiences, relationships, and other factors found in one's collegiate environment (e.g., co-curricular involvement, mentoring); and outcomes, such as students' characteristics after exposure to the college environment (e.g., Social Change Model values, social change behaviors, leadership self-efficacy, complex cognitive skills, social perspective taking, resiliency). In 2021, 74 institutions participated in the MSL, with over 450 participating institutions to date across a range of institutional types (Multi-Institutional Study of Leadership, n.d.). Germane to the scope of this chapter, crises, such as the COVID-19 pandemic and subsequent national incidents that occurred in recent years, disrupt the environment and the lived experience of those impacted most directly by the crisis.

Data Collection and Sample

Rutgers University–New Brunswick is one of more than 70 institutions who participated in the 2018 and 2021 administrations of the MSL. Following MSL protocol, the Office of Institutional Research generated a random sample of 4,000 undergraduate students who were invited to complete the survey.

The MSL was administered in February of 2018 and 2021. Data collection was conducted entirely online. Students received a series of email invitations and reminders. Each student received a pre-notification email informing them of the forthcoming survey, an e-mail invitation to complete the survey, and a series of three reminder emails that were only sent to students who had not completed the survey. Overall, the response rate for both years was below the national average of participating institutions, with an 18.5% response rate in 2018 and 12.4% response rate in 2021 resulting in a final sample of 740 students.

Table 1 describes the student characteristics of both the 2018 and 2021 samples, including distribution of gender, race/ethnicity, and status as first-generation college student. Apart from the breakdown by gender, the sample was representative of the overall undergraduate student population. Females tend to be overrepresented in survey research (Kwak & Radler, 2002; Sax, Gilmartin, & Bryant, 2003; Wu, Zhao, & Fils-Aime, 2022). Related to racial groups, the sample overrepresented African American / Black students and underrepresented multiracial students in comparison to campus enrollment during the 2018 and 2021 academic years.

Table 1. Demographic Characteristics

	2018 n	2018 Percent	2021 N	2021 Percent
Middle Eastern North African	73	4.8	14	4.4
African American / Black	134	8.8	25	7.9
Latinx / Hispanic	207	13.6	36	11.4
Asian American, American Indian Alaska Nativa, Native Hawaiian Pacific Islander	496	32.6	112	35.6
White / Caucasian	562	37.0	116	36.8
Multiracial	65	4.3	12	3.8
Race not listed	56	3.7	15	4.8
Man	493	24.3	102	20.5
Woman	1006	49.7	202	40.6
Transgender	11	0.5	8	1.6
First generation college student	272	18.2	261	85

Measures and Descriptive Statistics

Our variables of interest are breadth and depth of on- and off- campus organizational involvement, on campus employment, participation in leadership roles, frequency and forms of community service involvement, academic engagement experiences, participation in leadership development programs, and mentoring relationships. Prior research demonstrates these measures as forms of involvement cultivate important skills for college students and cultivate sense of belonging. Table 2 describes differences in campus involvement from before and during the COVID-19 pandemic, and Table 3 explains the differences in the frequency of students' engagement in these forms of involvement both prior to and during the COVID-19 pandemic. Each of these variables were included in the regression analysis. A detailed description of all items including variable definitions and coding schemes is located in the Appendix.

Table 2. Differences in Campus Involvement, Before and During the COVID-19 Pandemic

	2018		2021	
	n	Percent	N	Percent
Peer Helper	363	22.1%	78	16.5%
Engaged in learning community	380	19.8%	90	18.9%
Participated in a leadership training	715	44.2%	79	21.5%

Table 3. Differences in the Frequency of Student Engagement, Before and During the COVID-19 Pandemic

	2018		2021	
	Total n	Many Times + Much Of The Time	Total n	Many Times + Much Of The Time
Held a leadership position	1643	32.9%	381	19.1%
	Total n	Often + Very Often	Total n	Often + Very Often
Performed community service	1668	20.4%	387	12.9%
Mentored by a peer student	1619	29.5%	372	24.2%
Talked about different lifestyles/customs	1615	68.6%	370	25.9%
Held discussions with students whose personal values were very different from your own	1615	60.3%	370	19.5%
Discussed major social issues such as peace, human rights, and justice	1613	56.7%	370	27.0%
Held discussions with students whose religious beliefs were very different from your own	1613	51.5%	370	17.6%
Discussed your views about multiculturalism and diversity	1613	56.7%	369	24.4%
Held discussions with students whose political opinions were very different from your own	1614	45.2%	370	17.3%

To understand the degree to which the experiences of COVID-19 impacted undergraduate SOB, we looked to see how answers to these questions correlated with sense of belonging.

DATA ANALYSIS AND RESULTS

Factor Analysis

Confirmatory factor analysis was used to reduce the number of dependent variables. Given that there are common scales used to describe sense of belonging in the literature (Hurtado and Carter, 1997; Locks et al., 2008; Maestas et al., 2007), confirmatory factor analysis was performed to verify the survey items on the MSL explain sense of belonging similar to factor scales used in the literature (Hurtado and Carter, 1997; Locks et al., 2008; Maestas et al., 2007). Three survey items were entered into the factor analysis. Students were asked their level of agreement with the following three survey items:

(1) I feel valued as a person at this school.
(2) I feel accepted as a part of the community.
(3) I feel I belong on this campus.

First, principal axis factoring using promax to maximize the strength of each unique factor was performed on a sample of greater than 100 cases (Russell, 2002). Next, the default method of extracting factors with eigenvalues greater than 1 was applied. To be included in the factor, according to Agresti and Finlay (1997), variables should carry a loading of greater than 0.35 to be included, and each item maintained a loading of 0.50 and above (0.519, 0.594, and 0.578) and were included in the factor. Then, the Cronbach's Alpha was analyzed to determine the factor's internal consistency, interrelatedness and reliability, the Cronbach's Alpha were analyzed and resulted in 0.865, which is deemed acceptable as it is greater than the acceptable score of 0.65 as defined by scholars (Cortina, 1993; DeVellis & Thorpe, 2021).

Regression Analysis

Linear stepwise multiple regression analysis explored the unique effects of involvement and leadership experiences and education environment on college students' sense of belonging. All variables were blocked in a temporal sequence as discussed previously. The primary independent variable representing education environment were entered after controlling for demographic characteristics, involvement, and leadership experiences.

Multivariate Results: Variables Predicting Sense of Belonging

The research questions explored the association between involvement and leadership experiences on sense of belonging, and assessed how education environment, race, and status as a first-generation or continuing generation college student moderated the association. Table 3 displays the final regression results for the outcome measure used to define the dependent variable, sense of belonging. Included in Table 3 are the variables placed in the initial model. Standardized beta coefficients are listed if the variable was significant in the final model; blank cells indicate that a variable did not enter nor was significant in the final model.

The total proportion of variance accounted for by variables in the model explaining sense of belonging was 27%. Interestingly, education environment accounted for a significant amount of the explained variance (1%); however, involvement and leadership experiences accounted for 10% and leadership capacity and engagement accounted for the majority (13%). In this case, the year variable, which was significant until the third block, lost significance when frequency holding a leadership position entered the model. Of particular note, the outcome starts to get accounted for more strongly by the variables that describe involvement and leadership experiences.

While the primary focus of this research is the effect of the education environment on sense of belonging, after controlling for involvement and leadership experiences and the impact of race and status as a first-generation college student, the results of each regression block will be discussed in turn.

The first block included six variables to describe racial groups (e.g., African American/Black, Middle Eastern North African, Latinx/Hispanic, Multiracial, a combination of Asian American, American Indian/Alaskan Native, Native Hawaiian/Pacific Islander, and those who did not list a race). White/Caucasian was used as the comparison group and omitted from the model. Highest level of parent education was collapsed into a dichotomous measure to describe the status of first-generation or continuing generation college student. Of the seven variables that were placed into the first block, two emerged as significant. Among demographic characteristics, continuing-generation college students tended to report higher levels of sense of belonging and African American/Black college students indicated lower sense of belonging. It is important to note that identifying racially as African American/Black remained a significant predictor of sense of belonging with a negative association, while identifying as a continuing generation college student lost its significant association when the year variable entered the model.

Survey year was used to describe the education environment, the primary variable of importance in this study. As described previously, the MSL was administered during 2018, prior to the COVID-19 pandemic when education instruction took place in person, and in 2021, while the university operated primarily remote in a virtual environment as the world was continuing to navigate the COVID-19 pandemic. One of the primary goals of this regression analysis was to determine whether the survey year variable had a significant association with sense of belonging. In other words, did change in education environment from a traditional in-person format to remote and virtual learning have an impact on students' feeling of belonging and connection to the campus environment? While the mode of education environment variable did enter the regression as significant initially, it lost significance marginally by the final model. Given that 2021 (during the pandemic) was coded as the higher value, the results show that students in the 2021 sample had a lower sense of belonging than students in the 2018 sample. Therefore, students who were enrolled in 2021 during the pandemic when the university operated in a remote environment reported having less of a connection to the university or lower levels of sense of belonging than when the university operated in a traditional in-person environment.

Among the third block of variables, two variables describing involvement and leadership experiences were shown to be significant predictors of sense of belonging. Both the frequency of holding leadership positions in a college organization and the frequency of performing community service were significant and positive predictors of sense of belonging.

Moving to the fourth block of variables, two variables describing learning and mentoring as it relates to leadership were shown to be significant predictors of sense of belonging. Peer mentoring and engaging in learning communities or other formal programs where groups of students take two or more classes together were significant and positive predictors of sense of belonging.

Three variables describing leadership capacity and engagement were entered into the fifth and final block of the model and shown to be significant predictors of sense of belonging. The overall measure of leadership capacity was a strong and positive predictor of sense of belonging. The frequency in which students held discussions with other students whose religious beliefs were very different from their own had a positive association with sense of belonging. On the other hand, the frequency in which students engaged in discussions with students whose political opinions were very different from their own was a negative predictor of sense of belonging. In other words, students who engaged in these conversations more frequently had a lower sense of belonging. While the data does not allow us to imply causality, there are a variety of possible explanations and ways to interpret this negative finding. Perhaps engaging in such political discussions were on topics deemed controversial and sensitive, and especially during the pandemic, politics did influence attitudes around response measures, policies, and practices. If students do not feel they have consensus among peers, they are more likely to feel alone in a larger community. The type of discussion is unknown; however, what is known is the remote environment may have made it more challenging to engage in these types of discussions.

Table 4. Regression Predicting Sense of Belonging (N = 1674)

	r		final beta	
Block 1: Demographic Characteristics				
Status as a continuing generation college student	0.077	**	0.001	
Race: African American / Black	-0.050	*	-0.060	**
Race: Middle Eastern / North African	0.000			
Race: Latinx / Hispanic	0.009			
Race: Multiracial	-0.025			
Race: Race not listed	-0.008			
Race: Asian American, American Indian / Alaskan Native, Native Hawaiian / Pacific Islander	-0.022			
			($R^2 = 0.008$)	
Block 2: Mode of Instruction				
Survey year: In-person instruction vs. Remote learning	-0.099	***	-0.049	
			($R^2 = 0.013$)	
Block 3: Involvement and Leadership Experiences				
Frequency: Held a leadership position in a college organization	0.279	***	0.117	***
Frequency of engagement: Performed community service	0.229	***	0.041	
			($R^2 = 0.098$)	
Block 4: Learning and Mentorship				
Mentored by other students	0.252	***	0.111	***
Engagement: Learning community or other formal program where groups of students take two or more classes together	0.138	***	0.065	**
			($R^2 = 0.134$)	
Block 5: Leadership Capacity and Engagement				
Overall measure of leadership capacity	0.447	***	0.367	***
Frequency: Held discussions with other students whose religious beliefs were very different from your own	0.24	***	0.115	***
Frequency: Held discussions with students whose political opinions were very different from your own	0.156	***	-0.089	**
			($R^2 = 0.265$)	

Coefficients shown only for variables that entered the model. Significance indicated by *$p<0.05$, **$p<0.01$, ***$p<0.001$.

Limitations and Future Research

There are a few limitations associated with this study that require acknowledgement. First, the survey was a self-report of students' perceived experiences in involvement and leadership. Future research should examine utilization data, such as attendance and participation data captured through identification card swipe data

Relationship Between Student Involvement, Leadership

(e.g., the number and types of programs, events, and meetings). The survey results only capture data from the students who are most likely to respond to surveys.

While single institution studies limit the generalizability of the results, the combination of data from two distinct timepoints and the students' response to how the institution shifted its practices during the pandemic provide a compelling glimpse into leadership and involvement during a time of crisis. The university's response rate is significantly lower than the national average, which is common at this institution. This institution has a difficult time recruiting student participation on all surveys, and the even greater reduced sample in 2021 is perhaps explained by the challenges of the pandemic.

Finally, we cannot infer causality in the impact of the pandemic on changes in involvement and leadership participation and experiences because of limitations in the data and analytic techniques performed. There are a number of potential factors to explain the results and a variety of questions left unexplained by the data. When analyzing a national survey instrument, the study is at the discretion of the measures included on the survey instrument. The COVID-19 pandemic took an extraordinary toll on mental health, which already is a pressing priority and concern for college students. The topic of mental health was not covered on the Multi Institutional Study of Leadership Survey; however, it likely offers important context and explanation for students' decisions related to involvement and leadership choices and feelings of belonging during the pandemic. Future research delving into qualitative accounts of students' involvement and leadership experiences and emotional health both before, during, and post-pandemic are warranted to fully understand the impact of the pandemic on involvement and leadership.

DISCUSSION

The COVID-19 pandemic had a profound impact on institutions of higher education. As one of the largest residential housing programs in the nation, Rutgers University-New Brunswick was designed to be an in-person learning environment. When the pandemic abruptly evacuated the campus, it was unclear how students, faculty, and staff would transition to remote technology. While survey results showed students were overall satisfied with how the campus adapted, it was important to delve deeper into the MSL data in order to glean important insights that could be relevant for both our institution and other institutions of higher education. The results from this study point to a decline in student sense of belonging during the COVID-19 pandemic and the different variables that can positively impact college students' senses of belonging as we move forward. By focusing on these variables, institutions can likely see increases in their students' connection to campus overall post-pandemic. Rutgers University-New Brunswick's participation in the MSL in both 2018 (before the pandemic) and 2021 (during the pandemic) enabled us to examine the impact of the pandemic on involvement, leadership experiences, and sense of belonging. Involvement and leadership are fundamental to student success, providing necessary skills to foster student psychosocial development and to adequately prepare students for the pursuit of one's postgraduate aspirations.

The results from this study point to declines in student participation in campus organizations and declines in engagement in formal leadership opportunities, both of which may be attributed to the COVID-19 pandemic and the shift to a fully online teaching and learning environment. These findings can be explained by the lack of motivation in the remote setting, limited access or awareness of opportunities, or increased obligations at home as a result of the pandemic.

While the return to in-person instruction post-pandemic will likely increase rates of participation in student clubs and leadership involvement, the preliminary findings from this study highlight important lessons for those engaged in leadership education and development. First, it is important to understand where students learn about leadership opportunities. Students often learn about involvement opportunities, access information, and choose to attend events based on spontaneous interactions with peers and promotional materials; therefore, the remote environment reduced learning about involvement and leadership opportunities in this way. An in-person and residential learning environment serves as a catalyst for these spontaneous and casual interactions that result in involvement and learning, and the rapid shift to a fully online infrastructure did not allow adequate time to adapt all dimensions of the co-curricular and extra-curricular experience to a mediated setting.

As seen, there initially was a significant difference for first-generation students' sense of belonging compared to their continuing generation classmates. Many different factors may have directly impacted this disconnect for first-generation students, such as encountering pronounced difficulties related to online coursework and possibly needing to work in order to pay for their education. Through the use of university resources like specialized orientation programming and co-curricular programming to support their transition to the on-campus experience (e.g., Welcome Week), higher education institutions can continue to create avenues to meaningfully support first-generation students. Programming can also include specific experiences for the parents of first-generation students to advise them on how they can support their student's learning and connection to the institution. Altering times of programming can also help students who work to be able to access and attend campus events.

The findings show a negative association between students identifying as African American/Black and indicating a lower sense of belonging to their higher education institution (Johnson et al., 2007; Mwangi et al., 2018; Hunter, Case, & Harvey, 2019). Higher education institutions are majority white institutions both in student populations, faculty populations, and administratively. Black cultural centers, such as the Paul Robeson Cultural Center at Rutgers University–New Brunswick, provide a plethora of support systems, mentoring, and advising resources for students (Hunter, Case, & Harvey, 2019).

There is an indication of lower sense of belonging from the surveys completed in 2021 compared with 2018. While there is a smaller sample size from the individuals who responded in 2021, this could correlate to there being less connection to the institution while completing coursework in the virtual space. Many enrolled students in 2021 had never been to campus for more than a tour when looking at different schools. Their synchronous and asynchronous courses were primarily conducted via Zoom and Canvas. After hours spent engaging in formal coursework via mediated platforms, students experienced fatigue and may have been too tired to return to the computer to participate in student club meetings, gatherings, or other social events. Furthermore, finding student organizations may have been made difficult as a result of the shift to the fully remote environment. While the return to in-person instruction post-pandemic will likely increase rates of participation in student clubs and leadership involvement, the preliminary findings from this study highlight important lessons for those engaged in leadership education and development. First, it is important to understand where students learn about leadership opportunities. Students often learn about involvement opportunities, access information, and choose to attend events based on spontaneous interactions with peers and promotional materials; therefore, the remote environment reduced learning about involvement and leadership opportunities in this way. An in-person and residential learning environment serves as a catalyst for these spontaneous and casual interactions that result in involvement and learning, and the rapid shift to a fully online infrastructure did not allow adequate time to adapt all dimensions of the co-curricular and extra-curricular experience to a mediated setting. It is important for universities to reflect on and evaluate how the pandemic affected student leadership and involvement and to be proactive in creating inclusive environments for involvement in the design of the post-pandemic university. Finally, administrators need to be intentional about how best to support students in their development across a range of modalities including in-person, hybrid, or fully only. In turn, this will continue to increase student organization opportunities; therefore, expanding opportunities for students to cultivate leadership skills and experiences in college organizations and engaging students who have not traditionally accessed these learning opportunities.

Student exposure to mentoring opportunities foster relationships with advisors, coaches, faculty, and staff that have the potential to strengthen one's feeling of mattering and community. Universities should identify new student connection opportunities within academic and social groupings (e.g., majors, learning communities, and student organizations), as well as incentivize mentoring for engaged students. Peer mentoring is shown to be a very strong predictor of engaged learning and belonging (Flores & Estudillo, 2018). Mentorship and learning communities allow for connections with like-minded individuals, even through virtual spaces.

Rutgers University President, Jonathan Holloway, began his presidency during the COVID-19 pandemic. One of the core value propositions guiding the institution is a commitment to the cultivation of a beloved community, which is a community that promotes *tolerance, mutual respect, diversity, and the spirited exchange of opinions and ideas* (Rutgers Universty, n.d.). It is important to create environments where students experience empathy from their professors and advisors, and restorative practices are modeled when conflict occurs. Such examples will help students feel safe and encouraged to engage in discussions across different political and religious views. The university environment is an optimal setting to experiment with these challenging conversations. Varying levels of faculty and staff are available in classrooms, residence halls, student centers, and the outdoors to help facilitate and promote interactions across difference.

Furthermore, as supported by the data, student connection to the university and overall sense of belonging were affected by the pandemic, along with a reduction in conversations across difference. As institutions move towards a more flexible work arrangement for employees and an increase in hybrid and online offerings for students, institutions must remain steadfast in their focus on creating cultures of inclusion and belonging in an increasingly mediated environment—and to consider how best to support student leadership development in such an environment.

Additionally, the findings from this study raise important questions regarding how best to cultivate student belonging and student affiliation in a post-pandemic environment. For example, given decreases in involvement and participation in student organizations during the pandemic, there is a sense of address pressure to create meaningful experiences for current students and to ensure upperclassmen find pathways to involvement in the transition to a more in-person academic environment. At the same time, we are seeing increases in employee burnout and fatigue and many offices, especially in student affairs, with vacancies amid what has been labeled the "Great Resignation." Such an environment might require units and department to prioritize the programs, events, and initiatives that are most critical and to engage in more active sunset planning—a practice that historically has been a challenge for colleges and universities (Ruben et al., 2021). The pandemic, as supported by the findings from this study, create a unique opportunity to rethink what aspects of student involvement and leadership development are most critical, necessary, or advantageous—and to rethink what such efforts might look like an increasingly hybrid or online environment.

Finally, the findings from this study invite us to consider how to further integrate the social change model of leadership development into future undergraduate student leadership experiences, educate students on these desired outcomes, and align organizational and institutional practices with this framework.

CONCLUSION

As colleges and universities lean into a post-pandemic environment, it is an important moment to take stock of lessons learned from the pandemic itself. The findings detailed in this chapter provide a glimpse into the shift in student involvement and engagement in leadership opportunities, along with the impact on sense of belonging and community at two points in time, and these results likely mirror in some ways the experiences and trends found on other campuses during this shared crisis. In response to greater demands for online and hybrid courses and a preference for both in-person and virtual opportunities for co-curricular and extra-curricular services, along with increased faculty and staff fatigue and a collective reimaging of the post-pandemic university, the findings from this study raise important questions for those responsible for student leadership education and development. In addition to reclaiming our purpose in the leadership education and development of students (Guthrie & Osteen, 2016; Guthrie & Jenkins, 2018), this study invites a consideration of the following questions:

- How might we create opportunities for inclusion and belonging in both an in-person and virtual learning environment?
- How can we create conversations across difference in a virtual ecosystem?
- In what ways did we best serve and support students prior to the pandemic and during the pandemic, and how might these efforts extend into a post-pandemic setting?
- How did we facilitate student involvement and leadership during the pandemic—and what might we continue with or stop doing based on this experience?

The social change model provides a useful framework in thinking through leadership holistically, with attention centered on cultural awareness and cultural competency. As we lean into a post-pandemic environment, it remains an important moment for careful introspection regarding our core purpose as an institution of higher education, the ways in which we can best support student involvement and leadership development, and the approach we might take to create environments—physical and virtual—that help to cultivate a sense of inclusion and belonging.

REFERENCES

Agresti, A., & Finlay, B. (1997). *Statistical methods for the social sciences* (3rd ed.). Prentice Hall, Inc.

Apriceno, M., Levy, S. R., & London, B. (2020). Mentorship during college transition predicts academic self-efficacy and sense of belonging among STEM students. *Journal of College Student Development*, 61(5), 643–648. 10.1353/csd.2020.0061

Astin, A. W. (1993a). *What matters in college? Four critical years revisited.* Jossey-Bass.

Astin, A. W. (1993b). *Assessment for excellence: The philosophy and practice of assessment and evaluation in higher education.* Macmillan.

Astin, A. W., & Antonio, l. (2012). *Assessment for excellence: The philosophy and practice of assessment and evaluation in higher education.* Rowman & Littlefield Publishers.

Aucejo, E. M., French, J., Ugalde Araya, M. P., & Zafar, B. (2020). The impact of COVID-19 on student experiences and expectations: Evidence from a survey. *Journal of Public Economics*, 191, 104271. 10.1016/j.jpubeco.2020.10427132873994

Barringer, A., Papp, L. M., & Gu, P. (2023). College students' sense of belonging in times of disruption: Prospective changes from before to during the COVID-19 pandemic. *Higher Education Research & Development*, 42(6), 1309–1322. 10.1080/07294360.2022.213827537457647

Berger, J. B., & Milem, J. F. (1999). The role of student involvement and perceptions of integration in a causal model of student persistence. *Research in Higher Education*, 40(6), 641–664. 10.1023/A:1018708813711

Broady, K., Macklin, M., & O'Donnell, J. (2020, December 16). Preparing U.S. workers for the post-COVID economy: Higher education, workforce training and labor unions. *Brookings.* https://www.brookings.edu/research/preparing-u-s-workers-for-the-post-covid-economy-higher-education-workforce-training-and-labor-unions/

Correia-Harker, B. P., & Dugan, J. P. (2020). Beyond knowledge and skills: Exploring leadership motivation as a critical construct for student leadership development. *Journal of College Student Development*, 61(3), 299–316. 10.1353/csd.2020.0029

Correia-Harker, B. P., Snipes, J. T., Rockenbach, A. N., & Mayhew, M. J. (2019). Students' perceptions of and engagement with worldview diversity in college. In *Educating About Religious Diversity and Interfaith Engagement* (pp. 22-39). Routledge.

Cortina, J. M. (1993). What is a coefficient alpha? An examination of theory and applications. *The Journal of Applied Psychology*, 78(1), 98–104. https://www.psycholosphere.com/what%20is%20coefficient%20alpha%20by%20Cortina.pdf. 10.1037/0021-9010.78.1.98

DeVellis, R. F., & Thorpe, C. T. (2021). *Scale development: Theory and applications*. Sage publications.

Dugan, J. P., Bohle, C. W., Woelker, L. R., & Cooney, M. A. (2014). The role of social perspective-taking in developing students' leadership capacities. *Journal of Student Affairs Research and Practice*, 51(1), 1–15. 10.1515/jsarp-2014-0001

Dugan, J. P., Kodama, C. M., & Gebhardt, M. C. (2012). Race and leadership development among college students: The additive value of collective racial esteem. *Journal of Diversity in Higher Education*, 5(3), 174–189. 10.1037/a0029133

Dugan, J. P., Komives, S. R., & Segar, T. C. (2008). College Student Capacity for Socially Responsible Leadership: Understanding Norms and Influences of Race, Gender, and Sexual Orientation. *NASPA Journal*, 45(4), 475–500. 10.2202/1949-6605.2008

Duran, A., Dahl, L. S., Stipeck, C., & Mayhew, M. J. (2020). A critical quantitative analysis of students' sense of belonging: Perspectives on race, generation status, and collegiate environments. *Journal of College Student Development*, 61(2), 133–153. 10.1353/csd.2020.0014

Firang, D. (2020). The impact of COVID-19 pandemic on international students in Canada. *International Social Work*, 63(6), 820–824. 10.1177/0020872820940030

Flores, G., & Estudillo, A. (2018). Effects of a peer-to-peer mentoring program: Supporting first-year college students' academic and social integration on campus. *Journal of Human Services: Training, Research, and Practice*, 3(2). https://scholarworks.sfasu.edu/jhstrp/vol3/iss2/3

Freeman, T. M., Anderman, L. H., & Jensen, J. M. (2007). Sense of belonging in college freshmen at the classroom and campus levels. *Journal of Experimental Education*, 75(3), 203–220. 10.3200/JEXE.75.3.203-220

Gigliotti, R. A. (2020). Sudden shifts to fully online: Perceptions of campus preparedness and implications for leading through disruption. *The Journal of Literacy and Technology*, 21(2), 18–36.

Gigliotti, R. A. (2021). The impact of COVID-19 on academic department chairs: Heightened complexity, accentuated liminality, and competing perceptions of reinvention. Innovative Higher Education. Gillen-O'Neel, C. (2021). Sense of belonging and student engagement: A daily study of first-and continuing-generation college students. *Research in Higher Education*, 62(1), 45–71.

Gopalan, M., Linden-Carmichael, A., & Lanza, S. (2022). College students' sense of belonging and mental health amidst the COVID-19 pandemic. *The Journal of Adolescent Health*, 70(2), 228–233. 10.1016/j.jadohealth.2021.10.01034893423

Guthrie, K. L., & Jenkins, D. M. (2018). *The role of leadership educators: Transforming learning*. Information Age Publishing.

Guthrie, K. L., & Osteen, L. (Eds.). (2016). *Reclaiming higher education's purpose in leadership development. New directions for higher education, Number 174*. Wiley.

Hagerty, B. M., Williams, R. A., Coyne, J. C., & Early, M. R. (1996). Sense of belonging and indicators of social and psychological functioning. *Archives of Psychiatric Nursing*, 10(4), 235–244. 10.1016/S0883-9417(96)80029-X8799050

Hemer, K. M., Perez, R. J., & Harris, L. W. Jr. (2019b). An examination of factors that contribute to the development of perspective taking. *Journal of College and Character*, 20(2), 144–162. 10.1080/2194587X.2019.1591283

Higher Education Research Institute (HERI). (1996). *A social change model of leadership development: Guidebook version III*. National Clearinghouse for Leadership Programs.

Holloway-Friesen, H. (2018). On the road home: A Content analysis of commuters' sense of belonging. *The College Student Affairs Journal*, 36(2), 81–96. 10.1353/csj.2018.0017

Hsiao, K. P. (1992). First-generation college students. Retrieved from ERIC database. (ED351079)

Hunter, C. D., Case, A. D., & Harvey, I. S. (2019). Black college students' sense of belonging and racial identity. *International Journal of Inclusive Education*, 23(9), 950–966. 10.1080/13603116.2019.1602363

Hurtado, S., & Carter, D. F. (1997). Effects of college transition and perceptions of the campus racial climate on Latino college students' sense of belonging. *Sociology of Education*, 70(4), 324–345. 10.2307/2673270

Johnson, D. R., Soldner, M., Leonard, J. B., Alvarez, P., Inkelas, K. K., Rowan-Kenyon, H. T., & Longerbeam, S. D. (2007). Examining sense of belonging among first-year undergraduates from different racial/ethnic groups. *Journal of College Student Development*, 48(5), 525–542. 10.1353/csd.2007.0054

Johnson, M. R., Schuneman, M., & McClure, S. (2022). Comparing the effects of COVID-19 on fraternity & sorority members and unaffiliated college students. *Oracle: The Research Journal of the Association of Fraternity/Sorority Advisors*, 17(1), 17-30. DOI: 10.25774/ww8n-p985

Khalil, R., Mansour, A. E., Fadda, W. A., Almisnid, K., Aldamegh, M., Al-Nafeesah, A., Alkhalifah, A., & Al-Wutayd, O. (2020). The sudden transition to synchronized online learning during the COVID-19 pandemic in Saudi Arabia: A qualitative study exploring medical students' perspectives. *BMC Medical Education*, 20(285), 285. 10.1186/s12909-020-02208-z32859188

Kim, J. H. "Jane," Maria Claudia Soler, Zhe Zhao, and Erica Swirsky. 2024. Race and Ethnicity in Higher Education: 2024 Status Report Executive Summary. Washington, DC: American Council on Education.

Kodoma, C. M., & Dugan, J. P. (2013). Leveragin leadership efficacy for college students: Disaggregating data to examine unique predictors by race. *Equity & Excellence in Education*, 46(2), 184–201. 10.1080/10665684.2013.780646

Kwak, N., & Radler, B. (2002). A comparison between mail and web surveys: Response pattern, respondent profile, and data quality. *Journal of Official Statistics*, 18(2), 257.

Leupold, C., Lopina, E., & Skloot, E. (2020). An examination of leadership development and other experiential activities on student resilience and leadership efficacy. *Journal of Leadership Education*, 19(1), 53–64. 10.12806/V19/I1/R1

Lewis, J. S. (2020). Reconsidering the effects of work on college student leadership development: An empirical perspective. *Journal of College Student Development*, 61(5), 539–557. 10.1353/csd.2020.0054

Liu, T., Chen, Y., Hamilton, M., & Harris, K. (2022). Peer mentoring to enhance graduate students' sense of belonging and academic success. *Kinesiology Review*, 1(aop), 1-12.

Lockee, B. B. (2021). Online education in the post-COVID era. *Nature Electronics*, 4(1), 5–6. 10.1038/s41928-020-00534-0

Locks, A. M., Hurtado, S., Bowman, N. A., & Oseguera, L. (2008). Extending notions of campus climate and diversity to students' transition to college. *The Review of Higher Education, 31*(3), 257-285.Major, C. (2020). Unprecedented times and innovation. *Innovative Higher Education*, 45, 435–436. 10.1007/s10755-020-09528-4

Maestas, R., Vaquera, G. S., & Zehr, L. M. (2007). Factors impacting sense of belonging at a Hispanic- serving institution. *Journal of Hispanic Higher Education*, 6(3), 237–256. 10.1177/1538192707302801

Major, C. (2020). Innovations in teaching and learning during a time of crisis. *Innovative Higher Education*, 45(4), 265–266. 10.1007/s10755-020-09514-w32836726

Martinez, N., Sowcik, M. J., & Bunch, J. C. (2020). The impact of leadership education and cocurricular involvement on the development of socially responsible leadership outcomes in undergraduate students: An exploratory study. *Journal of Leadership Education*, 19(3), 32–43. 10.12806/V19/I3/R3

Mok, K. H., Xiong, W., Ke, G., & Cheung, J. (2021). Impact of COVID-19 pandemic on international higher education and student mobility: Student perspectives from mainland China and Hong Kong. *International Journal of Educational Research*, 105, 101718. 10.1016/j.ijer.2020.10171835719275

Multi-institutional study of leadership. Multi-Institutional Study of Leadership. (n.d.). Retrieved July 9, 2022, from https://www.leadershipstudy.net/

Museus, S. D., & Chang, T. H. (2021). The impact of campus environments on sense of belonging for first-generation college students. *Journal of College Student Development*, 62(3), 367–372. 10.1353/csd.2021.0039

Museus, S. D., Yi, V., & Saelua, N. (2017). The impact of culturally engaging campus environments on sense of belonging. *Review of Higher Education*, 40(2), 187–215. 10.1353/rhe.2017.0001

Museus, S. D., Yi, V., & Saelua, N. (2017). The impact of culturally engaging campus environments on sense of belonging. *Review of Higher Education*, 40(2), 187–215. 10.1353/rhe.2017.0001

Mwangi, C. A. G., Thelamour, B., Ezeofor, I., & Carpenter, A. (2018). "Black elephant in the room": Black students contextualizing campus racial climate within US racial climate. *Journal of College Student Development*, 59(4), 456–474. 10.1353/csd.2018.0042

Ntsiful, A., Kwarteng, M. A., Pilík, M., & Osakwe, C. N. (2022). Transitioning to online teaching during the pandemic period: The role of innovation and psychological characteristics. *Innovative Higher Education*. Advance online publication. 10.1007/s10755-022-09613-w35698463

Oxendine, S. D., Taub, D. J., & Cain, E. J. (2020). Factors related to Native American students' perceptions of campus culture. *Journal of College Student Development*, 61(3), 267–280. 10.1353/csd.2020.0027

Pedler, M. L., Willis, R., & Nieuwoudt, J. E. (2022). A sense of belonging at university: Student retention, motivation and enjoyment. *Journal of Further and Higher Education*, 46(3), 397–408. 10.1080/0309877X.2021.1955844

Potts, C. (2021). Seen and unseen: First-year college students' sense of belonging during the COVID-19 pandemic. *The College Student Affairs Journal*, 39(2), 214–224. 10.1353/csj.2021.0018

Ramlo, S. E. (2021). Universities and the COVID-19 pandemic: Comparing views about how to address the financial impact. *Innovative Higher Education*, 46(6), 777–793. 10.1007/s10755-021-09561-x34177079

Reuter, P. R., Forster, B. L., & Kruger, B. J. (2021). A longitudinal study of the impact of COVID-19 restrictions on students' health behavior, mental health and emotional well-being. *PeerJ*, 9, e12528. 10.7717/peerj.1252834993018

Ribera, A. K., Miller, A. L., & Dumford, A. D. (2017). Sense of peer belonging and institutional acceptance in the first year: The role of high-impact practices. *Journal of College Student Development*, 58(4), 545–563. 10.1353/csd.2017.0042

Rosch, D. M., Collier, D., & Thompson, S. E. (2015). An exploration of students' motivation to lead: An analysis by race, gender, and student leadership behaviors. *Journal of College Student Development*, 56(3), 286–291. 10.1353/csd.2015.0031

Ruben, B. D., De Lisi, R., & Gigliotti, R. A. (2021). *A guide for leaders in higher education: Concepts, competencies, and tools*. Stylus Publishing, LLC.

Russell, D. W. (2002). In search of underlying dimensions: The use (and abuse) of factor analysis in Personality and Social Psychology Bulletin. *Personality and Social Psychology Bulletin*, 28(12), 1629–1646. 10.1177/014616702237645

Sax, L. J., Gilmartin, S. K., & Bryant, A. N. (2003). Assessing response rates and nonresponse bias in web and paper surveys. *Research in Higher Education*, 44(4), 409–432. https://link.springer.com/content/pdf/10.1023/A:1024232915870.pdf. 10.1023/A:1024232915870

Soria, K. M., Boettcher, B., & Hallahan, K. (2022). The Effects of Participation in Recreational Activities on Students' Resilience and Sense of Belonging. *Recreational Sports Journal*, 46(2), 184–192. 10.1177/15588661221125201

Soria, K. M., Hussein, D., & Vue, C. (2014). Leadership for whom? Socioeconomic factors predicting undergraduate students' positional leadership participation. *Journal of Leadership Education. Winter (14)*.

Soria, K. M., Werner, L., & Nath, C. (2019). Leadership experiences and perspective taking among college students. *Journal of Student Affairs Research and Practice*, 56(2), 138–152. 10.1080/19496591.2018.1490309

Stern, G. M. (2014). Part-Time Job Program for Latinos Boosts College Success. *Education Digest*, 79, 55–58.

Strayhorn, T. L. (2019). *College students' sense of belonging: A key to educational success for all students* (2nd ed.). Routledge.

Suhlmann, M., Sassenberg, K., Nagengast, B., & Trautwein, U. (2018). Belonging mediates effects of student-university fit on well-being, motivation, and dropout intention. *Social Psychology (Göttingen)*, 49(1), 16–28. 10.1027/1864-9335/a000325

Thwaite, S. V. (2022). Crisis is a powerful tool: Resilient leadership during a global health pandemic. *Journal of Leadership Education*, 21(1), 196–208. 10.12806/V21/I1/C1

Walton, G. M., & Cohen, G. L. (2007). A question of belonging: Race, social fit, and achievement. *Journal of Personality and Social Psychology*, 92(1), 82–96. 10.1037/0022-3514.92.1.8217201544

Whitaker, B. L., & Kniffin, L. E. (2022). Crisis as pedagogy: Recommendations for using the pandemic in leadership education. *Journal of Leadership Education*, 21(3), 1–16. 10.12806/V21/I3/A2

Wu, M. J., Zhao, K., & Fils-Aime, F. (2022). Response rates of online surveys in published research: A meta-analysis. *Computers in Human Behavior Reports*, 7, 100206. 10.1016/j.chbr.2022.100206

Young, N. D., Michael, C. N., & Smolinksi, J. A. (2019). *Captivating campuses: Proven practices that promote college student persistence, engagement and success*. Vernon Press.

APPENDIX

Table 5. Regression model blocks, variable definitions, and coding scheme

Dependent Variable	Variable Definitions and Coding Scheme
Sense of belonging	Three-item factor Indicate your level of agreement with the following statements about your experience on your current campus: ENV11a1. I feel valued as a person at this school. ENV11a2. I feel accepted as part of the campus community. ENV11a3. I feel I belong on this campus. Five-item agreement scale: 1= "Strongly Disagree" to 5= "Strongly Agree"
Independent Variables	**Coding Scheme**
Block 1: Demographic Characteristics	
Status as a continuing generation college student	Dichotomous: 0= "first-generation college student", 1= "continuing generation college student" Created new variable from DEM14. What is the highest level of formal education obtained by any of your parent(s) or guardian(s)? First-generation college student= Less than high school diploma or less than a GED + High school diploma or GED + Some college + Associates degree Continuing generation college student: Bachelors degree + Masters degree + Doctorate or professional degree (e.g., JD, MD, PhD) Excluded: Don't know
Race: African American / Black	Dichotomous: 0= "not marked", 1= "marked"
Race: Middle Eastern / North African	Dichotomous: 0= "not marked", 1= "marked"
Race: Latinx / Hispanic	Dichotomous: 0= "not marked", 1= "marked"
Race: Multiracial	Dichotomous: 0= "not marked", 1= "marked"
Race: Race not listed	Dichotomous: 0= "not marked", 1= "marked"
Race: Asian American, American Indian / Alaskan Native, Native Hawaiian / Pacific Islander	Dichotomous: 0= "not marked", 1= "marked" Aggregated= Asian American + American Indian / Alaskan Native + Native Hawaaian / Pacific Islander
Block 2: Mode of Instruction	
Survey year: In-person instruction vs. Remote instruction	Dichotomous: 1= "2018", 2= "2021"
Block 3: Involvement and Leadership Experiences	

continued on following page

Table 5. Continued

Dependent Variable	Variable Definitions and Coding Scheme
Frequency: Held a leadership position in a college organization	Since starting college, how often have you: ENV6B. Held a leadership position in a college organization(s) (e.g., officer in a club or organization, captain of athletic team, first chair in musical group, section editor of newspaper, chairperson of committee)? Five-item scale: 1= "Never" to 5= "Much Of The Time"
Frequency of engagement: Performed community service	How often have you engaged in the following activities during your college experience: ENV5A. Performed community service Four-item scale: 1= "Never" to 4= "Often"
Block 4: Learning and Mentorship	
Mentored by other students	A mentor is defined as a person who intentionally assists with your growth or connects you to opportunities for career or personal development. Since you started at your current college/university, have you ever been mentored by the following types of people? ENV8a6. Other Student Dichotomous: 1= "No", 2= "Yes"
Engagement: Learning community or other formal program where groups of students take two ore more classes together	Which of the following have you engaged in during your college experience: ENV4C. Learning community or other formal program where groups of students take two or more classes together – Which of the following have you engaged in during your college experience: Dichotomous: 1= "No", 2= "Yes"
Block 5: Leadership Capacity and Engagement	

continued on following page

Table 5. Continued

Dependent Variable	Variable Definitions and Coding Scheme
Overall measure of leadership capacity	Socially Responsible Leadership Scale (mean score) Five-item agreement scale: 1= "Strongly Disagree" to 5= "Strongly Agree" SRLS4. I am able to articulate my priorities. SRLS3. I value differences in others. SRLS52. Being seen as a person of integrity is important to me. SRLS33. I believe I have responsibilities to my community. SRLS29. I can make a difference when I work with others on a task. SRLS5. Hearing differences in opinions enriches my thinking. SRLS63. My behaviors reflect my beliefs. SRLS30. I actively listen to what others have to say. SRLS40. I work with others to make my communities better places. SRLS28. I am focused on my responsibilities. SRLS22. I know myself pretty well. SRLS42. I enjoy working with others toward common goals. SRLS13. My behaviors are congruent with my beliefs. SRLS23. I am willing to devote the time and energy to things that are important to me. SRLS48. Others would describe me as a cooperative group member. SRLS24. I stick with others through difficult times. SRLS16: I respect opinions other than my own. SRLS34. I could describe my personality. SRLS47. I participate in activities that contribute to the common good. SRLS51. I can be counted on to do my part. SRLS53. I follow through on my promises. SRLS41. I can describe how I am similar to other people. SRLS59. I am comfortable expressing myself. SRLS60. My contributions are recognized by others in the groups I belong to. SRLS54: I hold myself accountable for responsibilities I agree to. SRLS62. I share my ideas with others. SRLS27. It is important to me to act on my beliefs. SRLS10. I am seen as someone who works well with others. SRLS69. It is important to me that I play an active role in my communities. SRLS9. I am usually self confident. SRLS66. I value opportunities that allow me to contribute to my community. SRLS1. I am open to others' ideas. SRLS32. My actions are consistent with my values. SRLS71. I believe my work has a greater purpose for the larger community.
Frequency: Held discussions with other students whose religious beliefs were very different from your own	ENV9D. Held discussions with students whose religious beliefs were very different from your own – During interactions with other students outside of class, how often have you done each of the following in an average school year?
Frequency: Held discussions with other students whose political opinions were very different from your own	ENV9F. Held discussions with students whose political opinions were very different from your own – During interactions with other students outside of class, how often have you done each of the following in an average school year?

Compilation of References

Abedi, M., & Badragheh, A. (2011). Online classes vs. traditional classes: Comparison between two methods. *The Journal of American Science*, 7(4), 307–314.

Adams, J., & Corbett, A. (2010). Experiences of traditional and non-traditional college students. *Perspectives*, 2(1), 2.

ADEA & APHRC. (2023). *The Long-Term Impact of COVID-19 on Educational Systems in Africa: Perspectives of Education Stakeholders from sub-Saharan Africa.* Association for the Development of Education in Africa & African Population and Health Research Center.

Adom, D., Mensa, J. A., & Osei, M. (2021). The Psychological Distress and Mental Health Disorders from COVID-19 Stigmatization in Ghana. *Social Sciences & Humanities Open*, 4(1), 1–10. 10.1016/j.ssaho.2021.10018634250461

Agresti, A., & Finlay, B. (1997). *Statistical methods for the social sciences* (3rd ed.). Prentice Hall, Inc.

Aguliera, E., & Nightengale-Lee, B. (2020). Emergency remote teaching across urban and rural contexts: Perspectives on educational equity. *Information and Learning Science*, 121(5/6), 471–478. 10.1108/ILS-04-2020-0100

Alaimo, K., Olson, C. M., & Frongillo, E. A.Jr. (2001). Food insufficiency and American school-aged children's cognitive, academic, and psychosocial development. *Pediatrics*, 108(1), 44–53. 10.1542/peds.108.1.4411433053

Allen, I.E. & Seaman, J. (2006). Growing by degrees: Online education in the United States, 2005. Sloan Consortium (NJ1).

Anistranski, J. A., & Brown, B. B. (2023). A little help from their friends? How social factors relate to students' sense of belonging at a large public university. *Journal of College Student Retention*, 25(2), 305–325. 10.1177/1521025120985107

Anne, Y., Starkey, L., Egerton, B., & Flueggen, F. (2020). High school students' experience of online learning during COVID-19: The influence of technology and pedagogy. *Technology, Pedagogy and Education*, 01(30), 59–73.

Compilation of References

Apriceno, M., Levy, S. R., & London, B. (2020). Mentorship during college transition predicts academic self-efficacy and sense of belonging among STEM students. *Journal of College Student Development*, 61(5), 643–648. 10.1353/csd.2020.0061

Asbari, M., Purwanto, A., Fayzhall, M., Purnamasari, D., & Firdaus, R. A. (2020). Hard Skills or Soft Skills: Which are More Important for Indonesian Teachers Innovation. *International Journal of Control and Automation*, 13(02).

Astin, A. W. (1993a). *What matters in college? Four critical years revisited.* Jossey-Bass.

Astin, A. W. (1993b). *Assessment for excellence: The philosophy and practice of assessment and evaluation in higher education.* Macmillan.

Aucejo, E. M., French, J., Ugalde Araya, M. P., & Zafar, B. (2020). The impact of COVID-19 on student experiences and expectations: Evidence from a survey. *Journal of Public Economics*, 191, 104271. 10.1016/j.jpubeco.2020.10427132873994

Baker, V. L., & Griffin, K. A. (2010). Beyond mentoring and advising toward understanding the role of faculty 'developers' in student success. *About Campus: Enriching the Student Learning Experience*, 14(6), 2–8. 10.1002/abc.20002

Balfanz, R., & Byrnes, V. (2012). *The importance of being in school: A report on absenteeism in the nation's public schools.* Johns Hopkins University Center for Social Organization of Schools.

Balfanz, R., & Byrnes, V. (2018). Using data and the human touch: Evaluating the NYC inter-agency campaign to reduce chronic absenteeism. *Journal of Education for Students Placed at Risk*, 23(1–2), 107–121. 10.1080/10824669.2018.1435283

Banda, A., & Mpolomoka, D. L. (2023). A Critique of the Southern African Development Community's Protocol on Education and Training. In *Sustaining Higher Education Through Resource Allocation, Learning Design Models, and Academic Development.* IGI Global. 10.4018/978-1-6684-7059-6.ch009

Banda, S., Mpolomoka, D. L., Mbono, D., & Sampa, R. L. (2017). Use of Questions in Qualitative Research: How Questions guided Our Study. *International Journal of Developmental Research*, 7(12).

Banerjee, P. (2020). The Impact of COVID-19 in Higher Education: An Empirical Study from West Bengal. *Research & Exploration*, 116–122.

Barringer, A., Papp, L. M., & Gu, P. (2023). College students' sense of belonging in times of disruption: Prospective changes from before to during the COVID-19 pandemic. *Higher Education Research & Development*, 42(6), 1309–1322. 10.1080/07294360.2022.213827537457647

Bauer, L., Liu, P., Schanzenbach, D. W., & Shambaugh, J. (2018). *Reducing chronic absenteeism under the every student succeeds act.* The Brookings Institution.

Beck, D. E., Maranto, R., & Lo, W.-J. (2014). Determinants of student and parent satisfaction at a cyber charter school. *The Journal of Educational Research*, 107(3), 209–216. 10.1080/00220671.2013.807494

Behera, S. K., Ansary, M. S., & Roy, S. (2022). Perception of Undergraduate Students on Online Education during COVID-19 Pandemic in Purulia District of West Bengal. In *Digital Innovation for Pandemics* (pp. 113–134). Auerbach Publications. 10.1201/9781003328438-6

Bellaver, C. M. (2016). *A study to determine a relationship between a response to intervention math program and standardized math assessments* (Publication No. 3746431). [Doctoral dissertation, Capella University]. ProQuest Dissertations & Theses Global. (1760153044).

Belsha, K. (2020, November 23). *Across the U.S., fewer students are being identified as homeless. Educators say that's actually a bad sign.* Chalkbeat.

Benner, A. D., & Mistry, R. S. (2020). Child development during the COVID-19 pandemic through a life course theory lens. *Child Development Perspectives*, 14(4), 236–243. 10.1111/cdep.1238733230400

Berg, B. L., & Lune, H. (2017). *Qualitative research methods for social sciences* (9th ed.). Pearson Education Limited.

Berger, J. B., & Milem, J. F. (1999). The role of student involvement and perceptions of integration in a causal model of student persistence. *Research in Higher Education*, 40(6), 641–664. 10.1023/A:1018708813711

Blass, N. (2020). *Opportunities and risks to the education system in the time of the coronavirus: An overview*. Taub Center for Social Policies in Israel.

Blicharz, J. (2021). *The perceptions of English language learners on their level of preparedness to complete college courses taught in English: An interpretative phenomenological analysis drawing upon culturally responsive pedagogy* [Doctoral dissertation, Saint John's University]. Theses and Dissertations. https://scholar.stjohns.edu/theses_dissertations/318

Bozkurt, C., & Sharma, R. (2020). Emergency remote teaching in a time of global crisis due to Corona Virus pandemic. *Asian Journal of Distance Education*, 15(1).

Brand, C., & O'Conner, L. (2004). School refusal: It takes a team. *Children & Schools*, 26(1), 54–64. 10.1093/cs/26.1.54

Braun, V., & Clarke, V. (2012). Thematic Analysis. *APA Handbook of Research Methods in Psychology*, 2, 57-71 10.1037/13620-004

Bridgeland, J. M., DiIulio, J. J., & Morrison, K. B. (2006). *The silent epidemic: Perspectives of high school dropouts*. Bill & Melinda Gates Foundation.

Compilation of References

Broady, K., Macklin, M., & O'Donnell, J. (2020, December 16). Preparing U.S. workers for the post-COVID economy: Higher education, workforce training and labor unions. *Brookings*. https://www.brookings.edu/research/preparing-u-s-workers-for-the-post-covid-economy-higher-education-workforce-training-and-labor-unions/

Bryant, J. (2020, November 9). The pandemic is a crisis for students with special needs. *The Atlantic*.https://www.theatlantic.com/politics/archive/2020/11/pandemic-crisis-students-special-needs/616808/

Byun, S., Irvin, M. J., & Bell, B. A. (2015). Advanced math course taking: Effects on math achievement and college enrollment. *Journal of Experimental Education*, 83(4), 439–468. 10.1080/00220973.2014.91957026508803

Campbell, S., Greenwood, M., Prior, S., Shearer, T., Walkem, K., Young, S., Bywaters, D., & Walker, K. (2020). Purposive Sampling: Complex or Simple? Research Case Examples. *Journal of Research in Nursing*, 25(8), 652–661. 10.1177/1744987120927206343946876

Causey, C. J. (2014). *Measuring the effects of computer-assisted instruction on teacher confidence and student achievement in 8th grade math* (Publication No. 3630384). [Doctoral dissertation, Trevecca Navarene University]. ProQuest Dissertations & Theses Global.

Centers for Disease Control and Prevention (U.S.). Office of Public Health Preparedness and Response. (2011). Preparedness 101: zombie pandemic. Author.

Centers for Disease Control and Prevention. (2020). *Interim guidance for administrators of US K–12 schools and childcare programs: Plan, prepare, and respond to coronavirus disease (COVID-19)*. Centers for Disease Control and Prevention.

Chandler, N. (2013). Braced for turbulence: Understanding and managing resistance to change in the higher education sector. *Management*, 3(5), 243–251.

Chang, H., & Romero, M. (2008). *Present, engaged and accounted for: The critical importance of addressing chronic absence in the early grades*. National Center for Children in Poverty.

Cheng, S., Yang, Y., & Deng, M. (2021). Psychological stress and perceived school success among parents of children with developmental disabilities during the COVID-19 pandemic. *Journal of Autism and Developmental Disorders*, 52(1), 1–8.34322825

Chickering, A. (1981). *The modern American college: Responding to the new realities of diverse students and changing society*. Jossey-Bass, Inc.

Chickering, A., & Reisser, L. (1993). *Education and identity* (2nd ed.). Jossey-Bass, Inc.

Chiland, C., & Young, J. G. (1990). *Why children reject school*. Yale University Press.

Chingos, M. (2013). Questioning the quality of virtual schools. *Education Next*, 13(2), 1–8.

Cipriano, C., & Brackett, M. (2020). *Teacher interrupted: Leaning into the social-emotional learning crisis amid the COVID-19 crisis*. EdSurge News.

Cole, D. A., Nick, E. A., Zelkowitz, R. L., Roeder, K. M., & Spinelli, T. (2017). Online social support for young people: Does it recapitulate in-person social support; can it help? *Computers in Human Behavior*, 68, 456–464. 10.1016/j.chb.2016.11.05828993715

Collins, K. M., Green, P. C.III, Nelson, S. L., & Madahar, S. (2015). Cyber charter schools and students with disabilities: Rebooting the IDEA to address equity, access, and compliance. *Equity & Excellence in Education*, 48(1), 71–86. 10.1080/10665684.2015.991219

Coronavirus Aid, Relief, and Economic Security Act. (2020). Pub. L. No. Public Law 116-136, 9001 15 USC.

Correia-Harker, B. P., Snipes, J. T., Rockenbach, A. N., & Mayhew, M. J. (2019). Students' perceptions of and engagement with worldview diversity in college. In *Educating About Religious Diversity and Interfaith Engagement* (pp. 22-39). Routledge.

Correia-Harker, B. P., & Dugan, J. P. (2020). Beyond knowledge and skills: Exploring leadership motivation as a critical construct for student leadership development. *Journal of College Student Development*, 61(3), 299–316. 10.1353/csd.2020.0029

Cortina, J. M. (1993). What is a coefficient alpha? An examination of theory and applications. *The Journal of Applied Psychology*, 78(1), 98–104. https://www.psychosphere.com/what%20is%20coefficient%20alpha%20by%20Cortina.pdf. 10.1037/0021-9010.78.1.98

Cramer, M. (2020, October 5). Parents face murder charge in death of girl with severe lice. *The New York Times*.

Creswell, J. W. (2012). *Educational research: Planning, conducting, and evaluating quantitative and qualitative research*. Pearson.

Creswell, J., & Poth, C. N. (2018). *Qualitative inquiry and research design: Choosing among five traditions* (4th ed.). Sage Publications.

Dahl, G. B., & Lochner, L. (2005). The impact of family income on child achievement. *The American Economic Review*, 102(5), 1927–1956. 10.1257/aer.102.5.1927

Daniel, S. J. (2020). Education and the COVID-19 pandemic. *Prospects*, 49(1-2), 91–96. 10.1007/s11125-020-09464-332313309

Darling-Hammond, L., Schachner, A., & Edgerton, A. K. (2020). *Restarting and reinventing school: Learning in the time of COVID-19 and beyond*. Learning Policy Institute.

Dar, S. A., Khurshid, S. Q., Wani, Z. A., Khanam, A., Haq, I., Shah, N. N., Shahnawaz, M., & Mustafa, H. (2020). 'Stigma in Coronavirus Disease-19 Survivors in Kashmir, India: A Cross-Sectional Exploratory Study'. *PLoS One*, 15(12), e0244715. 10.1371/journal.pone.024471533362246

Datta, M., & Bhattacharya, S. (2022). Factors Affecting Undergraduate Medical Students' Perception of Online Education During the COVID Pandemic at a Teaching Hospital in Eastern India. *Journal of Medical Education*, 21(1). Advance online publication. 10.5812/jme-122541

Compilation of References

Dempsey, M., Geitner, L., Brennan, A., & McAvoy, J. (2022). A review of the success and failure factors for Change Management. *IEEE Engineering Management Review*, 50(1), 85–93. 10.1109/EMR.2021.3130989

DeVellis, R. F., & Thorpe, C. T. (2021). *Scale development: Theory and applications*. Sage publications.

Devi, P. B. (2008). *Content Analysis: A Method of Social Science Research*. Sage.

Di Gennaro, F., Pizzol, D., Marotta, C., Antunes, M., Racalbuto, V., Veronese, N., & Smith, L. (2020). 'Coronavirus Diseases (COVID-19) Current Status and Future Perspectives: A Narrative Review.'. *International Journal of Environmental Research and Public Health*, 17(2690), 1–11. 10.3390/ijerph1708269032295188

Di Pietro, G., Biagi, F., Costa, P., Karpinski, Z., & Mazza, J. (2020). *The likely Impact of COVID-19 on Education: Reflections based on the existing Literature and Recent International Datasets. European Union and JRC Technical Report, EUR 30272*. European Union.

Dodge, K. A. (1993). Social-cognitive mechanisms in the development of conduct disorder and depression. *Annual Review of Psychology*, 44(1), 559–584. 10.1146/annurev.ps.44.020193.0030158434896

Dolighan, T., & Owen, M. (2021). Teacher efficacy for online teaching during the COVID-19 pandemic. *Brock Education Journal*, 30(1), 95–95. 10.26522/brocked.v30i1.851

Dougherty, S. M., Goodman, J. S., Hill, D. V., Litke, E. G., & Page, L. C. (2015). Middle school math acceleration and equitable access to eighth-grade algebra: Evidence from the wake county public school system. *Educational Evaluation and Policy Analysis*, 37(1_suppl, 1S), 80S–101S. 10.3102/0162373715576076

Doyumğaç, A., Tanhan, A., & Kiymaz, M. S. (2021). Understanding the Most Important Facilitators and Barriers for Online Education during COVID-19 through Online Photovoice Methodology. *International Journal of Higher Education*, 10(1), 166. 10.5430/ijhe.v10n1p166

DQ Institute (2019). Outsmart the Cyber-pandemic: Empower every child with digital intelligence by 2020. Retrieved from file:///D:/COVID/DQEveryChild%20DQ%20Institute.html.

Dugan, J. P., Bohle, C. W., Woelker, L. R., & Cooney, M. A. (2014). The role of social perspective-taking in developing students' leadership capacities. *Journal of Student Affairs Research and Practice*, 51(1), 1–15. 10.1515/jsarp-2014-0001

Dugan, J. P., Kodama, C. M., & Gebhardt, M. C. (2012). Race and leadership development among college students: The additive value of collective racial esteem. *Journal of Diversity in Higher Education*, 5(3), 174–189. 10.1037/a0029133

Dugan, J. P., Komives, S. R., & Segar, T. C. (2008). College Student Capacity for Socially Responsible Leadership: Understanding Norms and Influences of Race, Gender, and Sexual Orientation. *NASPA Journal*, 45(4), 475–500. 10.2202/1949-6605.2008

Dung, D. T. H. (2020). The advantages and disadvantages of virtual learning. *IOSR Journal of Research & Method in Education*, 10(3), 45–48. 10.9790/7388-1003054548

Duran, A., Dahl, L. S., Stipeck, C., & Mayhew, M. J. (2020). A critical quantitative analysis of students' sense of belonging: Perspectives on race, generation status, and collegiate environments. *Journal of College Student Development*, 61(2), 133–153. 10.1353/csd.2020.0014

Dusenbury, L., Calin, S., Domitrovich, C., & Weissberg, R. P. (2015). *What does evidence-based instruction in social and emotional learning actually look like in practice? A Brief on findings from CASEL's program reviews.* Collaborative for Academic, Social, and Emotional Learning.

Edelson, D. C., & Joseph, D. M. (2012). The interest-driven learning design framework: motivating learning through usefulness. In *Embracing Diversity in the Learning Sciences* (pp. 166–173). Routledge.

EdSource. (2020). Coronavirus: Highlighting strategies for student success. Retrieved from https://edsource.org/topic/coronavirus

Education Commission of the States. (2019). *High School Graduation Requirements: 50 state comparison.* Education commission of the States: Your education policy team. https://c0arw235.caspio.com/dp/b7f930000e16e10a822c47b3baa2

Ek, H., & Eriksson, R. (2013). Psychological factors behind truancy, school phobia, and school refusal: A literature study. *Child & Family Behavior Therapy*, 35(3), 228–248. 10.1080/07317107.2013.818899

El Said, G. R. (2021). How did the COVID-19 pandemic affect higher education learning experience? An empirical investigation of learners' academic performance at a university in a developing country. *Advances in Human-Computer Interaction*, 2021, 1–10. 10.1155/2021/6649524

Elliott, J. (1999). Practitioner review: School refusal: Issues of conceptualization, assessment, and treatment. *Journal of Child Psychology and Psychiatry, and Allied Disciplines*, 40(7), 1001–1012. 10.1111/1469-7610.0051910576531

Families First Coronavirus Response Act. (2020). Pub. L. No. Public Law 116-127, 2601 29 USC.

Fang, D., Thomsen, M. R., & Nayga, R. M.Jr. (2021). The association between food insecurity and mental health during the COVID-19 pandemic. *BMC Public Health*, 21(1), 1–8. 10.1186/s12889-021-10631-033781232

Farrell, D., & Greig, F. 2017. The online platform economy: Has growth peaked? Available at *SSRN* 2911194. 10.2139/ssrn.2911194

Fauci, A. S., Lane, H. C., & Redfield, R. R. (2020). COVID-19—Navigating the uncharted. *The New England Journal of Medicine*, 382(13), 1268–1269. 10.1056/NEJMe200238732109011

Feinberg, M. E. A., Mogle, J., Lee, J. K., Tornello, S. L., Hostetler, M. L., Cifelli, J. A., & Hotez, E. (2022). Impact of the COVID-19 pandemic on parent, child, and family functioning. *Family Process*, 61(1), 361–374. 10.1111/famp.1264933830510

Compilation of References

Ferri, F., Grifoni, P., & Guzzo, T. (2020). Online learning and emergency remote teaching: Opportunities and challenges in emergency situations. *Societies (Basel, Switzerland)*, 10(4), 86. 10.3390/soc10040086

Firang, D. (2020). The impact of COVID-19 pandemic on international students in Canada. *International Social Work*, 63(6), 820–824. 10.1177/0020872820940030

Fisher, D., Frey, N., & Hattie, J. (2021). *The distance learning playbook: Teaching for engagement & impact in any setting.* Corwin.

Flores, G., & Estudillo, A. (2018). Effects of a peer-to-peer mentoring program: Supporting first-year college students' academic and social integration on campus. *Journal of Human Services: Training, Research, and Practice*, 3(2). https://scholarworks.sfasu.edu/jhstrp/vol3/iss2/3

Francois, C., & Weiner, J. (2020). Accountability during school closures: moving from external to internal. CPRE Policy Briefs. Retrieved from https://repository.upenn.edu/cpre_policybriefs/91

Franklin, T., & Peng, L. (2008). Mobile math: Math educators and students engage in mobile learning. *Journal of Computing in Higher Education*, 20(2), 69–80. 10.1007/s12528-008-9005-0

Freeman, T. M., Anderman, L. H., & Jensen, J. M. (2007). Sense of belonging in college freshmen at the classroom and campus levels. *Journal of Experimental Education*, 75(3), 203–220. 10.3200/JEXE.75.3.203-220

Freemont, W. (2003). School refusal in children and adolescents. *American Family Physician*, 68(8), 1555–1561.14596443

Fruehwirth, J. C., Biswas, S., & Perreira, K. M. (2021). The COVID-19 pandemic and mental health of first-year college students: Examining the effect of COVID-19 stressors using longitudinal data. *PLoS One*, 16(3), e0247999. 10.1371/journal.pone.024799933667243

Gallè, E., Sabella, E. A., Da Molin, G., De Giglio, O., Caggiano, G., Di Onofrio, V., Ferracuti, S., Montagna, M. T., Liguori, G., Orsi, G. B., & Napoli, C. (2020). Understanding Knowledge and Behaviors Related to CoVID–19 Epidemic in Italian Undergraduate Students: The EPICO Study. *International Journal of Environmental Research and Public Health*, 17(10), 3481. 10.3390/ijerph1710348132429432

Garbe, A., Ogurlu, U., Logan, N., & Cook, P. (2020). COVID-19 and remote learning: Experiences of parents with children during the pandemic. *American Journal of Qualitative Research*, 4(3), 45–65.

Garvey, W. P., & Hegrenes, J. R. (1966). Desensitization techniques in the treatment of school phobia. *The American Journal of Orthopsychiatry*, 36(1), 147–152. 10.1111/j.1939-0025.1966.tb02301.x5904485

Gee, K. A., Hough, H., & Chavez, B. (2023). Chronic absenteeism postpandemic: let's not make this our "new normal." *Ed Policy*. https://edpolicyinca.org/newsroom/chronic-absenteeism-post-pandemic

Gee, K. A., Asmundson, V., & Vang, T. (2023). Educational impacts of the COVID-19 pandemic in the United States: Inequities by race, ethnicity, and socioeconomic status. *Current Opinion in Psychology*, 52, 101643. 10.1016/j.copsyc.2023.10164337442079

Genova, H. M., Arora, A., & Botticello, A. L. (2021, November). Effects of school closures resulting from COVID-19 in autistic and neurotypical children. *Frontiers in Education*, 6, 761485. 10.3389/feduc.2021.761485

Gentles, S. J., Charles, C., Ploeg, J., & McKibbon, K. N. (2015). Sampling in Qualitative research: Insights from an overview of the methods literature. *The Qualitative Report*, 20(11), 1777–1789. 10.46743/2160-3715/2015.2373

Gigliotti, R. A. (2020). Sudden shifts to fully online: Perceptions of campus preparedness and implications for leading through disruption. *The Journal of Literacy and Technology*, 21(2), 18–36.

Gigliotti, R. A. (2021). The impact of COVID-19 on academic department chairs: Heightened complexity, accentuated liminality, and competing perceptions of reinvention. Innovative Higher Education. Gillen-O'Neel, C. (2021). Sense of belonging and student engagement: A daily study of first-and continuing-generation college students. *Research in Higher Education*, 62(1), 45–71.

Goldberg, A. E., Allen, K. R., & Smith, J. Z. (2021). Divorced and separated parents during the COVID-19 pandemic. *Family Process*, 60(3), 866–887. 10.1111/famp.1269334227099

Goldstein, D. (2020, April 6). When can we go to school? *The New York Times*. https://www.nytimes.com/2020/04/06/us/coronavirus-schools-reopen.html

Gonzalez, T., De la Rubia, M. A., Hincz, K. P., Comas-Lopez, M., Subirats, L., Fort, S., & Sacha, G. M. (2020). Influence of COVID-19 Confinement on Students' Performance in Higher Education. *PLoS One*, 15(10), e0239490. 10.1371/journal.pone.023949033035228

Goodman, J., Melkers, J., & Pallais, A. (2019). Can online delivery increase access to education? *Journal of Labor Economics*, 37(1), 1–34. 10.1086/698895

Gopalan, M., Linden-Carmichael, A., & Lanza, S. (2022). College students' sense of belonging and mental health amidst the COVID-19 pandemic. *The Journal of Adolescent Health*, 70(2), 228–233. 10.1016/j.jadohealth.2021.10.01034893423

Gottfried, M. A. (2015). Can center-based childcare reduce the odds of early chronic absenteeism? *Early Childhood Research Quarterly*, 32, 160–173. 10.1016/j.ecresq.2015.04.002

Goudeau, S., Sanrey, C., Stanczak, A., Manstead, A., & Darnon, C. (2021). Why lockdown and distance learning during the COVID-19 pandemic are likely to increase the social class achievement gap. *Nature Human Behaviour*, 5(10), 1273–1281. 10.1038/s41562-021-01212-734580440

Gray, J. (2020, July 21). *Fordham fall opening plans and campus life update*. Fordham News. https://news.fordham.edu/university-news/fordham-fall-opening-plans-and-campus-life-update/

GRZ. (2020). *Statement by His Excellency, Dr. Edgar Chagwa Lungu, President of the Republic of Zambia, on the COVID-19 Pandemic, 25th March, 2020*. GRZ.

Compilation of References

Gulley, B. (2009). A computer based education (CBE) program for middle school mathematics intervention. *Journal of Computers in Mathematics and Science Teaching*, 28(4), 381–404.

Gulosino, C., & Miron, G. (2017). Growth and performance of fully online and blended K–12 public schools. *Education Policy Analysis Archives*, 25(124), 124. 10.14507/epaa.25.2859

Gundersen, C., & Ziliak, J. P. (2015). Food insecurity and health outcomes. *Health Affairs*, 34(11), 1830–1839. 10.1377/hlthaff.2015.064526526240

Guthrie, K. L., & Jenkins, D. M. (2018). *The role of leadership educators: Transforming learning*. Information Age Publishing.

Guthrie, K. L., & Osteen, L. (Eds.). (2016). *Reclaiming higher education's purpose in leadership development. New directions for higher education, Number 174*. Wiley.

Gutiérrez-Maldonado, J., Magallón-Neri, E., Rus-Calafell, M., & Peñaloza-Salazar, C. (2009). Virtual reality exposure for school phobia. *Anuario de Psicología*, 40(2), 223–236.

Haavik, M. (2020, October 12). % of Minnesota's educators are considering quitting. *KARE News Minneapolis*.

Hagerty, B. M., Williams, R. A., Coyne, J. C., & Early, M. R. (1996). Sense of belonging and indicators of social and psychological functioning. *Archives of Psychiatric Nursing*, 10(4), 235–244. 10.1016/S0883-9417(96)80029-X8799050

Haller, T., & Novita, S. (2021). Parents' perceptions of school support during COVID-19: What satisfies parents? *Frontiers in Education*, 6, 700441. 10.3389/feduc.2021.700441

Hallgarten, J. (2020). Evidence on Efforts to Mitigate the Negative Educational Impact of Past Disease Outbreak. *KD4 Helpdesk Report No. 793*. Education Development Trust.

Hampden-Thompson, G. (2013). Family policy, family structure, and children's educational achievement. *Social Science Research*, 42(3), 804–817. 10.1016/j.ssresearch.2013.01.00523521996

Hanushek, E., & Woessmann, L. (2020). *The economic impacts of learning losses*. OCED.

Hapompwe, C. C., Kukano, C., & Siwale, J. (2020). Impact of COVID-19 on Zambia's 2020 General Education Examination Candidates' Academic Performance in Lusaka: E-Learning Issues. *International Journal of Scientific and Research Publications*, 10(5), 647–654. 10.29322/IJSRP.10.05.2020.p10175

Härkönen, J., Bernardi, F., & Boertien, D. (2017). Family dynamics and child outcomes: An overview of research and open questions. *European Journal of Population*, 33(2), 163–184. 10.1007/s10680-017-9424-630976231

Harnett, B. M. (2015). *The value of Content Analysis as a Qualitative Research Method: Research Proposal*. The British University in Dubai.

Harris, A., & Goodall, J. (2008). Do parents know they matter? Engaging all parents in learning. *Educational Research*, 50(3), 277–289. 10.1080/00131880802309424

Havik, T., Bru, E., & Ertesvåg, S. K. (2015). School factors associated with school refusal- and truancy-related reasons for school non-attendance. *Social Psychology of Education*, 18(2), 221–240. 10.1007/s11218-015-9293-y

Hemer, K. M., Perez, R. J., & Harris, L. W.Jr. (2019b). An examination of factors that contribute to the development of perspective taking. *Journal of College and Character*, 20(2), 144–162. 10.1080/2194587X.2019.1591283

Herold, B. (2013, August 6). Federal indictment fuels concerns about Pa. cyber charters. *EdWeek*.

Higher Education Research Institute (HERI). (1996). *A social change model of leadership development: Guidebook version III*. National Clearinghouse for Leadership Programs.

Hodges, C. B., Moore, S., Lockee, B. B., Trust, T., & Bond, M. A. (2020). The difference between emergency remote teaching and online learning. https://er.educause.edu/articles/2020/3/the-difference-between-emergency-remote-teaching-and-online-learning

Holloway-Friesen, H. (2018). On the road home: A Content analysis of commuters' sense of belonging. *The College Student Affairs Journal*, 36(2), 81–96. 10.1353/csj.2018.0017

Honickman, T. K. (2023). *A qualitative study using ecological systems theory to understand the lived experience of students with academic risks during the return to in-person classrooms following the COVID-19 pandemic*. Available from ProQuest One Academic. (2843777412). Retrieved from https://www.proquest.com/dissertations-theses/qualitative-study-using-ecological-systems-theory/docview/2843777412/se-2

Houtrow, A., Harris, D., Molinero, A., Levin-Decanini, T., & Robichaud, C. (2020). Children with disabilities in the United States and the COVID-19 pandemic. *Journal of Pediatric Rehabilitation Medicine*, 13(3), 415–424. 10.3233/PRM-20076933185616

Hsiao, K. P. (1992). First-generation college students. Retrieved from ERIC database. (ED351079)

Hung, M., Smith, W. A., Voss, M. W., Franklin, J. D., Gu, Y., & Bounsanga, J. (2020). Exploring student achievement gaps in school districts across the United States. *Education and Urban Society*, 52(2), 175–193. 10.1177/0013124519833442

Hunter, C. D., Case, A. D., & Harvey, I. S. (2019). Black college students' sense of belonging and racial identity. *International Journal of Inclusive Education*, 23(9), 950–966. 10.1080/13603116.2019.1602363

Hunting, R. (2010). *Little people, big play and big mathematical ideas*. Conference report. Mathematics Education Reference Group of Australasia, 33, 725–730.

Hurtado, S., & Carter, D. F. (1997). Effects of college transition and perceptions of the campus racial climate on Latino college students' sense of belonging. *Sociology of Education*, 70(4), 324–345. 10.2307/2673270

ILO. (2020). *Terms of Reference for an Assessment on the Impact of COVID-19 on the Informal Sector in Zambia*.

Compilation of References

Jabareen, Y. (2008). Building a Conceptual Framework: Philosophy, Definitions and Procedure. International Journal of Qualitative Methods, 8(4), 49-62. doi:10.1177/160940690900406

Jensen, E. (2009). *Teaching with poverty in mind: What being poor does to kids' brains and what schools can do about it*. ASCD.

Johnson, D. R., Soldner, M., Leonard, J. B., Alvarez, P., Inkelas, K. K., Rowan-Kenyon, H. T., & Longerbeam, S. D. (2007). Examining sense of belonging among first-year undergraduates from different racial/ethnic groups. *Journal of College Student Development*, 48(5), 525–542. 10.1353/csd.2007.0054

Johnson, M. R., Schuneman, M., & McClure, S. (2022). Comparing the effects of COVID-19 on fraternity & sorority members and unaffiliated college students. *Oracle: The Research Journal of the Association of Fraternity/Sorority Advisors, 17*(1), 17-30. DOI: 10.25774/ww8n-p985

Jones, S. M., & Doolittle, E. J. (2017). Social and Emotional Learning: Introducing the Issue. *The Future of Children*, 27(1), 3–11. https://www.jstor.org/stable/44219018. 10.1353/foc.2017.0000

Kapasia, N., Paul, P., Roy, A., Saha, J., Zaveri, A., Mallick, R., Barman, B., Das, P., & Chouhan, P. (2020). Impact of lockdown on learning status of undergraduate and postgraduate students during COVID-19 pandemic in West Bengal, India. *Children and Youth Services Review*, 116, 105194. 10.1016/j.childyouth.2020.10519432834270

Karakulak, A., Tepe, B., Dimitrova, R., Abdelrahman, M., Akaliyski, P., Alaseel, R., Alkamali, Y. A., Amin, A., Lizarzaburu Aguinaga, D. A., Andres, A., Aruta, J. J. B. R., Assiotis, M., Avanesyan, H., Ayub, N., Bacikova-Sleskova, M., Baikanova, R., Bakkar, B., Bartoluci, S., Benitez, D., & Rudnev, M. (2023). Trust in government moderates the association between fear of COVID-19 as well as empathic concern and preventive behaviour. *Communications Psychology*, 1(43), 1–16. 10.1038/s44271-023-00046-5

Kearney, C. A. (2007). *Getting your child to say "yes" to school: A guide for parents of youth with school refusal behavior*. Oxford University Press. 10.1093/oso/9780195306309.001.0001

Kearney, C. A., & Beasley, J. F. (1994). The clinical treatment of school refusal behavior: A survey of referral and practice characteristics. *Psychology in the Schools*, 31(2), 128–132. 10.1002/1520-6807(199404)31:2<128::AID-PITS2310310207>3.0.CO;2-5

Kearney, C. A., & Graczyk, P. (2014). A response to intervention model to promote school attendance and decrease school absenteeism. *Child and Youth Care Forum*, 43(1), 1–25. 10.1007/s10566-013-9222-1

Khalil, R., Mansour, A. E., Fadda, W. A., Almisnid, K., Aldamegh, M., Al-Nafeesah, A., Alkhalifah, A., & Al-Wutayd, O. (2020). The sudden transition to synchronized online learning during the COVID-19 pandemic in Saudi Arabia: A qualitative study exploring medical students' perspectives. *BMC Medical Education*, 20(285), 285. 10.1186/s12909-020-02208-z32859188

Kim, J. H. "Jane," Maria Claudia Soler, Zhe Zhao, and Erica Swirsky. 2024. Race and Ethnicity in Higher Education: 2024 Status Report Executive Summary. Washington, DC: American Council on Education.

Kinfu, Y., Alamu, U., & Achoki, T. (2020). COVID-19 Pandemic in the African Continent: Forecasts of Cumulative Cases, New Infections and Mortality. MedRxiv*: Preprint Server for Health Sciences.* 10.1101/2020.04.09.20059154

Kodoma, C. M., & Dugan, J. P. (2013). Leveragin leadership efficacy for college students: Disaggregating data to examine unique predictors by race. *Equity & Excellence in Education*, 46(2), 184–201. 10.1080/10665684.2013.780646

Kraft, M. A., Simon, N. S., & Lyon, M. A. (2021). Sustaining a sense of success: The importance of teacher working conditions during the COVID-19-19 pandemic. *Journal of Research on Educational Effectiveness*, 14(4), 727–769. 10.1080/19345747.2021.1938314

Kuhn, T. L. (2008). Historical foundations of academic advising. In Gordon, V. N., Habley, W. R., & Grites, T. J. (Eds.), *Academic advising: A comprehensive handbook* (pp. 3–16). Jossey-Bass.

Kumah, D., Malviya, R., & Sharma, P. K. (2020). Corona Virus: A Review of COVID-19 History and Origin. *EJMO*, 4(1), 8–25.

Kwak, N., & Radler, B. (2002). A comparison between mail and web surveys: Response pattern, respondent profile, and data quality. *Journal of Official Statistics*, 18(2), 257.

Lake, R., & Worthen, M. (2021). *State Accountability Systems in the COVID Era and Beyond*. Center on Reinventing Public Education.

Lane, I. F. (2007). Change in higher education: Understanding and responding to individual and organizational resistance. *Journal of Veterinary Medical Education*, 34(2), 85–92. 10.3138/jvme.34.2.8517446632

Laumer, S., & Eckhardt, A. (2012). Why do people reject technologies: A review of user resistance theories. *Information Systems Theory: Explaining and Predicting Our Digital Society*, 1, 63–86. 10.1007/978-1-4419-6108-2_4

Layne, A. E., Bernstein, G. A., Egan, E. A., & Kushner, M. G. (2003). Predictors of treatment response in anxious-depressed adolescent with school refusal. *Journal of the American Academy of Child and Adolescent Psychiatry*, 42(3), 319–326. 10.1097/00004583-200303000-0001212595785

Lederman, D. (2020). (March 18, Will shift to remote teaching be boon or bane for inline learning? Inside Higher Ed. Retrieved from file:///D:/COVID/Most%20teaching%20is%20going%20remote.%20Will%20that%20help%20or%20hurt%20online%20learning.html

Lee, S. J., Ward, K. P., Chang, O. D., & Downing, K. M. (2021). Parenting activities and the transition to home-based education during the COVID-19 pandemic. *Children and Youth Services Review*, 122, 105585. 10.1016/j.childyouth.2020.10558533071407

Compilation of References

Leupold, C., Lopina, E., & Skloot, E. (2020). An examination of leadership development and other experiential activities on student resilience and leadership efficacy. *Journal of Leadership Education*, 19(1), 53–64. 10.12806/V19/I1/R1

Lewis, J. S. (2020). Reconsidering the effects of work on college student leadership development: An empirical perspective. *Journal of College Student Development*, 61(5), 539–557. 10.1353/csd.2020.0054

Liu, T., Chen, Y., Hamilton, M., & Harris, K. (2022). Peer mentoring to enhance graduate students' sense of belonging and academic success. *Kinesiology Review, 1*(aop), 1-12.

Liu, D., Baumeister, R. F., Veilleux, J. C., Chen, C., Liu, W., Yue, Y., & Zhang, S. (2020). Risk Factors associated with Mental Illness in Hospital Discharged Patients infected with COVID-19 in Wuhan, China. *Psychiatry Research*, 292, 1–9. 10.1016/j.psychres.2020.11329732707218

Li, X., & Guo, X. (2022). COVID-19 *Survivors: How Pandemic Precautions Result in Lingering Discrimination in China.*10.21203/rs.3.rs-2336680/v1

Lockee, B. B. (2021). Online education in the post-COVID era. *Nature Electronics*, 4(1), 5–6. 10.1038/s41928-020-00534-0

Locks, A. M., Hurtado, S., Bowman, N. A., & Oseguera, L. (2008). Extending notions of campus climate and diversity to students' transition to college. *The Review of Higher Education, 31*(3), 257-285.Major, C. (2020). Unprecedented times and innovation. *Innovative Higher Education*, 45, 435–436. 10.1007/s10755-020-09528-4

Lopez, K. A., & Willis, D. G. (2004). Descriptive Versus Interpretive Phenomenology: Their Contributions to Nursing Knowledge. *Qualitative Health Research*, 14(5), 726–235. 10.1177/1049732304263638151 07174

Love, S. M., & Marshall, D. T. (2022). Teacher experience during COVID-19. *COVID-19 and the classroom: How schools navigated the great disruption*, 21-65.

Luchembe, M. (2021). Preventive Measures against the Spread of COVID-19: Exploring Policy Responses in Selected Primary Schools in Lusaka, Zambia. *Kokusai Kyoiku Kyoryoku Ronshu*, 24(2), 97–111.

Maestas, R., Vaquera, G. S., & Zehr, L. M. (2007). Factors impacting sense of belonging at a Hispanic- serving institution. *Journal of Hispanic Higher Education*, 6(3), 237–256. 10.1177/1538192707302801

Major, C. (2020). Innovations in teaching and learning during a time of crisis. *Innovative Higher Education*, 45(4), 265–266. 10.1007/s10755-020-09514-w32836726

Malkus, N., Christensen, C., & West, L. (2020). *School district response to the COVID-19 pandemic: Round 1, districts' initial responses*. American Enterprise Institute.

Mann, B., Kotok, S., Frankenberg, E., Fuller, E., & Schafft, K. (2016). Choice, cyber charter schools, and the educational marketplace for rural districts. *Rural Educator*, 37(3), 17–29.

Martinez, N., Sowcik, M. J., & Bunch, J. C. (2020). The impact of leadership education and cocurricular involvement on the development of socially responsible leadership outcomes in undergraduate students: An exploratory study. *Journal of Leadership Education*, 19(3), 32–43. 10.12806/V19/I3/R3

Mayo Clinic Staff. (2020). *Severe acute respiratory syndrome (SARS)*. Mayo Clinic. https://www.mayoclinic.org/diseases-conditions/sars/symptoms-causes/syc-20351765

McAuliffe, G. (2002). *Working with troubled youth in schools: A guide for all school staff*. Bergin & Garvey. 10.5040/9798216038818

McNeely, C., Chang, H. N., & Gee, K. A. (2023). *Disparities in Unexcused Absences across California Schools*. Policy Analysis for California Education (PACE).

McShane, J. (2020a, March 13). *University operations. Fordham forward*. Fordham News. https://news.fordham.edu/university-news/university-operations-update-march-13-2020-8-p-m/

McShane, J. (2020b, April 24). *University COVID-19 update*. Fordham News. https://news.fordham.edu/university-news/university-COVID-19-update-friday-april-24-2020/

Merriam, S. (1998). *Qualitative research and case study applications in education*. Jossey-Bass Publishers.

Mhlanga, D., & Moloi, T. (2020). COVID-19 and the Digital Transformation of Education: What are we learning on 4IR in South Africa? *Education Science*, 10(180), 1-11. Available on https://bmjopen.bmj.com/

Miles, M. B., Huberman, A. M., & Saldana, J. (2014). *Qualitative Data Analysis: A Methods Sourcebook* (3rd ed.). SAGE Publishers.

MoE. (2020a). Education Contingency Plan for Novel Coronavirus. Lusaka: GRZ.

MoE. (2020b). *Ministry Statement on Re-opening of Schools*. GRZ.

MoE. (2021c). *Ministerial Statement on Re-Opening of Schools*. GRZ.

MoH. (2020). *Updates*. Lusaka: MOH.

MoH. (2021). *Updates*. Lusaka: MOH.

Mok, K. H., Xiong, W., Ke, G., & Cheung, J. (2021). Impact of COVID-19 pandemic on international higher education and student mobility: Student perspectives from mainland China and Hong Kong. *International Journal of Educational Research*, 105, 101718. 10.1016/j.ijer.2020.10171835719275

Moreland, A., Herlihy, C., Tynan, M. A., Sunshine, G., McCord, R. F., Hilton, C., & Popoola, A. (2020). Timing of state and territorial COVID-19 stay-at-home orders and changes in population movement, United States, March 1-May 31, 2020. *MMWR. Morbidity and Mortality Weekly Report*, 69(35), 1198–1203. 10.15585/mmwr.mm6935a232881851

Compilation of References

Morrison-Gutman, G., & McLoyd, V. (2000). Parents management of their children's education within the home, at school, and in the community: An examination of African-American families living in poverty. *The Urban Review*, 32(1), 1–24. 10.1023/A:1005112300726

Mpolomoka, D. L., Banda, A. M., Mushibwe, M., Banda, S., Nherera, S., Muvombo, M., Mainde, D., & Shawa, R. (2023). *Promoting Health and Well-Being of Secondary School Students in Chibombo District*. Paper presented at the International Conference on Making Sense of Educational Systems for Sustainable Development, Kibaha Kwa Mfipa, Tanzania.

Mukhtar, K., Javed, K., Arooj, M., & Sethi, A. (2020). Advantages, Limitations and Recommendations for online learning during COVID-19 pandemic era. *Pakistan Journal of Medical Sciences, 36*(S4), S27.

Multi-institutional study of leadership. Multi-Institutional Study of Leadership. (n.d.). Retrieved July 9, 2022, from https://www.leadershipstudy.net/

Munsaka, J., & Rukweza, J. (2021). Lived Experiences of Survivors of COVID-19 Disease at Hwange Hospital, Zimbabwe. *European Journal of Medical and Health Sciences*, 3(6), 95–100. 10.24018/ejmed.2021.3.6.1084

Museus, S. D., & Chang, T. H. (2021). The impact of campus environments on sense of belonging for first-generation college students. *Journal of College Student Development*, 62(3), 367–372. 10.1353/csd.2021.0039

Museus, S. D., Yi, V., & Saelua, N. (2017). The impact of culturally engaging campus environments on sense of belonging. *Review of Higher Education*, 40(2), 187–215. 10.1353/rhe.2017.0001

Mushibwe, C. P., Mpolomoka, D. L., Mwelwa, A., Mushima, M., & Kakoma, M. (2024). Socio-Economic Implications of COVID-19 in Densely Populated Compounds (Komboni) in Lusaka, Zambia. *Journal of Culture. Social Development*, 73, 45–59. 10.7176/JCSD/73-05

Muthuprasad, T., Aiswarya, S., Aditya, K. S., & Jha, G. K. (2021). Students' perception and preference for online education in India during COVID -19 pandemic. *Social Sciences & Humanities Open*, 3(1), 100101. 10.1016/j.ssaho.2020.10010134173507

Muvombo, M., Mpolomoka, D. L., Kabungo, C. J., Banda, A. M., Chikopela, R., & Mayamba, S. (2023). *Narratives by parents of what early childhood learners were doing during CoviD 19 in communities in Western and Eastern Provinces, Zambia: A Post-mortem and Binoculars lens*. Paper presented at the International Conference on Making Sense of Educational Systems for Sustainable Development, Kibaha Kwa Mfipa, Tanzania.

Mwangi, C. A. G., Thelamour, B., Ezeofor, I., & Carpenter, A. (2018). "Black elephant in the room": Black students contextualizing campus racial climate within US racial climate. *Journal of College Student Development*, 59(4), 456–474. 10.1353/csd.2018.0042

National Center for Education Statistics. (2011). *Findings in brief: Reading and mathematics 2011—National assessment of educational progress at Grades 4 and 8*. https://nces.ed.gov/nationsreportcard/pdf/main2011/2012459.pdf

National Center for Education Statistics. (2018). *Percentage of public school districts with students enrolled in technology-based distance education courses and number of enrollments in such courses by instructional level and district characteristics*. NCES.

National Center for Education Statistics. (2019). *What percentage of elementary and secondary schools offer distance education?* NCES.

Neuman, A., & Guterman, O. (2016). Academic achievements and homeschooling—It all depends on the goals. *Studies in Educational Evaluation*, 51, 1–6. 10.1016/j.stueduc.2016.08.005

New Jersey Department of Education. (2019). *NJ school performance report*. Author.

New Jersey Department of Education. (2021, April 14). *USED's determination regarding NJ's requirements to administer 2020-2021 statewide assessments*.https://www.nj.gov/education/broadcasts/2021/april/USEDsDeterminationRegardingNJsRequirementstoAdminister2020-2021 StatewideAssessments.pdf

New Jersey Department of Education. (2023). *NJ school performance report*.

Next Generation Science Standards. (2013). http://www.nextgenscience.org/next-generation-science-standards

Northall, T., Chang, E., Hatcher, D., & Nicholls, D. (2020). The Application and Tailoring of Colaizzi's Phenomenological Approach to a Hospital Setting. *Nurse Researcher*, 28(2), 20–25. Advance online publication. 10.7748/nr.2020.e170032309916

Ntsiful, A., Kwarteng, M. A., Pilík, M., & Osakwe, C. N. (2022). Transitioning to online teaching during the pandemic period: The role of innovation and psychological characteristics. *Innovative Higher Education*. Advance online publication. 10.1007/s10755-022-09613-w35698463

Official Site for the State of New Jersey. (2020, June 26). *Murphy administration announces reopening guidance for New Jersey schools*.https://nj.gov/governor/news/news/562020/approved/20200626b.shtml

Official Site for the State of New Jersey. (2020, May 4). *Governor murphy announces that schools will remain closed through the end of the academic year*.https://www.nj.gov/governor/news/news/562020/20200504a.shtml#:~:text=TRENTON%20%E2%80%93%20Citing%20the%20need%20to,the%202019%2D2020%20academic%20year

Okonofua, F., Ntoimo, L. F. C., Onoh, V. I., Omonkhua, A. A., Alex-Ojei, C. A., & Balogun, J. (2022). Lived Experiences of Recovered COVID-19 Persons in Nigeria: A Phenomenological Study. *PLoS One*, 17(8), e0268109. 10.1371/journal.pone.026810935969603

Olufadewa, I. I., Adesina, M. A., Oladokun, B., Baru, A., Oladele, R. I., Iyanda, T. O., Ajibade, O. J., & Abudu, F. (2020). I Was Scared I Might Die Alone: A Qualitative Study of the Physiological and Psychological Experience of COVID-19 Survivors and the Quality of Care Received at Health Facilities. *International Journal of Travel Medicine and Global Health*, 8(2), 51–57. 10.34172/ijtmgh.2020.09

Compilation of References

Omodon, B. I. (2020). The Vindication of decoloniality and the reality of COVID-19 as an emergency of unknown in rural universities, *International Journal of Sociology of Education*. 10.17583/rise.2020.5495

Oppong, S., Appiah, R., Hapunda, G., & Kheswa, J. G. (2023). Editorial: Contextualizing psychological assessment in Africa: COVID-19 and beyond. *Frontiers in Psychology*, 14, 1150387. 10.3389/fpsyg.2023.115038736895746

O'Shea, S. M. (2010). *A study of school phobic students on selected psychodynamic variables*. Available from ProQuest Central; ProQuest Dissertations & Theses Global. (756399330).

Oxendine, S. D., Taub, D. J., & Cain, E. J. (2020). Factors related to Native American students' perceptions of campus culture. *Journal of College Student Development*, 61(3), 267–280. 10.1353/csd.2020.0027

Oyinloye, O. (2020). The Possible Impact of COVID-19 on Senior Secondary School Students' Performance in Science Education in Nigeria. *Journal of Pedagogical and Psychology*, 2(2), 80–85. 10.33902/JPSP.2020263901

Patrick, S. W., Henkhaus, L. E., Zickafoose, J. S., Lovell, K., Halvorson, A., Loch, S., & Davis, M. M. (2020). Well-being of parents and children during the COVID-19 pandemic: A national survey. *Pediatrics*, 146(4), e2020016824. 10.1542/peds.2020-01682432709738

Patton, M. Q. (2015). *Qualitative research and evaluation methods* (4th ed.). Sage.

Pedler, M. L., Willis, R., & Nieuwoudt, J. E. (2022). A sense of belonging at university: Student retention, motivation and enjoyment. *Journal of Further and Higher Education*, 46(3), 397–408. 10.1080/0309877X.2021.1955844

Peprah, P., & Gyasi, R. M. (2021). Stigma and COVID-19 Crisis: A Wake-Up Call. *The International Journal of Health Planning and Management*, 36(1), 215-218. 10.1002/hpm.3065

Phillips, J., & Klein, J. D. (2023). Change Management: From Theory to Practice. *TechTrends*, 67(1), 189–197. https://link.springer.com/article/10.1007/s11528-022-00775-0#citeas. 10.1007/s11528-022-00775-036105238

Piasta, S. B. (2016). Current understandings of what works to support the development of emergent literacy in early childhood classrooms. *Child Development Perspectives*, 10(4), 234–239. 10.1111/cdep.12188

Poonam & Aggarwal, K. K. (2023). Analysis of the impact of COVID-19 on the stock market and capability of investing strategies. *AIP Conference Proceedings, 2782*. 10.1063/5.0154174

Porter, A. (2007). Rethinking the achievement gap. *PennGSE: A Review of Research, 5*(1), 1.

Potts, C. (2021). Seen and unseen: First-year college students' sense of belonging during the COVID-19 pandemic. *The College Student Affairs Journal*, 39(2), 214–224. 10.1353/csj.2021.0018

Putri, R. S., Purwanto, A., Pramono, R., Asbari, M., Wijayanti, L. M., & Hyun, C. C. (2020). Impact of the COVID-19 Pandemic on Online Home Learning: An Explorative Study of Primary Schools in Indonesia. *International Journal of Advanced Science and Technology*, 29(5), 4809–4818.

Ramlo, S. E. (2021). Universities and the COVID-19 pandemic: Comparing views about how to address the financial impact. *Innovative Higher Education*, 46(6), 777–793. 10.1007/s10755-021-09561-x34177079

Ramsetty, A., & Adams, C. (2020). Impact of the digital divide in the age of COVID-19. *Journal of the American Medical Informatics Association : JAMIA*, 27(7), 1147–1148. 10.1093/jamia/ocaa07832343813

Rayle, A. D., & Chung, K.-Y. (2007). Revisiting first-year college students' mattering: Social support, academic stress, and the mattering experience. *Journal of College Student Retention*, 9(1), 21–37. 10.2190/X126-5606-4G36-8132

Ren, J., Li, X., Chen, S., Chen, S., & Nie, Y. (2020). The influence of factors such as parenting stress and social support on the state anxiety in parents of special needs children during the COVID-19 epidemic. *Frontiers in Psychology*, 11, 565393. 10.3389/fpsyg.2020.56539333362628

Reuter, P. R., Forster, B. L., & Kruger, B. J. (2021). A longitudinal study of the impact of COVID-19 restrictions on students' health behavior, mental health and emotional well-being. *PeerJ*, 9, e12528. 10.7717/peerj.1252834993018

Ribera, A. K., Miller, A. L., & Dumford, A. D. (2017). Sense of peer belonging and institutional acceptance in the first year: The role of high-impact practices. *Journal of College Student Development*, 58(4), 545–563. 10.1353/csd.2017.0042

Richardson, K. L., Weiss, N. S., & Halbach, S. (2018). Chronic school absenteeism of children with chronic kidney disease. *The Journal of Pediatrics*, 199, 267–271. 10.1016/j.jpeds.2018.03.03129706492

Rillo, J. A., Uy, T. M. E., Macapagal, C. D., Mariano, C. R., Melosantos, M. F., Villena, C. M. D., Flores, E. A., & Catabona, Z. B. (2022). Quarantine Victors: Lived Experiences of Hospitalized COVID-19 Survivors. *Proceeding Series on Health and Medical Sciences: Proceedings of the 2nd International Nursing and Health Sciences*, 2, 21-41. Available on https://conferenceproceedings.ump.ac.id/index.php/pshms.issue/view/10

Robert Wood Johnson Foundation. (2016). *The relationship between school attendance and health*. Robert Wood Johnson Foundation.

Rogers, T., & Feller, A. (2016). Reducing student absences at scale. Working paper, Harvard University, Cambridge MA.

Romulo, S. G., & Urbano, R. C. (2022). *Separation and Discrimination: The Lived Experiences of COVID19 Survivors in Philippine Isolation Centres*. Sage Publication Journals.

Roots of Holistic Education. (2020). *Holistic Application of Google Platform to Education*. Googlesites.

Compilation of References

Rosch, D. M., Collier, D., & Thompson, S. E. (2015). An exploration of students' motivation to lead: An analysis by race, gender, and student leadership behaviors. *Journal of College Student Development*, 56(3), 286–291. 10.1353/csd.2015.0031

Roy, A. K., Breaux, R., Sciberras, E., Patel, P., Ferrara, E., Shroff, D. M., Cash, A. R., Dvorsky, M. R., Langberg, J. M., Quach, J., Melvin, G., Jackson, A., & Becker, S. P. (2022). A preliminary examination of key strategies, challenges, and benefits of remote learning expressed by parents during the COVID-19 pandemic. *School Psychology*, 37(2), 147–159. 10.1037/spq000046535266770

Ruben, B. D., De Lisi, R., & Gigliotti, R. A. (2021). *A guide for leaders in higher education: Concepts, competencies, and tools.* Stylus Publishing, LLC.

Russell, D. W. (2002). In search of underlying dimensions: The use (and abuse) of factor analysis in Personality and Social Psychology Bulletin. *Personality and Social Psychology Bulletin*, 28(12), 1629–1646. 10.1177/014616702237645

Saiz-Gonzalez, P., Fernández-Río, J. & Iglesias, D. (2023). Lessons from COVID's social distancing in the physical education class. *Apunts. Educació Física i Esports*, (154), 52-60. https://doi.org/.(2023/4).154.05 10.5672/apunts.2014-0983.es

Sarikas, C. (2020). *The High School Science Classes You Should Take.* Prepscholar. https://blog.prepscholar.com/the-high-school-science-classes-you-should-take https://www.nj.gov/education/standards/science/Sci9-12.shtml

Sarkar, B., Islam, N., Das, P., Miraj, A., Dakua, M., Debnath, M., & Roy, R. (2023). Digital learning and the lopsidedness of the education in government and private primary schools during the COVID-19 pandemic in West Bengal, India. *E-Learning and Digital Media*, 20(5), 473–497. 10.1177/20427530221117327

Sassano, J. M. (2022). Student satisfaction outcomes for autonomy, competency, and relatedness in different learning environments (29257205) Doctoral dissertation, Grand Canyon University. ProQuest.

Sax, L. J., Gilmartin, S. K., & Bryant, A. N. (2003). Assessing response rates and nonresponse bias in web and paper surveys. *Research in Higher Education*, 44(4), 409–432. https://link.springer.com/content/pdf/10.1023/A:1024232915870.pdf. 10.1023/A:1024232915870

Schelbe, L., Becker, M. S., Spinelli, C., & McCray, D. (2019). First-generation college students' perceptions of an academic retention program. *The Journal of Scholarship of Teaching and Learning*, 19(5), 61–76. 10.14434/josotl.v19i5.24300

Schonert-Reichl, K. A. (2017). Social and emotional learning and teachers. *The Future of Children*, 27(1), 137–155. 10.1353/foc.2017.0007

Schwartz, S. (2020, May 13). States all over the map on remote learning rigor, detail. *EdWeek*.

Schwartz, K. D., Exner-Cortens, D., McMorris, C. A., Makarenko, E., Arnold, P., Van Bavel, M., Williams, S., & Canfield, R. (2021). COVID-19 and student well-being: Stress and mental health during return-to-school. *Canadian Journal of School Psychology*, 36(2), 166–185. 10.1177/0829573521100165334040284

Sen, S., Chatterje, S., & Das, A. (2020). Problem of online education system in South Bengal during the COVID-19 pandemic: An appraisal. *IOSR J. Humanit. Soc. Sci*, 25(10), 7-20.

Shamburg, C., Amerman, T., Zieger, L., & Bahna, S. (2022). When school bells last rung: New Jersey schools and the reaction to COVID-19. *Education and Information Technologies*, 27(1), 23–44. 10.1007/s10639-021-10598-w34226818

Siegel, D., Acharya, P., & Sivo, S. (2017). Extending the technology acceptance model to improve usage & decrease resistance toward a new technology by faculty in higher education. *The Journal of Technology Studies*, 43(2), 58–69. 10.21061/jots.v43i2.a.1

Silwal, S., Khadgi, D., Mahato, A., Basnet, S., Thapa, S., & Niraula, A. (2021). 'Lived Experiences of COVID-19 Survivors in Nepal: A Phenomenological Analysis'. *JCMS Nepal*, 17(4), 298–307. 10.3126/jcmsn.v17i4.41887

Sintema, E. J. (2020). Effects of COVID-19 on the Performance of Grade 12 Students: Implications for STEM Education. *Eurasia Journal of Mathematics, Science and Technology Education*, 16(7), 1–6. 10.29333/ejmste/7893

Siracusano, M., Riccioni, A., Gialloreti, L. E., Segatori, E., Arturi, L., Vasta, M., Porfirio, M. C., Terribili, M., Galasso, C., & Mazzone, L. (2021). Parental stress and disability in offspring: A snapshot during the COVID-19 pandemic. *Brain Sciences*, 11(8), 1040. 10.3390/brainsci1108104034439660

Smith, J. A., & Fieldsend, M. (2021). Interpretative phenomenological analysis. In Camic, P. M. (Ed.), *Qualitative research in psychology: Expanding perspectives in methodology and design* (2nd ed., pp. 147–166). American Psychological Association. 10.1037/0000252-008

Soni, V. D. 2020. Global Impact of E-learning during COVID 19. Available at *SSRN* 3630073. 10.2139/ssrn.3630073

Soria, K. M., Hussein, D., & Vue, C. (2014). Leadership for whom? Socioeconomic factors predicting undergraduate students' positional leadership participation. *Journal of Leadership Education. Winter (14)*.

Soria, K. M., Boettcher, B., & Hallahan, K. (2022). The Effects of Participation in Recreational Activities on Students' Resilience and Sense of Belonging. *Recreational Sports Journal*, 46(2), 184–192. 10.1177/15588661221125201

Soria, K. M., Werner, L., & Nath, C. (2019). Leadership experiences and perspective taking among college students. *Journal of Student Affairs Research and Practice*, 56(2), 138–152. 10.1080/19496591.2018.1490309

Compilation of References

Stempel, H., Cox-Martin, M., Bronsert, M., Dickinson, L. M., & Allison, M. A. (2017). Chronic school absenteeism and the role of adverse childhood experiences. *Academic Pediatrics*, 17(8), 837–843. 10.1016/j.acap.2017.09.01328927940

Stern, G. M. (2014). Part-Time Job Program for Latinos Boosts College Success. *Education Digest*, 79, 55–58.

Strayhorn, T. L. (2019). *College students' sense of belonging: A key to educational success for all students* (2nd ed.). Routledge.

Suhlmann, M., Sassenberg, K., Nagengast, B., & Trautwein, U. (2018). Belonging mediates effects of student-university fit on well-being, motivation, and dropout intention. *Social Psychology (Göttingen)*, 49(1), 16–28. 10.1027/1864-9335/a000325

Sundler, A. J., Lindberg, E., Nilsson, C., & Palmer, L. (2019). Qualitative Thematic Analysis based on Descriptive Phenomenology. *Nursing Open*, 6(3), 1–7. 10.1002/nop2.27531367394

Tanner-Smith, E. E., & Fisher, B. W. (2020). Open schools, COVID-19, and child and teacher morbidity in Sweden. *The New England Journal of Medicine*, 383(15), 1484–1485.

Taunan, M., Domingo Barcelona, S. R., Sandoval, R. N. P., & Flaviano, R. L. (2021). Lived Experiences of the Senior High School Learners at Goshen of Technology and Humanities During the COVID-19 Pandemic. *International Journal of Multidisciplinary: Applied Business and Education Research*, 2(6), 679–484. 10.11594/ijmaber.02.06.03

Terry, S. (2004). *Soil Triangle Diagram*. Media Storehouse. https://www.mediastorehouse.com/science-photo-library/soil-triangle-diagram-6342015.html

Thompson, C. N., Baumgartner, J., Pichardo, C., Toro, B., Li, L., Arciuolo, R., Chan, P. Y., Chen, J., Culp, G., Davidson, A., Devinney, K., Dorsinville, A., Eddy, M., English, M., Fireteanu, A. M., Graf, L., Geevarughese, A., Greene, S. K., Guerra, K., & Fine, A. (2020). COVID-19 outbreak — New York city, February 29–June 1, 2020. *MMWR. Morbidity and Mortality Weekly Report*, 69(46), 1725–1729. 10.15585/mmwr.mm6946a233211680

Thwaite, S. V. (2022). Crisis is a powerful tool: Resilient leadership during a global health pandemic. *Journal of Leadership Education*, 21(1), 196–208. 10.12806/V21/I1/C1

Timmons, K. (2018). Educator expectations in full-day kindergarten: Comparing the factors that contribute to the formation of early childhood educator and teacher expectations. *Early Childhood Education Journal*, 46(6), 613–628. 10.1007/s10643-018-0891-0

Timmons, K., Cooper, A., Bozek, E., & Braund, H. (2021). The impacts of COVID-19 on early childhood education: Capturing the unique challenges associated with remote teaching and learning in K-2. *Early Childhood Education Journal*, 49(5), 887–901. 10.1007/s10643-021-01207-z34007140

Tinto, V. (1997). Classrooms as communities: Exploring the educational character of student persistence. *The Journal of Higher Education*, 68(6), 599–623. 10.1080/00221546.1997.11779003

Tinto, V. (2017). Reflections on student persistence. *Student Success*, 8(2), 1–8. 10.5204/ssj.v8i2.376

Toppin, I. N., & Toppin, S. M. (2016). Virtual schools: The changing landscape of K–12 education in the U.S. *Education and Information Technologies*, 21(6), 1571–1581. 10.1007/s10639-015-9402-8

Townsley, M. (2020). Grading principles in pandemic-era learning: Recommendations and implications for secondary school leaders. *Journal of School Administration Research and Development*, 5(1), 8–14. 10.32674/jsard.v5iS1.2760

Trotman Reid, P., & Roberts, S. K. (2006). Gaining options: A mathematics program for potentially talented at-risk adolescent girls. *Merrill-Palmer Quarterly*, 52(2), 288–304. 10.1353/mpq.2006.0019

TUAC-OECD. (2020). *Impact and Implications of the COVID-19 Crisis on Education Systems and Households. TUAC Secretariat Briefing*. TUAC.

Tyrell, M. (2005). School phobia. *Journal of Nursing (Luton, England)*, 21(3), 147–151. 15898849

UN OCHA. (2020). Zambia Cluster Status: Education. *Situation Report*. Retrieved from: https://reports.unocha.org/en/country/zambia/

UN. (2020). *Policy Brief: Education during COVID-19 and Beyond*. New York: UN.

UNESCO, WHO, & UNICEF. (2020). *Considerations for School-related Public Health Measures in the Context of COVID-19*. WHO, UNESCO and UNICEF.

UNESCO. COVID-19 Educational Disruption and Response. (2020). The impact of COVID-19 on student voice: Testimonies from students and teachers. https://en.unesco.org/covid19 (accessed on 29 October 2023).

UNESCO.org. (2022, July 7). https://www.unesco.org/en/articles/impact-COVID-19-student-voice-testimonies-students-and-teachers

UNHCR. (2020). Supporting continued Access to Education during COVID-19. *Emerging Promising Practices*. Copehagen: UNHCR.

United Nations. (2015). United Nations Sustainable Development Goals. https://sdgs.un.org/goals/goal4

Uzobo, E., Nwanwene, I., & Ojo, T. F. (2022). The Lived Social Experiences of COVID-19 Survivors in Southwestern Nigeria. *Journal of Social, Behavioral and Health Sciences*, 6(1), 211–225. 10.5590/JSBHS.2022.16.1.15

Vidergor, H. E. (2023). The effect of teachers' self-innovativeness on accountability, distance learning self-efficacy, and teaching practices. *Computers & Education*, 199, 104777. 10.1016/j.compedu.2023.10477736919161

Compilation of References

Villani, M.T. (2022). *First things first: Mission, relevancy and supporting persistence of first-generation college students* (Publication No. AAI28970073) [Doctoral dissertation, Fordham University]. ETD Collection for Fordham University. https://research.library.fordham.edu/dissertations/AAI28970073

Vlachopoulos, D. (2020). COVID-19: Threat or opportunity for online education? *Higher Learning Research Communications*, 10(1), 16–19. 10.18870/hlrc.v10i1.1179

Wahab. (2020). Online and Remote Learning in Higher Education Institutes: A Necessity in light of COVID-19 Pandemic. *Higher Education Studies, 10*(3).

Walton, G. M., & Cohen, G. L. (2007). A question of belonging: Race, social fit, and achievement. *Journal of Personality and Social Psychology*, 92(1), 82–96. 10.1037/0022-3514.92.1.8217201544

Waters, L. H., Barbour, M. K., & Menchaca, M. P. (2014). The nature of online charter schools: Evolution and emerging concerns. *Journal of Educational Technology & Society*, 17(4), 379–389.

Wayne, I. (2019, February 4). Benefits of homeschooling. *The New American Magazine*.

Whitaker, B. L., & Kniffin, L. E. (2022). Crisis as pedagogy: Recommendations for using the pandemic in leadership education. *Journal of Leadership Education*, 21(3), 1–16. 10.12806/V21/I3/A2

White, C. J. (2005). *Research: a practical guide*. Ithuthuko Investment.

WHO. (2020). Pneumonia of an Unknown Cause – China. https://www.who.int/emergencies/disease-outbreak-news/item/2020-DON229

WHO. (2020a). *Coronavirus Disease 2019 (COVID-19) Situation Report – 41*. WHO.

WHO. (2020b). *Coronavirus Disease 2019 (COVID-19) Situation Report – 94*. WHO.

Wimmer, M. B. (2013). Implementing evidence-based practices for school refusal and truancy. *National Association of School Psychologists Communique*, 42(4), 18–20.

Wirihana, L., Welch, A., Williamsin, M., Christensen, M., Bakon, S., & Craft, J. (2018). Using Colaizzi's Method of Data Analysis to Explore the Experiences of Nurse Academics Teaching on Satellite Campuses. *Nurse Researcher*, 25(4), 30–34. 10.7748/nr.2018.e151629546965

Wojnar, D. M., & Swanson, K. M. (2007). 'Phenomenology: An exploration'. *Journal of Holistic Nursing*, 25(3), 172–180. 10.1177/08980101106295172217724386

Woolfolk, A. (2014). *Educational Psychology: Active learner edition* (12th ed.). Pearson.

Wu, M. J., Zhao, K., & Fils-Aime, F. (2022). Response rates of online surveys in published research: A meta-analysis. *Computers in Human Behavior Reports*, 7, 100206. 10.1016/j.chbr.2022.100206

Xu, D., & Jaggars, S. S. (2014). Performance gaps between online and face-to-face courses: Differences across types of students and academic subject areas. *The Journal of Higher Education*, 85(5), 633–659. 10.1080/00221546.2014.11777343

Yamamura, E., & Tsustsui, Y. (2021). The impact of closing schools on working from home during the COVID-19 pandemic: Evidence using panel data from Japan. *Review of Economics of the Household*, 19(1), 41–60. 10.1007/s11150-020-09536-533456424

Yin, R. K. (2018). *Case study research and applications* (Vol. 6). Sage.

Yin, R. K. (2018). *Case study research and applications: Design and methods* (6th ed.). Sage.

Young-Jones, A. D., Burt, T. D., Dixon, S., & Hawthorne, M. J. (2013). Academic advising: Does it really impact student success? *Quality Assurance in Education*, 21(1), 7–19. 10.1108/09684881311293034

Young, N. D., Michael, C. N., & Smolinksi, J. A. (2019). *Captivating campuses: Proven practices that promote college student persistence, engagement and success.* Vernon Press.

Yuan, Y., Zhao, Y. J., Zhang, Q. E., Zhang, L., Cheung, T., Jackson, T., Jiang, G. Q., & Xiang, Y. T. (2021). COVID-19 'Related Stigma and its Socio-demographic Correlate: A Comparative Study'. *Globalization and Health*, 17(1), 17–54. 10.1186/s12992-021-00705-433962651

Yukhymenko-Lescroart, M. A., & Sharma, G. (2023). Sense of purpose and progress towards degree in freshman college students. *Journal of College Student Retention*, 25(1), 187–207. 10.1177/1521025120975134

Zezima, K., Craig, T., Wan, W., & Sonmez, F. (2020). *Coronavirus Now a Global Pandemic as U.S., World Scramble to Control Outbreak*. Washington, DC: The Washington Post.

Zhang, Q., Sauval, M., & Jenkins, J. M. (2023). Impacts of the COVID-19 pandemic on the childcare sector: Evidence from North Carolina. *Early Childhood Research Quarterly*, 62, 17–30. 10.1016/j.ecresq.2022.07.00335999900

Zhu, H., Wei, L., & Niu, P. (2020). The Novel Coronavirus Outbreak in Wuhan, China. *Global Health Research and Policy*, 5(1), 1–3. 10.1186/s41256-020-00135-632226823

Related References

To continue our tradition of advancing academic research, we have compiled a list of recommended IGI Global readings. These references will provide additional information and guidance to further enrich your knowledge and assist you with your own research and future publications.

Aburezeq, I. M., & Dweikat, F. F. (2017). Cloud Applications in Language Teaching: Examining Pre-Service Teachers' Expertise, Perceptions and Integration. *International Journal of Distance Education Technologies*, 15(4), 39–60. 10.4018/IJDET.2017100103

Acharjya, B., & Das, S. (2022). Adoption of E-Learning During the COVID-19 Pandemic: The Moderating Role of Age and Gender. *International Journal of Web-Based Learning and Teaching Technologies*, 17(2), 1–14. https://doi.org/10.4018/IJWLTT.20220301.oa4

Adams, J. L., & Thomas, S. K. (2022). Non-Linear Curriculum Experiences for Student Learning and Work Design: What Is the Maximum Potential of a Chat Bot? In Ramlall, S., Cross, T., & Love, M. (Eds.), *Handbook of Research on Future of Work and Education: Implications for Curriculum Delivery and Work Design* (pp. 299–306). IGI Global. https://doi.org/10.4018/978-1-7998-8275-6.ch018

Adera, B. (2017). Supporting Language and Literacy Development for English Language Learners. In Keengwe, J. (Ed.), *Handbook of Research on Promoting Cross-Cultural Competence and Social Justice in Teacher Education* (pp. 339–354). Hershey, PA: IGI Global. 10.4018/978-1-5225-0897-7.ch018

Ahamer, G. (2017). Quality Assurance for a Developmental "Global Studies" (GS) Curriculum. In I. Management Association (Ed.), *Educational Leadership and Administration: Concepts, Methodologies, Tools, and Applications* (pp. 438–477). Hershey, PA: IGI Global. https://doi.org/10.4018/978-1-5225-1624-8.ch023

Ahamer, G. (2017). Quality Assurance for a Developmental "Global Studies" (GS) Curriculum. In I. Management Association (Ed.), *Educational Leadership and Administration: Concepts, Methodologies, Tools, and Applications* (pp. 438–477). Hershey, PA: IGI Global. https://doi.org/10.4018/978-1-5225-1624-8.ch023

Akayoğlu, S., & Seferoğlu, G. (2019). An Analysis of Negotiation of Meaning Functions of Advanced EFL Learners in Second Life: Negotiation of Meaning in Second Life. In Kruk, M. (Ed.), *Assessing the Effectiveness of Virtual Technologies in Foreign and Second Language Instruction* (pp. 61–85). IGI Global. https://doi.org/10.4018/978-1-5225-7286-2.ch003

Akella, N. R. (2022). Unravelling the Web of Qualitative Dissertation Writing!: A Student Reflects. In Zimmerman, A. (Ed.), *Methodological Innovations in Research and Academic Writing* (pp. 260–282). IGI Global. https://doi.org/10.4018/978-1-7998-8283-1.ch014

Alegre de la Rosa, O. M., & Angulo, L. M. (2017). Social Inclusion and Intercultural Values in a School of Education. In Mukerji, S., & Tripathi, P. (Eds.), *Handbook of Research on Administration, Policy, and Leadership in Higher Education* (pp. 518–531). Hershey, PA: IGI Global. 10.4018/978-1-5225-0672-0.ch020

Alexander, C. (2019). Using Gamification Strategies to Cultivate and Measure Professional Educator Dispositions. *International Journal of Game-Based Learning*, 9(1), 15–29. https://doi.org/10.4018/IJGBL.2019010102

Anderson, K. M. (2017). Preparing Teachers in the Age of Equity and Inclusion. In I. Management Association (Ed.), *Medical Education and Ethics: Concepts, Methodologies, Tools, and Applications* (pp. 1532-1554). Hershey, PA: IGI Global. 10.4018/978-1-5225-0978-3.ch069

Awdziej, M. (2017). Case Study as a Teaching Method in Marketing. In Latusek, D. (Ed.), *Case Studies as a Teaching Tool in Management Education* (pp. 244–263). Hershey, PA: IGI Global. 10.4018/978-1-5225-0770-3.ch013

Bakos, J. (2019). Sociolinguistic Factors Influencing English Language Learning. In Erdogan, N., & Wei, M. (Eds.), *Applied Linguistics for Teachers of Culturally and Linguistically Diverse Learners* (pp. 403–424). IGI Global. https://doi.org/10.4018/978-1-5225-8467-4.ch017

Banas, J. R., & York, C. S. (2017). Pre-Service Teachers' Motivation to Use Technology and the Impact of Authentic Learning Exercises. In Tomei, L. (Ed.), *Exploring the New Era of Technology-Infused Education* (pp. 121–140). Hershey, PA: IGI Global. 10.4018/978-1-5225-1709-2.ch008

Barton, T. P. (2021). Empowering Educator Allyship by Exploring Racial Trauma and the Disengagement of Black Students. In Reneau, C., & Villarreal, M. (Eds.), *Handbook of Research on Leading Higher Education Transformation With Social Justice, Equity, and Inclusion* (pp. 186–197). IGI Global. https://doi.org/10.4018/978-1-7998-7152-1.ch013

Benhima, M. (2021). Moroccan English Department Student Attitudes Towards the Use of Distance Education During COVID-19: Moulay Ismail University as a Case Study. *International Journal of Information and Communication Technology Education*, 17(3), 105–122. https://doi.org/10.4018/IJICTE.20210701.oa7

Beycioglu, K., & Wildy, H. (2017). Principal Preparation: The Case of Novice Principals in Turkey. In I. Management Association (Ed.), *Educational Leadership and Administration: Concepts, Methodologies, Tools, and Applications* (pp. 1152-1169). Hershey, PA: IGI Global. https://doi.org/10.4018/978-1-5225-1624-8.ch054

Bharwani, S., & Musunuri, D. (2018). Reflection as a Process From Theory to Practice. In M. Khosrow-Pour, D.B.A. (Ed.), *Encyclopedia of Information Science and Technology, Fourth Edition* (pp. 1529-1539). Hershey, PA: IGI Global. 10.4018/978-1-5225-2255-3.ch132

Bhushan, A., Garza, K. B., Perumal, O., Das, S. K., Feola, D. J., Farrell, D., & Birnbaum, A. (2022). Lessons Learned From the COVID-19 Pandemic and the Implications for Pharmaceutical Graduate Education and Research. In Ford, C., & Garza, K. (Eds.), *Handbook of Research on Updating and Innovating Health Professions Education: Post-Pandemic Perspectives* (pp. 324–345). IGI Global. https://doi.org/10.4018/978-1-7998-7623-6.ch014

Bintz, W., Ciecierski, L. M., & Royan, E. (2021). Using Picture Books With Instructional Strategies to Address New Challenges and Teach Literacy Skills in a Digital World. In Haas, L., & Tussey, J. (Eds.), *Connecting Disciplinary Literacy and Digital Storytelling in K-12 Education* (pp. 38–58). IGI Global. https://doi.org/10.4018/978-1-7998-5770-9.ch003

Bohjanen, S. L., Cameron-Standerford, A., & Meidl, T. D. (2018). Capacity Building Pedagogy for Diverse Learners. In Keengwe, J. (Ed.), *Handbook of Research on Pedagogical Models for Next-Generation Teaching and Learning* (pp. 195–212). Hershey, PA: IGI Global. 10.4018/978-1-5225-3873-8.ch011

Brewer, J. C. (2018). Measuring Text Readability Using Reading Level. In M. Khosrow-Pour, D.B.A. (Ed.), *Encyclopedia of Information Science and Technology, Fourth Edition* (pp. 1499-1507). Hershey, PA: IGI Global. 10.4018/978-1-5225-2255-3.ch129

Brookbanks, B. C. (2022). Student Perspectives on Business Education in the USA: Current Attitudes and Necessary Changes in an Age of Disruption. In Zhuplev, A., & Koepp, R. (Eds.), *Global Trends, Dynamics, and Imperatives for Strategic Development in Business Education in an Age of Disruption* (pp. 214–231). IGI Global. 10.4018/978-1-7998-7548-2.ch011

Brown, L. V., Dari, T., & Spencer, N. (2019). Addressing the Impact of Trauma in High Poverty Elementary Schools: An Ecological Model for School Counseling. In Daniels, K., & Billingsley, K. (Eds.), *Creating Caring and Supportive Educational Environments for Meaningful Learning* (pp. 135–153). IGI Global. https://doi.org/10.4018/978-1-5225-5748-7.ch008

Brown, S. L. (2017). A Case Study of Strategic Leadership and Research in Practice: Principal Preparation Programs that Work – An Educational Administration Perspective of Best Practices for Master's Degree Programs for Principal Preparation. In Wang, V. (Ed.), *Encyclopedia of Strategic Leadership and Management* (pp. 1226–1244). Hershey, PA: IGI Global. 10.4018/978-1-5225-1049-9.ch086

Brzozowski, M., & Ferster, I. (2017). Educational Management Leadership: High School Principal's Management Style and Parental Involvement in School Management in Israel. In Potocan, V., Üngan, M., & Nedelko, Z. (Eds.), *Handbook of Research on Managerial Solutions in Non-Profit Organizations* (pp. 55–74). Hershey, PA: IGI Global. 10.4018/978-1-5225-0731-4.ch003

Cahapay, M. B. (2020). Delphi Technique in the Development of Emerging Contents in High School Science Curriculum. *International Journal of Curriculum Development and Learning Measurement*, 1(2), 1–9. https://doi.org/10.4018/IJCDLM.2020070101

Camacho, L. F., & Leon Guerrero, A. E. (2022). Indigenous Student Experience in Higher Education: Implementation of Culturally Sensitive Support. In Pangelinan, P., & McVey, T. (Eds.), *Learning and Reconciliation Through Indigenous Education in Oceania* (pp. 254–266). IGI Global. https://doi.org/10.4018/978-1-7998-7736-3.ch016

Cannaday, J. (2017). The Masking Effect: Hidden Gifts and Disabilities of 2e Students. In Dickenson, P., Keough, P., & Courduff, J. (Eds.), *Preparing Pre-Service Teachers for the Inclusive Classroom* (pp. 220–231). Hershey, PA: IGI Global. 10.4018/978-1-5225-1753-5.ch011

Cederquist, S., Fishman, B., & Teasley, S. D. (2022). What's Missing From the College Transcript?: How Employers Make Sense of Student Skills. In Huang, Y. (Ed.), *Handbook of Research on Credential Innovations for Inclusive Pathways to Professions* (pp. 234–253). IGI Global. https://doi.org/10.4018/978-1-7998-3820-3.ch012

Cockrell, P., & Gibson, T. (2019). The Untold Stories of Black and Brown Student Experiences in Historically White Fraternities and Sororities. In Hoffman-Miller, P., James, M., & Hermond, D. (Eds.), *African American Suburbanization and the Consequential Loss of Identity* (pp. 153–171). IGI Global. https://doi.org/10.4018/978-1-5225-7835-2.ch009

Cohen, M. (2022). Leveraging Content Creation to Boost Student Engagement. In Driscoll, T.III, (Ed.), *Designing Effective Distance and Blended Learning Environments in K-12* (pp. 223–239). IGI Global. https://doi.org/10.4018/978-1-7998-6829-3.ch013

Contreras, E. C., & Contreras, I. I. (2018). Development of Communication Skills through Auditory Training Software in Special Education. In M. Khosrow-Pour, D.B.A. (Ed.), *Encyclopedia of Information Science and Technology, Fourth Edition* (pp. 2431-2441). Hershey, PA: IGI Global. 10.4018/978-1-5225-2255-3.ch212

Cooke, L., Schugar, J., Schugar, H., Penny, C., & Bruning, H. (2020). Can Everyone Code?: Preparing Teachers to Teach Computer Languages as a Literacy. In Mitchell, J., & Vaughn, E. (Eds.), *Participatory Literacy Practices for P-12 Classrooms in the Digital Age* (pp. 163–183). IGI Global. https://doi.org/10.4018/978-1-7998-0000-2.ch009

Cooley, D., & Whitten, E. (2017). Special Education Leadership and the Implementation of Response to Intervention. In Topor, F. (Ed.), *Handbook of Research on Individualism and Identity in the Globalized Digital Age* (pp. 265–286). Hershey, PA: IGI Global. 10.4018/978-1-5225-0522-8.ch012

Cosner, S., Tozer, S., & Zavitkovsky, P. (2017). Enacting a Cycle of Inquiry Capstone Research Project in Doctoral-Level Leadership Preparation. In I. Management Association (Ed.), *Educational Leadership and Administration: Concepts, Methodologies, Tools, and Applications* (pp. 1460-1481). Hershey, PA: IGI Global. 10.4018/978-1-5225-1624-8.ch067

Crawford, C. M. (2018). Instructional Real World Community Engagement. In M. Khosrow-Pour, D.B.A. (Ed.), *Encyclopedia of Information Science and Technology, Fourth Edition* (pp. 1474-1486). Hershey, PA: IGI Global. 10.4018/978-1-5225-2255-3.ch127

Crosby-Cooper, T., & Pacis, D. (2017). Implementing Effective Student Support Teams. In Dickenson, P., Keough, P., & Courduff, J. (Eds.), *Preparing Pre-Service Teachers for the Inclusive Classroom* (pp. 248–262). Hershey, PA: IGI Global. 10.4018/978-1-5225-1753-5.ch013

Curran, C. M., & Hawbaker, B. W. (2017). Cultivating Communities of Inclusive Practice: Professional Development for Educators – Research and Practice. In Curran, C., & Petersen, A. (Eds.), *Handbook of Research on Classroom Diversity and Inclusive Education Practice* (pp. 120–153). Hershey, PA: IGI Global. 10.4018/978-1-5225-2520-2.ch006

Dass, S., & Dabbagh, N. (2018). Faculty Adoption of 3D Avatar-Based Virtual World Learning Environments: An Exploratory Case Study. In I. Management Association (Ed.), *Technology Adoption and Social Issues: Concepts, Methodologies, Tools, and Applications* (pp. 1000-1033). Hershey, PA: IGI Global. https://doi.org/10.4018/978-1-5225-5201-7.ch045

Davison, A. M., & Scholl, K. G. (2017). Inclusive Recreation as Part of the IEP Process. In Curran, C., & Petersen, A. (Eds.), *Handbook of Research on Classroom Diversity and Inclusive Education Practice* (pp. 311–330). Hershey, PA: IGI Global. 10.4018/978-1-5225-2520-2.ch013

DeCoito, I. (2018). Addressing Digital Competencies, Curriculum Development, and Instructional Design in Science Teacher Education. In M. Khosrow-Pour, D.B.A. (Ed.), *Encyclopedia of Information Science and Technology, Fourth Edition* (pp. 1420-1431). Hershey, PA: IGI Global. https://doi.org/10.4018/978-1-5225-2255-3.ch122

DeCoito, I., & Richardson, T. (2017). Beyond Angry Birds™: Using Web-Based Tools to Engage Learners and Promote Inquiry in STEM Learning. In Levin, I., & Tsybulsky, D. (Eds.), *Digital Tools and Solutions for Inquiry-Based STEM Learning* (pp. 166–196). Hershey, PA: IGI Global. 10.4018/978-1-5225-2525-7.ch007

Delmas, P. M. (2017). Research-Based Leadership for Next-Generation Leaders. In Styron, R.Jr, & Styron, J. (Eds.), *Comprehensive Problem-Solving and Skill Development for Next-Generation Leaders* (pp. 1–39). Hershey, PA: IGI Global. 10.4018/978-1-5225-1968-3.ch001

Demiray, U., & Ekren, G. (2018). Administrative-Related Evaluation for Distance Education Institutions in Turkey. In Buyuk, K., Kocdar, S., & Bozkurt, A. (Eds.), *Administrative Leadership in Open and Distance Learning Programs* (pp. 263–288). Hershey, PA: IGI Global. 10.4018/978-1-5225-2645-2.ch011

Dickenson, P. (2017). What do we Know and Where Can We Grow?: Teachers Preparation for the Inclusive Classroom. In Dickenson, P., Keough, P., & Courduff, J. (Eds.), *Preparing Pre-Service Teachers for the Inclusive Classroom* (pp. 1–22). Hershey, PA: IGI Global. 10.4018/978-1-5225-1753-5.ch001

Ding, Q., & Zhu, H. (2021). Flipping the Classroom in STEM Education. In Keengwe, J. (Ed.), *Handbook of Research on Innovations in Non-Traditional Educational Practices* (pp. 155–173). IGI Global. https://doi.org/10.4018/978-1-7998-4360-3.ch008

Dixon, T., & Christison, M. (2021). Teaching English Grammar in a Hybrid Academic ESL Course: A Mixed Methods Study. In Kelch, K., Byun, P., Safavi, S., & Cervantes, S. (Eds.), *CALL Theory Applications for Online TESOL Education* (pp. 229–251). IGI Global. https://doi.org/10.4018/978-1-7998-6609-1.ch010

Donne, V., & Hansen, M. (2017). Teachers' Use of Assistive Technologies in Education. In Tomei, L. (Ed.), *Exploring the New Era of Technology-Infused Education* (pp. 86–101). Hershey, PA: IGI Global. 10.4018/978-1-5225-1709-2.ch006

Donne, V., & Hansen, M. A. (2018). Business and Technology Educators: Practices for Inclusion. In I. Management Association (Ed.), *Business Education and Ethics: Concepts, Methodologies, Tools, and Applications* (pp. 471-484). Hershey, PA: IGI Global. https://doi.org/10.4018/978-1-5225-3153-1.ch026

Dos Santos, L. M. (2022). Completing Student-Teaching Internships Online: Instructional Changes During the COVID-19 Pandemic. In Alaali, M. (Ed.), *Assessing University Governance and Policies in Relation to the COVID-19 Pandemic* (pp. 106–127). IGI Global. https://doi.org/10.4018/978-1-7998-8279-4.ch007

Dreon, O., Shettel, J., & Bower, K. M. (2017). Preparing Next Generation Elementary Teachers for the Tools of Tomorrow. In Grassetti, M., & Brookby, S. (Eds.), *Advancing Next-Generation Teacher Education through Digital Tools and Applications* (pp. 143–159). Hershey, PA: IGI Global. 10.4018/978-1-5225-0965-3.ch008

Durak, H. Y., & Güyer, T. (2018). Design and Development of an Instructional Program for Teaching Programming Processes to Gifted Students Using Scratch. In Cannaday, J. (Ed.), *Curriculum Development for Gifted Education Programs* (pp. 61–99). Hershey, PA: IGI Global. 10.4018/978-1-5225-3041-1.ch004

Egorkina, E., Ivanov, M., & Valyavskiy, A. Y. (2018). Students' Research Competence Formation of the Quality of Open and Distance Learning. In Mkrttchian, V., & Belyanina, L. (Eds.), *Handbook of Research on Students' Research Competence in Modern Educational Contexts* (pp. 364–384). Hershey, PA: IGI Global. 10.4018/978-1-5225-3485-3.ch019

Ekren, G., Karataş, S., & Demiray, U. (2017). Understanding of Leadership in Distance Education Management. In I. Management Association (Ed.), *Educational Leadership and Administration: Concepts, Methodologies, Tools, and Applications* (pp. 34-50). Hershey, PA: IGI Global. https://doi.org/10.4018/978-1-5225-1624-8.ch003

Elmore, W. M., Young, J. K., Harris, S., & Mason, D. (2017). The Relationship between Individual Student Attributes and Online Course Completion. In Shelton, K., & Pedersen, K. (Eds.), *Handbook of Research on Building, Growing, and Sustaining Quality E-Learning Programs* (pp. 151–173). Hershey, PA: IGI Global. 10.4018/978-1-5225-0877-9.ch008

Ercegovac, I. R., Alfirević, N., & Koludrović, M. (2017). School Principals' Communication and Co-Operation Assessment: The Croatian Experience. In I. Management Association (Ed.), *Educational Leadership and Administration: Concepts, Methodologies, Tools, and Applications* (pp. 1568-1589). Hershey, PA: IGI Global. https://doi.org/10.4018/978-1-5225-1624-8.ch072

Everhart, D., & Seymour, D. M. (2017). Challenges and Opportunities in the Currency of Higher Education. In Rasmussen, K., Northrup, P., & Colson, R. (Eds.), *Handbook of Research on Competency-Based Education in University Settings* (pp. 41–65). Hershey, PA: IGI Global. 10.4018/978-1-5225-0932-5.ch003

Farmer, L. S. (2017). Managing Portable Technologies for Special Education. In Wang, V. (Ed.), *Encyclopedia of Strategic Leadership and Management* (pp. 977–987). Hershey, PA: IGI Global. 10.4018/978-1-5225-1049-9.ch068

Farmer, L. S. (2018). Optimizing OERs for Optimal ICT Literacy in Higher Education. In Keengwe, J. (Ed.), *Handbook of Research on Mobile Technology, Constructivism, and Meaningful Learning* (pp. 366–390). Hershey, PA: IGI Global. 10.4018/978-1-5225-3949-0.ch020

Ferguson, B. T. (2019). Supporting Affective Development of Children With Disabilities Through Moral Dilemmas. In Ikuta, S. (Ed.), *Handmade Teaching Materials for Students With Disabilities* (pp. 253–275). IGI Global. 10.4018/978-1-5225-6240-5.ch011

Fındık, L. Y. (2017). Self-Assessment of Principals Based on Leadership in Complexity. In I. Management Association (Ed.), *Educational Leadership and Administration: Concepts, Methodologies, Tools, and Applications* (pp. 978-991). Hershey, PA: IGI Global. https://doi.org/10.4018/978-1-5225-1624-8.ch047

Flor, A. G., & Gonzalez-Flor, B. (2018). Dysfunctional Digital Demeanors: Tales From (and Policy Implications of) eLearning's Dark Side. In I. Management Association (Ed.), The Dark Web: Breakthroughs in Research and Practice (pp. 37-50). Hershey, PA: IGI Global. https://doi.org/10.4018/978-1-5225-3163-0.ch003

Floyd, K. K., & Shambaugh, N. (2017). Instructional Design for Simulations in Special Education Virtual Learning Spaces. In Kidd, T., & Morris, L.Jr., (Eds.), *Handbook of Research on Instructional Systems and Educational Technology* (pp. 202–215). Hershey, PA: IGI Global. 10.4018/978-1-5225-2399-4.ch018

Freeland, S. F. (2020). Community Schools: Improving Academic Achievement Through Meaningful Engagement. In Kronick, R. (Ed.), *Emerging Perspectives on Community Schools and the Engaged University* (pp. 132–144). IGI Global. https://doi.org/10.4018/978-1-7998-0280-8.ch008

Ghanbarzadeh, R., & Ghapanchi, A. H. (2019). Applied Areas of Three Dimensional Virtual Worlds in Learning and Teaching: A Review of Higher Education. In I. Management Association (Ed.), *Virtual Reality in Education: Breakthroughs in Research and Practice* (pp. 172-192). IGI Global. https://doi.org/10.4018/978-1-5225-8179-6.ch008

Giovannini, J. M. (2017). Technology Integration in Preservice Teacher Education Programs: Research-based Recommendations. In Grassetti, M., & Brookby, S. (Eds.), *Advancing Next-Generation Teacher Education through Digital Tools and Applications* (pp. 82–102). Hershey, PA: IGI Global. 10.4018/978-1-5225-0965-3.ch005

Good, S., & Clarke, V. B. (2017). An Integral Analysis of One Urban School System's Efforts to Support Student-Centered Teaching. In Keengwe, J., & Onchwari, G. (Eds.), *Handbook of Research on Learner-Centered Pedagogy in Teacher Education and Professional Development* (pp. 45–68). Hershey, PA: IGI Global. 10.4018/978-1-5225-0892-2.ch003

Guetzoian, E. (2022). Gamification Strategies for Higher Education Student Worker Training. In Lane, C. (Ed.), *Handbook of Research on Acquiring 21st Century Literacy Skills Through Game-Based Learning* (pp. 164–179). IGI Global. https://doi.org/10.4018/978-1-7998-7271-9.ch009

Hamidi, F., Owuor, P. M., Hynie, M., Baljko, M., & McGrath, S. (2017). Potentials of Digital Assistive Technology and Special Education in Kenya. In Ayo, C., & Mbarika, V. (Eds.), *Sustainable ICT Adoption and Integration for Socio-Economic Development* (pp. 125–151). Hershey, PA: IGI Global. 10.4018/978-1-5225-2565-3.ch006

Hamim, T., Benabbou, F., & Sael, N. (2022). Student Profile Modeling Using Boosting Algorithms. *International Journal of Web-Based Learning and Teaching Technologies*, 17(5), 1–13. https://doi.org/10.4018/IJWLTT.20220901.oa4

Henderson, L. K. (2017). Meltdown at Fukushima: Global Catastrophic Events, Visual Literacy, and Art Education. In Shin, R. (Ed.), *Convergence of Contemporary Art, Visual Culture, and Global Civic Engagement* (pp. 80–99). Hershey, PA: IGI Global. 10.4018/978-1-5225-1665-1.ch005

Hudgins, T., & Holland, J. L. (2018). Digital Badges: Tracking Knowledge Acquisition Within an Innovation Framework. In I. Management Association (Ed.), *Wearable Technologies: Concepts, Methodologies, Tools, and Applications* (pp. 1118-1132). Hershey, PA: IGI Global. https://doi.org/10.4018/978-1-5225-5484-4.ch051

Hwang, R., Lin, H., Sun, J. C., & Wu, J. (2019). Improving Learning Achievement in Science Education for Elementary School Students via Blended Learning. *International Journal of Online Pedagogy and Course Design*, 9(2), 44–62. https://doi.org/10.4018/IJOPCD.2019040104

Jančec, L., & Vodopivec, J. L. (2019). The Implicit Pedagogy and the Hidden Curriculum in Postmodern Education. In Vodopivec, J., Jančec, L., & Štemberger, T. (Eds.), *Implicit Pedagogy for Optimized Learning in Contemporary Education* (pp. 41–59). IGI Global. https://doi.org/10.4018/978-1-5225-5799-9.ch003

Janus, M., & Siddiqua, A. (2018). Challenges for Children With Special Health Needs at the Time of Transition to School. In I. Management Association (Ed.), *Autism Spectrum Disorders: Breakthroughs in Research and Practice* (pp. 339-371). Hershey, PA: IGI Global. 10.4018/978-1-5225-3827-1.ch018

Jesus, R. A. (2018). Screencasts and Learning Styles. In M. Khosrow-Pour, D.B.A. (Ed.), *Encyclopedia of Information Science and Technology, Fourth Edition* (pp. 1548-1558). Hershey, PA: IGI Global. 10.4018/978-1-5225-2255-3.ch134

John, G., Francis, N., & Santhakumar, A. B. (2022). Student Engagement: Past, Present, and Future. In Ramlall, S., Cross, T., & Love, M. (Eds.), *Handbook of Research on Future of Work and Education: Implications for Curriculum Delivery and Work Design* (pp. 329–341). IGI Global. https://doi.org/10.4018/978-1-7998-8275-6.ch020

Karpinski, A. C., D'Agostino, J. V., Williams, A. K., Highland, S. A., & Mellott, J. A. (2018). The Relationship Between Online Formative Assessment and State Test Scores Using Multilevel Modeling. In M. Khosrow-Pour, D.B.A. (Ed.), *Encyclopedia of Information Science and Technology, Fourth Edition* (pp. 5183-5192). Hershey, PA: IGI Global. 10.4018/978-1-5225-2255-3.ch450

Kats, Y. (2017). Educational Leadership and Integrated Support for Students with Autism Spectrum Disorders. In I. Management Association (Ed.), *Educational Leadership and Administration: Concepts, Methodologies, Tools, and Applications* (pp. 101-114). Hershey, PA: IGI Global. https://doi.org/10.4018/978-1-5225-1624-8.ch007

Kaya, G., & Altun, A. (2018). Educational Ontology Development. In M. Khosrow-Pour, D.B.A. (Ed.), *Encyclopedia of Information Science and Technology, Fourth Edition* (pp. 1441-1450). Hershey, PA: IGI Global. 10.4018/978-1-5225-2255-3.ch124

Keough, P. D., & Pacis, D. (2017). Best Practices Implementing Special Education Curriculum and Common Core State Standards using UDL. In Dickenson, P., Keough, P., & Courduff, J. (Eds.), *Preparing Pre-Service Teachers for the Inclusive Classroom* (pp. 107–123). Hershey, PA: IGI Global. 10.4018/978-1-5225-1753-5.ch006

Kilburn, M., Henckell, M., & Starrett, D. (2018). Factors Contributing to the Effectiveness of Online Students and Instructors. In M. Khosrow-Pour, D.B.A. (Ed.), *Encyclopedia of Information Science and Technology, Fourth Edition* (pp. 1451-1462). Hershey, PA: IGI Global. 10.4018/978-1-5225-2255-3.ch125

Koban Koç, D. (2021). Gender and Language: A Sociolinguistic Analysis of Second Language Writing. In Hancı-Azizoglu, E., & Kavaklı, N. (Eds.), *Futuristic and Linguistic Perspectives on Teaching Writing to Second Language Students* (pp. 161–177). IGI Global. https://doi.org/10.4018/978-1-7998-6508-7.ch010

Konecny, L. T. (2017). Hybrid, Online, and Flipped Classrooms in Health Science: Enhanced Learning Environments. In I. Management Association (Ed.), *Flipped Instruction: Breakthroughs in Research and Practice* (pp. 355-370). Hershey, PA: IGI Global. https://doi.org/10.4018/978-1-5225-1803-7.ch020

Kupietz, K. D. (2021). Gaming and Simulation in Public Education: Teaching Others to Help Themselves and Their Neighbors. In Drumhiller, N., Wilkin, T., & Srba, K. (Eds.), *Simulation and Game-Based Learning in Emergency and Disaster Management* (pp. 41–62). IGI Global. https://doi.org/10.4018/978-1-7998-4087-9.ch003

Kwee, C. T. (2022). Assessing the International Student Enrolment Strategies in Australian Universities: A Case Study During the COVID-19 Pandemic. In Alaali, M. (Ed.), *Assessing University Governance and Policies in Relation to the COVID-19 Pandemic* (pp. 162–188). IGI Global. https://doi.org/10.4018/978-1-7998-8279-4.ch010

Lauricella, S., & McArthur, F. A. (2022). Taking a Student-Centred Approach to Alternative Digital Credentials: Multiple Pathways Toward the Acquisition of Microcredentials. In Piedra, D. (Ed.), *Innovations in the Design and Application of Alternative Digital Credentials* (pp. 57–69). IGI Global. https://doi.org/10.4018/978-1-7998-7697-7.ch003

Llamas, M. F. (2019). Intercultural Awareness in Teaching English for Early Childhood: A Film-Based Approach. In Domínguez Romero, E., Bobkina, J., & Stefanova, S. (Eds.), *Teaching Literature and Language Through Multimodal Texts* (pp. 54–68). IGI Global. https://doi.org/10.4018/978-1-5225-5796-8.ch004

Lokhtina, I., & Kkese, E. T. (2022). Reflecting and Adapting to an Academic Workplace Before and After the Lockdown in Greek-Speaking Cyprus: Opportunities and Challenges. In Zhuplev, A., & Koepp, R. (Eds.), *Global Trends, Dynamics, and Imperatives for Strategic Development in Business Education in an Age of Disruption* (pp. 126–148). IGI Global. https://doi.org/10.4018/978-1-7998-7548-2.ch007

Lovell, K. L. (2017). Development and Evaluation of Neuroscience Computer-Based Modules for Medical Students: Instructional Design Principles and Effectiveness. In Stefaniak, J. (Ed.), *Advancing Medical Education Through Strategic Instructional Design* (pp. 262–276). Hershey, PA: IGI Global. 10.4018/978-1-5225-2098-6.ch013

Maher, D. (2019). The Use of Course Management Systems in Pre-Service Teacher Education. In Keengwe, J. (Ed.), *Handbook of Research on Blended Learning Pedagogies and Professional Development in Higher Education* (pp. 196–213). IGI Global. https://doi.org/10.4018/978-1-5225-5557-5.ch011

Makewa, L. N. (2019). Teacher Technology Competence Base. In Makewa, L., Ngussa, B., & Kuboja, J. (Eds.), *Technology-Supported Teaching and Research Methods for Educators* (pp. 247–267). IGI Global. https://doi.org/10.4018/978-1-5225-5915-3.ch014

Mallett, C. A. (2022). School Resource (Police) Officers in Schools: Impact on Campus Safety, Student Discipline, and Learning. In Crews, G. (Ed.), *Impact of School Shootings on Classroom Culture, Curriculum, and Learning* (pp. 53–70). IGI Global. https://doi.org/10.4018/978-1-7998-5200-1.ch004

Marinho, J. E., Freitas, I. R., Leão, I. B., Pacheco, L. O., Gonçalves, M. P., Castro, M. J., Silva, P. D., & Moreira, R. J. (2022). Project-Based Learning Application in Higher Education: Student Experiences and Perspectives. In Alves, A., & van Hattum-Janssen, N. (Eds.), *Training Engineering Students for Modern Technological Advancement* (pp. 146–164). IGI Global. https://doi.org/10.4018/978-1-7998-8816-1.ch007

McCleskey, J. A., & Melton, R. M. (2022). Rolling With the Flow: Online Faculty and Student Presence in a Post-COVID-19 World. In Ramlall, S., Cross, T., & Love, M. (Eds.), *Handbook of Research on Future of Work and Education: Implications for Curriculum Delivery and Work Design* (pp. 307–328). IGI Global. https://doi.org/10.4018/978-1-7998-8275-6.ch019

McCormack, V. F., Stauffer, M., Fishley, K., Hohenbrink, J., Mascazine, J. R., & Zigler, T. (2018). Designing a Dual Licensure Path for Middle Childhood and Special Education Teacher Candidates. In Polly, D., Putman, M., Petty, T., & Good, A. (Eds.), *Innovative Practices in Teacher Preparation and Graduate-Level Teacher Education Programs* (pp. 21–36). Hershey, PA: IGI Global. 10.4018/978-1-5225-3068-8.ch002

McDaniel, R. (2017). Strategic Leadership in Instructional Design: Applying the Principles of Instructional Design through the Lens of Strategic Leadership to Distance Education. In Wang, V. (Ed.), *Encyclopedia of Strategic Leadership and Management* (pp. 1570–1584). Hershey, PA: IGI Global. 10.4018/978-1-5225-1049-9.ch109

McKinney, R. E., Halli-Tierney, A. D., Gold, A. E., Allen, R. S., & Carroll, D. G. (2022). Interprofessional Education: Using Standardized Cases in Face-to-Face and Remote Learning Settings. In Ford, C., & Garza, K. (Eds.), *Handbook of Research on Updating and Innovating Health Professions Education: Post-Pandemic Perspectives* (pp. 24–42). IGI Global. https://doi.org/10.4018/978-1-7998-7623-6.ch002

Meintjes, H. H. (2021). Learner Views of a Facebook Page as a Supportive Digital Pedagogical Tool at a Public South African School in a Grade 12 Business Studies Class. *International Journal of Smart Education and Urban Society*, 12(2), 32–45. https://doi.org/10.4018/IJSEUS.2021040104

Melero-García, F. (2022). Training Bilingual Interpreters in Healthcare Settings: Student Perceptions of Online Learning. In LeLoup, J., & Swanson, P. (Eds.), *Handbook of Research on Effective Online Language Teaching in a Disruptive Environment* (pp. 288–310). IGI Global. https://doi.org/10.4018/978-1-7998-7720-2.ch015

Meletiadou, E. (2022). The Use of Peer Assessment as an Inclusive Learning Strategy in Higher Education Institutions: Enhancing Student Writing Skills and Motivation. In Meletiadou, E. (Ed.), *Handbook of Research on Policies and Practices for Assessing Inclusive Teaching and Learning* (pp. 1–26). IGI Global. https://doi.org/10.4018/978-1-7998-8579-5.ch001

Memon, R. N., Ahmad, R., & Salim, S. S. (2018). Critical Issues in Requirements Engineering Education. In I. Management Association (Ed.), *Computer Systems and Software Engineering: Concepts, Methodologies, Tools, and Applications* (pp. 1953-1976). Hershey, PA: IGI Global. 10.4018/978-1-5225-3923-0.ch081

Mendenhall, R. (2017). Western Governors University: CBE Innovator and National Model. In Rasmussen, K., Northrup, P., & Colson, R. (Eds.), *Handbook of Research on Competency-Based Education in University Settings* (pp. 379–400). Hershey, PA: IGI Global. 10.4018/978-1-5225-0932-5.ch019

Mense, E. G., Griggs, D. M., & Shanks, J. N. (2018). School Leaders in a Time of Accountability and Data Use: Preparing Our Future School Leaders in Leadership Preparation Programs. In Mense, E., & Crain-Dorough, M. (Eds.), *Data Leadership for K-12 Schools in a Time of Accountability* (pp. 235–259). Hershey, PA: IGI Global. 10.4018/978-1-5225-3188-3.ch012

Mense, E. G., Griggs, D. M., & Shanks, J. N. (2018). School Leaders in a Time of Accountability and Data Use: Preparing Our Future School Leaders in Leadership Preparation Programs. In Mense, E., & Crain-Dorough, M. (Eds.), *Data Leadership for K-12 Schools in a Time of Accountability* (pp. 235–259). Hershey, PA: IGI Global. 10.4018/978-1-5225-3188-3.ch012

Mestry, R., & Naicker, S. R. (2017). Exploring Distributive Leadership in South African Public Primary Schools in the Soweto Region. In I. Management Association (Ed.), *Educational Leadership and Administration: Concepts, Methodologies, Tools, and Applications* (pp. 1041-1064). Hershey, PA: IGI Global. 10.4018/978-1-5225-1624-8.ch050

Monaghan, C. H., & Boboc, M. (2017). (Re)Defining Leadership in Higher Education in the U.S. In Wang, V. (Ed.), *Encyclopedia of Strategic Leadership and Management* (pp. 567–579). Hershey, PA: IGI Global. 10.4018/978-1-5225-1049-9.ch040

Morall, M. B. (2021). Reimagining Mobile Phones: Multiple Literacies and Digital Media Compositions. In C. Moran (Eds.), *Affordances and Constraints of Mobile Phone Use in English Language Arts Classrooms* (pp. 41-53). IGI Global. https://doi.org/10.4018/978-1-7998-5805-8.ch003

Mthethwa, V. (2022). Student Governance and the Academic Minefield During COVID-19 Lockdown in South Africa. In Alaali, M. (Ed.), *Assessing University Governance and Policies in Relation to the COVID-19 Pandemic* (pp. 255–276). IGI Global. https://doi.org/10.4018/978-1-7998-8279-4.ch015

Muthee, J. M., & Murungi, C. G. (2018). Relationship Among Intelligence, Achievement Motivation, Type of School, and Academic Performance of Kenyan Urban Primary School Pupils. In M. Khosrow-Pour, D.B.A. (Ed.), *Encyclopedia of Information Science and Technology, Fourth Edition* (pp. 1540-1547). Hershey, PA: IGI Global. https://doi.org/10.4018/978-1-5225-2255-3.ch133

Naranjo, J. (2018). Meeting the Need for Inclusive Educators Online: Teacher Education in Inclusive Special Education and Dual-Certification. In Polly, D., Putman, M., Petty, T., & Good, A. (Eds.), *Innovative Practices in Teacher Preparation and Graduate-Level Teacher Education Programs* (pp. 106–122). Hershey, PA: IGI Global. 10.4018/978-1-5225-3068-8.ch007

Nkabinde, Z. P. (2017). Multiculturalism in Special Education: Perspectives of Minority Children in Urban Schools. In Keengwe, J. (Ed.), *Handbook of Research on Promoting Cross-Cultural Competence and Social Justice in Teacher Education* (pp. 382–397). Hershey, PA: IGI Global. 10.4018/978-1-5225-0897-7.ch020

Nkabinde, Z. P. (2018). Online Instruction: Is the Quality the Same as Face-to-Face Instruction? In Keengwe, J. (Ed.), *Handbook of Research on Digital Content, Mobile Learning, and Technology Integration Models in Teacher Education* (pp. 300–314). Hershey, PA: IGI Global. 10.4018/978-1-5225-2953-8.ch016

Nugroho, A., & Albusaidi, S. S. (2022). Internationalization of Higher Education: The Methodological Critiques on the Research Related to Study Overseas and International Experience. In Magd, H., & Kunjumuhammed, S. (Eds.), *Global Perspectives on Quality Assurance and Accreditation in Higher Education Institutions* (pp. 75–89). IGI Global. https://doi.org/10.4018/978-1-7998-8085-1.ch005

Nulty, Z., & West, S. G. (2022). Student Engagement and Supporting Students With Accommodations. In Bull, P., & Patterson, G. (Eds.), *Redefining Teacher Education and Teacher Preparation Programs in the Post-COVID-19 Era* (pp. 99–116). IGI Global. https://doi.org/10.4018/978-1-7998-8298-5.ch006

O'Connor, J. R.Jr, & Jackson, K. N. (2017). The Use of iPad® Devices and "Apps" for ASD Students in Special Education and Speech Therapy. In Kats, Y. (Ed.), *Supporting the Education of Children with Autism Spectrum Disorders* (pp. 267–283). Hershey, PA: IGI Global. 10.4018/978-1-5225-0816-8.ch014

Okolie, U. C., & Yasin, A. M. (2017). TVET in Developing Nations and Human Development. In Okolie, U., & Yasin, A. (Eds.), *Technical Education and Vocational Training in Developing Nations* (pp. 1–25). Hershey, PA: IGI Global. 10.4018/978-1-5225-1811-2.ch001

Pack, A., & Barrett, A. (2021). A Review of Virtual Reality and English for Academic Purposes: Understanding Where to Start. *International Journal of Computer-Assisted Language Learning and Teaching*, 11(1), 72–80. https://doi.org/10.4018/IJCALLT.2021010105

Pashollari, E. (2019). Building Sustainability Through Environmental Education: Education for Sustainable Development. In L. Wilson, & C. Stevenson (Eds.), *Building Sustainability Through Environmental Education* (pp. 72-88). IGI Global. https://doi.org/10.4018/978-1-5225-7727-0.ch004

Paulson, E. N. (2017). Adapting and Advocating for an Online EdD Program in Changing Times and "Sacred" Cultures. In I. Management Association (Ed.), *Educational Leadership and Administration: Concepts, Methodologies, Tools, and Applications* (pp. 1849-1876). Hershey, PA: IGI Global. https://doi.org/10.4018/978-1-5225-1624-8.ch085

Petersen, A. J., Elser, C. F., Al Nassir, M. N., Stakey, J., & Everson, K. (2017). The Year of Teaching Inclusively: Building an Elementary Classroom for All Students. In Curran, C., & Petersen, A. (Eds.), *Handbook of Research on Classroom Diversity and Inclusive Education Practice* (pp. 332–348). Hershey, PA: IGI Global. 10.4018/978-1-5225-2520-2.ch014

Pfannenstiel, K. H., & Sanders, J. (2017). Characteristics and Instructional Strategies for Students With Mathematical Difficulties: In the Inclusive Classroom. In Curran, C., & Petersen, A. (Eds.), *Handbook of Research on Classroom Diversity and Inclusive Education Practice* (pp. 250–281). Hershey, PA: IGI Global. 10.4018/978-1-5225-2520-2.ch011

Phan, A. N. (2022). Quality Assurance of Higher Education From the Glonacal Agency Heuristic: An Example From Vietnam. In Magd, H., & Kunjumuhammed, S. (Eds.), *Global Perspectives on Quality Assurance and Accreditation in Higher Education Institutions* (pp. 136–155). IGI Global. https://doi.org/10.4018/978-1-7998-8085-1.ch008

Preast, J. L., Bowman, N., & Rose, C. A. (2017). Creating Inclusive Classroom Communities Through Social and Emotional Learning to Reduce Social Marginalization Among Students. In Curran, C., & Petersen, A. (Eds.), *Handbook of Research on Classroom Diversity and Inclusive Education Practice* (pp. 183–200). Hershey, PA: IGI Global. 10.4018/978-1-5225-2520-2.ch008

Randolph, K. M., & Brady, M. P. (2018). Evolution of Covert Coaching as an Evidence-Based Practice in Professional Development and Preparation of Teachers. In Bryan, V., Musgrove, A., & Powers, J. (Eds.), *Handbook of Research on Human Development in the Digital Age* (pp. 281–299). Hershey, PA: IGI Global. 10.4018/978-1-5225-2838-8.ch013

Rell, A. B., Puig, R. A., Roll, F., Valles, V., Espinoza, M., & Duque, A. L. (2017). Addressing Cultural Diversity and Global Competence: The Dual Language Framework. In Leavitt, L., Wisdom, S., & Leavitt, K. (Eds.), *Cultural Awareness and Competency Development in Higher Education* (pp. 111–131). Hershey, PA: IGI Global. 10.4018/978-1-5225-2145-7.ch007

Richards, M., & Guzman, I. R. (2020). Academic Assessment of Critical Thinking in Distance Education Information Technology Programs. In I. Management Association (Ed.), *Learning and Performance Assessment: Concepts, Methodologies, Tools, and Applications* (pp. 1-19). IGI Global. https://doi.org/10.4018/978-1-7998-0420-8.ch001

Riel, J., Lawless, K. A., & Brown, S. W. (2017). Defining and Designing Responsive Online Professional Development (ROPD): A Framework to Support Curriculum Implementation. In Kidd, T., & Morris, L.Jr., (Eds.), *Handbook of Research on Instructional Systems and Educational Technology* (pp. 104–115). Hershey, PA: IGI Global. 10.4018/978-1-5225-2399-4.ch010

Roberts, C. (2017). Advancing Women Leaders in Academe: Creating a Culture of Inclusion. In Mukerji, S., & Tripathi, P. (Eds.), *Handbook of Research on Administration, Policy, and Leadership in Higher Education* (pp. 256–273). Hershey, PA: IGI Global. 10.4018/978-1-5225-0672-0.ch012

Rodgers, W. J., Kennedy, M. J., Alves, K. D., & Romig, J. E. (2017). A Multimedia Tool for Teacher Education and Professional Development. In Martin, C., & Polly, D. (Eds.), *Handbook of Research on Teacher Education and Professional Development* (pp. 285–296). Hershey, PA: IGI Global. 10.4018/978-1-5225-1067-3.ch015

Romanowski, M. H. (2017). Qatar's Educational Reform: Critical Issues Facing Principals. In I. Management Association (Ed.), *Educational Leadership and Administration: Concepts, Methodologies, Tools, and Applications* (pp. 1758-1773). Hershey, PA: IGI Global. https://doi.org/10.4018/978-1-5225-1624-8.ch080

Ruffin, T. R., Hawkins, D. P., & Lee, D. I. (2018). Increasing Student Engagement and Participation Through Course Methodology. In M. Khosrow-Pour, D.B.A. (Ed.), *Encyclopedia of Information Science and Technology, Fourth Edition* (pp. 1463-1473). Hershey, PA: IGI Global. 10.4018/978-1-5225-2255-3.ch126

Sabina, L. L., Curry, K. A., Harris, E. L., Krumm, B. L., & Vencill, V. (2017). Assessing the Performance of a Cohort-Based Model Using Domestic and International Practices. In I. Management Association (Ed.), *Educational Leadership and Administration: Concepts, Methodologies, Tools, and Applications*(pp. 913-929). Hershey, PA: IGI Global. https://doi.org/10.4018/978-1-5225-1624-8.ch044

Samkian, A., Pascarella, J., & Slayton, J. (2022). Towards an Anti-Racist, Culturally Responsive, and LGBTQ+ Inclusive Education: Developing Critically-Conscious Educational Leaders. In Cain-Sanschagrin, E., Filback, R., & Crawford, J. (Eds.), *Cases on Academic Program Redesign for Greater Racial and Social Justice* (pp. 150–175). IGI Global. https://doi.org/10.4018/978-1-7998-8463-7.ch007

Santamaría, A. P., Webber, M., & Santamaría, L. J. (2017). Effective School Leadership for Māori Achievement: Building Capacity through Indigenous, National, and International Cross-Cultural Collaboration. In I. Management Association (Ed.), *Educational Leadership and Administration: Concepts, Methodologies, Tools, and Applications* (pp. 1547-1567). Hershey, PA: IGI Global. https://doi.org/10.4018/978-1-5225-1624-8.ch071

Santamaría, L. J. (2017). Culturally Responsive Educational Leadership in Cross-Cultural International Contexts. In I. Management Association (Ed.), *Educational Leadership and Administration: Concepts, Methodologies, Tools, and Applications* (pp. 1380-1400). Hershey, PA: IGI Global. https://doi.org/10.4018/978-1-5225-1624-8.ch064

Segredo, M. R., Cistone, P. J., & Reio, T. G. (2017). Relationships Between Emotional Intelligence, Leadership Style, and School Culture. *International Journal of Adult Vocational Education and Technology*, 8(3), 25–43. 10.4018/IJAVET.2017070103

Shalev, N. (2017). Empathy and Leadership From the Organizational Perspective. In Nedelko, Z., & Brzozowski, M. (Eds.), *Exploring the Influence of Personal Values and Cultures in the Workplace* (pp. 348–363). Hershey, PA: IGI Global. 10.4018/978-1-5225-2480-9.ch018

Siamak, M., Fathi, S., & Isfandyari-Moghaddam, A. (2018). Assessment and Measurement of Education Programs of Information Literacy. In Bhardwaj, R. (Ed.), *Digitizing the Modern Library and the Transition From Print to Electronic* (pp. 164–192). Hershey, PA: IGI Global. 10.4018/978-1-5225-2119-8.ch007

Siu, K. W., & García, G. J. (2017). Disruptive Technologies and Education: Is There Any Disruption After All? In I. Management Association (Ed.), *Educational Leadership and Administration: Concepts, Methodologies, Tools, and Applications* (pp. 757-778). Hershey, PA: IGI Global. https://doi.org/10.4018/978-1-5225-1624-8.ch037

Slagter van Tryon, P. J. (2017). The Nurse Educator's Role in Designing Instruction and Instructional Strategies for Academic and Clinical Settings. In Stefaniak, J. (Ed.), *Advancing Medical Education Through Strategic Instructional Design* (pp. 133–149). Hershey, PA: IGI Global. 10.4018/978-1-5225-2098-6.ch006

Slattery, C. A. (2018). Literacy Intervention and the Differentiated Plan of Instruction. In *Developing Effective Literacy Intervention Strategies: Emerging Research and Opportunities* (pp. 41–62). Hershey, PA: IGI Global. 10.4018/978-1-5225-5007-5.ch003

Smith, A. R. (2017). Ensuring Quality: The Faculty Role in Online Higher Education. In Shelton, K., & Pedersen, K. (Eds.), *Handbook of Research on Building, Growing, and Sustaining Quality E-Learning Programs* (pp. 210–231). Hershey, PA: IGI Global. 10.4018/978-1-5225-0877-9.ch011

Souders, T. M. (2017). Understanding Your Learner: Conducting a Learner Analysis. In Stefaniak, J. (Ed.), *Advancing Medical Education Through Strategic Instructional Design* (pp. 1–29). Hershey, PA: IGI Global. 10.4018/978-1-5225-2098-6.ch001

Spring, K. J., Graham, C. R., & Ikahihifo, T. B. (2018). Learner Engagement in Blended Learning. In M. Khosrow-Pour, D.B.A. (Ed.), *Encyclopedia of Information Science and Technology, Fourth Edition* (pp. 1487-1498). Hershey, PA: IGI Global. 10.4018/978-1-5225-2255-3.ch128

Storey, V. A., Anthony, A. K., & Wahid, P. (2017). Gender-Based Leadership Barriers: Advancement of Female Faculty to Leadership Positions in Higher Education. In Wang, V. (Ed.), *Encyclopedia of Strategic Leadership and Management* (pp. 244–258). Hershey, PA: IGI Global. 10.4018/978-1-5225-1049-9.ch018

Stottlemyer, D. (2018). Develop a Teaching Model Plan for a Differentiated Learning Approach. In *Differentiated Instructional Design for Multicultural Environments: Emerging Research and Opportunities* (pp. 106–130). Hershey, PA: IGI Global. 10.4018/978-1-5225-5106-5.ch005

Stottlemyer, D. (2018). Developing a Multicultural Environment. In *Differentiated Instructional Design for Multicultural Environments: Emerging Research and Opportunities* (pp. 1–27). Hershey, PA: IGI Global. 10.4018/978-1-5225-5106-5.ch001

Swagerty, T. (2022). Digital Access to Culturally Relevant Curricula: The Impact on the Native and Indigenous Student. In Reeves, E., & McIntyre, C. (Eds.), *Multidisciplinary Perspectives on Diversity and Equity in a Virtual World* (pp. 99–113). IGI Global. https://doi.org/10.4018/978-1-7998-8028-8.ch006

Swami, B. N., Gobona, T., & Tsimako, J. J. (2017). Academic Leadership: A Case Study of the University of Botswana. In Baporikar, N. (Ed.), *Innovation and Shifting Perspectives in Management Education* (pp. 1–32). Hershey, PA: IGI Global. 10.4018/978-1-5225-1019-2.ch001

Swanson, K. W., & Collins, G. (2018). Designing Engaging Instruction for the Adult Learners. In M. Khosrow-Pour, D.B.A. (Ed.), *Encyclopedia of Information Science and Technology, Fourth Edition* (pp. 1432-1440). Hershey, PA: IGI Global. 10.4018/978-1-5225-2255-3.ch123

Swartz, B. A., Lynch, J. M., & Lynch, S. D. (2018). Embedding Elementary Teacher Education Coursework in Local Classrooms: Examples in Mathematics and Special Education. In Polly, D., Putman, M., Petty, T., & Good, A. (Eds.), *Innovative Practices in Teacher Preparation and Graduate-Level Teacher Education Programs* (pp. 262–292). Hershey, PA: IGI Global. 10.4018/978-1-5225-3068-8.ch015

Taliadorou, N., & Pashiardis, P. (2017). Emotional Intelligence and Political Skill Really Matter in Educational Leadership. In I. Management Association (Ed.), *Educational Leadership and Administration: Concepts, Methodologies, Tools, and Applications* (pp. 1274-1303). Hershey, PA: IGI Global. https://doi.org/10.4018/978-1-5225-1624-8.ch060

Tandoh, K. A., & Ebe-Arthur, J. E. (2018). Effective Educational Leadership in the Digital Age: An Examination of Professional Qualities and Best Practices. In Keengwe, J. (Ed.), *Handbook of Research on Digital Content, Mobile Learning, and Technology Integration Models in Teacher Education* (pp. 244–265). Hershey, PA: IGI Global. 10.4018/978-1-5225-2953-8.ch013

Tobin, M. T. (2018). Multimodal Literacy. In M. Khosrow-Pour, D.B.A. (Ed.), *Encyclopedia of Information Science and Technology, Fourth Edition* (pp. 1508-1516). Hershey, PA: IGI Global. 10.4018/978-1-5225-2255-3.ch130

Torres, K. M., Arrastia-Chisholm, M. C., & Tackett, S. (2019). A Phenomenological Study of Pre-Service Teachers' Perceptions of Completing ESOL Field Placements. *International Journal of Teacher Education and Professional Development*, 2(2), 85–101. https://doi.org/10.4018/IJTEPD.2019070106

Torres, M. C., Salamanca, Y. N., Cely, J. P., & Aguilar, J. L. (2020). All We Need is a Boost! Using Multimodal Tools and the Translanguaging Strategy: Strengthening Speaking in the EFL Classroom. *International Journal of Computer-Assisted Language Learning and Teaching*, 10(3), 28–47. 10.4018/IJCALLT.2020070103

Torres, M. L., & Ramos, V. J. (2018). Music Therapy: A Pedagogical Alternative for ASD and ID Students in Regular Classrooms. In Epler, P. (Ed.), *Instructional Strategies in General Education and Putting the Individuals With Disabilities Act (IDEA) Into Practice* (pp. 222–244). Hershey, PA: IGI Global. 10.4018/978-1-5225-3111-1.ch008

Toulassi, B. (2017). Educational Administration and Leadership in Francophone Africa: 5 Dynamics to Change Education. In Mukerji, S., & Tripathi, P. (Eds.), *Handbook of Research on Administration, Policy, and Leadership in Higher Education* (pp. 20–45). Hershey, PA: IGI Global. 10.4018/978-1-5225-0672-0.ch002

Umair, S., & Sharif, M. M. (2018). Predicting Students Grades Using Artificial Neural Networks and Support Vector Machine. In M. Khosrow-Pour, D.B.A. (Ed.), *Encyclopedia of Information Science and Technology, Fourth Edition* (pp. 5169-5182). Hershey, PA: IGI Global. 10.4018/978-1-5225-2255-3.ch449

Vettraino, L., Castello, V., Guspini, M., & Guglielman, E. (2018). Self-Awareness and Motivation Contrasting ESL and NEET Using the SAVE System. In M. Khosrow-Pour, D.B.A. (Ed.), *Encyclopedia of Information Science and Technology, Fourth Edition* (pp. 1559-1568). Hershey, PA: IGI Global. 10.4018/978-1-5225-2255-3.ch135

Wiemelt, J. (2017). Critical Bilingual Leadership for Emergent Bilingual Students. In I. Management Association (Ed.), *Educational Leadership and Administration: Concepts, Methodologies, Tools, and Applications* (pp. 1606-1631). Hershey, PA: IGI Global. 10.4018/978-1-5225-1624-8.ch074

Wolf, F., Seyfarth, F. C., & Pflaum, E. (2018). Scalable Capacity-Building for Geographically Dispersed Learners: Designing the MOOC "Sustainable Energy in Small Island Developing States (SIDS)". In Pandey, U., & Indrakanti, V. (Eds.), *Open and Distance Learning Initiatives for Sustainable Development* (pp. 58–83). Hershey, PA: IGI Global. 10.4018/978-1-5225-2621-6.ch003

Woodley, X. M., Mucundanyi, G., & Lockard, M. (2017). Designing Counter-Narratives: Constructing Culturally Responsive Curriculum Online. *International Journal of Online Pedagogy and Course Design*, 7(1), 43–56. 10.4018/IJOPCD.2017010104

Yell, M. L., & Christle, C. A. (2017). The Foundation of Inclusion in Federal Legislation and Litigation. In Curran, C., & Petersen, A. (Eds.), *Handbook of Research on Classroom Diversity and Inclusive Education Practice* (pp. 27–52). Hershey, PA: IGI Global. 10.4018/978-1-5225-2520-2.ch002

Zinner, L. (2019). Fostering Academic Citizenship With a Shared Leadership Approach. In Zhu, C., & Zayim-Kurtay, M. (Eds.), *University Governance and Academic Leadership in the EU and China* (pp. 99–117). IGI Global. https://doi.org/10.4018/978-1-5225-7441-5.ch007

About the Contributors

Leah Purpuri has served in the public education and non-profit sectors for nearly 15 years. As a professional helper, she has been the administrative lead over school and district-wide counseling teams, in addition to being a counselor and senior case manager. Further, Dr. Purpuri currently serves as the President of Ocean County Directors of Counseling and previously served as the President of Ocean County Guidance and Personnel Association. Both her Bachelors in Psychology and Masters in Counseling are from Messiah College (University). In 2021, she completed her Doctorate in Educational Leadership degree from Monmoouth University; her dissertation was titled Expressions of Superintendent Resiliency in the Wake of COVID-19. Dr. Leah Purpuri lives in New Jersey with her beloved husband, Luke, and their two children, Levi Mark and Judah Lily.

* * *

Keon N. Berry is a dynamic practicing scholar with a rich background in education management. Driven by a passion for positive social change, Dr. Berry utilizes core principles of equity, advocacy, and innovation to drive impactful transformations in higher education, early childhood education, education policy, academia, and social welfare. Throughout Dr. Berry's career, he has demonstrated a track record of unwavering commitment to empowering families and fostering favorable outcomes for youth of all ages. Through vision, passion, and service to all humanity, Dr. Keon N. Berry strives to help children and families envision and actualize their dreams of a prosperous future. Learn more about Dr. Keon N. Berry by visiting www.drkeonberry.com or https://www.linkedin.com/in/keonnberry/.

Jenna Cook, with over six years of experience in higher education, Ph.D., brings with her experiences from a multitude of educational sectors, including but not limited to academic advising, tutoring, learning support, admissions, and teaching. She is a passionate and dedicated academic leader who strives to provide quality advising and instruction to undergraduate students. In her current role as the Assistant Dean for Seniors at the Gabelli School of Business at Fordham University, Dr. Cook oversees the academic progress and graduation of approximately 650 students, collaborates with faculty and staff to ensure the alignment of the curriculum with the mission and objectives of the school, and implements strategies to improve retention and completion rates. In addition to her administrative role, she is an adjunct professor in the Communications and Media Management Area at the Gabelli School of Business teaching Career Exploration. She has also served as an adjunct professor of English at Berkeley College and Saint Peter's University, where she taught various writing, literature, and research courses. Dr. Cook holds a Ph.D. in Literacy from St. John's University, an M.A. in English and Creative Writing from Southern New Hampshire University, and a B.A. in English Language and Literature from New Jersey City University. Additionally, she has multiple tutoring, teaching, and supplemental instruction certifications. Dr. Cook has a strong background in online and in-person pedagogy, curriculum development, assessment, and academic support. Dr. Cook is deeply committed to the tenet of cura personalis, "care for the whole person," and strives to incorporate this phrase in her everyday work. In her spare time, Dr. Cook loves to spend time with her husband, daughter, and son. You can always find her reading, eating, dancing, or a combination of the three.

About the Contributors

Jessica DeLisa is a teacher at Long Branch Public Schools in central New Jersey. She received her Ed.D. in Educational Leadership at Monmouth University.

Liam Duffy has taught English internationally since 2008 in South Korea, Thailand, Vietnam, Russia, and China. He earned a Master of Education in Higher Education in 2014 and a Doctorate of Education in Organizational Leadership, focusing on Higher Education in 2023. His dissertation is titled: Exploring Expatriate Academics' Perceptions of Job Satisfaction Relating to Organizational Support at International Branch Campuses in China. His research interests include learning more about how transnational education administrators can support international faculty to keep them satisfied in their roles. He is interested in exploring whether expatriate academics are more satisfied living abroad when they are able to learn the local language. He is also interested in students' test-taking strategies, having written about IELTS and wanting to explore other exams.

Greg Dyer (he/him) is a student affairs professional with experience in residence life, programming, fundraising development, leadership engagement, and student wellness. Dyer is currently a Residence Life Coordinator at Rutgers University. He completed his Master's in Education, Higher Education Student Affairs at Kent State University (2022). His work during his graduate studies and professionally influences his passion for increasing access to education and student affairs assessment.

Michael Edmondson, Ph.D., serves as the Associate Provost for Continued Learning at the New Jersey Institute of Technology and as the Vice President of Professional and Corporate Education at the New Jersey Innovation Institute. Dr. Edmondson also serves as an adjunct at Drexel University, has published eight books with Business Experts Press, and is the Co-Editor of the Human Resource Management and Organizational Development Collection for Business Experts Press.

Ralph Gigliotti, Ph.D., serves as Assistant Vice President for Organizational Leadership in University Academic Affairs at Rutgers University. In this role, he directs the Rutgers Office of Organizational Leadership and provides executive leadership for a portfolio of signature leadership programs, consultation services, and research initiatives. He holds part-time faculty appointments in the Department of Communication, Ph.D. Program in Higher Education, Rutgers Business School Executive Education, and Department of Family Medicine and Community Health at Robert Wood Johnson Medical School. His research and consulting interests explore topics related to organizational communication, leadership, crisis, strategy, and training and development within the context of higher education.

Tori Glascock (she/her) is the Research Project Coordinator for the Division of Student Affairs at Rutgers University-New Brunswick. Tori holds a Bachelor of Science from Stevens Institute of Technology and a Master of Applied Psychology from the Graduate School of Applied and Professional Psychology, Rutgers University, where she is currently a doctoral student in organizational psychology. Tori's academic and professional experiences range from providing peer to peer mental health support to working as a DEI consultant with various organizations. Her current work with the Division of Student Affairs reflects her passion to ensure that people feel comfortable and safe to be their truest selves in their environment and develop a strong sense of belonging.

Gabriella Hall, Ed.D., is a proud mother, wife, and early childhood educator. She studied at Monmouth University where she earned her master's degree in special education and her doctorate degree in educational leadership. During her doctoral studies, she completed her dissertation on Inquiry-based STEM Learning in Preschool Education. She is an experienced classroom teacher who taught preschool special education in a NJ public school. Before teaching in the public school system, Gabriella taught in a private preschool and at behavioral health centers with children ages 4 to 17. Gabriella holds NJ teaching licenses in early childhood preK-3, Kindergarten through 6th, and special education. Gabriella also studied social-emotional learning and the benefits of mindfulness and yoga, and is a certified social-emotional learning facilitator and yoga instructor. She is currently a professional development specialist at Kodo Kids and teaches private classes for young children and their families.

About the Contributors

Sheenah Hartigan currently serves as the Executive Director of Enrollment Services at Ocean County College located in Toms River, NJ where she oversees the one stop shop, enrollment services, recruitment and admissions, retention services and early college. Sheenah worked to develop and launch the successful one stop shop at OCC and is currently piloting a retention model. Sheenah's work in implementing an AI chatbot at Ocean was recently awarded a national Bellwether award for 2022 in Planning, Governance and Finance. She has presented at national conferences and on panels for The Chronicle of Higher Education, Middle States Commission for Higher Education, Ellucian Live and others. Sheenah earned her bachelor's degree in Business Management from The College of New Jersey. Sher earned a Master's Degree in Student Service Administration and a doctorate in Higher Education Administration, both from Fairleigh Dickinson University. Sheenah is passionate about student enrollment and recruitment, streamlining processes, and change management. When she is not busy strategizing, she enjoys spending time with her husband and two small children outdoors, especially hiking and the beach, trying new foods and watching poorly-rated reality TV shows.

Catherine Hayes is Professor of Health Professions Pedagogy and Scholarship at the University of Sunderland, UK. She is a UK National Teaching Fellow and Principal Fellow of the UK Higher Education Academy. As a graduate of Podiatric Medicine in 1992, Catherine was a Founding Fellow of the Faculty of Podiatric Medicine at the Royal College of Physicians and Surgeons (Glasgow) in 2012 and was awarded Fellowship of the Royal College of Podiatry (London) in 2010. She is currently Programme Leader of the University of Sunderland's Professional Doctorate pathways for the DBA, EdD, DPM and DProf.

Jen Huey is a science teacher for the Toms River Regional School District.

Osama Ismail is a dedicated e-mobility engineer turned educator who is passionate about teaching engineering. Osama graduated from the University of Antwerp with a master's degree in Sustainable Automotive Engineering and then went on to work for various automotive companies. After many years in the automotive industry, Osama took the initiative for education. He wanted to share his love of engineering and technology with the next generation, so he decided to become an automotive engineering teacher alongside his research in the e-mobility sector.

Joseph Mandyata is currently a lecturer in special education, guidance and counselling in the School of Education at the University of Zambia. He has served in various academic and education positions such as: external and internal examiner of students at postgraduate level, Assistant Dean in the School of Education; Senior Inspector of Schools (special education); a District Inspector of schools, Head teacher of special education school, special education teacher and as a Secondary School teacher in the Zambian Ministry of Education. He has researched and published several articles in the field of special and inclusive education and guidance and counselling in local and international journals. He holds a Doctor of Philosophy degree in Special education, Master of Education in Special Education) and a Bachelor of Arts with Education degree of the University of Zambia. He lectures in Special Education and guidance and counselling courses at both post and undergraduate degree programmes. His research interests are; Policies in Special / Inclusive Education; Partnerships in Special / Inclusive Education; Guidance and Counseling, Disability, Education and Poverty for persons with disabilities.

Salvador Mena (he, him, el) serves as Senior Vice Chancellor for the Student Experience at Rutgers University–New Brunswick. In this role, Dr. Mena leads a comprehensive division of student affairs that focuses on health and wellness, student life and advocacy, campus engagement and belonging, and student services. Over the last 20 years, Dr. Mena has had the privilege to serve college students at different institutional types, including both public and private colleges and universities. Dr. Mena received his doctor of philosophy degree in higher education, student affairs, and international education policy from the University of Maryland, College Park and a master's degree in student development in higher education and bachelor's degree in political science from the University of Maine. Nationally, Dr. Mena has been involved with a number of higher education professional organizations, including the National Association of Student Personnel Administrators (NASPA). He is a regular presenter at national conferences and has published in the Journal of Student Affairs Research and Practice and contributed a book chapter in Cultural Centers in Higher Education: Perspectives on Identity, Theory, and Practice.

About the Contributors

Matthew Miranda is an educator at Rumson Public Schools in Monmouth County, New Jersey. He is a graduate of the EdD Program in Educational Leadership at Monmouth University, with a research focus on developing programs to boost resilience and retention in novice teachers. Dr. Miranda is an avid lifelong learner, committed to seeking solutions and strategies to some of the most important challenges facing our education systems.

Daniel L. Mpolomoka is the Dean of the School of Education, Humanities and Social Sciences at Unicaf University Zambia. Daniel holds a Master of Education in Special Education; and another Master of Education in Literacy Education and a Doctoral Degree in Literacy Education. He has 14 years of professional experience as a lecturer and researcher. Daniel taught at various government secondary schools before taking up lectureship at Zambian Open University (ZAOU), were he saved in many key administrative positions. He once served as a Masters Coordinator for a Project dubbed the Transformative Engagement Network (TEN), which involved Mynooth University (Ireland), Muzuzu University (Malawi), Mulungushi University (Zambia) and Zambian Open University (Zambia). He has won scholarships and awards too, one of them being the Harmonization, Accreditation and Quality Assurance in African Higher Education (HAQAA2), October, 2022–January, 2023, which culminated into a Diploma certification. His research interests include: Literacy Studies, Technological Education, Open and Distance Education in Higher Institutions of Learning, Adult Education, Special Education and Early Education Studies. Daniel has made paper presentations at local and international conferences. He has also published various articles in local and international refereed journals. He is an editorial board member / reviewer for many reputable scientific journals.

Tracy Mulvaney the Dean of the School of Education at the University of North Carolina at Pembroke. After a long career as a P-12 teacher and administrator, she entered the higher education space as the Chair of a teacher education program in Arizona. In 2016 she accepted the position of Assistant Dean of the School of Education at Monmouth University, a role she served for six years prior to returning to faculty to work directly with doctoral students. Dr. Mulvaney holds a B.S. in Rehabilitation and an M.A. in Special Education from the University of Arizona. Her Ed.D. was conferred from Northern Arizona University.

Petronella Mwaka is a Postgraduate Student at Zambian Open University. She is a sustentative Head of the Literature and Languages Department at a government school in Northern Province.

Carlos Rodriguez stands as a distinguished leader deeply engaged in data-informed decision-making. As the Vice President of Administrative and Strategic Analytics and Data Illumination at Kean University, he plays a crucial role in propelling the institution's strategic initiatives and overall efficacy. Prior to arriving at Kean, He worked for the New Jersey Department of Education for two decades. He concluded his career as an Executive County Superintendent of Schools. In that role, he represented the New Jersey Commissioner of Education, overseeing 28 school districts and managing a network of 147 schools that served approximately 83,000 students. Highlighting his commitment to advancing educational excellence and diversity, Dr. Rodriguez was recognized in 2021 as one of 25 fellows nationwide selected for the prestigious Hispanic Association of Colleges and Universities (HACU) Leadership Academy.

Jamie Sassano is a mom, a secondary educator, and an instructional data coach in New Jersey mentoring and encouraging teachers to push forward with new techniques involving educational technology and online learning. Dr. Sassano's published dissertation focused on pedagogy and specific instructional methods through a lens of self-determination theory, specifically regarding autonomy, competency, & relatedness in IBL and Didactic teaching environments. She earned her doctorate in Organizational Leadership in 2022, has an MA in Urban Education, with a second major focus in Educational Technology received from New Jersey City University, and a BA in English Literature from Rutgers University.

About the Contributors

Shantel M. Scott is a passionate educator with 20 years of experience teaching English in grades 7-12. She works to inspire, educate, empower, and build confidence in learners of all ages through the design of personalized, authentic, and impactful learning experiences. She considers it her life's mission to provide educational opportunities for students of every race and creed to claim their space in the world through vocal empowerment. She sees all classrooms as learning labs to build calm, confident communicators that can leverage technology tools to elevate their voice.

Kyle Seiverd is vice principal at The Grunin Performing Arts Academy at the Ocean County Vocational Technical School District and adjunct professor at Monmouth University.

Ranjit Singha is a Doctorate Research Fellow at Christ (Deemed to be University) and a distinguished American Psychological Association (APA) member. His expertise lies in research and development across various domains, including Mindfulness, Addiction Psychology, Women Empowerment, UN Sustainable Development Goals, and Data Science. He has earned certifications from renowned institutions, including IBM and The University of Oxford Mindfulness Centre, UK, in Mindfulness. Additionally, he holds certifications as a Microsoft Innovative Educator, Licensed Yoga Professional, Certified Mindfulness Teacher, and CBCT Teachers Training from Emory University, USA. Mr Ranjit's educational qualifications include PGDBA (GM), MBA (IB), MSc in Counseling Psychology, and completion of a Senior Diploma in Tabla (Musical Instrumentation). His dedication to continuous learning is evident through his involvement in the SEE Learning® (Social, Emotional, and Ethical) Learning program. As a committed researcher and educator, Mr Ranjit focuses on mindfulness and compassion-based interventions. He has an impressive publication record, having authored twenty-three research papers, ten chapters, four books, and five edited books. His research interests encompass various aspects of mindfulness, such as assessment, benefits of mindfulness-based programs, change mechanisms, professional training, mindfulness ethics, cognitive and neuropsychology, and studies related to high-risk behaviours. Apart from his research endeavours, Mr Ranjit has extensive teaching experience, instructing courses in diverse subjects like Forensic Psychology, Positive Psychology, Organizational Planning, Strategic Management, Psycho Metric Tests, Counseling Skills, Disaster Management, Basic Computer Science, Business Planning, Business Law, and Auditing. He has mentored numerous Postgraduate and undergraduate research projects, demonstrating his commitment to nurturing young minds in psychology. Ad Hoc Reviewer at International Journal of Cyber Behavior, Psychology and Learning (IJCBPL), Reviewer and author at IGI Global, and Editor and Reviewer at TNT Publication. Furthermore, Mr Ranjit actively provides personal counselling services, showcasing his genuine concern for his students' well-being and academic success. His unwavering dedication to research and education has solidified his position as a valuable contributor to psychology. ORCID iD: https://orcid.org/0000-0002-3541-8752.

Kaitlyn M. Sorochka, Ed.D., is an adjunct professor of mathematics education in the Department of Curriculum and Instruction at Monmouth University. Sorochka is also a full time middle school special education mathematics teacher in a New Jersey public school. She earned her Bachelor of Science degree at Skidmore College and her Master of Arts in Education at Georgian Court University (thesis focused on positive behavioral interventions and supports). Sorochka completed her doctorate in Educational Leadership in 2021 at Monmouth University, with Dr. Zambak serving as her chair. Her dissertation focused on a customized voluntary online learning intervention program for middle grades mathematics education.

Marisa Villani, Ph.D., has worked in a variety of higher ed spaces including academic affairs, development and alumni relations, and student affairs. Her recent work includes student success programming, persistence support and community building for first-generation college students, and strategic development for retention efforts. Marisa has experience in course development and in teaching first-year seminar courses and business leadership courses. She has guest lectured or served as a speaker on a variety of topics including organizational theory, student development theory, leadership and ethics, social justice, and DEI. Marisa is the Senior Assistant Dean for Undergraduate Studies at the Gabelli School of Business at Fordham University. She serves on the Board of Trustees of St. Catharine Academy. Marisa is a proud first-generation college student whose wildest academic dream was to obtain a Ph.D. Her research focuses on Mission and identity, academic advising, and persistence support for first-generation college students.

About the Contributors

Angello Villarreal is an award-winner Teacher of Spanish & Adjunct Professor who was born and raised in Lima, Peru. Previously, Dr. Villarreal taught Spanish and ESL at an urban school. He has utilized his experiences working with different types of demographics and educational needs to serve students better. Advocacy is a center of Dr. Villarreal's philosophy as all his research, work, community service, mentorship, and leadership are towards serving the students and their families needs. From creating after-school programs to leading different projects, Dr. Villarreal believes working with the community is critical for the student's success.

Dayna Weintraub (she/her) serves as Assistant Vice Chancellor for Strategy, Assessment, and Planning in Student Affairs and an Associate Member of the Faculty in the Graduate School of Education at Rutgers University–New Brunswick. Dayna leads and directs assessment, communication, strategic planning, and development processes. She has published research in academic journals, and presented her work on parental involvement, gender issues in STEM fields, and civic engagement in community colleges at conferences worldwide. Dayna brings an extensive career in residence life, faculty governance, and curriculum management. She holds a PhD in Higher Education and Organizational Change from the University of California, Los Angeles, a Masters in Higher Education and Student Affairs from Indiana University- Bloomington, and a Bachelor's Degree in Speech Communication from Ithaca College.

Silvana Zircher is a Chief School Administrator in Middlesex County, NJ. She is also an adjunct professor at Monmouth University in the Graduate School of Education. She is a board member on the Educational Services Commission of New Jersey, and is on the advisory council of Middlesex College. Dr. Zircher serves as a mentor for the state of New Jersey to support new principals, directors, and superintendents. As the county's representative on the New Jersey Association of Superintendents' Governmental Relations and Curriculum and Instruction Committees, she collaborates with superintendents throughout the state to inform legislators and the Department of Education on matters of interest and policy.

Index

A

Academic Advising 199, 201, 202, 203, 217, 224, 225, 226

B

Biology 99, 101, 111, 112

C

Chronic Absenteeism 1, 4, 5, 6, 7, 12, 13, 27, 28, 40, 50, 143
COVID-19 1, 2, 3, 4, 10, 11, 13, 19, 27, 29, 32, 33, 34, 35, 36, 37, 38, 39, 40, 42, 43, 47, 50, 51, 52, 53, 54, 55, 56, 57, 58, 59, 61, 63, 65, 66, 70, 71, 72, 74, 75, 77, 78, 79, 80, 81, 82, 88, 89, 90, 91, 92, 93, 96, 97, 115, 116, 117, 118, 119, 120, 121, 122, 123, 124, 125, 126, 127, 128, 129, 130, 131, 132, 133, 134, 135, 136, 137, 140, 141, 146, 147, 148, 149, 151, 153, 154, 155, 156, 157, 158, 159, 161, 162, 163, 165, 172, 181, 183, 184, 185, 186, 187, 188, 190, 191, 192, 193, 194, 196, 197, 198, 200, 204, 205, 206, 207, 208, 218, 223, 224, 225, 228, 229, 230, 231, 233, 234, 235, 236, 237, 238, 240, 241, 243, 244, 246, 248, 249, 250, 251, 252, 253
COVID-19 Pandemic 1, 3, 4, 13, 29, 32, 33, 34, 35, 37, 38, 47, 50, 51, 52, 53, 56, 61, 65, 70, 71, 74, 75, 77, 78, 79, 80, 81, 82, 88, 91, 92, 93, 97, 117, 125, 127, 130, 131, 133, 135, 137, 141, 147, 151, 153, 154, 155, 156, 158, 159, 162, 163, 172, 183, 184, 185, 186, 187, 188, 190, 191, 192, 193, 197, 200, 204, 223, 224, 228, 229, 230, 231, 233, 235, 236, 237, 238, 240, 241, 243, 244, 246, 248, 249, 250, 251, 252, 253

D

Discrimination 71, 117, 118, 119, 120, 122, 123, 124, 127, 131, 133

E

EdTech 185, 188, 190, 191, 192, 193, 194, 195
Educational Challenges 4, 32, 33, 78, 162
Educational Disparities 48, 162
Education Policy 28, 114, 116
Emergency Remote Teaching 56, 57, 58, 63, 70, 74, 183
Environmental Science 101, 102, 105, 106

F

Fordham University 197, 198, 204, 206, 225

G

GDP 185, 190, 192, 193, 195
Graduation Rates 200

H

Higher Education 33, 37, 76, 81, 94, 129, 130, 156, 157, 158, 160, 162, 182, 183, 184, 188, 193, 198, 199, 201, 223, 224, 225, 226, 229, 230, 234, 235, 243, 244, 247, 248, 249, 250, 251, 252, 253

I

ICT 126, 157, 158, 161, 172, 175, 181
Individualized Education Plan 36
Interactive Online Whiteboard 86
Intervention Strategies 3

L

Laboratory 96, 97, 98, 99, 100, 103, 112
Leadership Development 231, 233, 235, 236, 237, 246, 247, 248, 249, 250, 251
Learning 1, 2, 3, 4, 5, 6, 10, 11, 12, 13,

311

14, 16, 18, 19, 20, 21, 22, 24, 26, 27, 28, 29, 30, 31, 32, 33, 34, 35, 36, 37, 38, 39, 40, 41, 42, 43, 44, 45, 46, 47, 48, 50, 51, 52, 53, 54, 55, 57, 58, 59, 60, 61, 62, 63, 64, 65, 66, 67, 68, 69, 70, 71, 72, 73, 74, 75, 77, 78, 79, 80, 81, 82, 83, 84, 85, 86, 87, 88, 89, 90, 91, 92, 93, 94, 96, 97, 98, 99, 101, 102, 103, 104, 112, 113, 121, 124, 125, 126, 127, 129, 130, 131, 135, 136, 137, 138, 140, 141, 142, 143, 144, 145, 146, 147, 148, 150, 151, 152, 153, 154, 155, 156, 157, 158, 159, 160, 161, 162, 163, 165, 168, 170, 173, 176, 179, 181, 182, 183, 184, 185, 186, 187, 188, 189, 190, 192, 196, 198, 199, 200, 208, 209, 210, 211, 212, 213, 214, 215, 217, 219, 220, 222, 223, 225, 226, 229, 231, 232, 233, 234, 235, 238, 241, 242, 243, 244, 245, 246, 247, 250, 251, 252, 256

M

Mathematics Achievement 77, 78, 79, 81, 82, 92
Middle School 60, 69, 77, 78, 79, 80, 81, 82, 84, 85, 91, 92, 94

N

New Jersey Student Learning Assessment 79

O

Online Education 2, 57, 75, 156, 157, 158, 160, 161, 162, 163, 164, 165, 167, 169, 172, 175, 179, 181, 182, 183, 184, 185, 186, 187, 188, 190, 191, 192, 193, 195, 196, 251
Outbreak 76, 96, 105, 121, 130, 134, 185, 186, 198, 205, 225

P

Pandemic 1, 2, 3, 4, 11, 12, 13, 20, 29, 31, 32, 33, 34, 35, 37, 38, 39, 40, 41, 42, 43, 44, 46, 47, 48, 49, 50, 51, 52, 53, 54, 55, 56, 59, 61, 62, 63, 64, 65, 67, 68, 70, 71, 72, 74, 75, 77, 78, 79, 80, 81, 82, 83, 84, 88, 91, 92, 93, 97, 106, 117, 122, 125, 127, 130, 131, 133, 134, 135, 136, 137, 139, 140, 141, 142, 143, 144, 145, 146, 147, 148, 149, 150, 151, 152, 153, 154, 155, 156, 157, 158, 159, 160, 161, 162, 163, 167, 172, 175, 179, 181, 183, 184, 185, 186, 187, 188, 189, 190, 191, 192, 193, 194, 196, 197, 198, 199, 200, 203, 204, 205, 206, 207, 208, 209, 210, 211, 212, 213, 214, 215, 216, 217, 218, 219, 220, 221, 222, 223, 224, 228, 229, 230, 231, 233, 234, 235, 236, 237, 238, 240, 241, 243, 244, 245, 246, 247, 248, 249, 250, 251, 252, 253, 254
Parent-Child Interaction 32, 33
Post-Pandemic University 245, 247

R

Remote Instruction 10, 24, 63, 71, 87, 137, 140, 143, 233, 255
Remote Learning 1, 30, 35, 36, 37, 38, 39, 40, 41, 43, 44, 45, 46, 47, 50, 52, 58, 59, 61, 64, 65, 68, 69, 70, 72, 73, 81, 82, 83, 84, 86, 87, 88, 89, 90, 91, 121, 125, 126, 127, 136, 140, 148, 155, 184, 189, 196, 199, 208, 210, 211, 215, 217, 220, 222, 242
Retention Rates 13, 197, 204, 206, 207, 209
Rural-Urban Gap 156, 157, 163, 167

S

Safety 6, 11, 40, 83, 98, 99, 103, 116, 121, 136, 147, 149, 150, 151, 185, 186, 190, 207, 208, 214
School Phobia 6, 7, 8, 9, 28, 31
Science 27, 51, 66, 67, 74, 94, 96, 97, 98,

99, 100, 101, 102, 105, 106, 110, 111, 112, 114, 129, 131, 133, 151, 160, 162, 163, 164, 169, 170, 171, 184
Screencast 80, 81
Secondary School Learners 115, 116
SEL 26, 62, 63, 64, 66
Sense of Belonging 203, 213, 223, 229, 230, 231, 232, 233, 235, 237, 239, 240, 241, 242, 243, 244, 245, 246, 247, 248, 249, 250, 251, 252, 253, 254, 255
Special Education 17, 18, 34, 43, 44, 47, 48, 49, 66, 72, 77, 78, 81, 84, 85, 87, 88
Stigma 25, 42, 117, 118, 119, 122, 123, 124, 127, 129, 133, 134
Student Communities 197
Student Engagement 12, 26, 33, 84, 142, 198, 209, 214, 220, 221, 233, 238, 250
Student Involvement 208, 228, 229, 231, 235, 246, 247, 248
Student Leadership 222, 229, 231, 234, 235, 245, 246, 247, 248, 251, 253
Student Persistence 197, 200, 203, 204, 205, 213, 215, 225, 226, 248, 254
Student Success 66, 77, 80, 84, 137, 196, 203, 223, 225, 226, 230, 244

V

Virtual Learning 1, 2, 3, 4, 10, 11, 12, 13, 14, 16, 18, 19, 20, 21, 22, 24, 26, 35, 45, 72, 78, 80, 81, 84, 85, 89, 93, 94, 96, 97, 98, 101, 102, 112, 113, 141, 142, 143, 144, 146, 211, 214, 231, 234, 241, 247

Publishing Tomorrow's Research Today

Uncover Current Insights and Future Trends in Education
with IGI Global's Cutting-Edge Recommended Books

Print Only, E-Book Only, or Print + E-Book.
Order direct through IGI Global's Online Bookstore at www.igi-global.com or through your preferred provider.

Artificial Intelligence Applications Using ChatGPT in Education: Case Studies and Practices
ISBN: 9781668493007
© 2023; 234 pp.
List Price: US$ 215

Generative AI in Teaching and Learning
ISBN: 9798369300749
© 2024; 383 pp.
List Price: US$ 230

Dynamic Curriculum Development and Design Strategies for Effective Online Learning in Higher Education
ISBN: 9781668486467
© 2023; 471 pp.
List Price: US$ 215

Illuminating and Advancing the Path for Mathematical Writing Research
ISBN: 9781668465387
© 2024; 389 pp.
List Price: US$ 215

Cases on Economics Education and Tools for Educators
ISBN: 9781668475836
© 2024; 359 pp.
List Price: US$ 215

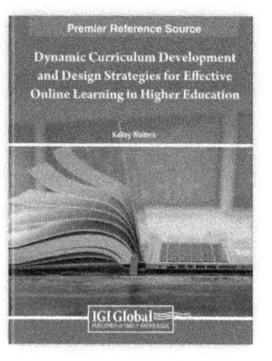

Emerging Trends and Historical Perspectives Surrounding Digital Transformation in Education: Achieving Open and Blended Learning Environments
ISBN: 9781668444238
© 2023; 334 pp.
List Price: US$ 240

Do you want to stay current on the latest research trends, product announcements, news, and special offers?
Join IGI Global's mailing list to receive customized recommendations, exclusive discounts, and more.
Sign up at: www.igi-global.com/newsletters.

Scan the QR Code here to view more related titles in Education.

www.igi-global.com | Sign up at www.igi-global.com/newsletters | facebook.com/igiglobal | twitter.com/igiglobal | linkedin.com/igiglobal

Ensure Quality Research is Introduced to the Academic Community

Become a Reviewer for IGI Global Authored Book Projects

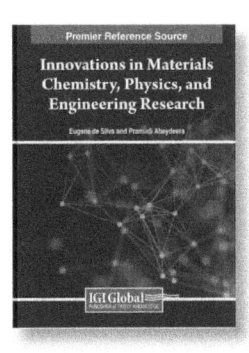

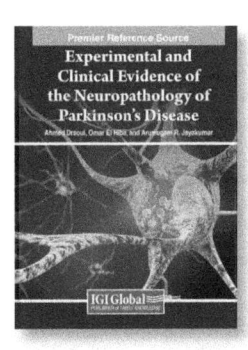

The overall success of an authored book project is dependent on quality and timely manuscript evaluations.

Applications and Inquiries may be sent to:
development@igi-global.com

Applicants must have a doctorate (or equivalent degree) as well as publishing, research, and reviewing experience. Authored Book Evaluators are appointed for one-year terms and are expected to complete at least three evaluations per term. Upon successful completion of this term, evaluators can be considered for an additional term.

If you have a colleague that may be interested in this opportunity, we encourage you to share this information with them.

IGI Global's Open Access Journal Program

Publishing Tomorrow's Research Today

Including Nearly 200 Peer-Reviewed, Gold (Full) Open Access Journals across IGI Global's Three Academic Subject Areas: Business & Management; Scientific, Technical, and Medical (STM); and Education

Consider Submitting Your Manuscript to One of These Nearly 200 Open Access Journals for to Increase Their Discoverability & Citation Impact

Web of Science Impact Factor	Journal
6.5	Journal of Organizational and End User Computing
4.7	Journal of Global Information Management
3.2	International Journal on Semantic Web and Information Systems
2.6	Journal of Database Management

Choosing IGI Global's Open Access Journal Program Can Greatly Increase the Reach of Your Research

Higher Usage
Open access papers are 2-3 times more likely to be read than non-open access papers.

Higher Download Rates
Open access papers benefit from 89% higher download rates than non-open access papers.

Higher Citation Rates
Open access papers are 47% more likely to be cited than non-open access papers.

Submitting an article to a journal offers an invaluable opportunity for you to share your work with the broader academic community, fostering knowledge dissemination and constructive feedback.

Submit an Article and Browse the IGI Global Call for Papers Pages

We can work with you to find the journal most well-suited for your next research manuscript.
For open access publishing support, contact: journaleditor@igi-global.com

Publishing Tomorrow's Research Today
IGI Global
e-Book Collection

Including Essential Reference Books Within Three Fundamental Academic Areas

Business & Management
Scientific, Technical, & Medical (STM)
Education

- Acquisition options include Perpetual, Subscription, and Read & Publish
- No Additional Charge for Multi-User Licensing
- No Maintenance, Hosting, or Archiving Fees
- Continually Enhanced Accessibility Compliance Features (WCAG)

| Over **150,000+** Chapters | Contributions From **200,000+** Scholars Worldwide | More Than **1,000,000+** Citations | Majority of e-Books Indexed in Web of Science & Scopus | Consists of Tomorrow's Research Available Today! |

Recommended Titles from our e-Book Collection

Innovation Capabilities and Entrepreneurial Opportunities of Smart Working
ISBN: 9781799887973

Advanced Applications of Generative AI and Natural Language Processing Models
ISBN: 9798369305027

Using Influencer Marketing as a Digital Business Strategy
ISBN: 9798369305515

Human-Centered Approaches in Industry 5.0
ISBN: 9798369326473

Modeling and Monitoring Extreme Hydrometeorological Events
ISBN: 9781668487716

Data-Driven Intelligent Business Sustainability
ISBN: 9798369300497

Information Logistics for Organizational Empowerment and Effective Supply Chain Management
ISBN: 9798369301593

Data Envelopment Analysis (DEA) Methods for Maximizing Efficiency
ISBN: 9798369302552

Request More Information, or Recommend the IGI Global e-Book Collection to Your Institution's Librarian

For More Information or to Request a Free Trial, Contact IGI Global's e-Collections Team: eresources@igi-global.com | 1-866-342-6657 ext. 100 | 717-533-8845 ext. 100

Milton Keynes UK
Ingram Content Group UK Ltd.
UKHW011953080824
446595UK00005B/140